Strategies for Writers

Strategies for Writers

A READER

Sheena Gillespie

Queensborough Community College

Longman

New York   San Francisco   Boston
London   Toronto   Sydney   Tokyo   Singapore   Madrid
Mexico City   Munich   Paris   Cape Town   Hong Kong   Montreal

Vice President, Humanities: Joseph Opiela
Editorial Assistant: Mary Beth Varney
Marketing Manager: Kate Sheehan
Editorial-Production Service: Omegatype Typography, Inc.
Composition and Prepress Buyer: Linda Cox
Manufacturing Buyer: Suzanne Lareau
Cover Administrator: Linda Knowles
Electronic Composition: Omegatype Typography, Inc.

Copyright © 2000
A Pearson Education Company
160 Gould Street
Needham Heights, MA 02494

Library of Congress Cataloging-in-Publication Data

Strategies for writers : a reader / [compiled by] Sheena Gillespie.
     p.   cm.
   Includes index.
   ISBN 0-205-29001-9 (alk. paper)
   1. College readers.   2. English language—Rhetoric Problems,
exercises, etc.   3. Report writing Problems, exercises, etc.
I. Gillespie, Sheena.
PE1417.S7656   2000
427—dc21   99-34334
                                                     CIP

Printed in the United States of America

10 9 8 7 6 5 4 3   04 03

To F. G., Gabriel, and Amanda—friends forever.

Contents

6   Description   80

10 Definition   225

13 Persuasion 338

14 Further Reading 385

Thematic Contents

Education and Work

Maturation

Cultural Differences

Social Issues

Human Values

Language and Writing

Nature and Science

Preface

"LEARNING TO READ BOOKS—or pictures, or film—is not just a matter of acquiring information from texts, it is a matter of learning to read and write the texts of our lives." In these words, writer and critic Robert Scholes points to the integral relationship between reading and writing, and this interconnection is an essential aspect of this anthology.

Why do writers read and write? Emily Dickinson, a nineteenth-century poet, viewed reading as a means of traveling to far-off places: "There is no frigate like a book." Jorge Luis Borges, a contemporary Latin American novelist, thought of reading as a way of revitalizing the self: "I have always come to life after coming to books." African American writer Toni Morrison, a Nobel Prize–winning author, believes in the power of narrative to help us understand ourselves and others: "Narrative is radical, creating us at the very moment it is being created." Morrison is particularly concerned that the writer's words and stories be the windows through which both writer and reader gain knowledge not only of the self but also of the self in relation to people of other ethnic groups and cultures. In other words, writers write to be read; they write for you, their audience. They communicate their insights to you in the hope that you will recognize aspects of your own thoughts and experiences in their essays and stories.

The readings in this text are on topics I think will interest you. I have chosen classic and contemporary writers of nonfiction who share their ideas on such issues as family and community, the media, education and work, cultural differences, nature and science, and gender. Because reading, as well as writing, is often made easier by applying strategies that will help you become a critical reader, Chapter 1 begins with a guided reading section preceding Brent Staples's essay, "A Brother's Murder." This guided reading section suggests several questions to ask before and after reading your assignments.

I also include three rhetorical sections—Chapters 2 through 4— on writing and revising. Sherwood Anderson's "Discovery of a Father" is the model for discussing techniques for planning an essay, and Maya

Angelou's "Sister Flowers" provides the framework for organizing a paper. Emily Hegarty's "*Meanie* and Me" is followed by her analysis of the various stages of the process she went through, from thinking about an essay, writing a first draft, and revising for a final product. Guidelines for revising an essay conclude this section of the text.

The readings are grouped in nine chapters ranging from narration, or storytelling (Chapter 5); description (Chapter 6); comparison and contrast (Chapter 11); and persuasion (Chapter 13). These methods of developing an essay are not rigidly adhered to by the writers you will read. In fact, you will find that they seldom stick to one method in writing their essays. For example, although Lewis Thomas, in "Death in the Open," chooses cause and effect (Chapter 12) to explain his theory that only when our population doubles and we can no longer avoid the thought of death, then death will finally be in the open, he also cites many illustrations and examples (Chapter 7) to reinforce his thesis. Similarly, Jim Fusilli, in "Becoming American, by Degrees," selects process analysis (Chapter 8) as his method of organization, but he also includes comparison and contrast (Chapter 11) as well as definition (Chapter 10) to explain his changing concepts of what it means to be an American.

Each group of readings in Chapters 5 through 13 includes an introduction explaining the patterns of essay development, followed by guidelines to expand that method. A brief author biography precedes each essay and study questions follow the essay. Questions on meaning require critical thinking and interpretation. Questions on method call attention to specific rhetorical features used by the writer and form the basis for the writing topics that follow each essay.

Two other features of the book will help you apply the readings to your study of writing. The additional writing topics at the end of each chapter require you to conduct interviews, engage in debate, take positions, or reach conclusions. A rhetorical and cultural Glossary at the end of the book defines terminology essential to any writing class. Finally, Chapter 14 provides additional reading selections for further study.

ACKNOWLEDGMENTS

We would like to extend special thanks to Joe Opiela, who conceived this project, to Mary Bernardez for her research assistance, and to Kathleen Howard and Patricia Gorton for their generous assistance in the preparation of the manuscript.

Strategies for Writers

1

On Reading an Essay: The Reader's Responsibility

"I WAS INTRODUCED TO MORTALITY, not by the old and failing, but by beautiful young men who lay wrecked after sudden explosions of violence," writes Brent Staples in a poignant essay about the murder of his twenty-two-year-old brother. Staples's purpose in writing about this intensely personal experience is not only to reveal the complexity of his relationship with his brother but also to inform his readers of the terrifying reality of ghetto life in the United States.

Before reading Staples's narrative, it is useful to explore your responsibility—to yourself and to the author—to understand what you are reading. A reader's responsibility involves discovering how to read a text and why it should be read. Sometimes you have to learn how to read a piece of writing before you can work up enthusiasm for wanting to read it. Other times you may be motivated to read a piece before knowing quite how to go about doing so.

In either case, previewing a piece of writing first will give you some ideas about it, perhaps enough ideas to motivate you to want to read further. Thinking about what type of writing this is, about the title, about the writer's name, about any headings, about footnotes,

1

about length of paragraphs, about any other features of the text that stand out gives you a foundation on which to build. Then, asking questions about it based on your preview will add further incentive. Skimming for main ideas is a final stage in this prereading process.

After reading the text through, writing down what you have learned encourages you to record the main ideas, mull over the issues raised, and fit the writer's **thesis** into what you know about the subject in general.

FULFILLING THE READER'S RESPONSIBILITY

Procedures to Follow in Fulfilling the Reader's Responsibility

Before reading the text:

1. Preview—ask yourself the following questions:

   a.   What type of writing is this: an essay or article, a story, a text-book chapter, a report, a set of instructions? What do I know about the typical structure of this type of writing?

   b.   What are the title and subtitle, if any? What do they suggest to me that I already know about?

   c.   Have I heard of the author before? If so, what do I know about him or her? If not, who does he or she seem to be—is there a title included, such as M.D., or is a brief biography included?

   d.   What does the text itself look like? Are there headings, foot-notes, illustrations? What do they suggest to me?

2. Question—based on your preview, ask yourself questions about the text, questions that you want to know the answers to, questions that will help you understand the text, and questions that will help you relate the text to your previous reading and experience. These questions might include specific versions of the following general questions:

   a.   What is this text about?

   b.   Who is the author writing for?

   c.   What does he or she want the reader to understand?

   d.   How does this text relate to what I know about the subject already, either from my reading or from my experience?

At this point, you should also be able to answer the question, "Why should I read this text?" If your answer is simply that you must fulfill an assignment, ask yourself the question again to see if you can't find a motivation that engages you more deeply, one that would encourage you to continue even if you were not assigned to do so.

A Brother's Murder

Brent Staples (b. 1951) is from Chester, Pennsylvania, and has a Ph.D. in psychology from the University of Chicago. He is currently on the editorial board of the New York Times, *where he writes on culture and politics. His autobiography,* Parallel Time: Growing Up Black and White, *was published in 1994.*

IT HAS BEEN MORE THAN TWO YEARS since my telephone rang with the news that my younger brother Blake—just 22 years old—had been murdered. The young man who killed him was only 24. Wearing a ski mask, he emerged from a car, fired six times at close range with a massive .44 Magnum, then fled. The two had once been inseparable friends. A senseless rivalry—beginning, I think, with an argument over a girlfriend—escalated from posturing, to threats, to violence, to murder. The way the two were living, death could have come to either of them from anywhere. In fact, the assailant had already survived multiple gunshot wounds from an incident much like the one in which my brother lost his life.

As I wept for Blake I felt wrenched backward into events and circumstances that had seemed light-years gone. Though a decade apart, we both were raised in Chester, Pa., an angry, heavily black, heavily poor, industrial city southwest of Philadelphia. There, in the 1960's, I was introduced to mortality, not by the old and failing, but by beautiful young men who lay wrecked after sudden explosions of violence. The first, I remember from my 14th year—Johnny, brash lover of fast cars, stabbed to death two doors from my house in a fight over a pool game. The next year, my teenage cousin, Wesley, whom I loved very much, was shot dead. The summers blur. Milton, an angry young neighbor, shot a crosstown rival, wounding him badly. William, another teenage neighbor, took a shotgun blast to the shoulder in some urban drama and displayed his bandages proudly. His brother, Leonard, severely beaten, lost an eye and donned a black patch. It went on.

I recall not long before I left for college, two local Vietnam vet-   3
erans—one from the Marines, one from the Army—arguing fiercely,
nearly at blows about which outfit had done the most in the war. The
most killing, they meant. Not much later, I read a magazine article that
set that dispute in a context. In the story, a noncommissioned officer—
a sergeant, I believe—said he would pass up any number of affluent,
suburban-born recruits to get hard-core soldiers from the inner city.
They jumped into the rice paddies with "their manhood on their
sleeves," I believe he said. These two items—the veterans arguing and
the sergeant's words—still characterize for me the circumstances under
which black men in their teens and 20's kill one another with such frequency. With a touchy paranoia born of living battered lives, they are
desperate to be *real* men. Killing is only *machismo* taken to the extreme.
Incursions to be punished by death were many and minor, and they remain so: they include stepping on the wrong toe, literally; cheating in
a drug deal; simply saying "I dare you" to someone holding a gun;
crossing territorial lines in a gang dispute. My brother grew up to wear
his manhood on his sleeve. And when he died, he was in that group—
black, male and in its teens and early 20's—that is far and away the
most likely to murder or be murdered.

I left the East Coast after college, spent the mid- and late-1970's in   4
Chicago as a graduate student, taught for a time, then became a journalist. Within 10 years of leaving my hometown, I was overeducated and
"upwardly mobile," ensconced on a quiet, tree-lined street where voices
raised in anger were scarcely ever heard. The telephone, like some grim
umbilical, kept me connected to the old world with news of deaths, im-
prisonings and misfortune. I felt emotionally beaten up. Perhaps to protect myself, I added a psychological dimension to the physical distance I
had already achieved. I rarely visited my hometown. I shut it out.

As I fled the past, so Blake embraced it. On Christmas of 1983, I   5
traveled from Chicago to a black section of Roanoke, Va., where he
then lived. The desolate public housing projects, the hopeless, idle
young men crashing against one another—these reminded me of the
embittered town we'd grown up in. It was a place where once I would
have been comfortable, or at least sure of myself. Now, hearing of my
brother's forays into crime, his scrapes with police and street thugs, I
was scared, unsteady on foreign terrain.

I saw that Blake's romance with the street life and the hustler im-   6
age had flowered dangerously. One evening that late December, standing in some Roanoke dive among drug dealers and grim, hair-trigger

losers, I told him I feared for his life. He had affected the image of the tough he wanted to be. But behind the dark glasses and the swagger, I glimpsed the baby-faced toddler I'd once watched over. I nearly wept. I wanted desperately for him to live. The young think themselves immortal, and a dangerous light shone in his eyes as he spoke laughingly of making fools of the policemen who had raided his apartment looking for drugs. He cried out as I took his right hand. A line of stitches lay between the thumb and index finger. Kickback from a shotgun, he explained, nothing serious. Gunplay had become part of his life.

I lacked the language simply to say: Thousands have lived this for you and died. I fought the urge to lift him bodily and shake him. This place and the way you are living smells of death to me, I said. Take some time away, I said. Let's go downtown tomorrow and buy a plane ticket anywhere, take a bus trip, anything to get away and cool things off. He took my alarm casually. We arranged to meet the following night—an appointment he would not keep. We embraced as though through glass. I drove away. 7

As I stood in my apartment in Chicago holding the receiver that evening in February 1984, I felt as though part of my soul had been cut away. I questioned myself then, and I still do. Did I not reach back soon enough or earnestly enough for him? For weeks I awoke crying from a recurrent dream in which I chased him, urgently trying to get him to read a document I had, as though reading it would protect him from what had happened in waking life. His eyes shining like black diamonds, he smiled and danced just beyond my grasp. When I reached for him, I caught only the space where he had been. 8

The following guided examination of "A Brother's Murder" should help you understand the reader's responsibility to interact with the text. You might consider approaching your analysis of Staples's essay as a detective trying to solve a crime. Arm yourself with a dictionary and a thesaurus, and be on the alert for the many textual hints and rhetorical clues the author has supplied for you. Pay close attention to the essay by analyzing how the author uses nouns, adjectives, figurative language, images, and symbols to construct his narrative.

Questions on Meaning

1. What do we learn about Blake's way of life from the first paragraph of the essay?

We learn that Blake is a young African American man who lives in the ghetto surrounded by violence.

2. What examples does Staples give in paragraph 2 to convey that he "was introduced to mortality, not by the old and failing, but by beautiful young men who lay wrecked after sudden explosions of violence"?

   He cites several examples of the other young men he knew, such as Johnny, Milton, and William, as well as his cousin Wesley, who were shot or stabbed or who perpetrated violence themselves.

3. Why does Staples include the argument between the Vietnam veterans? How does it add to your understanding of his thesis that "killing is only *machismo* taken to the extreme"? Do you agree with him? Why or why not?

   Staples establishes that the victims of the Vietnam War were poor African Americans from the ghetto rather than middle-class white youths. He also blames their Vietnam experiences for their obsession with violence and death. Open for discussion.

4. How did the narrator escape the fate of the other young men in the ghetto of Chester, Pennsylvania? Does the fact that he made it out alter your opinion of those who didn't? Explain.

   Staples escaped by going to college. Open for discussion.

5. "As I fled the past, so Blake embraced it." How does this choice affect the relationship of the two brothers?

   The difference in their choices made it more difficult for the brothers to relate to each other, and Staples's attempts to "reach" Blake were usually unsuccessful.

6. In the concluding paragraph, Staples reveals that he is still haunted by his brother's death and feels guilty about what he could have done to prevent it. Are his guilty feelings justified? Do you think anything he could have done would have altered his brother's destiny? Explain.

   Open for discussion.

Questions on Method

1. Staples records his personal anguish about his brother's death, but he also focuses on the plight of a whole generation growing up in the ghetto. Do you think his purpose is primarily to inform his audience, or is he also trying to influence his readers? Cite evidence from the essay to support your point of view. What effect does the essay have on you?

   Because Staples's essay was published in the "About Men" column of the New York Times Magazine, *he was obviously trying not only to inform but also to influence his readers by engaging their interest in the seriousness of the situation. His introducing the Vietnam War and his many examples of the wasted lives of*

African American men in the ghetto point to the discrepancy between the future of the affluent as opposed to that of the poor. Open for discussion.

2. How do techniques such as flashbacks enable Staples to place his brother's murder in a larger context? What other effective narrative techniques does he use?

   Staples's use of flashback engages the reader's attention immediately; he then moves from the particular to the more general. He also uses contrast and comparison to highlight the implications of his own choices as opposed to those of his brother. By concluding the essay with his own reaction to Blake's death, he places the experience again into a larger context—should society feel guilty about the Blakes of the ghetto?

3. Staples tries to maintain an objective tone in his essay. Are there points at which his tone becomes more personal? What, for example, is the effect of concluding the essay with his recurrent dreams?

   Staples's tone becomes more emotional when he recalls personal experiences with Blake. By ending the essay with his recurrent dream, he conveys to the reader the extent to which he is still tortured by his brother's death.

4. Does Staples convey his attitude toward the young African Americans for whom gunplay had become a way of life? Explain your answer.

   In the final paragraph of the essay, Staples expresses an impatience with those for whom "gunplay had become a way of life," but he mainly agonizes over his failure to find language that would reach them.

2

Creating an Effective Subject

ONE OF THE FIRST STEPS in writing is to create an effective topic. This stage in the writing process usually occurs before you put pen to paper. As you read "Discovery of a Father," ask yourself how Anderson went about creating an effective subject—not only deciding whom to write about but also choosing what aspects of the person's life to emphasize. Further discussion of this important step in your writing process follows Anderson's essay (pp. 15–17).

Discovery of a Father

Sherwood Anderson (1876–1941), American novelist and short-story writer, was born in a small town in Ohio and spent most of his life there. His collection of short stories, Winesburg, Ohio *(1919), reflects life in a small Midwestern town. Although these stories are fictional, Anderson's early life experiences are obvious influences in his writing as he has captured the details of small-town life so well. Anderson was convinced that the growth of urban centers would result in the disintegration of the personal life. His interest both in small-town life and its effect on people is evident in his autobiographical essay "Discovery of a Father."*

YOU HEAR IT SAID that fathers want their sons to be what they feel they cannot themselves be, but I tell you it also works the other way. A boy wants something very special from his father. I know that as a small boy I wanted my father to be a certain thing he was not. I wanted him to be a proud, silent, dignified father. When I was with other boys and he passed along the street, I wanted to feel a flow of pride. "There he is. That is my father." 1

But he wasn't such a one. He couldn't be. It seemed to me then that he was always showing off. Let's say someone in our town had got up a show. They were always doing it. The druggist would be in it, the shoe-store clerk, the horse doctor, and a lot of women and girls. My father would manage to get the chief comedy part. It was, let's say, a Civil War play and he was a comic Irish soldier. He had to do the most absurd things. They thought he was funny, but I didn't. 2

I thought he was terrible. I didn't see how mother could stand it. She even laughed with the others. Maybe I would have laughed if it hadn't been my father. 3

Or there was a parade, the Fourth of July or Decoration Day. He'd be in that, too, right at the front of it, as Grand Marshal or something, on a white horse hired from a livery stable. 4

He couldn't ride for shucks. He fell off the horse and everyone hooted with laughter, but he didn't care. He even seemed to like it. I 5 remember once when he had done something ridiculous, and right out on Main Street, too. I was with some other boys and they were laughing and shouting at him and he was shouting back and having as good a time as they were. I ran down an alley back of some stores and there in the Presbyterian Church sheds I had a good long cry.

Or I would be in bed at night and father would come home a lit- 6
tle lit up and bring some men with him. He was a man who was never alone. Before he went broke, running a harness shop, there were always a lot of men loafing in the shop. He went broke, of course, because he gave too much credit. He couldn't refuse it and I thought he was a fool. I had got to hating him.

There'd be men I didn't think would want to be fooling around 7
with him. There might even be the superintendent of our schools and a quiet man who ran the hardware store. Once I remember there was a white-haired man who was a cashier of the bank. It was a wonder to me they'd want to be seen with such a windbag. That's what I thought he was. I know now what it was that attracted them. It was because life in our town, as in all small towns, was at times pretty dull and he livened it up. He made them laugh. He could tell stories. He'd even get them to singing.

If they didn't come to our house they'd go off, say at night, to 8
where there was a grassy place by a creek. They'd cook food there and drink beer and sit about listening to his stories.

He was always telling stories about himself. He'd say this or that 9
wonderful thing had happened to him. It might be something that made him look like a fool. He didn't care.

If an Irishman came to our house, right away father would say he 10
was Irish. He'd tell what county in Ireland he was born in. He'd tell things that happened there when he was a boy. He'd make it seem so real that, if I hadn't known he was born in southern Ohio, I'd have believed him myself.

If it was a Scotchman the same thing happened, He'd get a burr 11
into his speech. Or he was a German or a Swede. He'd be anything the other man was. I think they all knew he was lying but they seemed to like him just the same. As a boy that was what I couldn't understand.

And there was mother. How could she stand it? I wanted to ask 12
but never did. She was not the kind you asked such questions.

I'd be upstairs in my bed, in my room above the porch, and father 13
would be telling some of his tales. A lot of father's stories were about the Civil War. To hear him tell it he'd been in about every battle. He'd

known Grant, Sherman, Sheridan and I don't know how many others. He'd been particularly intimate with General Grant so that when Grant went East to take charge of all the armies, he took father along.

"I was an orderly at headquarters and Sim Grant said to me,   14
'Irve,' he said, 'I'm going to take you along with me.'"

It seems he and Grant used to slip off sometimes and have a quiet   15
drink together. That's what my father said. He'd tell about the day Lee surrendered and how, when the great moment came, they couldn't find Grant.

"You know," my father said, "about General Grant's book, his   16
memoirs. You've read of how he said he had a headache and how, when he got word that Lee was ready to call it quits, he was suddenly and miraculously cured.

"Huh," said father. "He was in the woods with me.   17

"I was in there with my back against a tree. I was pretty well   18
corned. I had got hold of a bottle of pretty good stuff.

"They were looking for Grant. He had got off his horse and   19
come into the woods. He found me. He was covered with mud.

"I had the bottle in my hand. What'd I care? The war was over. I   20
knew we had them licked."

My father said that he was the one who told Grant about Lee. An   21
orderly riding by had told him, because the orderly knew how thick he was with Grant. Grant was embarrassed.

"But, Irve, look at me. I'm all covered with mud," he said to   22
father.

And then, my father said, he and Grant decided to have a drink   23
together. They took a couple of shots and then, because he didn't want Grant to show up potted before the immaculate Lee, he smashed the bottle against the tree.

"Sim Grant's dead now and I wouldn't want it to get out on   24
him," my father said.

That's just one of the kind of things he'd tell. Of course the men   25
knew he was lying, but they seemed to like it just the same.

When we got broke, down and out, do you think he ever brought   26
anything home? Not he. If there wasn't anything to eat in the house, he'd go off visiting around at farmhouses. They all wanted him. Sometimes he'd stay away for weeks, mother working to keep us fed, and then home he'd come bringing, let's say, a ham. He'd got it from some farmer friend. He'd slap it on the table in the kitchen. "You bet I'm going to see that my kids have something to eat," he'd say, and mother would just

stand smiling at him. She'd never say a word about all the weeks and months he'd been away, not leaving us a cent for food. Once I heard her speaking to a woman in our street. Maybe the woman had dared to sympathize with her. "Oh," she said, "it's all right. He isn't ever dull like most of the men in this street. Life is never dull when my man is about."

But often I was filled with bitterness, and sometimes I wished he 27
wasn't my father. I'd even invent another man as my father. To protect my mother I'd make up stories of a secret marriage that for some strange reason never got known. As though some man, say the president of a railroad company or maybe a Congressman, had married my mother, thinking his wife was dead and then it turned out she wasn't.

So they had to hush it up but I got born just the same. I wasn't 28
really the son of my father. Somewhere in the world there was a very dignified, quite wonderful man who was really my father. I even made myself half believe these fancies.

And then there came a certain night. He'd been off somewhere 29
for two or three weeks. He found me alone in the house, reading by the kitchen table.

It had been raining and he was very wet. He sat and looked at me 30
for a long time, not saying a word. I was startled, for there was on his face the saddest look I had ever seen. He sat for a time, his clothes dripping. Then he got up.

"Come on with me," he said. 31

I got up and went with him out of the house. I was filled with 32
wonder but I wasn't afraid. We went along a dirt road that led down into a valley, about a mile out of town, where there was a pond. We walked in silence. The man who was always talking had stopped his talking.

I didn't know what was up and had the queer feeling that I was 33
with a stranger. I don't know whether my father intended it so. I don't think he did.

The pond was quite large. It was still raining hard and there were 34
flashes of lightning followed by thunder. We were on a grassy bank at the pond's edge when my father spoke, and in the darkness and rain his voice sounded strange.

"Take off your clothes," he said. Still filled with wonder, I began to 35
undress. There was a flash of lightning and I saw that he was already naked.

Naked, we went into the pond. Taking my hand he pulled me in. 36
It may be that I was too frightened, too full of a feeling of strangeness, to speak. Before that night my father had never seemed to pay any attention to me.

"And what is he up to now?" I kept asking myself. I did not 37
swim very well, but he put my hand on his shoulder and struck out
into the darkness.

He was a man with big shoulders, a powerful swimmer. In the 38
darkness I could feel the movement of his muscles. We swam to the far
edge of the pond and then back to where we had left our clothes. The
rain continued and the wind blew. Sometimes my father swam on his
back and when he did he took my hand in his large powerful one and
moved it over so that it rested always on his shoulder. Sometimes there
would be a flash of lightning and I could see his face clearly.

It was as it was earlier, in the kitchen, a face filled with sadness. 39
There would be the momentary glimpse of his face and then again the
darkness, the wind, and the rain. In me there was a feeling I had never
known before.

It was a feeling of closeness. It was something strange. It was as 40
though there were only we two in the world. It was as though I had
been jerked suddenly out of myself, out of my world of the schoolboy,
out of a world in which I was ashamed of my father.

He had become blood of my blood; he the strong swimmer and 41
I the boy clinging to him in the darkness. We swam in silence and in
silence we dressed in our wet clothes, and went home.

There was a lamp lighted in the kitchen and when we came in, 42
the water dripping from us, there was my mother. She smiled at us. I
remember that she called us "boys."

"What have you boys been up to," she asked, but my father did 43
not answer. As he had begun the evening's experience with me in silence, so he ended it. He turned and looked at me. Then he went, I
thought, with a new and strange dignity out of the room.

I climbed the stairs to my own room, undressed in the darkness 44
and got into bed. I couldn't sleep and did not want to sleep. For the
first time I knew that I was the son of my father. He was a storyteller
as I was to be. It may be that I even laughed a little softly there in the
darkness. If I did, I laughed knowing that I would never again be
wanting another father.

Questions on Meaning

1. In the first part of the essay, what impression of his father does Anderson
   create? What examples of his father's behavior are given to achieve this
   impression?

2. What differences does the boy discover about his father in the swimming scene?
3. Explain the phrase "a face filled with sadness," which is used at least twice in the second part of the essay.
4. Anderson gains recognition about himself and his father as a result of this encounter. What does he find out?
5. What kind of man was Anderson's father? Why was he a clown? Why didn't he support his family? Would a father like Anderson's have embarrassed and angered you if you had been in Anderson's place?

Questions on Method

1. Why does Anderson focus on the swimming scene in writing about his father?
2. What effect does he create by using dialogue and anecdotes?
3. How would you classify Anderson's level of language? What does that suggest about the audience he is trying to reach? Explain your answer.

CREATING AN EFFECTIVE SUBJECT

How Did Anderson Create an Effective Subject?

At some point in his thinking and writing about his father, Anderson decided that his purpose should be to convey his childhood feelings about him. He therefore decided to eliminate all information about his father except that which was necessary to explain their evolving relationship. He also made a decision to focus on the swimming scene because this one event served best to indicate what he had learned about his father. He both eliminated and added material to fulfill his purpose.

He decided to show us his father in action so that we would understand both his early hatred and his subsequent admiration of the man. He chose to write an autobiographical personal essay filled with conversation and anecdote. His informality and simple vocabulary indicate that his desired audience was the common reader—the majority of Americans, regardless of the level of their education.

Creating an Effective Subject

In choosing a subject, several considerations must be kept in mind: the purpose of your writing, the **audience** to whom you are writing, your knowledge of your subject, and the proposed length of the piece. Once you have taken these aspects into account, you can begin to formulate an effective subject.

In writing for English classes, your purpose is usually to write an informative essay, and your audience is usually your instructor and your classmates. However, your instructor may also ask you to write an autobiographical essay, a business letter, an evaluative report, a scientific research essay, an editorial, or an informative magazine article. Likewise, you may be asked to write for various audiences during the semester: your peers, an employer, your coworkers, or the readers common to a particular publication, such as your college newspaper or a magazine. If your purpose and your audience vary, your choice or presentation of a subject will also vary. What is suitable to one purpose and one audience is not suitable to another.

For example, as you read the other essays in this anthology, you will notice that they are written for different audiences and with different purposes. The simple vocabulary level, the use of dialogue, and the relatively uncomplicated ideas indicate that Maya Angelou's informal autobiographical essay, like Sherwood Anderson's, is written for the average person. Other essays, such as "The Allegory of the Cave" or "A Modest Proposal," are aimed at a more sophisticated audience, as indicated by the author's allusions and vocabulary level.

A third consideration in choosing an effective subject is your knowledge of it. You write most easily about what you know best. Unless you are given an assignment to research your subject, choose one with which you are familiar, about which you have knowledge sufficient for your purpose. A good way to tell how much you know about a subject is to freewrite about it; if you cannot produce much freewriting on a subject, then you might consider another subject.

A final consideration is length. Most assignments in English classes call for much shorter essays than those written by many professional writers—usually in the 500- to 1,000-word range. You will therefore want to focus more narrowly than they in order not to sacrifice the concreteness of detail that is the mark of any successful essay. It is much more effective to devote full attention to one specific aspect of your subject than to try to tell everything about it in a short space. If you have many pages of freewriting or many entries in your journal, you might consider narrowing your subject to just one aspect of it.

Once you have taken into account purpose, audience, your knowledge of the subject, and the length called for, you should be able to shape an effective subject.

Procedures to Follow in Creating an Effective Subject

1. Define your purpose in writing. Is it to express your feelings, give information, persuade? How would each purpose affect your presentation of your material?

2. Consider your audience. What is your reader most likely to be interested in and know about? If you are writing an informal essay to your classmates, then consider how the material might best be presented in an essay written for this audience. If you are given the assignment of writing instead for your instructor, consider how your presentation of the material will differ.

3. Determine how much writing will be necessary to develop your purpose specifically, even dramatically. If you find you have too much material for the length of your paper, reexamine your material for an aspect or aspects that you can develop specifically in the allotted space.

4. In order to be as specific as possible, explore your subject further through freewriting or, if further knowledge is required, conduct some research.

5. Phrase a sentence to clarify for yourself exactly what you intend to write about. Be as specific as possible. For example, Anderson's thesis sentence might have been, "While for many of my childhood years I was ashamed of my clownish father, I one night came to realize his serious side, which made me proud to be his son." While Anderson did not include this sentence in his essay, you may wish to include your thesis sentence in your introductory paragraph.

3

Organizing the Essay

How did Maya Angelou organize her essay on Sister Flowers? As you read the essay, you will discover that Angelou is obviously telling about a person she knew as a child. However, she narrates the experience as vividly as though it were taking place in the present. Ask yourself how Angelou organized the details she recalled of Sister Flowers's clothes, her smile, the odor in her house, and the appearance of her rooms. Further discussion of this important step in your writing process follows Angelou's essay (pp. 25–28).

Sister Flowers

Born in St. Louis, Missouri, Maya Angelou (b. 1928) is an author, poet, playwright, professional stage and screen producer, director, performer, and singer. She won the National Book Award in 1970 for I Know Why the Caged Bird Sings *and a Pulitzer Prize nomination in 1972 for* Just Give Me a Cool Drink of Water 'fore I Die. *In 1976 she was named Woman of the Year in Communications and was nominated for a Tony Award for best supporting actress in* Roots. *Angelou, who is a prolific writer and poet, has an extensive list of publications that includes* Gather in My Name *(1974);* Oh Pray My Wings Are Gonna Fit Me Well, *poetry (1975);* Singin' and Swingin' and Gettin' Merry Like Christmas, *an autobiography (1976);* And Still I Rise, *poetry (1978);* The Heart of a Woman, *an autobiography (1981);* Shaker Why Don't You Sing?, *poetry (1983);* All God's Children Need Traveling Shoes, *an autobiography (1986);* Mrs. Flowers: A Moment of Friendship, *fiction (1986);* Poems: Maya Angelou, *four volumes (1987);* Now Sheba Sings the Song *(1987);* I Shall Not Be Moved, *poetry (1990); and the inaugural poem she wrote for President Clinton,* On the Pulse of Morning *(1993).*

FOR NEARLY A YEAR, I sopped around the house, the Store, the school and the church, like an old biscuit, dirty and inedible. Then I met, or rather got to know, the lady who threw me my first life line. [1]

Mrs. Bertha Flowers was the aristocrat of Black Stamps. She had the grace of control to appear warm in the coldest weather, and on the Arkansas summer days it seemed she had a private breeze which swirled around, cooling her. She was thin without the taut look of wiry people, and her printed voile dresses and flowered hats were as right for her as denim overalls for a farmer. She was our side's answer to the richest white woman in town. [2]

Her skin was a rich black that would have peeled like a plum if snagged, but then no one would have thought of getting close enough to Mrs. Flowers to ruffle her dress, let alone snag her skin. She didn't encourage familiarity. She wore gloves too. [3]

I don't think I ever saw Mrs. Flowers laugh, but she smiled often.   4
A slow widening of her thin black lips to show even, small white teeth,
then the slow effortless closing. When she chose to smile on me, I always wanted to thank her. The action was so graceful and inclusively
benign.

Mrs. She was one of the few gentlewomen I have ever known, and has   5
remained throughout my life the measure of what a human being can
be.

Momma had a strange relationship with her. Most often when   6
she passed on the road in front of the Store, she spoke to Momma in
that soft yet carrying voice, "Good day, Mrs. Henderson." Momma
responded with "How you, Sister Flowers?"

Mrs. Flowers didn't belong to our church, nor was she Momma's   7
familiar. Why on earth did she insist on calling her Sister Flowers?
Shame made me want to hide my face. Mrs. Flowers deserved better
than to be called Sister. Then, Momma left out the verb. Why not ask,
"How *are* you, *Mrs.* Flowers?" With the unbalanced passion of the
young, I hated her for showing her ignorance to Mrs. Flowers. It
didn't occur to me for many years that they were as alike as sisters, separated only by formal education.

Although I was upset, neither of the women was in the least   8
shaken by what I thought an unceremonious greeting. Mrs. Flowers
would continue her easy gait up the hill to her little bungalow, and
Momma kept on shelling peas or doing whatever had brought her to
the front porch.

Occasionally, though, Mrs. Flowers would drift off the road and   9
down to the Store and Momma would say to me, "Sister, you go on
and play." As she left I would hear the beginning of an intimate conversation. Momma persistently using the wrong verb, or none at all.

"Brother and Sister Wilcox is sho'ly the meanest—" "Is,"   10
Momma? "Is"? Oh, please, not "is," Momma, for two or more. But
they talked, and from the side of the building where I waited for the
ground to open up and swallow me, I heard the soft-voiced Mrs.
Flowers and the textured voice of my grandmother merging and melting. They were interrupted from time to time by giggles that must
have come from Mrs. Flowers (Momma never giggled in her life).
Then she was gone.

She appealed to me because she was like people I had never met   11
personally. Like women in English novels who walked the moors
(whatever they were) with their loyal dogs racing at a respectful dis-

tance. Like the women who sat in front of roaring fireplaces, drinking tea incessantly from silver trays full of scones and crumpets. Women who walked over the "heath" and read morocco-bound books and had two last names divided by a hyphen. It would be safe to say that she made me proud to be Negro, just by being herself.

She acted just as refined as whitefolks in the movies and books 　12 and she was more beautiful, for none of them could have come near that warm color without looking gray by comparison.

It was fortunate that I never saw her in the company of powhite- 　13 folks. For since they tend to think of their whiteness as an evenizer, I'm certain that I would have had to hear her spoken to commonly as Bertha, and my image of her would have been shattered like the un-mendable Humpty-Dumpty.

One summer afternoon, sweet-milk fresh in my memory, she 　14 stopped at the Store to buy provisions. Another Negro woman of her health and age would have been expected to carry the paper sacks home in one hand, but Momma said, "Sister Flowers, I'll send Bailey up to your house with these things."

She smiled that slow dragging smile, "Thank you, Mrs. Hender- 　15 son. I'd prefer Marguerite, though." My name was beautiful when she said it. "I've been meaning to talk to her, anyway." They gave each other age-group looks.

Momma said, "Well, that's all right then. Sister, go and change 　16 your dress. You going to Sister Flowers's."

The chifforobe was a maze. What on earth did one put on to go 　17 to Mrs. Flowers's house? I knew I shouldn't put on a Sunday dress. It might be sacrilegious. Certainly not a house dress, since I was already wearing a fresh one. I chose a school dress, naturally. It was formal without suggesting that going to Mrs. Flowers's house was equivalent to attending church.

I trusted myself back into the Store. 　18

"Now, don't you look nice." I had chosen the right thing, for 　19 once....

There was a little path beside the rocky road, and Mrs. Flowers 　20 walked in front swinging her arms and picking her way over the stones.

She said, without turning her head, to me, "I hear you're doing 　21 very good school work, Marguerite, but that it's all written. The teachers report that they have trouble getting you to talk in class." We passed the triangular farm on our left and the path widened to allow us to walk together. I hung back in the separate unasked and unanswerable questions.

"Come and walk along with me, Marguerite." I couldn't have refused even if I wanted to. She pronounced my name so nicely. Or more correctly, she spoke each word with such clarity that I was certain a foreigner who didn't understand English could have understood her.   22

"Now no one is going to make you talk—possibly no one can. But bear in mind, language is man's way of communicating with his fellow man and it is language alone which separates him from the lower animals." That was a totally new idea to me, and I would need time to think about it.   23

"Your grandmother says you read a lot. Every chance you get. That's good, but not good enough. Words mean more than what is set down on paper. It takes the human voice to infuse them with the shades of deeper meaning."   24

I memorized the part about the human voice infusing words. It seemed so valid and poetic.   25

She said she was going to give me some books and that I not only must read them, I must read them aloud. She suggested that I try to make a sentence sound in as many different ways as possible.   26

"I'll accept no excuse if you return a book to me that has been badly handled." My imagination boggled at the punishment I would deserve if in fact I did abuse a book of Mrs. Flowers's. Death would be too kind and brief.   27

The odors in the house surprised me. Somehow I had never connected Mrs. Flowers with food or eating or any other common experience of common people. There must have been an outhouse, too, but my mind never recorded it.   28

The sweet scent of vanilla had met us as she opened the door.   29

"I made tea cookies this morning. You see, I had planned to invite you for cookies and lemonade so we could have this little chat. The lemonade is in the icebox."   30

It followed that Mrs. Flowers would have ice on an ordinary day, when most families in our town bought ice late on Saturdays only a few times during the summer to be used in the wooden ice-cream freezers.   31

She took the bags from me and disappeared through the kitchen door. I looked around the room that I had never in my wildest fantasies imagined I would see. Browned photographs leered or threatened from the walls and the white, freshly done curtains pushed against   32 themselves and against the wind. I wanted to gobble up the room entire and take it to Bailey, who would help me analyze and enjoy it.

"Have a seat, Marguerite. Over there by the table." She carried a 33 platter covered with a tea towel. Although she warned that she hadn't tried her hand at baking sweets for some time, I was certain that like everything else about her the cookies would be perfect.

They were flat round wafers, slightly browned on the edges and 34 butter-yellow in the center. With the cold lemonade they were sufficient for childhood's lifelong diet. Remembering my manners, I took nice little lady-like bites off the edges. She said she had made them expressly for me and that she had a few in the kitchen that I could take home to my brother. So I jammed one whole cake in my mouth and the rough crumbs scratched the insides of my jaws, and if I hadn't had to swallow, it would have been a dream come true.

As I ate she began the first of what we later called "my lessons in 35 living." She said that I must always be intolerant of ignorance but understanding of illiteracy. That some people, unable to go to school, were more educated and even more intelligent than college professors. She encouraged me to listen carefully to what country people called mother wit. That in those homely sayings was couched the collective wisdom of generations.

When I finished the cookies she brushed off the table and 36 brought a thick, small book from the bookcase. I had read *A Tale of Two Cities* and found it up to my standards as a romantic novel. She opened the first page and I heard poetry for the first time in my life.

"It was the best of times and the worst of times..." Her voice slid 37 in and curved down through and over the words. She was nearly singing. I wanted to look at the pages. Were they the same that I had read? Or were there notes, music, lined on the pages, as in a hymn book? Her sounds began cascading gently. I knew from listening to a thousand preachers that she was nearing the end of her reading, and I hadn't really heard, heard to understand, a single word.

"How do you like that?" 38

It occurred to me that she expected a response. The sweet vanilla 39 flavor was still on my tongue and her reading was a wonder in my ears. I had to speak.

I said, "Yes, ma'am." It was the least I could do, but it was the 40 most also.

"There's one more thing. Take this book of poems and memo- 41 rize one for me. Next time you pay me a visit, I want you to recite."

I have tried often to search behind the sophistication of years for the enchantment I so easily found in those gifts. The essence escapes but its aura remains. To be allowed, no, invited, into the private lives of strangers, and to share their joys and fears, was a chance to exchange the Southern bitter wormwood for a cup of mead with Beowulf or a hot cup of tea and milk with Oliver Twist. When I said aloud, "It is a far, far better thing that I do, than I have ever done..." tears of love filled my eyes at my selflessness.

On that first day, I ran down the hill and into the road (few cars ever came along it) and had the good sense to stop running before I reached the Store.

I was liked, and what a difference it made. I was respected not as Mrs. Henderson's grandchild or Bailey's sister but for just being Marguerite Johnson.

Childhood's logic never asks to be proved (all conclusions are absolute). I didn't question why Mrs. Flowers had singled me out for attention, nor did it occur to me that Momma might have asked her to give me a little talking to. All I cared about was that she had made tea cookies for *me* and read to *me* from her favorite book. It was enough to prove that she liked me.

Questions on Meaning

1. What is Marguerite like before Sister Flowers takes an interest in her? Why is the attention of Sister Flowers important to her?
2. Marguerite calls Sister Flowers "one of the few gentlewoman" she has ever known. What does she mean? What is it that makes Sister Flowers a gentlewoman in her eyes?
3. What sort of lessons does Sister Flowers give Marguerite? Why does she encourage Marguerite to be "intolerant of ignorance but understanding of illiteracy"? Why does she insist that Marguerite read aloud?
4. After she has grown up, what does Marguerite realize about her relationship with Sister Flowers?
5. Marguerite says that Sister Flowers made her "proud to be Negro." How does Sister Flowers do that? Is this the most important thing she does for Marguerite?

Questions on Method

1. Why does Angelou choose to write about Sister Flowers? Which sentence best explains the significance of her subject for her?

2. In what ways does Angelou contrast Momma with Sister Flowers? In what ways does she contrast herself as a child with each woman? How do these contrasts help us to understand Marguerite better?

3. Angelou chooses to focus on the first time Marguerite goes to Sister Flowers's house. What do we learn about Marguerite through this experience? What, for example, do we learn about her when Angelou writes that the odors in the house surprised her?

4. Angelou begins the essay by comparing herself to "an old biscuit, dirty and inedible." What does this image tell us about her? How does the image of the tea cookies help us to understand the kind of effect Sister Flowers will have on her?

ORGANIZING AN ESSAY

What Framework Is Evident in Angelou's Essay?

Maya Angelou introduces her essay with a one-sentence description of her life before meeting Sister Flowers and then introduces her subject in the final sentence of the first paragraph: "Then I met, or rather got to know, the lady who threw me my first life line." In her next four paragraphs, she describes Sister Flowers's appearance and demeanor as a gentlewoman.

She devotes paragraphs 6–10 to Momma's relationship with Sister Flowers and 11–13 to the reasons why Sister Flowers appealed to her, and then in paragraph 14, beginning "One summer afternoon...," she begins narrating her visit to Sister Flowers's home. She proceeds chronologically from Sister Flowers's invitation to her subsequent preparation for the visit, her walk with Sister Flowers to her home, her eating the cookies Sister Flowers had prepared, and finally the first of her "lessons in living." She concludes her essay with her jubilant reaction to the interest this gentlewoman had taken in her.

Like Anderson's, Angelou's essay is divided into two major sections, the first giving background, the second focusing on one event that best dramatizes her thesis, the visit to Sister Flowers's house. Her outline might look like this:

I. Introduction (Paragraph 1)

II. My admiration for Sister Flowers from afar (Paragraphs 1–13)

    A. Sister Flowers, the aristocrat (Paragraphs 2–5)

        1. Her grace

        2. Her clothing

3. Her reserve

   B. Momma's relationship with Sister Flowers (Paragraphs 6–10)

      1. Momma called her by the familiar name "Sister"

      2. Momma used the wrong verb

      3. Only as an adult does Angelou realize they were alike as sisters, separated only by formal education

   C. Sister Flowers's appeal to Angelou (Paragraphs 11–13)

      1. She reminds her of heroines in novels

      2. She acted as refined as whitefolks

III. One summer afternoon's visit to Sister Flowers's home (Paragraphs 14–43)

   A. The invitation

   B. The preparation

   C. The discussion about talking as well as reading

   D. The odors in the house

   E. The cookies

   F. The first "lesson in living"

   G. The reading from *A Tale of Two Cities*

   H. The gift of the book of poems

   I. The exit running down the hill

IV. Conclusion: reaction to being liked (Paragraphs 44–45)

Organizing the Essay

Good writing results from much effort. One important step in writing the essay, which is time-consuming but necessary, is developing the outline. The outline helps you focus sharply on a subject by eliminating wandering from the subject, repeating earlier points, or neglecting major aspects of the subject. The outline also helps you focus on the order in which you will present your points.

There are at least two ways of approaching the organization of an essay through outlining. The traditional method is to list all aspects of a topic, arrange them in appropriate sequence, and proceed to write. Many writers find that a second method works better because they do not know what they want to say until they actually begin writing. These writers prefer to make their outlines after they have engaged in freewriting or have written a first draft. With all of their ideas on paper, they then sort them into a logical sequence. After changing, rearranging, eliminating, and/or adding, they proceed to the final draft.

There are various patterns of organization, and you will explore many of these in subsequent chapters, including Chapter 5 (narrative arrangement), Chapter 6 (descriptive arrangement), Chapter 8 (process analysis), Chapter 11 (comparison and contrast), and Chapter 13 (persuasion).

These patterns apply largely to the middle, or body, of the essay. The introduction has a dual function: to interest the reader in the essay and to give him or her some idea of its purpose (the thesis statement is usually located in this paragraph). The **introduction** should present the subject in such a way as to make the audience aware that the writer is interested in the reader's reactions to his or her subject matter.

The **conclusion** to a short essay should do more than simply summarize the paper; only in long essays, in which the reader might forget earlier points, is the summary conclusion effective. The conclusion instead should present to the reader aspects of the subject about which he or she might think further. It should also leave an impact on the reader's mind. Most important, it should have a note of finality that assures the reader that the essay has been concluded.

Procedures to Follow in Organizing Your Essay

1. Write your thesis sentence at the top of the page, making sure it is phrased as clearly as possible.

2. Make an outline under the first method.

   a. List all of the ideas that occur to you in thinking about your topic.

   b. Once you have made an extensive list, rearrange the items into headings and subheadings. Your headings will form the major points that will later constitute the body of your paper.

   c. Group all the other items under the major headings, eliminating those that, on second thought, obviously do not fit in. Your subheadings should develop your headings, just as your headings develop your essay topic.

   d. Check to see that each division is distinct from the others to avoid overlapping.

   e. Determine if any major points have been omitted.

   f. Arrange your points in a logical order.

3. If you prefer the second method of outlining, begin with free-writing or a first draft of your topic. Next, make an outline based on what you have written. Scrutinize your outline carefully. Does each heading belong? Are any repeated? Are the points arranged in a logical order? What other points can you now think of to include? Once you have answered these questions and made the necessary adjustments, you are ready to begin what may be your final draft.

4

On Writing and Revising an Essay

EMILY HEGARTY WROTE "*Meanie* and Me" specifically for this book, and her description of her writing and revision process follows the essay. As you read "*Meanie* and Me," focus on how effectively Hegarty's introductory paragraph prepares you for what follows in the essay. Try to determine her purpose in writing the essay. You already know that she wrote for a particular audience—college students like yourself. To what extent is she successful in reaching that audience? Although Hegarty is writing about her first experience reading her poetry in public, how does her inclusion of specific details about people and the process of producing a poetry magazine make her essay more effective?

Meanie *and* Me

Emily Hegarty (b. 1964) is an English instructor at Nassau Community College and lives and writes mostly joyfully in Brooklyn. She would like to acknowledge the kind cooperation of Jim Behrle, Mike Bucell, and Fred Marchant, who graciously consented to be interviewed for this article. Meanie welcomes submissions and can be contacted through their website at www.meanie.behrle.com.

I AM NOT MUCH OF A POET. I am an academic, a college English 1 teacher. I study poetry and teach poetry but I haven't written much of it myself, and what I have written I rarely show to anyone. Even though I grade hundreds of freshman essays each semester, I don't like it when the tables are turned and my own personal writing is judged. I am afraid to be laughed at. So when my friend Jim Behrle started a poetry magazine in Boston, I encouraged him. I cheered him on. I went to the readings. But I didn't participate.

Jim started the magazine in December 1995, during a time when 2 some other things in his life weren't working out. He explains: "I had failed out of college. I was living at home at that point. It was my senior year and I wasn't going to graduate." At college, Jim had been editing the campus literary journal *Venture,* but found the process difficult: "I decided I wanted to start my own poetry magazine. I was having terrible problems with *Venture* and wondered what it would be like to run my own poetry magazine my way."

The new magazine was called *Meanie,* after an "awful love poem" 3 he had written years before. Jim says his poem was "about this person I was achingly, desperately in love with, and who was always cruel to me." In the first issue of *Meanie,* he defends "the thought behind" the awful love poem: "Often in everyday life, we express affection through animosity. We pull pigtails on the recess field because we love you. We make fun of you because we love you. That's what this magazine is about. Finding something grand in an unexpected place."

The first issue of *Meanie* was clearly an amateur production. It   4
was twenty-eight pages photocopied on plain paper and side-stapled.
On the cover, under the title, was the cover of a religious pamphlet
distributed by fanatics in the subway: "Repent now! The End is
Near!" The illustrations were doodled cartoons and a few collages
made of "found" objects arranged on the photocopier glass: loose
change, coupons for free coffee, receipts from used bookstores. There
were ten poems by ten different contributors, and an introduction to
each poet on the page facing his or her poem. Most of the poets were
students who had also been involved with *Venture*. It cost a dollar. Jim
sold thirty copies on campus out of his backpack.

Reactions to early editions of *Meanie* were mixed. Jim frankly   5
says: "They thought it sucked. The first ten contributors were friends
I had solicited poems from." By this time, Jim had left college and
found a job at Waterstones, a bookstore chain with several outlets in
Boston. He continued to publish *Meanie*. When his friend Mike Bucell
moved back to Boston from California, Jim enlisted his help as co-
editor. Asked why he decided to get involved, Mike is characteristi-
cally low-key: "I had a computer and he didn't. It's a good excuse to
get drunk together." But when he wasn't drinking, Mike created a
website for the magazine which has become a source of many submissions. *Meanie* held a few open mike readings at a local coffeehouse.
Meanwhile, Jim convinced his employers at the bookstore to let him
sell copies of *Meanie* and hold regular readings in their main store in
Boston's Back Bay.

Now that he had a job, Jim worked out a discount rate with a local   6
printing shop and created more elaborate colored covers for the magazine. Illustrator Steve Donaruma and cartoonist Rob Morse provided
witty artwork, and the "found object" collages grew more elaborate.
Recent issues have included reproductions of brochures from self-help
groups ("Change your life!"), grade-school "punishment" essays on
"why I can't behave," scolding notes to roommates who leave the bathroom a mess, and even a curt letter from a bookstore refusing to stock
Meanie on the grounds that it is "poetically challenged." Slowly but
surely, *Meanie* has grown, increasing in length and price. The most recent, eleventh issue was seventy-eight pages long and cost three dollars.
Jim and Mike estimate that they have sold about 700 copies of *Meanie* in
the past three years. Even at three dollars, the price doesn't cover the
cost of printing. Jim pays the difference himself, and intends to keep

publishing *Meanie* as long as he can afford it. He has included free ads for supporters like the print shop and the coffeehouse, but has rejected advertisers who have approached him. He says, "*Meanie* has resisted growing and changing because *Meanie* just sort of is what it is."

As the magazine has grown, so has the range of contributors. Jim's 7 attention to the local poetry community has won *Meanie* the support of more established Boston poets who appreciate what he and Mike are trying to do. Poet William Corbett, author of *New York Literary Lights* and the memoir *Furthering My Education,* has appeared in *Meanie*. Corbett has also included Jim's work in a group of Boston poets featured in the literary magazine *lingo*. Especially charming was *lingo*'s photograph of sixty-five Boston poets lined up on the steps of the august Boston Public Library in Copley Square. Jim and Mike are right in the middle, grinning broadly, as is Poet Laureate Robert Pinsky in the lower left, though Nobel Prize winner Seamus Heaney is pokerfaced in the lower right. The *Boston Globe* published a human interest feature on *Meanie*. Most recently, Jim has been featured in a "Roving Poet" radio program for WBUR-FM, Cambridge's NPR affiliate.

Publishing a literary magazine, however, is not all hobnobbing 8 with the literati. Every three months, Jim and Mike actually put the magazine together. They compile and review all of the submissions. They accept almost all of them, although sometimes Jim will suggest revisions to improve a poem. They deliberately avoid outright rejecting people; Jim explains:

> One of the strengths of what *Meanie* is is to not be editorial or hierarchical which people associate too much with poetry.... In the eleven issues that we've published, we've probably published over a hundred people for the first time. Poetry is an increasingly intimidating genre of writing and the less intimidating we can make it and the more fun we can make it seem, the better it is for the future of all poetry everywhere.

Their strategy is to resist claiming the authority inherent in the title "Editor" by making fun of the idea of editors. Jim's biographical statement reads: "Jim Behrle grows more corrupt every day, the power bloating the sides of his head like a water balloon." Mike spoofs the notion of poetry publication as a commodity: "We hand-pick only the freshest, most ripe poems we can find, and then flash-freeze them to preserve their juicy goodness."

Poet Fred Marchant, author of *Tipping Point,* acknowledges that   9
"Jim has an intuitive sense of how to combine the high-art impulse
with the down and dirty subversive impulse." But Marchant also pre-
dicts that as *Meanie* continues to grow, Jim and Mike will have to resign
themselves to rejecting some poems for reasons of space if not aesthetics. But another poet, Elizabeth Savage, disagrees. She praises *Meanie's*
open editorial policy as a "deliberate abandonment of authority" that
allows a redefinition of risk for young poets. By making publication
possible for everyone, Savage argues, *Meanie* decertifies publication as
proof of "goodness." Instead, publication becomes part of the process
of writing. Writers can begin to move away from judgmental ideas
about what's good and what's bad, thereby "forgoing traditional com-
petitiveness" and making space for more interesting conversations
about writing and poetry in general.

After each issue's poems are selected, Jim and Mike retype them   10
to fit the *Meanie* layout. Then it's time to brainstorm each issue's far too
personal interview questions. After the first issue, Jim replaced each
poet's introduction with an interview. The interviews take as much
space as the poems, and are something like a game of Truth or Consequences. Each poet answers questions like: What does God look like?
If you could invent anything, what would you invent? What's the
worst thing you have ever done? What makes you nervous? If you became a vampire, who would you bite first? What would you like to be
wearing when you die? Who was the first person you ever loved? Do
you have any memories of when you were two? What wouldn't you
want published about you? If you could change something about your
appearance, what would it be? What do you pray for? These interviews
have become one of the attractions of the magazine. Regular contributors begin to anticipate each other's answers and speak to each other.
Sometimes contributors resist the interviews, speaking past Jim to the
readers or to other poets in the community. Some write letters, scrawl
notes, or send greeting cards, all of which are faithfully photocopied
and included.

Once the interviews are done, there is a rush to get the issue to   11
the printer, and then *Meanie* is ready for release and preparations for the
new issue's reading can begin. The readings are even more accessible
than the magazine. Anyone who shows up is allowed to read, whether
they have contributed to *Meanie* or not. The well-publicized readings
can draw up to forty people on good night, and the audience usually
includes contributors, friends, poetry fans, and various customers who

happen to be in the bookstore when the reading starts. Obviously, the material is highly varied. Sometimes a poet reading a fifteen-second haiku is followed by a novelist reading from his work-in-progress. Coffee, wine, and snacks are provided, and every reader is applauded, although with varying degrees of enthusiasm. At times, the readings become emotional, a sure sign that a community is forming. One issue of *Meanie* was dedicated to Michael Plante, a writer and friend who had recently died, whose poetry was read *in absentia*. The most emotional reading I've seen there was by a nervous but jubilant young woman with cerebral palsy, who read: "They say I have cerebral palsy and I can't write poetry, but I can!" "The readings," Jim says,

> foster a camaraderie between poets where people who are writing at the same time can converse with one another. There is a community for younger starting poets. You don't have to go to Harvard and get an MFA to be in a community of poets. There are cheaper and easier ways to find community that are just as fulfilling.

Even though *Meanie* readings create a friendly, nonjudgmental, and kind community, it took more than a year for me to get up the courage to read one of my own poems. I felt that my own nervousness was ridiculous. After all, as a teacher I stand up and talk in front of a roomful of people a dozen times a week. But I hadn't counted on the difference between talking about a homework assignment or the importance of transitional sentences and the completely other experience of reading my own poem. Classroom discussion is in a sense impersonal; it's about the matters we're studying, the text at hand. I didn't write it; I only teach it. If people don't like it, that just means they don't like English or they don't like the homework assignment. It's nothing to do with me. But my poem *is* me. Standing in front of that audience, everything I knew about the difference between the author and the author's persona went right out of my head. At the microphone, I was horrified to find that my hands were shaking too much to hold my poem steady; I had to put it down on the podium to read it. I felt sick to my stomach and my voice sounded funny and shaky. I tried to read slowly, in hopes of hitting at least a normal speed instead of the jittery dash in my head. It didn't help that I had written a sad love poem, and now risked being rejected for writing badly about being rejected.

Somewhere in the middle of the third line, I had a revelation. That sick feeling in my stomach wasn't illness; it was excitement. And that jit-

12

13

tery feeling was adrenaline, not fear. I was amazed to realize that I was more excited at that moment about that poem than I had been about anything I'd written in years. I was excited precisely because I didn't know if my poem was good or not. I was thrillingly unsure, with not even a notion of a thesis statement, nor a single footnote to fall back on.

The audience clapped when I finished, but I wasn't worried anymore about rejection. I was too excited. Reading my poem had made *me* like it, because I finally owned it, out loud and in front of people. Reading my poem made me wonder why everything I wrote wasn't exciting. I saw finally how often I hid the real me behind footnotes and academic jargon. Even more, reading my poem made me see that I really love writing, but had been, after years of judged and graded academic work, too fearful of rejection to write anything real. Since then, I've written a lot more often and a lot more honestly. I'm still not much of a poet, but I'm a happier writer. *Meanie* taught me about my need for writing to be joyful, and I'd been teaching for years before I even knew I needed to learn that.

14

Questions on Meaning

1. What portrait emerges of Hegarty from the first paragraph of the essay? What other examples does the author include at the end of her essay to reinforce her introduction?
2. What did you learn about producing a poetry magazine from reading "*Meanie* and Me"?
3. Why does Hegarty include so many details about Jim and Mike? Which did you find most effective?
4. What purposes do the poetry readings serve?

Questions on Method

1. How does Hegarty's title provide the framework for her essay?
2. What is her purpose in writing this essay? Is she merely informing her audience about the process involved in producing a poetry magazine, or is she seeking to persuade them that this is a worthwhile task? What is your response to her essay?
3. How effective is Hegarty's use of humor? Cite examples you appreciated.

How I Wrote "Meanie *and Me*"

MY WRITING PROCESS for this essay was more streamlined than usual, because I was under deadline pressure. Here are the steps I followed:

1. I decided on *Meanie* as a topic. *Meanie* had been for some months the context in which I did most of my thinking about writing. I thought I already knew everything about *Meanie,* so writing about it would be easy. That turned out not to be true.

2. I interviewed the *Meanie* editors. I thought they would be easy to interview, since we are friends and we have had many great conversations about their magazine and the issues it raises for them. However, once they knew they were being interviewed for an article, they got self-conscious and had little to say. Later on, I did a supplemental phone interview with Jim Behrle, which went better. My advice: Don't conduct interviews in bars.

3. One morning, some weeks later, sitting on the commuter train to work, I realized the deadline was getting very close. I took out a notebook and freewrote about *Meanie.*

4. When I got home, I used a flowchart program on the computer to diagram the main ideas of my freewrite. A lot of what I'd written had gone off on irrelevant tangents. They were interesting to me, but I left them out.

   The flowchart program is great for outlining, because after you finish making the diagram, you can click a button to put the categories into an outline format. Shifting back and forth between the two views—diagram and outline—really lets you see different relationships between ideas and information. I changed the order of topics frequently while I was writing. I also found that several of my favorite ideas and quotes didn't really fit into any category, no matter how much I rearranged them, so I left them out.

5. I reread my notes from the interview and put some of the quotes into appropriate categories. Some of the quotes gave me ideas for new categories.

6. I got my stack of old *Meanie* magazines from the bookshelf and read through all of them, adding ideas and descriptions to my outline as I went along. I was tempted to include some of the poetry, but decided my article was more about writing than about poetry. I knew that I wanted to frame the essay with my own experience at a poetry reading, but I wanted to focus on my experience reading. If I started to include poetry, it would only make sense to include my poem. I didn't want to do that, because I thought it would distract people from my main point about the experience of reading one's work. There was the chance readers would think, "What a terrible poem! She was right to be scared! She should never have read this!" If that happened, my main point would be ruined.

7. I emailed a few people familiar with *Meanie* to see if they wanted to add any suggestions or quotes. Fred Marchant emailed me back fastest, and was interesting, so I used his quote. I also liked that he was an authority, and thought that including him added a fuller perspective to my article.

8. By now I had a very long outline. I saved it as a word processing document and started filling in the outline, writing a paragraph or two for each major point. My first draft was done! Steps 4 through 8 took all of one day.

9. The next evening, I reread my first draft and notice it was rambling and too personal. It wasn't right to talk so much about myself in an article primarily about *Meanie*. Also, much of the personal information failed the "Who cares?" test. I couldn't imagine anyone being that interested. I also worried that no one would be interested in any part of the essay, but I fought off that irrational fear and continued.

10. I started editing the essay, mostly by cutting things out of it. I did most of the cutting in the introduction, which had far too much boring and irrelevant personal rambling. I also deleted an opening paragraph that was mostly a memo to myself about what I was trying to do. Throughout the rest of the essay, especially in the conclusion, I tried to make the writing clearer. I had written lots of compound sentences with many dependent clauses and semicolons. I broke those down into shorter, declarative sentences, leaving out irrelevant details and extra examples. Because I had been writing swiftly, my vocabulary in my first draft was

sloppy. I had used the first words I thought of and gone on to the next paragraph. During this edit, I thought of better and more precise words to use in places where I had been vague and unclear.

11. I did a final proofread. I reformatted the essay so it had standard margins and a standard font. I ran a spellchecking program and fixed my spelling errors. I double-checked my quotes and my punctuation.

Steps 9 through 11 lasted one entire evening. When I was finished, I faxed the essay to the editor and congratulated myself on missing the deadline by only one day.

Questions on Hegarty's Revision Process

1. How valuable is Hegarty's freewriting exercise described in Steps 3 and 4 for her revision of "*Meanie* and Me"?
2. How does the flowchart program assist her in outlining and rearranging her ideas?
3. What techniques for preserving the essay's unity emerge in Steps 6 and 9?
4. In Step 10, Hegarty focuses on deletion, sentence structure, and vocabulary. What editing strategies do you find most effective?
5. Why does Hegarty record the time spent in completing Steps 4–8 and 9–11? How many drafts does she complete before her final proofread in Step 11?

REVISING THE ESSAY

In order to focus and unify a piece of writing, writers will adopt one or more of several revision strategies. They may add, delete, rearrange, substitute, consolidate, or distribute.

Adding means that material—a word, sentence, or paragraph—is inserted to clarify the subject.

Deleting means that material that distracts from what is being said about the subject is cut.

Rearranging means that parts are moved around in order to make the organization more effective.

Substituting means that material—a word, sentence, or paragraph—is changed to make the meaning clearer.

Consolidating means that because too many references to an aspect of the subject detract from the importance of that aspect or destroy the overall unity of the subject, all material on that aspect is brought to-gether in one part of the essay.

Distributing is the opposite of consolidating. It means that an aspect of the subject that in the original was mentioned only once is now mentioned throughout because of its importance for creating unity.

Procedures for Revising Your Essay

Whether you used freewriting in starting to compose your first draft or tried to write an already organized piece of writing, you might consider whether your essay would benefit from any of the revision strategies. If you work in groups, your group members may give you feedback as well.

1. Has important information or transitional material been left out that you might add now?

2. Does every sentence and every paragraph contribute directly to your subject, or should some material be deleted?

3. Do your points follow in a logical order such as least important to most important or, as in a narrative, from beginning to end, or should they be rearranged for a greater impact?

4. Paragraphs that often need substitutions are the introduction and conclusion. Are you happy with yours, or might you substitute better ones?

5. Have you scattered references to an important aspect of your sub-ject throughout the essay, thus reducing its impact or mentioning it before it is effective to do so? If so, you might consolidate your discussion in one part of the essay.

6. Have you mentioned an important theme and then dropped it? Or have you neglected to introduce a theme that you should have mentioned from the very beginning? If so, you will want to dis-tribute mention of this theme throughout the essay.

5

Narration

NARRATION IS STORYTELLING that makes a point. This definition implies that the purpose of a narrative is to share a main idea, and the meaning of a narrative is the main point to be shared. A good narration includes a meaningful event, thoughtful organization, a clear point of view, and telling details that evoke interest and contribute to meaning. Many events seem to happen at random, either because they are unexpected or because the participants do not invest them with meaning. In narrating an event, however, you, as narrator, should decide beforehand what meaning you wish to convey to the reader. This meaning will give unity to your essay if you select your organization, point of view, and details with this theme in mind. This meaning does not have to be earth-shattering, just as the event you write about need not be cataclysmic; it must, however, matter to you.

Beyond these requirements, narration demands attention to *point of view, pacing, chronology,* and *transitions.* Whether you are writing fiction or nonfiction, you will have to choose a *point of view.* In everyday language the term *point of view* means opinion or attitude, as in the question, "What is your point of view on capital punishment?" In narration, however, **point of view** is a technical term meaning the consciousness through whom the story is conveyed, or simply, who is telling the story. There are four possible points of view, depending on the number of persons whose thoughts and feelings are revealed—not by their speech or action but by "getting into their heads."

1. *First person*—narrator reveals *only his or her own* thoughts and feelings.
2. *Third-person omniscient*—author reveals thoughts and feelings of *any number* of characters.
3. *Third-person limited omniscient*—author reveals thoughts and feelings of *only one* character.
4. *Third-person objective*—author reveals thoughts and feelings of *none* of the characters, as is usual in drama.

For an essay in which you are a participant, first person with you as your own storyteller will probably seem the natural choice:

> It was early morning when I went out to chop some wood for the kitchen. I had split hardly a dozen sticks when I turned toward the shed and saw a pair of green eyes staring from a hole in the wall. "Russell, bring me my shotgun," I yelled.

But you could change the perspective by allowing Russell, another participant, to tell the story:

> Al had just gone to the woodlot when all of a sudden I heard him yell to me to bring him his gun.

Or you might want "green eyes" to be your narrator:

> It's not easy finding shelter in these woods, so when I found an old woodshed I made it my home for the night. Whacks of an ax woke me the next morning, and I peered out a crack between the shingles to see, not five feet away....

Another way you can control how the narrative is told is to change the point of view to a third-person form.

> Alan Smith paused after chopping half a dozen sticks of firewood to find a pair of green eyes peering out of a crack in the

woodshed wall. Remembering the story he had heard last night, he yelled, "Russell, bring me my gun!"

Deciding on a point of view is as important as choosing the events, the persons, and the setting of your essay. Experiment with various points of view, and choose the one that best serves your purpose.

Pacing is the amount of detail apportioned to the various parts or scenes of your story. In some scenes every step of the action must be told; in others, it must be sketched only in the boldest strokes. If you are writing about a race, for example, when is it important to detail every movement, when you are warming up or when you cross the finish line?

Chronology refers to the time sequence of an event. Many writers, like Frederick Douglass in "Learning to Read and Write," prefer to narrate an event chronologically, that is, as it actually occurred, starting at the beginning and stopping at the end. Others, like Hana Wehle in "The Return," make use of flashbacks to enrich their narratives. Notice how her mind darts back and forth across her life in no discernible pattern on her train ride back to Prague after years in various concentration camps. Other choices to be made also involve time. You may find it useful to imagine a clock or calendar in your story; you can build to a climax by crowding more and more incidents into a shorter and shorter period of time. Do you want to end with a surprise or to create suspense? A surprise ending is achieved simply by withholding information; but to create suspense you must feed your readers bits of information to awaken their curiosity. Flashbacks are especially useful for creating suspense, leaving unanswered the burning question "What happened next?" while telling what happened earlier.

Transition—words, phrases, or sentences—is important in all writing, but especially in narration. Use familiar words with such ordering expressions as "first," "second," and "finally" to direct the traffic in your stories. If you use flashbacks, become accustomed to using words and phrases like "earlier," "all at once," and "at 3:41 sharp."

Telling details also flesh out the framework provided by meaning, organization, and point of view. Without them, the narrative is a spindly skeleton indeed. Telling a good story is an ancient art, and people still like to hear one. They enjoy the suspense and appreciate the meaning, but above all they remember the details, because through details the narrative springs to life.

WRITING NARRATION

1. Choose an event that you have witnessed or an experience you have had that you wish to convey to the reader. Impart the meaning of the event to the reader as you narrate the experience.

2. Organize your essay to establish a narrative pattern—either straight chronology or a flashback arrangement.

3. Decide on your point of view as narrator. Will you be an actor in the event or a spectator on the sidelines—or somewhere in between?

4. Select telling details that will grab the imagination of the reader.

5. Use transitional words or phrases to move from one phase of your narrative to the next.

Learning to Read and Write

Frederick Douglass (1817–1895) was born a slave. Douglass never revealed the identity of his white father, and he barely knew his black mother. At the age of twenty-one, he escaped slavery in Maryland. He lectured in New England and Great Britain for the abolitionist cause. He published his Narrative of the Life of Frederick Douglass *in 1845, sixteen years before the start of the Civil War.*

I LIVED IN MASTER HUGH'S FAMILY about seven years. During this time, I succeeded in learning to read and write. In accomplishing this, I was compelled to resort to various stratagems. I had no regular teacher. My mistress, who had kindly commenced to instruct me, had, in compliance with the advice and direction of her husband, not only ceased to instruct, but had set her face against my being instructed by any one else. It is due, however, to my mistress to say of her, that she did not adopt this course of treatment immediately. She at first lacked the depravity indispensable to shutting me up in mental darkness. It was at least necessary for her to have some training in the exercise of irresponsible power, to make her equal to the task of treating me as though I were a brute.

My mistress was, as I have said, a kind and tender-hearted woman; and in the simplicity of her soul she commenced, when I first went to live with her, to treat me as she supposed one human being ought to treat another. In entering upon the duties of a slaveholder, she did not seem to perceive that I sustained to her the relation of a mere chattel, and that for her to treat me as a human being was not only wrong, but dangerously so. Slavery proved as injurious to her as it did to me. When I went there, she was a pious, warm, and tender-hearted woman. There was no sorrow or suffering for which she had not a tear. She had bread for the hungry, clothes for the naked, and comfort for every mourner that came within her reach. Slavery soon proved its ability to divest her of these heavenly qualities. Under its influence, the tender heart became stone, and the lamblike disposition gave way to one of tiger-like fierceness. The first step in her downward course was in her ceasing to instruct me. She now commenced to practise her husband's precepts. She finally became even more violent in her opposition than her husband himself. She was not satisfied with simply doing as well as he had commanded; she seemed anxious to do better. Nothing seemed to make her more angry than to see me with a newspaper. She seemed to think that here lay the danger. I have had her rush at me with a face made all up of fury, and snatch from me a newspaper, in a manner that fully revealed her apprehension. She was an apt woman; and a little experience soon demonstrated, to her satisfaction, that education and slavery were incompatible with each other.

From this time I was most narrowly watched. If I was in a separate room any considerable length of time, I was sure to be suspected of having a book, and was at once called to give an account of myself. All this, however, was too late. The first step had been taken. Mistress, in teaching me the alphabet, had given me the *inch,* and no precaution could prevent me from taking the *ell.*

3

The plan which I adopted, and the one by which I was most successful, was that of making friends of all the little white boys whom I met in the street. As many of these as I could, I converted into teachers. With their kindly aid, obtained at different times and in different places, I finally succeeded in learning to read. When I was sent on errands, I always took my book with me, and by doing one part of my errand quickly, I found time to get a lesson before my return. I used also to carry bread with me, enough of which was always in the house, and to which I was always welcome; for I was much better off in this regard than many of the poor white children in our neighborhood. This bread I used to bestow upon the hungry little urchins, who, in return, would give me that more valuable bread of knowledge. I am strongly tempted to give the names of two or three of those little boys, as a testimonial of the gratitude and affection I bear them; but prudence forbids;—not that it would injure me, but it might embarrass them; for it is almost an unpardonable offence to teach slaves to read in this Christian country. It is enough to say of the dear little fellows, that they lived on Philpot Street, very near Durgin and Bailey's ship-yard. I used to talk this matter of slavery over with them. I would sometimes say to them, I wished I could be as free as they would be when they got to be men. "You will be free as soon as you are twenty-one, *but I am a slave for life!* Have not I as good a right to be free as you have?" These words used to trouble them; they would express for me the

4

liveliest sympathy, and console me with the hope that something would occur by which I might be free.

I was now about twelve years old, and the thought of being *a slave for life* began to bear heavily upon my heart. Just about this time, I got hold of a book entitled "The Columbian Orator." Every opportunity I got, I used to read this book. Among much of other interesting matter, I found in it a dialogue between a master and his slave. The slave was represented as having run away from his master three times. The dialogue represented the conversation which took place between them, when the slave was retaken the third time. In this dialogue, the whole argument in behalf of slavery was brought forward by the master, all of which was disposed of by the slave. The slave was made to say some very smart as well as impressive things in reply to his master— things which had the desired though unexpected effect; for the conversation resulted in the voluntary emancipation of the slave on the part of the master.   5

In the same book, I met with one of Sheridan's mighty speeches on and in behalf of Catholic emancipation: These were choice documents to me. I read them over and over again with unabated interest. They gave tongue to interesting thoughts of my own soul, which had frequently flashed through my mind, and died away for want of utterance. The moral which I gained from the dialogue was the power of truth over the conscience of even a slaveholder. What I got from Sheridan was a bold denunciation of slavery, and a powerful vindication of human rights. The reading of these documents enabled me to utter my thoughts, and to meet the arguments brought forward to sustain slavery; but while they relieved me of one difficulty, they brought on another even more painful than the one of which I was relieved. The more I read, the more I was led to abhor and detest my enslavers. I could regard them in no other light than a band of successful robbers, who had left their homes, and gone to Africa, and stolen us from our homes, and in a strange land reduced us to slavery. I loathed them as being the meanest as well as the most wicked of men. As I read and contemplated the subject, behold! that very discontentment which Master Hugh had predicted would follow my learning to read had already come, to torment and sting my soul to unutterable anguish. As I writhed under it, I would at times feel that learning to read had been a curse rather than a blessing. It had given me a view of my wretched condition, without the remedy. It opened my eyes to the horrible pit, but to no ladder upon which to get out. In moments of agony, I envied   6 my fellow-slaves for their stupidity. I have often wished myself a beast. I preferred the condition of the meanest reptile to my own. Any thing, no matter what, to get rid of thinking! It was this everlasting thinking of my condition that tormented me. There was no getting rid of it. It was pressed upon me by every object within sight or hearing, animate or inanimate. The silver trump of freedom had roused my soul to eternal wakefulness. Freedom now appeared, to disappear no more forever. It was heard in every sound, and seen in every thing. It was ever present to torment me with a sense of my wretched condition. I saw nothing without seeing it, I heard nothing without hearing it, and felt nothing without feeling it. It looked from every star, it smiled in every calm, breathed in every wind, and moved in every storm.

I often found myself regretting my own existence, and wishing myself dead; and but for the hope of being free, I have no doubt but that I should have killed myself, or done something for which I should have been killed. While in this state of mind, I was eager to hear any one speak of slavery. I was a ready listener. Every little while, I could hear something about the abolitionists. It was some time before I found what the word meant. It was always used in such connections as to make it an interesting word to me. If a slave ran away and succeeded in getting clear, or if a slave killed his master, set fire to a barn, or did any thing very wrong in the mind of a slaveholder, it was spoken of as the fruit of *abolition*. Hearing the word in this connection very often, I set about learning what it meant. The dictionary afforded me little or no help. I found it was "the act of abolishing"; but then I did not know what was to be abolished. Here I was perplexed. I did not dare to ask any one about its meaning, for I was satisfied that it was something they wanted me to know very little about. After a patient waiting, I got one of our city papers, containing an account of the number of petitions from the north, praying for the abolition of slavery in the District of Columbia, and of the slave trade between the States. From this time I understood the words *abolition* and *abolitionist,* and always drew near when that word was spoken, expecting to hear something of importance to myself and fellow-slaves. The light broke in upon me by degrees. I went one day down to the wharf of Mr. Waters; and seeing two Irishmen unloading a scow of stone, I went, unasked, and helped them. When we had finished, one of them came to me and asked me if I were a slave. I told him I was. He asked, "Are ye a slave for life?" I told him that I was. The good Irishman seemed to be deeply affected by the statement. He said to the other that it was a pity so fine a little

7

fellow as myself should be a slave for life. He said it was a shame to hold me. They both advised me to run away to the north; that I should find friends there, and that I should be free. I pretended not to be interested in what they said, and treated them as if I did not understand them; for I feared they might be treacherous. White men have been known to encourage slaves to escape, and then, to get the reward, catch them and return them to their masters. I was afraid that these seemingly good men might use me so; but I nevertheless remembered their advice, and from that time I resolved to run away. I looked forward to a time at which it would be safe for me to escape. I was too young to think of doing so immediately; besides, I wished to learn how to write, as I might have occasion to write my own pass. I consoled myself with the hope that I should one day find a good chance. Meanwhile, I would learn to write.

The idea as to how I might learn to write was suggested to me by being in Durgin and Bailey's ship-yard, and frequently seeing the ship carpenters, after hewing, and getting a piece of timber ready for use, write on the timber the name of that part of the ship for which it was intended. When a piece of timber was intended for the larboard side, it would be marked thus—"L." When a piece was for the starboard side, it would be marked thus—"S." A piece for the larboard side forward, would be marked thus—"L. F." When a piece was for starboard side forward, it would be marked thus—"S. F." For larboard aft, it would be marked thus—"L. A." For starboard aft, it would be marked thus— "S. A." I soon learned the names of these letters, and for what they were intended when placed upon a piece of timber in the ship-yard. I immediately commenced copying them, and in a short time was able to make the four letters named. After that, when I met with any boy who I knew could write, I would tell him I could write as well as he. The next word would be, "I don't believe you. Let me see you try it." I would then make the letters which I had been so fortunate as to learn, and ask him to beat that. In this way I got a good many lessons in writing, which it is quite possible I should never have gotten in any other way. During this time, my copy-book was the board fence, brick wall, and pavement; my pen and ink was a lump of chalk. With these, I learned mainly how to write. I then commenced and continued copying the Italics in Webster's Spelling Book, until I could make them all without looking on the book. By this time, my little Master Thomas had gone to school, and learned how to write, and had written over a number of copy-books. These had been brought home, and shown to some of our near neighbors, and then laid aside. My mistress used to go to class meeting at the Wilk Street meetinghouse every Monday afternoon, and leave me to take care of the house. When left thus, I used to spend the time in writing in the spaces left in Master Thomas's copy-book, copying what he had written. I continued to do this until I could write a hand very similar to that of Master Thomas. Thus, after a long, tedious effort for years, I finally succeeded in learning how to write.

Questions on Meaning

1. What portrait of Douglass's mistress emerges from paragraphs 1 and 2?
2. Why would slaveholders wish slaves to remain illiterate?
3. What does Douglass learn from reading "The Columbian Orator"?
4. Why did Douglass decide that it was essential that he learn to write before trying to escape?

Questions on Method

1. Select two or three paragraphs from Douglass's essay and show how his examples support his thesis in each case.
2. How does Douglass use the statement in paragraph 1, "I was compelled to resort to various stratagems," to organize his account of learning to read and write?
3. How many examples of such stratagems can you find? Why do you think Douglass chose this particular word?
4. Douglass uses irony and figurative language to enhance his narrative. Cite examples.

Writing Topics

1. Acquiring mastery of language changes Douglass's self-concept. How did you learn to read and write? Were there obstacles you had to overcome? Freewrite about your memories of this experience and expand on them for a fully developed essay.
2. Douglass's determination to educate himself involves acts of rebellion and self-reliance. To what extent does he succeed in challenging and refuting racial stereotypes about African American slaves?
3. Write an essay responding to the statement that an "education is not a product—rank, diploma, job, money—in that order: It is a process, a never-ending one."

The Misery of Silence

Maxine Hong Kingston (b. 1940) grew up in the Chinese American community of Stockton, California, and graduated from the University of California. Her award-winning autobiographies The Woman Warrior *(1976) and* China Men *(1980) focus on growing up female as a first-generation Chinese American. In 1988 she published a novel,* Tripmaster Monkey: His Fake Book. *As a writer, Kingston often blends myth, history, and autobiography to illustrate the importance of stories in the lives and culture of Chinese Americans.*

WHEN I WENT TO KINDERGARTEN and had to speak English for the first time, I became silent. A dumbness—a shame—still cracks my voice in two, even when I want to say "hello" casually, or ask an easy question in front of the check-out counter, or ask directions of a bus driver. I stand frozen, or I hold up the line with the complete, grammatical sentence that comes squeaking out at impossible length. "What did you say?" says the cab driver, or "Speak up," so I have to perform again, only weaker the second time. A telephone call makes my throat bleed and takes up that day's courage. It spoils my day with self-disgust when I hear my broken voice come skittering out into the open. It makes people wince to hear it. I'm getting better, though. Recently I asked the postman for special-issue stamps; I've waited since childhood for postmen to give me some of their own accord. I am making progress, a little every day.

My silence was thickest—total—during the three years that I covered my school paintings with black paint. I painted layers of black over houses and flowers and suns, and when I drew on the blackboard, I put a layer of chalk on top. I was making a stage curtain, and it was the moment before the curtain parted or rose. The teachers called my parents to school, and I saw they had been saving my pictures, curling and cracking, all alike and black. The teachers pointed to the pictures and looked serious, talked seriously too, but my parents did not understand English. ("The parents and teachers of criminals were executed," said my father.)

My parents took the pictures home. I spread them out (so black and full of possibilities) and pretended the curtains were swinging open, flying up, one after another, sunlight underneath, mighty operas.

During the first silent year I spoke to no one at school, did not ask   3
before going to the lavatory, and flunked kindergarten. My sister also said nothing for three years, silent in the playground and silent at lunch. There were other quiet Chinese girls not of our family, but most of them got over it sooner than we did. I enjoyed the silence. At first it did not occur to me I was supposed to talk or to pass kindergarten. I talked at home and to one or two of the Chinese kids in class. I made motions and even made some jokes. I drank out of a toy saucer when the water spilled out of the cup, and everybody laughed, pointing at me, so I did it some more. I didn't know that Americans don't drink out of saucers.

I liked the Negro students (Black Ghosts) best because they   4
laughed the loudest and talked to me as if I were a daring talker too. One of the Negro girls had her mother coil braids over her ears Shanghai-style like mine; we were Shanghai twins except that she was covered with black like my paintings. Two Negro kids enrolled in Chinese school, and the teachers gave them Chinese names. Some Negro kids walked me to school and home, protecting me from the Japanese kids, who hit me and chased me and stuck gum in my ears. The Japanese kids were noisy and tough. They appeared one day in kindergarten, released from concentration camp, which was a tic-tac-toe mark, like barbed wire, on the map.

It was when I found out I had to talk that school became a mis-   5
ery, that the silence became a misery. I did not speak and felt bad each time that I did not speak. I read aloud in first grade, though, and heard the barest whisper with little squeaks come out of my throat. "Louder," said the teacher, who scared the voice away again. The other Chinese girls did not talk either, so I knew the silence had to do with being a Chinese girl.

Reading out loud was easier than speaking because we did not   6
have to make up what to say, but I stopped often, and the teacher would think I'd gone quiet again. I could not understand "I." The Chinese "I" has seven strokes, intricacies. How could the American "I," assuredly wearing a hat like the Chinese, have only three strokes, the middle so straight? Was it out of politeness that this writer left off the strokes the way a Chinese has to write her own name small and crooked? No, it was not politeness; "I" is a capital and "you" is lower-case. I stared at that middle line and waited so long for its black center

to resolve into tight strokes and dots that I forgot to pronounce it. The other troublesome word was "here," no strong consonant to hang on to, and so flat, when "here" is two mountainous ideographs. The teacher, who had already told me every day how to read "I" and "here," put me in the low corner under the stairs again, where the noisy boys usually sat.

When my second grade class did a play, the whole class went to the auditorium except the Chinese girls. The teacher, lovely and Hawaiian, should have understood about us, but instead left us behind in the classroom. Our voices were too soft or nonexistent, and our parents never signed the permission slips anyway. They never signed anything unnecessary. We opened the door a crack and peeked out, but closed it again quickly. One of us (not me) won every spelling bee, though.

I remember telling the Hawaiian teacher, "We Chinese can't sing 'land where our fathers died.'" She argued with me about politics, while I meant because of curses. But how can I have that memory when I couldn't talk? My mother says that we, like the ghosts, have no memories.

After American school, we picked up our cigar boxes, in which we had arranged books, brushes, and an inkbox neatly, and went to Chinese school, from 5:00 to 7:30 P.M. There we chanted together, voices rising and falling, loud and soft, some boys shouting, everybody reading together, reciting together and not alone with one voice. When we had a memorization test, the teacher let each of us come to his desk and say the lesson to him privately, while the rest of the class practiced copying or tracing. Most of the teachers were men. The boys who were so well behaved in the American school played tricks on them and talked back to them. The girls were not mute. They screamed and yelled during recess, when there were no rules; they had fistfights. Nobody was afraid of children hurting themselves or of children hurting school property. The glass doors to the red and green balconies with the gold joy symbols were left wide open so that we could run out and climb the fire escapes. We played capture-the-flag in the auditorium, where Sun Yat-sen and Chiang Kai-shek's pictures hung at the back of the stage, the Chinese flag on their left and the American flag on their right. We climbed the teak ceremonial chairs and made flying leaps off the stage. One flag headquarters was behind the glass door and the other on stage right. Our feet drummed on the hollow stage. During recess the teachers locked themselves up in their offices with the shelves of books, copybooks, inks from China. They drank tea and warmed their hands at a stove. There was no play super-vision. At recess we had the school to ourselves, and also we could roam as far as we could go—downtown, Chinatown stores, home—as long as we returned before the bell rang.

At exactly 7:30 the teacher again picked up the brass bell that sat on his desk and swung it over our heads, while we charged down the stairs, our cheering magnified in the stairwell. Nobody had to line up.   10

Not all of the children who were silent at American school found voice at Chinese school. One new teacher said each of us had to get up and recite in front of the class, who was to listen. My sister and I had memorized the lesson perfectly. We said it to each other at home, one chanting, one listening. The teacher called on my sister to recite first. It was the first time a teacher had called on the second-born to go first. My sister was scared. She glanced at me and looked away; I looked down at my desk. I hoped that she could do it because if she could, then I wouldn't have to. She opened her mouth and a voice came out that wasn't a whisper, but it wasn't a proper voice either. I hoped that she would not cry, fear breaking up her voice like twigs underfoot. She sounded as if she were trying to sing through weeping and strangling. She did not pause or stop to end the embarrassment. She kept going until she said the last word, and then she sat down. When it was my turn, the same voice came out, a crippled animal running on broken legs. You could hear splinters in my voice, bones rubbing jagged against one another. I was loud, though. I was glad I didn't whisper.   11

How strange that the emigrant villagers are shouters, hollering face to face. My father asks, "Why is it I can hear Chinese from blocks away? Is it that I understand the language? Or is it they talk loud?" They turn the radio up full blast to hear the operas, which do not seem to hurt their ears. And they yell over the singers that wail over the drums, everybody talking at once, big arm gestures, spit flying. You can see the disgust on American faces looking at women like that. It isn't just the loudness. It is the way Chinese sounds, ching-chong ugly, to American ears, not beautiful like Japanese sayonara words with the consonants and vowels as regular as Italian. We make guttural peas-ant noise and have Ton Duc Thang names you can't remember. And the Chinese can't hear Americans at all; the language is too soft and western music unbearable. I've watched a Chinese audience laugh, visit, talk-story, and holler during a piano recital, as if the musician could not hear them. A Chinese-American, somebody's son, was   12 playing Chopin, which has no punctuation, no cymbals, no gongs. Chinese piano music is five black keys. Normal Chinese women's voices are strong and bossy. We American-Chinese girls had to whisper to make ourselves American-feminine. Apparently we whispered even more softly than the Americans. Once a year the teachers referred my sister and me to speech therapy, but our voices would straighten out, unpredictably normal, for the therapists. Some of us gave up, shook our heads, and said nothing, not one word. Some of us could not even shake our heads. At times shaking my head no is more self-assertion than I can manage. Most of us eventually found some voice, however faltering. We invented an American-feminine speaking personality.

Questions on Meaning

1. In paragraph 1, Kingston reveals her agony about speaking English. What is the relationship between her silence in school and the paintings she did in kindergarten?
2. What does she reveal about her school experience through her portrayal of the other students in paragraph 4? Was her experience in any way similar to yours? How?
3. What was the main reason for the difference in the children's behavior in Chinese school as opposed to American school? Why did Kingston include this comparison in her essay?
4. What distinctions does she make between Chinese and American speech patterns in the last paragraph? What is your reaction to her point that "We American-Chinese girls had to whisper to make ourselves American-feminine"?
5. Is Kingston's experience one with which you can empathize? Why or why not?

Questions on Method

1. What is Kingston's thesis statement? Where in the essay does this generalization occur?
2. Reread the essay's introduction and conclusion. Is her technique of moving from the particular to the general effective?
3. What was Kingston's purpose in recording this experience?
4. How effectively does Kingston support the generalizations in her topic sentences? Are the examples that she cites convincing to you? Why or why not?

Writing Topics

1. Kingston experiences alienation as a Chinese American student grappling with English in an American school. If you have also experienced alienation, possibly in a similar situation, write an essay focusing on your emotional reactions to it.

2. Kingston writes about an experience many children have: realizing that parents are fallible and cannot protect them. If you have a similar memory, develop it into an essay, explaining the effect on you.

3. Kingston describes her family's and her own interactions with language. What role does English play in her essay? How does language affect their interactions with the dominant culture?

Coloring Lessons

David Updike (b. 1957) is a graduate of Harvard and Columbia Universities and teaches English at Roxbury Community College in Boston. He has published a collection of short stories, Out on the Marsh *(1988), and a number of works for juveniles, including* A Winter Journey *(1985) and* An Autumn Tale *(1988). He has also contributed articles to the* New York Times Magazine.

IT WAS THE BIG ANNUAL FAIR at Shady Hill, a private school nestled away in one of our city's finer neighborhoods. Though October, it was warm and the ash gray clouds were giving way to soft, swelling shapes of blue. There were lots of kids already, their parents working the various concessions—apple bobbing and doughnut biting, water-balloon throwing at a heckling buffoon—all ploys to harvest money for the school's scholarship fund.

It seemed like the perfect event to bring an almost-4-year-old to, but my son, Wesley, was dragging on my arm, nervously surveying the scene. Getting tired of pulling him, disappointed that he was not having more fun, I stopped finally, kneeled down and asked him what was the matter.

He hesitated, looked around, chewing on his sleeve. "Too many pink people," he said softly. I laughed, but Wesley failed to see the humor of it and kept peering out through the thickening throng. "Too many pink people," he repeated. But along with my laugh came a twinge of nervousness—the parent's realization that our apprehensions are not entirely unfounded and that racial awareness comes even to 3-year-olds. I suspected, half wished, that his state of unhappiness had less to do with too many "pink" people than with too many people.

And we had taught him to use "pink" in the first place, in preference to the more common adjective used for people of my complexion. For my wife, we had opted for "brown" because that's the color she actually is: Wesley was learning his colors, after all, and it seemed silly and misleading to be describing people by colors they clearly are not.

The issue had arisen at his first day care—predominantly African- 5
American—from which he had returned one day and asked whether
he really was "gray." We told him no, he wasn't gray, more brown, but
a lighter, pinker shade than his mother.

A few months later he came home from his new day care, this 6
time predominantly European-American, and asked, "Mommy, are we
brown?"

"Yes," she said. "Why?" 7

"Melissa said we're b_____." 8

"She did?" 9

"Yeah." 10

The whole question caused me to wonder what these two words, 11
b_____ and w_____—so frequently used and so heavily laden with historical and social baggage—actually mean. I looked in a dictionary: the
lighter of the two, I learned, is "the color of pure snow…reflecting
nearly all the rays of sunlight, or a similar light…."

The other means "lacking hue and brightness; absorbing light 12
without reflecting any of the rays composing it…gloomy, pessimistic
or dismal…without any moral light or goodness."

I am not the color of pure snow, and my wife and son reflect a 13
good deal of light; they seem much closer in the spectrum to brown,
"a dark shade with a yellowish or reddish hue." In any event, perhaps
my problem with the two words is that they are, in the spectrum and
in people's minds, absolutes and polar opposites, absorbing light or reflecting it but admitting no shades in between except gray—the pallor
of the recently departed on the mortuary slab, blood drained from
their earthly vessel.

All of which is likely to raise the hackles ("hairs on a dog's neck 14
that bristle when the dog is ready to fight") of the anti-politically-
correct thought police, who are fed up with all this precious talk about
what we should call one another. They resist African-American—too
many syllables, so hard to say—though they seem to be comfortable
with Italian-American.

Let me enrage them further by suggesting that w_____ may also 15
have outlived its usefulness in describing people, and that we should
take up European-American, instead, in keeping with the now-
accepted Native, Asian- and African-American. Or maybe just plain
"pink" will do, the color even the palest of us turn when push comes
to shove and we reveal our humanity—when angry, say, or while
laughing or having sex or lying in the sun, trying to turn brown.

W _ _ _ _ and b _ _ _ _ are colors no one really is, monolithic and   16
redolent with historical innuendo and social shading, and the words
encourage those of us who use them—everyone—to continue to think
in binary terms, like computers. I am not suggesting the terms be
abandoned, tossed onto the scrap heap of language with other discarded words—just that they are used too easily and often and should
be traded in, occasionally, for words that admit that issues of race and
ethnicity are more complicated than these monosyllables imply. Try
not saying them, once or twice, and see how it feels. And if you are
teaching a child his or her colors, you might want to adopt a vocabulary that holds true for skin tones and for crayons.

But at the fair, things were improving slowly. I had, with misgiv-   17
ings, pointed out to Wesley that I am "pink," like some of his cousins
and grandparents and uncles and aunts and school friends, and that it's
not nice to say there are "too many" of us.

We walked around, mulling all this over, and I bought us a dough-   18
nut. We went into a gym and looked at old sports equipment, and I
fought the temptation to buy something. We went outside again into
the soft yellow sunlight and found happiness at a wading pool where,
using fishing poles with magnets dangling from the lines, you could
catch plastic fish with paper-clip noses. He caught a few and we traded
them for prizes he then clutched tightly in his small, strong hands.

But he was still tired, and when I suggested we go home, he nod-   19
ded and started to suck his thumb. I picked him up and carried him,
and as we approached the gate he triumphantly called my attention to
a "brown boy" with a baseball hat, who was just then coming in.

Again, his observation elicited in me a vague discomfort, and I   20
wondered if we couldn't get away from all this altogether. But how?

"Wesley," I finally offered. "Do you have to call him 'brown   21
boy'? Why don't you just say, 'That tall boy' or 'the boy with the blue
hat' or 'the boy in the green sweatshirt'?" He mulled over my suggestion, but then rejected it.

"No," he said firmly. "He's brown."   22

Questions on Meaning

1. Why was Wesley upset at the annual fair? How effectively does the narrator respond to his son's complaint?
2. How appropriate is Updike's title? How many lessons are taught and by
   whom?

Questions on Method

1. Review paragraphs 11–16 in which Updike presents definitions of race as they pertain to his own family and to people in general. What is your response to his suggestion that "w____ may also have outlived its usefulness in describing people"?
2. Review the last three paragraphs of the essay. How do they contribute to meaning?

Writing Topics

1. The parent–child relationship is a focus of "Coloring Lessons." What adjectives would you use to describe the emotional relationship of father and son? What did the father learn about his son through their visit to the fair?
2. Race is a significant factor in "Coloring Lessons." Narrate an event in which the issue of race was important to you. Focus on as many specifics as you can, including where you were, who was part of the experience, what occurred, how you responded, and what you learned from the situation.

A Hanging

George Orwell (1903–1950) was born in India to British parents, and he spent much of his adult life there. For many years he served with the imperial police of Burma. His best-known novels are Animal Farm *and* 1984, *both of which are political satires.*

IT WAS IN BURMA, a sodden morning of the rains. A sickly light, like yellow tinfoil, was slanting over the high walls into the jail yard. We were waiting outside the condemned cells, a row of sheds fronted with double bars, like small animal cages. Each cell measured about ten feet by ten and was quite bare within except for a plank bed and a pot for drinking water. In some of them brown, silent men were squatting at the inner bars, with their blankets draped round them. These were the condemned men, due to be hanged within the next week or two.

One prisoner had been brought out of his cell. He was a Hindu, a puny wisp of a man, with a shaven head and vague liquid eyes. He had a thick, sprouting mustache, absurdly too big for his body, rather like the mustache of a comic man in the films. Six tall Indian warders were guarding him and getting him ready for the gallows. Two of them stood by with rifles and fixed bayonets, while the others handcuffed him, passed a chain through his handcuffs and fixed it to their belts, and lashed his arms tight to his sides. They crowded very close about him, with their hands always on him in a careful, caressing grip, as though all the while feeling him to make sure he was there. It was like men handling a fish which is still alive and may jump back into the water. But he stood quite unresisting, yielding his arms limply to the ropes, as though he hardly noticed what was happening.

Eight o'clock struck and a bugle call, desolately thin in the wet air, floated from the distant barracks. The superintendent of the jail, who was standing apart from the rest of us, moodily prodding the gravel with his stick, raised his head at the sound. He was an army doctor, with a grey toothbrush mustache and a gruff voice. "For God's

sake, hurry up, Francis," he said irritably. "The man ought to have
been dead by this time. Aren't you ready yet?"

Francis, the head jailer, a fat Dravidian in a white drill suit and   4
gold spectacles, waved his black hand. "Yes sir, yes sir," he bubbled.
"All iss satisfactorily prepared. The hangman iss waiting. We shall
proceed."

"Well, quick march, then. The prisoners can't get their breakfast   5
till this job's over."

We set out for the gallows. Two warders marched on either side of   6
the prisoner, with their rifles at the slope; two others marched close
against him, gripping him by arm and shoulder, as though at once pushing and supporting him. The rest of us, magistrates and the like, followed
behind. Suddenly, when we had gone ten yards, the procession stopped
short without any order or warning. A dreadful thing had happened—a
dog, come goodness knows whence, had appeared in the yard. It came
bounding among us with a loud volley of barks and leapt round us wag-
ging its whole body, wild with glee at finding so many human beings together. It was a large woolly dog, half Airedale, half pariah. For a
moment it pranced around us, and then, before anyone could stop it, it
had made a dash for the prisoner, and jumping up tried to lick his face.
Everybody stood aghast, too taken aback even to grab the dog.

"Who let that bloody brute in here?" said the superintendent an-   7
grily. "Catch it, someone!"

A warder detached from the escort charged clumsily after the   8
dog, but it danced and gambolled just out of his reach, taking everything as part of the game. A young Eurasian jailer picked up a handful
of gravel and tried to stone the dog away, but it dodged the stones and
came after us again. Its yaps echoed from the jail walls. The prisoner, in
the grasp of the two warders, looked on incuriously, as though this was
another formality of the hanging. It was several minutes before someone managed to catch the dog. Then we put my handkerchief through
its collar and moved off once more, with the dog still straining and
whimpering.

It was about forty yards to the gallows. I watched the bare brown   9
back of the prisoner marching in front of me. He walked clumsily with
his bound arms, but quite steadily, with that bobbing gait of the Indian
who never straightens his knees. At each step his muscles slid neatly
into place, the lock of hair on his scalp danced up and down, his feet
printed themselves on the wet gravel. And once, in spite of the men

who gripped him by each shoulder, he stepped lightly aside to avoid a puddle on the path.

It is curious; but till that moment I had never realized what it   10
means to destroy a healthy, conscious man. When I saw the prisoner step aside to avoid the puddle, I saw the mystery, the unspeakable wrongness, of cutting a life short when it is in full tide. This man was not dying, he was alive just as we are alive. All the organs of his body were working—bowels digesting food, skin renewing itself, nails growing, tissues forming—all toiling away in solemn foolery. His nails would still be growing when he stood on the drop, when he was falling through the air with a tenth-of-a-second to live. His eyes saw the yellow gravel and the grey walls, and his brain still remembered, foresaw, reasoned—even about puddles. He and we were a party of men walking together, seeing, hearing, feeling, understanding the same world; and in two minutes, with a sudden snap, one of us would be gone—one mind less, one world less.

The gallows stood in a small yard, separate from the main   11
grounds of the prison, and overgrown with tall prickly weeds. It was a brick erection like three sides of a shed, with planking on top, and above that two beams and a crossbar with the rope dangling. The hangman, a greyhaired convict in the white uniform of the prison, was waiting beside his machine. He greeted us with a servile crouch as we entered. At a word from Francis the two warders, gripping the prisoner more closely than ever, half led, half pushed him to the gallows and helped him clumsily up the ladder. Then the hangman climbed up and fixed the rope round the prisoner's neck.

We stood waiting, five yards away. The warders had formed in a   12
rough circle round the gallows. And then, when the noose was fixed, the prisoner began crying out to his god. It was a high, reiterated cry of "Ram! Ram! Ram! Ram!" not urgent and fearful like a prayer or cry for help, but steady, rhythmical, almost like the tolling of a bell. The dog answered the sound with a whine. The hangman, still standing on the gallows, produced a small cotton bag like a flour bag and drew it down over the prisoner's face. But the sound, muffled by the cloth, still persisted, over and over again: "Ram! Ram! Ram! Ram! Ram!"

The hangman climbed down and stood ready, holding the lever.   13
Minutes seemed to pass. The steady, muffled crying from the prisoner went on and on, "Ram! Ram! Ram!" never faltering for an instant. The superintendent, his head on his chest, was slowly poking the ground with his stick; perhaps he was counting the cries, allowing the

prisoner a fixed number—fifty, perhaps, or a hundred. Everyone had changed colour. The Indians had gone grey like bad coffee, and one or two of the bayonets were wavering. We looked at the lashed, hooded man on the drop, and listened to his cries—each cry another second of life; the same thought was in all our minds; oh, kill him quickly, get it over, stop that abominable noise!

Suddenly the superintendent made up his mind. Throwing up his head he made a swift motion with his stick. "Chalo!" he shouted almost fiercely.   14

There was a clanking noise, and then dead silence. The prisoner had vanished, and the rope was twisting on itself. I let go of the dog, and it galloped immediately to the back of the gallows; but when it got there it stopped short, barked, and then retreated into a corner of the yard, where it stood among the weeds, looking timorously out at us. We went round the gallows to inspect the prisoner's body. He was dangling with his toes pointed straight downwards, very slowly revolving, as dead as a stone.   15

The superintendent reached out with his stick and poked the bare brown body; it oscillated slightly. "*He's* all right," said the superintendent. He backed out from under the gallows, and blew out a deep breath. The moody look had gone out of his face quite suddenly. He glanced at his wristwatch. "Eight minutes past eight. Well, that's all for this morning, thank God."   16

The warders unfixed bayonets and marched away. The dog, sobered and conscious of having misbehaved itself, slipped after them. We walked out of the gallows yard, past the condemned cells with their waiting prisoners, into the big central yard of the prison. The convicts, under the command of warders armed with lathis, were already receiving their breakfast. They squatted in long rows, each man holding a tin pannikin, while two warders with buckets marched around ladling out rice; it seemed quite a homely, jolly scene, after the hanging. An enormous relief had come upon us now that the job was done. One felt an impulse to sing, to break into a run, to snigger. All at once everyone began chattering gaily.   17

The Eurasian boy walking beside me nodded towards the way we had come, with a knowing smile: "Do you know sir, our friend (he meant the dead man), when he heard his appeal had been dismissed, he pissed on the floor of his cell. From fright. Kindly take one of my cigarettes, sir. Do you not admire my new silver case, sir? From the box-wallah, two rupees eight annas. Classy European style."   18

Several people laughed—at what, nobody seemed certain.   19

Francis was walking by the superintendent, talking garrulously: 20
"Well, sir, all has passed off with the utmost satisfactoriness. It was all
finished—flick! Like that. It iss not always so—oah, no! I have known
cases where the doctor was obliged to go beneath the gallows and pull
the prissoner's legs to ensure decease. Most disagreeable!"

"Wriggling about, eh? That's bad," said the superintendent.   21

"Ach, sir, it iss worse when they become refractory! One man, I   22
recall, clung to the bars of hiss cage when we went to take him out.
You will scarcely credit, sir, that it took six warders to dislodge him,
three pulling at each leg. We reasoned with him, 'My dear fellow,' we
said, 'think of all the pain and trouble you are causing to us!' But no,
he would not listen! Ach, he wass very troublesome!"

I found that I was laughing quite loudly. Everyone was laughing.   23
Even the superintendent grinned in a tolerant way. "You'd better all
come out and have a drink," he said quite genially. "I've got a bottle of
whisky in the car. We could do with it."

We went through the big double gates of the prison into the   24
road. "Pulling at his legs!" exclaimed a Burmese magistrate suddenly,
and burst into a loud chuckling. We all began laughing again. At that
moment Francis' anecdote seemed extraordinarily funny. We all had a
drink together, native and European alike, quite amicably. The dead
man was a hundred yards away.

Questions on Meaning

1. How do you explain the superintendent's impatience?
2. The narrator focuses on the dog at several points in his narrative. What
   thematic significance do you attach to the various actions of the dog?
3. What is your response to the questions raised by Orwell in paragraph 10?
4. To what factors do you attribute the laughter and talk that followed the
   hanging?

Questions on Method

1. Orwell uses chronological order through most of the narrative. Where
   does he change his time sequence? To what effect?
2. How does Orwell use point of view to enhance the meaning of his narrative? Consider, for example, the roles of the superintendent, Francis,
   and the Eurasian boy.
3. What is the effect of Orwell's including in paragraph 2 a detailed description of the prisoner?

Writing Topics

1. Write an essay on the thematic significance of the last sentence of Orwell's narrative.
2. Write a narrative essay that teaches a moral or lesson. Try to avoid explaining the lesson or moral; instead let your narration communicate the meaning through your selection of events and details.
3. According to the writer Césare Pavese, "We do not remember days, we remember moments." Freewrite about a moment of special significance for you. Then expand the memory and its importance in a fully developed essay. Why do you remember it so vividly? What do you remember? How might you best explain its effects on you?

The Return

Hana Wehle (1917–1997) was born in Czechoslovakia (now Czech Republic). She survived Theresienstadt, Auschwitz, and Stutthof concentration camps. Her first husband was killed by the SS in Terezin. After the Nazis' defeat in 1945, she returned to Czechoslovakia, where she remarried. In 1951 she and her husband, also a survivor of Auschwitz, emigrated to the United States. She published several essays about her concentration camp experiences.

THE AIR RAID SIRENS are quiet, the bombers are grounded, the bowels of the crematoria furnaces are covered with human ashes—the war is over.

My face presses against the cool windowpane of the train carrying repatriates from various parts of Europe. My destination: Prague, Czechoslovakia. As the black engine hisses through the German countryside, the cities of the Reich stare at me from under the ashes and ruins. I plunge again into the nightmare of the recent past, to be awakened occasionally by the penetrating sound of the engine whistle.

"QUARANTINE"—the big letters obstruct my view. I am lying among the many half-corpses on the wooden planks. My body is tossing restlessly with typhoid fever. My lips are parched, my eyes are searching for water. Unconsciously, my head is turning toward the slowly opening door of the barracks. I see my mother's pale, frightened face. She forces a smile as she nods. She has come to say goodbye before I die. Or—is it she who is parting from me? With glassy eyes I am trying desperately to send her a smile. The monotonous sound of the clattering wheels overshadows the mirage of my mother's face. The wheels are turning on the shiny rails as the train crawls around a bend. My hollowed-out soul struggles to separate my thoughts of the bottomless pit of death from the sounds of whistle and clatter....

The engine puffs out the last cloud of steam and the train comes to a stop. Clutching my shabby bundle of belongings, I uncertainly descend the steps of the train. Soon I am swallowed up by the once so familiar noise and smell of the railroad station. My legs march with the crowds. Once I belonged to them as they belonged to me. There was a balance and harmony in which everyone was both himself and a part of others. Today, a strange, invisible wall of loneliness and fear separates me from them. I never knew that the arrival would be as hard as the departure. In the camps, freedom had seemed so unattainable, glorious and beautiful!

Now I am not marching as I dreamed I would. My body is filling 5 up mercilessly with pain. I see the Square of Saint Wenceslas, the beautiful center of the city of Prague, as it unfolds in front of me. Its pavement, it seems, still reverberates with the sound of marching boots; the frozen eyes, half hidden under the caps of the SS uniforms, form a net of hatred. They pierce the Star of David, no longer fastened on my coat but still scorching my heart.

The sky is gray. The fine drizzle is wetting the roofs of the city. I 6 stand in front of the National Museum, waiting for a trolley car. I feel the moisture mixing with the tears rolling down my cheeks. Twenty-two years ago, I stood here with my mother and my sister, Helen. Then also we waited for a trolley car to come. We were on our way to visit our grandmother. Holding onto our mother's hands, we laughed as I mischievously pulled on Helen's blond braids. The brightly painted cars announced their coming and going with chimelike bells. It was Eastertime. The air was full of holiday mood and the smell of spring. The aroma of the golden chicken soup, lovingly prepared by our grandmother, filled my imagination. The little dumplings moved playfully around the floating rings of fat in the hot liquid which steamed from the fine china designed with a blue onion pattern.

From the bend of a side street, a rattling sound draws my atten- 7 tion. I am forced to emerge from the state of elation, in which everything in me has melted with happiness. In front of me a faded trolley car stops with a squeak. I board the half-empty car mechanically. I feel alone, so alone! As through a veil, my eyes slide from one passenger to another, my body sways from side to side with the music of the wheels. Did my sister survive? Will I find her under the same address? When I left her, three years ago, she was protected by her non-Jewish husband. Did he divorce her? And what about their children? What do I tell them all? How can it be told! Who will believe that I survived my own death? Why me, while our mother, father, and brother had to die? Can they understand? I survived and I have a message from the dead. But what words will I choose to tell it all?

The downpour of thoughts cuts through the silence around me.   8
Yes, I have arrived at my destination. A sudden jerk of the trolley car
brings me to my feet. As if in a daze, I walk the familiar street—tracing
the gray building in front of me. Here is my sister's house! I need to
loosen the stranglehold around my heart as I slowly mount the twisting
staircase in the dark hallway. I inhale the collective aromas of the dinners, slipping through and around the many apartment doors in the
hall. A small rectangular label shines on a door. This is unmistakably
Helen's place! My shaky hand timidly presses the little doorbell. A
click of the lock; a slow movement of the opening door lets a wedge of
light into the dark hall....Two happy shouts echo through the building. My sister and I look at each other in amazement. We both sense a
miracle—we both survived! The invisible wall thrust between us
through the Nuremberg Laws★ can no longer separate us.

Helen's and my faces are drenched with tears of happiness and   9
sorrow as we cling together in the open doorway. This mixture,
streaming down our cheeks, suddenly forms the unspoken words I
have been so anxiously searching for. There is one kind of knowledge:
we both are together again, we each have a different story to tell....

Questions on Meaning

1. Hana Wehle tells us near the end of her essay that her mother died in the
   concentration camp. Where does the author give the first evidence of
   her possible death? Explain.
2. The memories of the author constantly overwhelm her. At how many
   points in the essay does she succumb to them? What scenes in the past do
   these thoughts revive?
3. Why does the author feel the arrival is "as hard as the departure"? Why
   is her present freedom not as "glorious and beautiful" as she had thought
   it would be while she was in the concentration camp?
4. Why does Wehle believe that the Nazis might not have sent her sister to
   a camp? Why is she nevertheless not sure that her sister survived?
5. Why does Wehle fear that she will not know how to tell her sister about
   her experience in the concentration camp? Why do their tears at the end
   form "the unspoken words" she has been "so anxiously searching for"?

★In 1939, the Reich's Protector of Bohemia and Moravia placed the Jews under
German jurisdiction in accordance with the so-called Nuremberg Laws, adopted by
the German parliament (Reichstag) in 1935. These comprehensive decrees defined
the status of the Jews and limited their rights, thus establishing anti-Semitism in law.

Questions on Method

1. The author uses the past tense ("I belonged to them") in relating some of her memories, but she uses the progressive tense ("I am lying") in relating others. Why doesn't she use the past tense throughout? What function does the progressive tense fulfill?
2. Why is it significant that the sky is gray and that it is drizzling out? What other details take on symbolic overtones?
3. What is the function of flashbacks in this particular narrative?

Writing Topics

1. Wehle writes about the passage of time and the changes that this brings. Write an essay on the attitude that she takes toward the passage of time. How is her concept of time similar to or different from yours?
2. In Wehle's essay, the meaning of the narrative is rendered symbolically. Discuss in an essay how she uses symbolic images to convey information about her experiences in "The Return."
3. Most writers of narratives choose events and experiences that are of value to their readers. If you have witnessed an event or have had an experience that other people can learn from, write an essay in which you relate that event in chronological order. Include any insights you gained from the experience that you want to share.

Three Days to See

Helen Keller (1880–1968) was an American memoirist, essayist, and coun-selor on international relations for the American Foundation of the Blind. She was deaf and blind from the age of nineteen months. The story of how her teacher, Annie Sullivan, broke through the barrier of silence to reach her has been dramatized in The Miracle Worker. *Through Sullivan, Keller learned to communicate, first by using sign language and later through voice lessons. Despite her physical handicaps, Keller had a keen awareness and in-sight into human nature and the world around her. She graduated with hon-ors from Radcliffe and received critical acclaim for her autobiography* Story of My Life *(1902). Among her other works are* Optimism *(1903),* The World I Live In *(1908), and* Out of the Dark *(1913).*

IF I WERE THE PRESIDENT of a university I should establish a com-pulsory course in "How to Use Your Eyes." The professor would try to show his pupils how they could add joy to their lives by really seeing what passes unnoticed before them. He would try to awake their dor-mant and sluggish faculties. 1

Perhaps I can best illustrate by imagining what I should most like to see if I were given the use of my eyes, say, for just three days. And while I am imagining, suppose you, too, set your mind to work on the problem of how you would use your own eyes if you had only three more days to see. If with the oncoming darkness of the third night you knew that the sun would never rise for you again, how would you spend those three precious intervening days? What would you most want to let your gaze rest upon? 2

I, naturally, should want most to see the things which have be-come dear to me through my years of darkness. You, too, would want to let your eyes rest long on the things that have become dear to you so that you could take the memory of them with you into the night that loomed before you. 3

If, by some miracle, I were granted three seeing days, to be followed by a relapse into darkness, I should divide the period into three parts. 4

On the first day, I should want to see the people whose kindness and gentleness and companionship have made my life worth living. First I should like to gaze long upon the face of my dear teacher, Mrs. Anne Sullivan Macy, who came to me when I was a child and opened the outer world to me. I should want not merely to see the outline of her face, so that I could cherish it in my memory, but to study that face and find in it the living evidence of the sympathetic tenderness and patience with which she accomplished the difficult task of my education. I should like to see in her eyes that strength of character which has enabled her to stand firm in the face of difficulties, and that compassion for all humanity which she has revealed to me so often.

I do not know what it is to see into the heart of a friend through that "window of the soul," the eye. I can only "see" through my fingertips the outline of a face. I can detect laughter, sorrow, and many other obvious emotions. I know my friends from the feel of their faces. But I cannot really picture their personalities by touch. I know their personalities, of course, through other means, through the thoughts they express to me, through whatever of their actions are revealed to me. But I am denied that deeper understanding of them which I am sure would come through sight of them, through watching their reactions to various expressed thoughts and circumstances, through noting the immediate and fleeting reactions of their eyes and countenance.

Friends who are near to me I know well, because through the months and years they reveal themselves to me in all their phases; but of casual friends I have only an incomplete impression, an impression gained from a handclasp, from spoken words which I take from their lips with my fingertips, or which they tap into the palm of my hand.

How much easier, how much more satisfying it is for you who can see to grasp quickly the essential qualities of another person by watching the subtleties of expression, the quiver of a muscle, the flutter of a hand. But does it ever occur to you to use your sight to see into the inner nature of a friend or acquaintance? Do not most of you seeing people grasp casually the outward features of a face and let it go at that?

For instance, can you describe accurately the faces of five good friends? Some of you can, but many cannot. As an experiment, I have questioned husbands of long standing about the color of their wives' eyes, and often they express embarrassed confusion and admit that they do not know. And, incidentally, it is a chronic complaint of wives that their husbands do not notice new dresses, new hats, and changes in household arrangements.

The eyes of seeing persons soon become accustomed to the rou-   10
tine of their surroundings, and they actually see only the startling and
spectacular. But even in viewing the most spectacular sights the eyes
are lazy. Court records reveal every day how inaccurately "eyewitnesses" see. A given event will be "seen" in several different ways by as
many witnesses. Some see more than others, but few see everything
that is within the range of their vision.

Oh, the things that I should see if I had the power of sight for just   11
three days!

The first day would be a busy one. I should call to me all my dear   12
friends and look long into their faces, imprinting upon my mind the
outward evidences of the beauty that is within them. I should let my
eyes rest, too, on the face of a baby, so that I could catch a vision of the
eager, innocent beauty which precedes the individual's consciousness
of the conflicts which life develops.

And I should like to look into the loyal, trusting eyes of my   13
dogs—the grave, canny little Scottie, Darkie, and the stalwart, understanding Great Dane, Helga, whose warm, tender, and playful friendships are so comforting to me.

On that busy first day I should also view the small simple things   14
of my home. I want to see the warm colors in the rugs under my feet,
the pictures on the walls, the intimate trifles that transform a house
into home. My eyes would rest respectfully on the books in raised type
which I have read, but they would be more eagerly interested in the
printed books which seeing people can read, for during the long night
of my life the books I have read and those which have been read to me
have built themselves into a great shining lighthouse, revealing to me
the deepest channels of human life and the human spirit.

In the afternoon of that first seeing day, I should take a long walk   15
in the woods and intoxicate my eyes on the beauties of the world of
Nature, trying desperately to absorb in a few hours the vast splendor
which is constantly unfolding itself to those who can see. On the way
home from my woodland jaunt my path would lie near a farm so that
I might see the patient horses plowing in the field (perhaps I should see
only a tractor!) and the serene content of men living close to the soil.
And I should pray for the glory of a colorful sunset.

When dusk had fallen, I should experience the double delight of   16
being able to see by artificial light, which the genius of man has created
to extend the power of his sight when Nature decrees darkness.

In the night of that first day of sight, I should not be able to sleep,   17
so full would be my mind of the memories of the day.

The next day—the second day of sight—I should arise with the 18
dawn and see the thrilling miracle by which night is transformed into
day. I should behold with awe the magnificent panorama of light with
which the sun awakens the sleeping earth.

This day I should devote to a hasty glimpse of the world, past and 19
present. I should want to see the pageant of man's progress, the kaleidoscope of the ages. How can so much be compressed into one day?
Through the museums, of course. Often I have visited the New York
Museum of Natural History to touch with my hands many of the objects there exhibited, but I have longed to see with my eyes the con-
densed history of the earth and its inhabitants displayed there—animals
and the races of men pictured in their native environment; gigantic
carcasses of dinosaurs and mastodons which roamed the earth long before man appeared, with his tiny stature and powerful brain, to conquer the animal kingdom; realistic presentations of the processes of
evolution in animals, in man, and in the implements which man has
used to fashion for himself a secure home on this planet; and a thousand and one other aspects of natural history.

I wonder how many readers of this article have viewed this pan- 20
orama of the face of living things as pictured in that inspiring museum.
Many, of course, have not had the opportunity, but I am sure that
many who *have* had the opportunity have not made use of it. There,
indeed, is a place to use your eyes. You who see can spend many fruit-
ful days there, but I, with my imaginary three days of sight, could only
take a hasty glimpse, and pass on.

My next stop would be the Metropolitan Museum of Art, for just 21
as the Museum of Natural History reveals the material aspects of the
world, so does the Metropolitan show the myriad facets of the human
spirit. Throughout the history of humanity the urge to artistic expression has been almost as powerful as the urge for food, shelter, and procreation. And here, in the vast chambers of the Metropolitan Museum,
is unfolded before me the spirit of Egypt, Greece, and Rome, as expressed in their art. I know well through my hands the sculptured gods
and goddesses of the ancient Nile-land. I have felt copies of Parthenon
friezes, and I have sensed the rhythmic beauty of charging Athenian
warriors. Apollos and Venuses and the Winged Victory of Samothrace
are friends of my fingertips. The gnarled, bearded features of Homer
are dear to me, for he, too, knew blindness.

My hands have lingered upon the living marble of Roman sculp- 22
ture as well as that of later generations. I have passed my hands over a
plaster cast of Michelangelo's inspiring and heroic Moses; I have sensed

the power of Rodin; I have been awed by the devoted spirit of Gothic wood carving. These arts which can be touched have meaning for me, but even they were meant to be seen rather than felt, and I can only guess at the beauty which remains hidden from me. I can admire the simple lines of a Greek vase, but its figured decorations are lost to me.

So on this, my second day of sight, I should try to probe into the soul of man through his art. The things I knew through touch I should now see. More splendid still, the whole magnificent world of painting would be opened to me, from the Italian Primitives, with their serene religious devotion, to the Moderns, with their feverish visions. I should look deep into the canvases of Raphael, Leonardo da Vinci, Titian, Rembrandt. I should want to feast my eyes upon the warm colors of Veronese, study the mysteries of El Greco, catch a new vision of Nature from Corot. Oh, there is so much rich meaning and beauty in the art of the ages for you who have eyes to see! 23

Upon my short visit to this temple of art I should not be able to review a fraction of that great world of art which is open to you. I should be able to get only a superficial impression. Artists tell me that for a deep and true appreciation of art one must educate the eye. One must learn through experience to weigh the merits of line, of composition, of form and color. If I had eyes, how happily would I embark upon so fascinating a study! Yet I am told that, to many of you who have eyes to see, the world of art is a dark night, unexplored and unilluminated. 24

It would be with extreme reluctance that I should leave the Metropolitan Museum, which contains the key to beauty—a beauty so neglected. Seeing persons, however, do not need a Metropolitan to find this key to beauty. The same key lies waiting in smaller museums, and in books on the shelves of even small libraries. But naturally, in my limited time of imaginary sight, I should choose the place where the key unlocks the greatest treasures in the shortest time. 25

The evening of my second day of sight I should spend at a theater or at the movies. Even now I often attend theatrical performances of all sorts, but the action of the play must be spelled into my hand by a companion. But how I should like to see with my own eyes the fascinating figure of Hamlet, or the gusty Falstaff amid colorful Elizabethan trappings! How I should like to follow each movement of the graceful Hamlet, each strut of the hearty Falstaff! And since I could see only one play, I should be confronted by the many-horned dilemma, for there are scores of plays I should want to see. You who have eyes can see any you like. How many of you, I wonder, when you gaze at a play, 26 a movie, or any spectacle, realize and give thanks for the miracle of sight which enables you to enjoy its color, grace, and movement?

I cannot enjoy the beauty of rhythmic movement except in a sphere restricted to the touch of my hands. I can vision only dimly the grace of a Pavlova, although I know something of the delight of rhythm, for often I can sense the beat of music as it vibrates through the floor. I can well imagine that cadenced motion must be one of the most pleasing sights in the world. I have been able to gather something of this by tracing with my fingers the lines in sculptured marble; if this static grace can be so lovely, how much more acute must be the thrill of seeing grace in motion.

One of my dearest memories is of the time when Joseph Jefferson allowed me to touch his face and hands as he went through some of the gestures and speeches of his beloved Rip Van Winkle. I was able to catch thus a meager glimpse of the world of drama, and I shall never forget the delight of that moment. But, oh, how much I must miss, and how much pleasure you seeing ones can derive from watching and hearing the interplay of speech and movement in the unfolding of a dramatic performance! If I could see only one play, I should know how to picture in my mind the action of a hundred plays which I have read or had transferred to me through the medium of the manual alphabet.

So, through the evening of my second imaginary day of sight, the great figures of dramatic literature would crowd sleep from my eyes.

The following morning, I should again greet the dawn, anxious to discover new delights, for I am sure that, for those who have eyes which really see, the dawn of each day must be a perpetually new revelation of beauty.

This, according to the terms of my imagined miracle, is to be my third and last day of sight. I shall have no time to waste in regrets or longings; there is too much to see. The first day I devoted to my friends, animate and inanimate. The second revealed to me the history of man and Nature. Today I shall spend in the workaday world of the present, amid the haunts of men going about the business of life. And where can one find so many activities and conditions of men as in New York? So the city becomes my destination.

I start from my home in the quiet little suburb of Forest Hills, Long Island. Here, surrounded by green lawns, trees, and flowers, are neat little houses, happy with the voices and movements of wives and children, havens of peaceful rest for men who toil in the city. I drive across the lacy structure of steel which spans the East River, and I get a new and startling vision of the power and ingenuity of the mind of man. Busy boats chug and scurry about the river—racy speedboats, stolid, snorting tugs. If I had long days of sight ahead, I should spend many of them watching the delightful activity upon the river.

I look ahead, and before me rise the fantastic towers of New York, a city that seems to have stepped from the pages of a fairy story. What an awe-inspiring sight, these glittering spires, these vast banks of stone and steel—structures such as the gods might build for themselves! This animated picture is a part of the lives of millions of people every day. How many, I wonder, give it so much as a second glance? Very few, I fear. Their eyes are blind to this magnificent sight because it is so familiar to them.

I hurry to the top of one of those gigantic structures, the Empire State Building, for there, a short time ago, I "saw" the city below through the eyes of my secretary. I am anxious to compare my fancy with reality. I am sure I should not be disappointed in the panorama spread out before me, for to me it would be a vision of another world.

Now I begin my rounds of the city. First, I stand at a busy corner, merely looking at people, trying by sight of them to understand something of their lives. I see smiles, and I am happy. I see determination, and I am proud. I see suffering, and I am compassionate.

I stroll down Fifth Avenue. I throw my eyes out of focus so that I see no particular object but only a seething kaleidoscope of color. I am certain that the colors of women's dresses moving in a throng must be a gorgeous spectacle of which I should never tire. But perhaps if I had sight I should be like most other women—too interested in styles and the cut of individual dresses to give much attention to the splendor of color in the mass. And I am convinced, too, that I should become an inveterate window shopper, for it must be a delight to the eye to view the myriad articles of beauty on display.

From Fifth Avenue I make a tour of the city—to Park Avenue, to the slums, to factories, to parks where children play. I take a stay-at-home trip abroad by visiting the foreign quarters. Always my eyes are open wide to all the sights of both happiness and misery so that I may probe deep and add to my understanding of how people work and live. My heart is full of the images of people and things. My eye passes lightly over no single trifle; it strives to touch and hold closely each thing its gaze rests upon. Some sights are pleasant, filling the heart with happiness; but some are miserably pathetic. To these latter I do not shut my eyes, for they, too, are part of life. To close the eye on them is to close the heart and mind.

33

34

35

36

37

My third day of sight is drawing to an end. Perhaps there are 38
many serious pursuits to which I should devote the few remaining
hours, but I am afraid that on the evening of that last day I should again
run away to the theater, to a hilariously funny play, so that I might appreciate the overtones of comedy in the human spirit.

At midnight my temporary respite from blindness would cease, and 39
permanent night would close in on me again. Naturally in those three
short days I should not have seen all I wanted to see. Only when darkness had again descended upon me should I realize how much I had left
unseen. But my mind would be so crowded with glorious memories
that I should have little time for regrets. Thereafter the touch of every
object would bring a glowing memory of how that object looked.

Perhaps this short outline of how I should spend three days of 40
sight does not agree with the program you would set for yourself if you
knew that you were about to be stricken blind. I am, however, sure
that if you actually faced that fate your eyes would open to things you
had never seen before, storing up memories for the long night ahead.
You would use your eyes as never before. Everything you saw would
become dear to you. Your eyes would touch and embrace every object
that came within your range of vision. Then, at last, you would really
see, and a new world of beauty would open itself before you.

I who am blind can give one hint to those who see—one admo- 41
nition to those who would make full use of the gift of sight: Use your
eyes as if tomorrow you would be stricken blind. And the same
method can be applied to the other senses. Hear the music of voices,
the song of a bird, the mighty strains of an orchestra, as if you would be
stricken deaf tomorrow. Touch each object you want to touch as if tomorrow your tactile sense would fail. Smell the perfume of flowers,
taste with relish each morsel, as if tomorrow you could never smell and
taste again. Make the most of every sense; glory in all the facets of
pleasure and beauty which the world reveals to you through the several
means of contact which Nature provides. But of all the senses, I am
sure that sight must be the most delightful.

Questions on Meaning

1. Do we take our senses for granted as well as our life? Do only the deaf
   and blind appreciate hearing and seeing?
2. What priorities does Keller establish for what she would like to see in her
   three allotted days of sight? She says others would not agree with her
   program. How would your priorities compare with hers?

3. Do you agree that you have to see people really to know them? Why does she think so? Do you agree that we are as unobservant about even our close friends as she claims?
4. Why would she visit museums on her second day of sight? Why does she say that our "urge to artistic expression has been almost as powerful as the urge for food, shelter, and procreation"? How does her desire to visit the theater relate to her visit to the museums?

Questions on Method

1. Where does Keller's introduction end? Where does her thesis statement occur? What technique does she employ in this rather lengthy introduction?
2. Why does she choose three days rather than two, four, or any other number?
3. What is her purpose in constantly referring to and asking questions of the reader?
4. Keller's illustration of how to appreciate life grows very naturally out of her own experience as a person blind from infancy. What other illustrations of her theme does she mention? Can you think of illustrations other than that which she mentioned of having only three days to see?
5. To what extent does her conclusion build a frame around her essay? Does it refer to the introduction in any way?

Writing Topics

1. What would you include in your curriculum for a college course in "How to Use Your Eyes"?
2. Imagine yourself as having only three more days to see, and write an account of how you would spend them.
3. "Sometimes I have thought it would be an excellent rule to live each day as if we should die tomorrow. Such an attitude would emphasize sharply the values of life." Write an essay responding to Helen Keller's keen awareness that people should utilize their freedom to appreciate life.

Narration
Writing Topics

For each of the essay assignments below, make an appropriate narrative choice in terms of point of view, narrative speed, and chronological arrangement.

1. Narrate an experience in which you felt yourself to be an outsider. Discuss the value of the experience to you.

2. Choose an experience you have had—dating, school, camping, traveling—and form a conclusion about that experience that can be of value to other people. For example, you might conclude that dating many types of people is an education itself. Use your conclusion as a thesis statement, and develop an essay in which your own experience supplies the details and examples. Try analyzing your experience rather than relating it in chronological order.

3. Past experiences—their own or others—play an important role in the essays of Kingston, Douglass, and Wehle. Does the fact that each essay is concerned with an ethnic group have any relevance to the writer's purpose? Is there an experience you have had as a member of an ethnic group that could be valuable to record? If so, write an essay about it.

4. Write an essay on one of the following topics using flashbacks. Begin with a scene in the present—one that holds conflict for you—then recall earlier events. Create suspense by concealing until the end how your conflict is resolved.
   a. an educational experience outside school, such as something learned on the streets, in the family, or on a trip
   b. an experience in strange and frightening surroundings
   c. an experience with a bully

5. Narrate an event in such a way that the personalities of the participants are revealed. Use dialogue, active verbs, description of appearance, and dramatization of key actions in conveying the characters' personalities.

6

Description

WHEREAS NARRATION DEALS PRIMARILY IN ACTION AND VERBS, **description** relies mainly on adjectives, nouns, and **figures of speech.** Like narration, it is a kind of writing you encounter every day. Description involves both content and arrangement. You need to be concerned both with what you want to say and the manner in which you present your subject to the reader.

Description of a place, for example, generally involves two aspects: how a place is experienced sensuously—by the senses—and how it is experienced emotionally. A good description may concentrate on either the sensuous or the emotional, or it may combine them. The sensuous description usually evokes primarily visual details, because sight is ordinarily our strongest sense and the one on which we depend the most, although smells, sounds, and even taste and touch may be brought to bear on what the writer wishes the reader to experience. A mood description, which seeks to implant a particular emotion about a place, may use sensuous details, or the writer may employ emotional scenes or encounters in the description of the place. In this chapter, E. B. White's essay is largely a mood piece infused with sensuous detail.

Visual detail is present, as are sound, smell, taste, and touch, and he uses them very skillfully in conveying his emotional reactions to the lake.

The object of description is to aid your reader in sharing your experience of the place. This sharing is done by supplying details that paint a picture or evoke a mood. The more vividly these details are presented, the more vividly the scene is shared by the reader.

The arrangement of description depends on one's purpose in writing. If purely sensuous description is the aim, then the writer can choose one of several spatial or visual patterns or orientations for describing the place:

Left to right (for rooms, stages, or landscapes)

Top to bottom (for buildings, people, or objects)

Outer to inner (for buildings, or other places that permit several perspectives; the Grand Canyon, for example)

Main impression to detail (similar to the film technique of "panning"; for places, objects, or people)

Other sense impressions can be described as one moves along visually, or the essay can be divided into sections for the different senses: sight, sounds, smells. It is also possible, of course, to describe a place as though you were blind and to let the senses other than sight dominate.

In writing a mood piece, any spatial pattern can be used to organize the description. However, main-impression-to-detail (or its reverse) is the most frequent pattern of arrangement. The writer states the main impression (mood) of the place and then proceeds to support that impression with details, or uses details to lead to a conclusion about the emotional atmosphere. The writer of a mood description may also work out two arrangements simultaneously: one for the mood of the piece, the other for the sensuous details.

Another consideration you need to be aware of is the level of emotion that you will put into your description—its level of **objectivity** or **subjectivity.** Objective description is factual and exact. A laboratory technician, for example, must describe what he or she sees under the microscope in language stripped of personal and emotional overtones. Similarly, a witness in a courtroom must reproduce in words the defendant's or the victim's appearance detail by detail without embellishment. The purpose of subjective description, in contrast, is to give an emotional or personal interpretation or to create a mood; this type of description capitalizes on a *connotative* vocabulary that plays on the reader's values and attitudes.

If you are writing a subjective description, decide what *dominant impression* you require and choose vocabulary with the appropriate **connotations.** Puns and figures of speech such as **simile, metaphor, personification, understatement,** and **hyperbole** (see Figure of Speech in the Glossary) can often convey more than a literal statement; for example, in the description of a sinister scene *creeper* can contribute more than the word *vine*.

Because description is united around a dominant impression, if you can decide what impression you want to create—sinister, lyrical, grotesque, innocent, calm, grand, or intimate, for example—you may be able to provide more **unity** through your choice of vocabulary. Notice how Loren Eiseley achieves a climactic effect as he describes the reunion of his sparrow hawks by focusing on the cry of the female as she catches sight of her mate.

> I was young then and had seen little of the world, but when I heard that cry my heart turned over. It was not the cry of the hawk I had captured; for, by shifting my position against the sun, I was now seeing further up. Straight out of the sun's eye, where she must have been soaring restlessly above us for untold hours, hurtled his mate. And from far up, ringing from peak to peak of the summits over us, came a cry of such unutterable and ecstatic joy that it sounds down across the years and tingles among the cups on my quiet breakfast table.

One last consideration is audience. How much information will your reader need? Is the described thing familiar? Try to give your reader new eyes, to make the familiar new and fresh. Or, if you are describing unusual objects, you may need to make the unusual familiar. In that case, use additional information, a simplified vocabulary, or a well-chosen comparison.

Narration and description complement each other; after all, stories happen in specific places that may exert a powerful influence and so need to be made real to your reader. Because of the way these two techniques work together and in association with the other **modes** to be described in the following chapters, you will probably want to include narration and description in most of your essays.

WRITING DESCRIPTION

1. Select your details carefully; you can't include everything.

2. Determine your purpose. Do you want to provide a factual, scientific, objective description? If so, use a step-by-step spatial arrangement or a progression from least to most important (or the reverse).

3. Determine how best to present your description. The following are two useful organization patterns that work for both types of description:

   a. Begin with an overall impression and then add contributing details.

   b. Begin with details and conclude with an overall impression for a climactic effect.

4. For purely sensuous description, choose a pattern that works from left to right, inner to outer, top to bottom, or the reverse of any of these. Follow your order carefully so as not to confuse your reader.

5. In subjective description, choose sensuous details and a vocabulary that creates a dominant impression.

Once More to the Lake

E. B. White (1899–1985), born in Mount Vernon, New York, was a humorist, poet, storyteller, and essayist who began his career as a journalist with the New Yorker in 1926. His contributions of essays, editorials, and other features to "The Talk of the Town" helped build his reputation for wit and good writing. He also wrote a monthly column for Harper's in which he expressed his views on contemporary life. His keen wit and succinct, highly refined prose style earned him the reputation as one of America's finest essayists. In 1963 White was among the first group of Americans to receive the Presidential Medal of Freedom, with a citation that called him "an essayist whose concise comment...has revealed to yet another age the vigor of the English sentence." White's books include Charlotte's Web *(1952), a beloved children's book that reflects some of his own life on a Maine farm,* The Second Tree from the Corner *(1954), and* The Points on My Compass *(1962). Collections of his letters, essays, poems, and sketches were published between 1976 and 1981.*

AUGUST 1941

ONE SUMMER, along about 1904, my father rented a camp on a lake in Maine and took us all there for the month of August. We all got ringworm from some kittens and had to rub Pond's Extract on our arms and legs night and morning, and my father rolled over in a canoe with all his clothes on; but outside of that the vacation was a success and from then on none of us ever thought there was any place in the world like that lake in Maine. We returned summer after summer—always on August 1 for one month. I have since become a salt-water man, but sometimes in summer there are days when the restlessness of the tides and the fearful cold of the sea water and the incessant wind that blows across the afternoon and into the evening make me wish for the placidity of a lake in the woods. A few weeks ago this feeling got so strong I bought myself a couple of bass hooks and a spinner and re-

turned to the lake where we used to go, for a week's fishing and to re-
visit old haunts.

I took along my son, who had never had any fresh water up his
nose and who had seen lily pads only from train windows. On the journey over to the lake I began to wonder what it would be like. I wondered how time would have marred this unique, this holy spot—the
coves and streams, the hills that the sun set behind, the camps and the
paths behind the camps. I was sure that the tarred road would have found
it out, and I wondered in what other ways it would be desolated. It is
strange how much you can remember about places like that once you allow your mind to return into the grooves that lead back. You remember
one thing, and that suddenly reminds you of another thing. I guess I remembered clearest of all the early mornings, when the lake was cool and
motionless, remembered how the bedroom smelled of the lumber it was
made of and of the wet woods whose scent entered through the screen.
The partitions in the camp were thin and did not extend clear to the top
of the rooms, and as I was always the first up I would dress softly so as not
to wake the others, and sneak out into the sweet outdoors and start out
in the canoe, keeping close along the shore in the long shadows of the
pines. I remembered being very careful never to rub my paddle against
the gunwale for fear of disturbing the stillness of the cathedral.

The lake had never been what you would call a wild lake. There
were cottages sprinkled around the shores, and it was in farming country although the shores of the lake were quite heavily wooded. Some
of the cottages were owned by nearby farmers, and you would live at
the shore and eat your meals at the farmhouse. That's what our family
did. But although it wasn't wild, it was a fairly large and undisturbed
lake and there were places in it that, to a child at least, seemed infinitely remote and primeval.

I was right about the tar: It led to within half a mile of the shore.
But when I got back there, with my boy, and we settled into a camp
near a farmhouse and into the kind of summertime I had known, I
could tell that it was going to be pretty much the same as it had been
before—I knew it, lying in bed the first morning smelling the bedroom and hearing the boy sneak quietly out and go off along the shore
in a boat. I began to sustain the illusion that he was I, and therefore, by
simple transposition, that I was my father. This sensation persisted,
kept cropping up all the time we were there. It was not an entirely new
feeling, but in this setting it grew much stronger. I seemed to be living
a dual existence. I would be in the middle of some simple act, I would

be picking up a bait box or laying down a table fork, or I would be saying something and suddenly it would be not I but my father who was
saying the words or making the gesture. It gave me a creepy sensation.

We went fishing the first morning. I felt the same damp moss   5
covering the worms in the bait can, and saw the dragonfly alight on
the tip of my rod as it hovered a few inches from the surface of the water. It was the arrival of this fly that convinced me beyond any doubt
that everything was as it always had been, that the years were a mirage
and that there had been no years. The small waves were the same,
chucking the rowboat under the chin as we fished at anchor, and the
boat was the same boat, the same color green and the ribs broken in
the same places, and under the floorboards the same fresh water leav-
ings and debris—the dead hellgrammite, the wisps of moss, the rusty
discarded fishhook, the dried blood from yesterday's catch. We stared
silently at the tips of our rods, at the dragonflies that came and went. I
lowered the tip of mine into the water, tentatively, pensively dislodging
the fly, which darted two feet away, poised, darted two feet back, and
came to rest again a little farther up the rod. There had been no years
between the ducking of this dragonfly and the other one—the one
that was part of memory. I looked at the boy, who was silently watching his fly, and it was my hands that held his rod, my eyes watching. I
felt dizzy and didn't know which rod I was at the end of.

We caught two bass, hauling them in briskly as though they were   6
mackerel, pulling them over the side of the boat in a businesslike manner without any landing net, and stunning them with a blow on the
back of the head. When we got back for a swim before lunch, the lake
was exactly where we had left it, the same number of inches from the
dock, and there was only the merest suggestion of a breeze. This
seemed an utterly enchanted sea, this lake you could leave to its own
devices for a few hours and come back to, and find that it had not
stirred, this constant and trustworthy body of water. In the shallows,
the dark, water-soaked sticks and twigs, smooth and old, were undu-
lating in clusters on the bottom against the clean ribbed sand, and the
track of the mussel was plain. A school of minnows swam by, each
minnow with its small individual shadow, doubling the attendance, so
clear and sharp in the sunlight. Some of the other campers were in
swimming, along the shore, one of them with a cake of soap, and the
water felt thin and clear and unsubstantial. Over the years there had
been this person with the cake of soap, this cultist, and here he was.
There had been no years.

Up to the farmhouse to dinner through the teeming dusty field, 7
the road under our sneakers was only a two-track road. The middle
track was missing, the one with the marks of the hooves and the
splotches of dried, flaky manure. There had always been three tracks to
choose from in choosing which track to walk in; now the choice was
narrowed down to two. For a moment I missed terribly the middle alternative. But the way led past the tennis court, and something about
the way it lay there in the sun reassured me; the tape had loosened
along the backline, the alleys were green with plantains and other
weeds, and the net (installed in June and removed in September)
sagged in the dry noon, and the whole place steamed with midday
heat and hunger and emptiness. There was a choice of pie for dessert,
and one was blueberry and one was apple, and the waitresses were the
same country girls, there having been no passage of time, only the illusion of it as in a dropped curtain—the waitresses were still fifteen; their
hair had been washed, that was the only difference—they had been to
the movies and seen the pretty girls with the clean hair.

Summertime, oh, summertime, pattern of life indelible with fade- 8
proof lake, the woods unshatterable, the pasture with the sweetfern and
the juniper forever and ever, summer without end; this was the background, and the life along the shore was the design, the cottagers with
their innocent and tranquil design, their tiny docks with the flagpole
and the American flag floating against the white clouds in the blue sky,
the little paths over the roots of the trees leading from camp to camp
and the paths leading back to the outhouses and the can of lime for
sprinkling, and at the souvenir counters at the store the miniature
birchbark canoes and the postcards that showed things looking a little
better than they looked. This was the American family at play, escap-
ing the city heat, wondering whether the newcomers in the camp at
the head of the cove were "common" or "nice," wondering whether
it was true that the people who drove up for Sunday dinner at the
farmhouse were turned away because there wasn't enough chicken.

It seemed to me, as I kept remembering all this, that those times 9
and those summers had been infinitely precious and worth saving.
There had been jollity and peace and goodness. The arriving (at the
beginning of August) had been so big a business in itself, at the railway
station the farm wagon drawn up, the first smell of the pine-laden air,
the first glimpse of the smiling farmer, and the great importance of the
trunks and your father's enormous authority in such matters, and the
feel of the wagon under you for the long ten-mile haul, and at the top

of the last long hill catching the first view of the lake after eleven
months of not seeing this cherished body of water. The shouts and
cries of the other campers when they saw you, and the trunks to be
unpacked, to give up their rich burden. (Arriving was less exciting
nowadays, when you sneaked up in your car and parked it under a tree
near the camp and took out the bags and in five minutes it was all over,
no fuss, no loud wonderful fuss about trunks.)

Peace and goodness and jollity. The only thing that was wrong   10
now, really, was the sound of the place, an unfamiliar nervous sound of
the outboard motors. This was the note that jarred, the one thing that
would sometimes break the illusion and set the years moving. In those
other summertimes all motors were inboard; and when they were at a
little distance, the noise they made was a sedative, an ingredient of
summer sleep. They were one-cylinder and two-cylinder engines, and
some were make-and-break and some were jump-spark, but they all
made a sleepy sound across the lake. The one-lungers throbbed and
fluttered, and the twin-cylinder ones purred and purred, and that was
a quiet sound, too. But now the campers all had outboards. In the daytime, in the hot mornings, these motors made a petulant irritable
sound; at night in the still evening when the afterglow lit the water,
they whined about one's ears like mosquitoes. My boy loved our
rented outboard, and his great desire was to achieve single-handed
mastery over it, and authority, and he soon learned the trick of chok-
ing it a little (but not too much), and the adjustment of the needle
valve. Watching him I would remember the things you could do with
the old one-cylinder engine with the heavy flywheel, how you could
have it eating out of your hand if you got really close to it spiritually.
Motorboats in those days didn't have clutches, and you would make a
landing by shutting off the motor at the proper time and coasting in
with a dead rudder. But there was a way of reversing them, if you
learned the trick, by cutting the switch and putting it on again exactly
on the final dying revolution of the flywheel, so that it would kick
back against compression and begin reversing. Approaching a dock in
a strong following breeze, it was difficult to slow up sufficiently by the
ordinary coasting method, and if a boy felt he had complete mastery
over his motor, he was tempted to keep it running beyond its time and
then reverse it a few feet from the dock. It took a cool nerve, because
if you threw the switch a twentieth of a second too soon you would
catch the flywheel when it still had speed enough to go up past center,
and the boat would leap ahead, charging bull-fashion at the dock.

We had a good week at the camp. The bass were biting well and   11
the sun shone endlessly, day after day. We would be tired at night and
lie down in the accumulated heat of the little bedrooms after the long
hot day and the breeze would stir almost imperceptibly outside and the
smell of the swamp drift in through the rusty screens. Sleep would
come easily and in the morning the red squirrel would be on the roof,
tapping out his gay routine. I kept remembering everything, lying in
bed in the mornings—the small steamboat that had a long rounded
stern like the lip of a Ubangi, and how quietly she ran on the moon-
light sails, when the older boys played their mandolins and the girls
sang and we ate doughnuts dipped in sugar, and how sweet the music
was on the water in the shining night, and what it had felt like to think
about girls then. After breakfast we would go up to the store and the
things were in the same place—the minnows in a bottle, the plugs and
spinners disarranged and pawed over by the youngsters from the boys'
camp, the Fig Newtons and the Beeman's gum. Outside, the road was
tarred and cars stood in front of the store. Inside, all was just as it had
always been, except there was more Coca-Cola and not so much
Moxie and root beer and birch beer and sarsaparilla. We would walk
out with the bottle of pop apiece and sometimes the pop would backfire up our noses and hurt. We explored the streams, quietly, where the
turtles slid off the sunny logs and dug their way into the soft bottom;
and we lay on the town wharf and fed worms to the tame bass. Everywhere we went I had trouble making out which was I, the one walking
at my side, the one walking in my pants.

One afternoon while we were there at the lake a thunderstorm   12
came up. It was like the revival of an old melodrama that I had seen
long ago with childish awe. The second-act climax of the drama of the
electrical disturbance over a lake in America had not changed in any
important respect. This was the big scene, still the big scene. The
whole thing was so familiar, the first feeling of oppression and heat and
a general air around camp of not wanting to go very far away. In mid-
afternoon (it was all the same) a curious darkening of the sky, and a lull
in everything that had made life tick; and then the way the boats suddenly swung the other way at their moorings with the coming of a
breeze out of the new quarter, and the premonitory rumble. Then the
kettle drum, then the snare, then the bass drum and cymbals, then
crackling light against the dark, and the gods grinning and licking their
chops in the hills. Afterward the calm, the rain steadily rustling in the
calm lake, the return of light and hope and spirits, and the campers

running out in joy and relief to go swimming in the rain, their bright cries perpetuating the deathless joke about how they were getting simply drenched, and the children screaming with delight at the new sensation of bathing in the rain, and the joke about getting drenched linking the generations in a strong indestructible chain. And the comedian who waded in carrying an umbrella.

When the others went swimming, my son said he was going in, too. He pulled his dripping trunks from the line where they had hung all through the shower and wrung them out. Languidly, and with no thought of going in, I watched him, his hard little body, skinny and bare, saw him wince slightly as he pulled up around his vitals the small, soggy, icy garment. As he buckled the swollen belt, suddenly my groin felt the chill of death.

13

Questions on Meaning

1. White describes the Maine lake as a "holy spot." What details from the essay defend this description?
2. What particular features distinguish this lake from others?
3. What does the author mean by "I seemed to be living a dual existence"? What importance does this statement have for the essay?
4. "Arriving was less exciting nowadays." What other differences does the author discover between his childhood and adult visits to the lake?
5. What does the last sentence mean? Does it have any connection with the rest of the essay?

Questions on Method

1. White describes the reflection of the tall pines on the surface of the lake as a "cathedral." What other similes and metaphors does he use?
2. Did White have to limit his topic? What might his broader topic have been? What sentence might be his thesis sentence?
3. What was White's purpose in writing his essay? How would you categorize the audience he is writing for?
4. Does White at any point in the essay foreshadow the last sentence? Does he prepare us for it in any way?

Writing Topics

1. E. B. White's essay is largely a mood piece infused with sensuous detail. Visual details are present as are sounds, smells, taste, and touch. Has a

place affected you as intensely as the lake did White? Describe this place, conveying your response to it through your use of sensuous detail.

2. In "Once More to the Lake," place evokes an important insight for the author. Write about a place that had a similar effect on you *or* discuss the interaction between person and place in White's essay that made this insight possible.

3. We all have places of our own that may seem unappealing to others but that we like very much. Your room, for example, may be messy and chaotic but a refuge nevertheless. Write an essay describing a place that is **paradoxal** in this way. Include what is both unappealing and appealing at the same time.

Sparrow Hawks

Born in Lincoln, Nebraska, Loren Eiseley (1907–1977) was an American educator, anthropologist, poet, and author. He had a unique talent for combining a poetic style with scientific subject matter, reflecting his conceit that reason alone, without vision and imagination, would be detrimental to humanity. His best-known works include The Immense Journey *(1957),* Darwin's Century *(1958), and* The Unexpected Universe *(1969).*

I JOINED SOME COLLEAGUES heading into a remote windy tableland where huge bones were reputed to protrude like boulders from the turf.... There had been talk of birds in connection with my duties. Birds are intense, fast-living creatures—reptiles, I suppose one might say, that have escaped out of the heavy sleep of time, transformed fairy creatures dancing over sunlit meadows. It is a youthful fancy, no doubt, but because of something that happened up there among the escarpments of that range, it remains with me a lifelong impression. I can never bear to see a bird imprisoned.

We came into that valley through the trailing mists of a spring night. It was a place that looked as though it might never have known the foot of man, but our scouts had been ahead of us and we knew all about the abandoned cabin of stone that lay far up on one hillside. It had been built in the land rush of the last century and then lost to the cattlemen again as the marginal soils failed to take to the plow.

There were spots like this all over that country. Lost graves marked by unlettered stones and old corroding rim-fire cartridge cases lying where somebody had made a stand among the boulders that rimmed the valley. They are all that remain of the range wars; the men are under the stones now. I could see our cavalcade winding in and out through the mist below us: torches, the reflection of the truck lights on our collecting tins, and the far-off bumping of a loose dinosaur thigh bone in the bottom of a trailer. I stood on a rock a moment looking down and thinking what it cost in money and equipment to capture the past.

We had, in addition, instructions to lay hands on the present. The
word had come through to get them alive—birds, reptiles, anything. A
zoo somewhere abroad needed restocking. It was one of those recipro-
cal matters in which science involves itself. Maybe our museum needed
a stray ostrich egg and this was the payoff. Anyhow, my job was to help
capture some birds and that was why I was there before the trucks.

The cabin had not been occupied for years. We intended to clean
it out and live in it, but there were holes in the roof and the birds had
come in and were roosting in the rafters. You could depend on it in a
place like this where everything blew away, and even a bird needed
some place out of the weather and away from coyotes. A cabin going
back to nature in a wild place draws them till they come in, listening at
the eaves, I imagine, pecking softly among the shingles till they find a
hole and then suddenly the place is theirs and man is forgotten....

I got the door open softly and I had the spotlight all ready to turn
on and blind whatever birds there were so they couldn't see to get out
through the roof. I had a short piece of ladder to put against the far
wall where there was a shelf on which I expected to make the biggest
haul. I had all the information I needed just like any skilled assassin. I
pushed the door open, the hinges squeaking only a little. A bird or two
stirred—I could hear them—but nothing flew and there was a faint
starlight through the holes in the roof.

I padded across the floor, got the ladder up and the light ready,
and slithered up the ladder till my head and arms were over the shelf.
Everything was dark as pitch except for the starlight at the little place
back of the shelf near the eaves. With the light to blind them, they'd
never make it. I had them. I reached my arm carefully over in order to
be ready to seize whatever was there and I put the flash on the edge of
the shelf where it would stand by itself when I turned it on. That way
I'd be able to use both hands.

Everything worked perfectly except for one detail—I didn't
know what kinds of birds were there. I never thought about it at all,
and it wouldn't have mattered if I had. My orders were to get something interesting. I snapped on the flash and sure enough there was a
great beating and feathers flying, but instead of my having them, they,
or rather he, had me. He had my hand, that is, and for a small hawk
not much bigger than my fist he was doing all right. I heard him give
one short metallic cry when the light went on and my hand descended
on the bird beside him; after that he was busy with his claws and his
beak was sunk in my thumb. In the struggle I knocked the lamp over

on the shelf, and his mate got her sight back and whisked neatly through the hole in the roof and off among the stars outside. It all happened in fifteen seconds and you might think I would have fallen down the ladder, but no, I had a professional assassin's reputation to keep up, and the bird, of course, made the mistake of thinking the hand was the enemy and not the eyes behind it. He chewed my thumb up pretty effectively and lacerated my hand with his claws, but in the end I got him, having two hands to work with.

He was a sparrow hawk and a fine young male in the prime of life.   9
I was sorry not to catch the pair of them, but as I dripped blood and folded his wings carefully, holding him by the back so that he couldn't strike again, I had to admit the two of them might have been more than I could have handled under the circumstances. The little fellow had saved his mate by diverting me, and that was that. He was born to it, and made no outcry now, resting in my hand hopelessly, but peering toward me in the shadows behind the lamp with a fierce, almost indifferent glance. He neither gave nor expected mercy and something out of the high air passed from him to me, stirring a faint embarrassment.

I quit looking into that eye and managed to get my huge carcass   10
with its fist full of prey back down the ladder. I put the bird in a box too small to allow him to injure himself by struggle and walked out to welcome the arriving trucks. It had been a long day, and camp still to make in the darkness. In the morning that bird would be just another episode. He would go back with the bones in the truck to a small cage in a city where he would spend the rest of his life. And a good thing, too. I sucked my aching thumb and spat out some blood. An assassin has to get used to these things. I had a professional reputation to keep up.

In the morning, with the change that comes on suddenly in that   11
high country, the mist that had hovered below us in the valley was gone. The sky was a deep blue, and one could see for miles over the high outcroppings of stone. I was up early and brought the box in which the little hawk was imprisoned out onto the grass where I was building a cage. A wind as cool as a mountain spring ran over the grass and stirred my hair. It was a fine day to be alive. I looked up and all around and at the hole in the cabin roof out of which the other little hawk had fled. There was no sign of her anywhere that I could see.

"Probably in the next county by now," I thought cynically, but be-   12
fore beginning work I decided I'd have a look at my last night's capture.

Secretively, I looked again all around the camp and up and down   13
and opened the box. I got him right out in my hand with his wings

folded properly and I was careful not to startle him. He lay limp in my grasp and I could feel his heart pound under the feathers but he only looked beyond me and up.

I saw him look that last look away beyond me into a sky so full of light that I could not follow his gaze. The little breeze flowed over me again, and nearby a mountain aspen shook all its tiny leaves. I suppose I must have had an idea then of what I was going to do, but I never let it come up into consciousness. I just reached over and laid the hawk on the grass.

He lay there a long minute without hope, unmoving, his eyes still fixed on that blue vault above him. It must have been that he was already so far away in heart that he never felt the release from my hand. He never even stood. He just lay with his breast against the grass.

In the next second after that long minute he was gone. Like a flicker of light, he had vanished with my eyes full on him, but without actually seeing even a premonitory wing beat. He was gone straight into that towering emptiness of light and crystal that my eyes could scarcely bear to penetrate. For another long moment there was silence. I could not see him. The light was too intense. Then from far up somewhere a cry came ringing down.

I was young then and had seen little of the world, but when I heard that cry my heart turned over. It was not the cry of the hawk I had captured; for, by shifting my position against the sun, I was now seeing further up. Straight out of the sun's eye, where she must have been soaring restlessly above us for untold hours, hurtled his mate. And from far up, ringing from peak to peak of the summits over us, came a cry of such unutterable and ecstatic joy that it sounds down across the years and tingles among the cups on my quiet breakfast table.

I saw them both now. He was rising fast to meet her. They met in a great soaring gyre that turned to a whirling circle and a dance of wings. Once more, just once, their two voices, joined in a harsh wild medley of question and response, struck and echoed against the pinnacles of the valley. Then they were gone forever somewhere into those upper regions beyond the eyes of men.

Questions on Meaning

1. Why had Eiseley come to capture the birds?
2. Do you think you would have freed the bird after being attacked by it as Eiseley was? Why or why not?

3. "I was young then and had seen little of the world, but when I heard that cry my heart turned over." Do you think Eiseley would have reacted in the same way had he been older? Should he have been more concerned about fulfilling his professional responsibilities?
4. Was freeing the bird a sentimental act? Is a sentimental act bad? Good? Sometimes bad, sometimes good? Explain.
5. What is your overall response to the essay?

Questions on Method

1. What clue does Eiseley give in the first paragraph that foreshadows the decision he will make later?
2. What is the significance of Eiseley's referring to himself as an "assassin" in paragraphs 6, 8, and 10?
3. For what audience is Eiseley writing?
4. What is his purpose in recalling this experience?
5. Look up the meaning of "epiphany." Why is that an appropriate term to describe Eiseley's experience in paragraphs 17 and 18? What was your reaction to his description of his experience?

Writing Topics

1. To what senses does Eiseley appeal in his use of figurative language? Write an essay citing examples from "Sparrow Hawks" that you found effective.
2. Eiseley's unexpected choice results in his experiencing an epiphany. Write an essay describing the circumstances about a choice you made that had deep significance for you emotionally and intellectually.
3. Analyze how viewing things scientifically affects a person. In what ways does a scientific perspective increase one's understanding of what is observed? Are there ways such a perspective might limit one's understanding?

False Gold

Fae Myenne Ng (b. 1967) was born in San Francisco where as a child she helped her mother in the Chinatown sweatshops. Ng recalls, "One of my duties was to write the little code number of my mother's sewing machine onto the laundering tabs." She studied English at the University of California at Berkeley and received an M.F.A. from Columbia University; she now resides in Brooklyn. Her prose has been published in numerous anthologies and periodicals including Harper's, The American Voice, *and* The City Lights Review. *Her novel* Bone *(1993), which narrates her parents' struggle in America, is an account of the attempts of an Asian American family in San Francisco's Chinatown to cope with the suicide of the second of three daughters. Ng says of her novel, "The whole ritual of sending the bones back to China was fascinating to me," a reference to the desire of many early Asian immigrants to be buried in their homeland. "Bone is what lasts, and I wanted to honor the quality of the endurance of the human spirit." Because her parents do not speak English, Ng has told them what her novel is about: "I tell them that the book celebrates the hard work and living they endured in order to give future generations a better life."*

IT'S THAT SAME OLD, same old story. We all have an immigrant ancestor, one who believed in America; one who, daring or duped, took sail. The Golden Venture emigrants have begun the American journey, suffering and sacrificing, searching for the richer, easier life. I know them; I could be one of their daughters. Like them, my father took the sacrificial role of being the first to venture. Now, at the end of his life, he calls it a bitter, no-luck life. I have always lived with his question, Was it worth it? As a child, I saw the bill-by-bill payback and I felt my own unpayable emotional debt. Obedience and Obligation: the Confucian curse. 1

For $4,000 my father became the fourth son of a legal Chinese immigrant living in San Francisco. His paper-father sent him a coaching book, detailing complicated family history. It was 1940; my father paid ninety more dollars for passage on the s.s. *Coolidge.* He had little hand luggage, a change of clothes, herbs and seeds and a powder for soup. To 2 soothe his pounding heart during the fifteen-day voyage he recited the coaching book over and over again. It was not a floating hell. "The food was Chinese. We traveled third-class. A bunk was good enough space." He was prepared for worse. He'd heard about the Peruvian ships that transported Chinese coolies★ for plantation labor in the 1850s. (Every generation has a model.) One hundred and twenty days. Two feet by six for each man. Were these the first ships to be called floating hells?

Gold Mountain was the name of my father's America. In February, when the Golden Venture immigrants sailed from Bangkok, they were shouting, *Mei Guo! Mei Guo!* "Beautiful Country" was the translation they preferred. America is the land of light and hope. But landing here is only the beginning of a long tale. When I saw the photos of the shipwrecked Chinese on the beach, I was reminded of the men kept on Angel Island, the detention center in the middle of San Francisco Bay. A sea of hats on the deck of the ship. Triple-decked bunkers. Men in loose pants playing volleyball. "Was volleyball fun?" I wanted to know. My father shrugged, "Nothing else to do. It helped pass the day." Our fathers spent months detained on Angel Island. Their name for it was Wooden House. What, I wonder, are the Chinese calling the detention center in Bethlehem, Pennsylvania?

After his release from Angel Island, my father lived at a bachelor hotel on Waverly Place with a dozen other bachelors in one room, communal toilets, no kitchen. He had breakfast at Uncle's Cafe, dinners at the Jackson Cafe, midnight noodles at Sam Wo's. Drinks at the Li Po Bar or Red's Place, where fat burlesque queens sat on his lap. Marriage for duty. Sons for tradition. My father left the hotel but kept the habits. He still eats like a mouse, in the middle of the night, cooking on a hot plate in his room. (I do my version of the same.) He keeps his money under the floorboard. When I have it, I like to have a grip, bill by bill. Like everyone, too little money upsets me; but more money than I can hold upsets me too. I feel obliged to give it away. Is it a wonder that money has a dirty feel? Get it and get it fast. Then get rid of it.

I remember this Angel Island photograph. Thirty bare-chested Chinese men are waiting for a medical examination. The doctor, a hunching man with a scraping stare, sits at a small desk, elbows and thick hands over a black book. At his side, a guard in knee-high boots measures a boy's forehead. Arranged by height, baby-eyed boys stand stoop-shouldered on the outer edge. The men, at least a head taller,

3

4

5

★*Coolie:* (Urdu, hireling) in Asia, an unskilled native worker, employed cheaply.

stand toward the center of the room, staring at the examiner. Those eyes scare me. Bold and angry and revengeful. Eyes that owe. Eyes that will make you pay. Humiliation with a vengeance.

As boldly, the Golden Venture men have looked into American cameras. (If they believed a foot on soil would make them legal, a photo in an American newspaper would be as good as a passport.) There was a "See me!" bounce in their faces. They'd arrived, and now they wanted to send their news back home. And back home, a grateful father jumped when he picked out his son as one of the survivors, "He's alive! My son made it." 6

Another photo. A Golden Venture man looks out from a locked door, his face framed by a tight window. He has a jail-view of the Beautiful Country. How would he describe his new world? I imagine he'd use his own body as a measure. "Window, two head high. Sun on both ears." Can we forget the other "face" photograph taken earlier this century? The sold and smuggled prostitute, demoted from brothel to a crib, a wooden shack with barred windows that barely fits a cot. Looking out from her fenced window, she has the same downcast eyes, the same bitter-strange lips that seem to be smiling as well as trembling. The caption quotes her price: "Lookee two bits, feelee floor bits, doee six bits." 7

Life was and still is weighed in gold. People buy people. Sons and wives and slaves. There was the imperial edict that forbade Chinese to leave China; there was China's contribution to France during World War I, in which tens of thousands of Chinese lived horrible lives as indentured slaves. I've heard parents threaten to sell children who misbehave. (Mine threatened to throw me into the garbage can where they claimed they found me.) There's the story of Old Man Jeong, the one on Beckett Alley. Lonely after his wife died, fearful no one would care for him in his senile retirement, he went back to his home village and bought himself a wife. A woman born in 1956. 8

Listen to the animal names. Snakes sneak into America. The Golden Venture was a snake ship. The emigrants are snake cargo; the middleman, a snakehead. In my father's time, a pig was sold to America. A pig gets caught, a pig gets cheated. My father feels cheated, sold, on an easy story. 9

On a recent visit to my father's house in Guangzhou, I found his original coaching book. I knew it had been untouched since he last held it. In my hand, the loosely bound papers felt like ashes. I thought about how when he committed everything to memory, he became another 10

man's son. There's an elaborate map of the family compound; each page
is lined with questions and answers, some marked with red circles. Tedious questions and absurd details. How much money did Second
Brother send to Mother? How much farmland did Mother have and
what vegetables were harvested? Third Brother's wife's feet, were they
big or bound? The book has a musty smell that reaches into my throat.

One out of every four relations let me know they wanted to   11
come to America. At the end of my visit, a distant relation and her 13-
year-old daughter followed me into the rice paddies. "I'm selling her,"
the mother told me.

"What did you say? Say again?" I replied.   12

She held a palm over her (golden) lower teeth, and said it again,   13
"Don't know what I'm saying? Sell. We sell her."

I stared at her. She laughed some more and then just walked   14
away, back toward the village. The girl followed me, quiet till we got to
the river, where she posed for some pictures and then asked for my address. I wrote it on the back of a business card. (I considered giving her
my post office box.) I hope never to be surprised. I hope never to see
this child at my door holding the card like a legal document.

"Don't add and don't take away" was the advice of an uncle who   15
heard that I wrote things. Stay safe. Keep us safe. How right that
"China" is written with the character "middle." Obedience is a safe
position. The Golden Venture men trusted the stories they heard.
Their clansmen entrusted their dreams to them. The question is not
how bad it is in China. The question is how good it can be in America. My father believes the Golden Venturers have only passed through
the first hell. In coming to America, he laments (there is no other
word) that he trusted too much. Ironic that in Chinese he bought a
name that reads, To Have Trust.

Questions on Meaning

1. "For $4,000 my father became the fourth son of a legal Chinese immi-
   grant living in San Francisco." How do you respond to his decision to assume a new identity in a new land? To what extent is it possible to
   reinvent oneself?
2. In paragraph 9, the author indicates that her father felt cheated. What are
   his reasons? Were his expectations about opportunities in the United
   States unrealistic? Why or why not?
3. In paragraph 4, Ng discusses her attitude toward money. How is it similar
   to or different from her father's? From yours?

Questions on Method

1. Ng uses gold as the dominant symbol in her essay. Make a list of the references to gold and money throughout the text and analyze their meaning in the author's family history as well as to Chinese immigrants in general.
2. Characterize the tone of the essay. Is it **ironic,** bitter, serious, pessimistic? Cite evidence to support your answer.

Writing Topics

1. Throughout the essay, Ng cites evidence to support her thesis that "life was and still is weighed in gold." To what extent do you agree or disagree that money is important in contemporary culture regardless of the ethnic group to which one belongs? Cite examples.
2. Write an essay describing a part of your cultural heritage you might someday want to share with your children.

The Allegory of the Cave

Plato (c. 427–347 B.C.E.) was a Greek philosopher and writer who came from a wealthy aristocratic family. He served in the military against Sparta and traveled to Egypt, Syracuse, and Sicily. As far as is known, he never married. Plato, best known for his philosophical dialogues, probably first presented his philosophy in the academy, which he founded. The student body consisted of aristocratic young men who could study a multifaceted curriculum free of charge. He became actively involved in the politics of the Athenian state. He, like his friend and mentor Socrates, protested against the tyranny that corrupted Athenian democracy. His rebellion, coupled with his reaction to the death of Socrates, who received the death penalty for corrupting the young men of Athens and for challenging the authority of the gods through his philosophical methods, led Plato to search for an alternative lifestyle. Plato's philosophical and political ideas have had a significant influence on Western thought.

AND NOW, I SAID, let me show in a figure how far our nature is enlightened or unenlightened: Behold! human beings living in an underground den, which has a mouth open towards the light and reaching all along the den; here they have been from their childhood, and have their legs and necks chained so that they cannot move, and can only see before them, being prevented by the chains from turning round their heads. Above and behind them a fire is blazing at a distance, and between the fire and the prisoners there is a raised way; and you will see, if you look, a low wall built along the way, like the screen which marionette players have in front of them, over which they show the puppets. 1

I see. 2

And do you see, I said, men passing along the wall carrying all sorts of vessels, and statues and figures of animals made of wood and stone and various materials, which appear over the wall? Some of them are talking, others silent. 3

You have shown me a strange image, and they are strange prisoners. 4

Like ourselves, I replied; and they see only their own shadows, or 5
the shadows of one another, which the fire throws on the opposite wall
of the cave?

True, he said; how could they see anything but the shadows if 6
they were never allowed to move their heads?

And of the objects which are being carried in like manner they 7
would only see the shadows?

Yes, he said. 8

And if they were able to converse with one another, would they 9
not suppose that they were naming what was actually before them?

Very true. 10

And suppose further that the prison had an echo which came 11
from the other side, would they not be sure to fancy when one of the
passers-by spoke that the voice which they heard came from the passing shadow?

No question, he replied. 12

To them, I said, the truth would be literally nothing but the shad- 13
ows of the images.

That is certain. 14

And now look again, and see what will naturally follow if the 15
prisoners are released and disabused of their error. At first, when any of
them is liberated and compelled suddenly to stand up and turn his
neck round and walk and look towards the light, he will suffer sharp
pains; the glare will distress him and he will be unable to see the realities of which in his former state he had seen the shadows; and then
conceive some one saying to him, that what he saw before was an illusion, but that now, when he is approaching nearer to being and his eye
is turned towards more real existence, he has a clearer vision—what
will be his reply? And you may further imagine that his instructor is
pointing to the objects as they pass and requiring him to name them—
will he not be perplexed? Will he not fancy that the shadows which he
formerly saw are truer than the objects which are now shown to him?

Far truer. 16

And if he is compelled to look straight at the light, will he not 17
have a pain in his eyes which will make him turn away to take refuge in
the objects of vision which he can see, and which he will conceive to
be in reality clearer than the things which are now being shown to him?

True, he said. 18

And suppose once more, that he is reluctantly dragged up a steep 19
and rugged ascent, and held fast until he is forced into the presence of

the sun himself, is he not likely to be pained and irritated? When he approaches the light his eyes will be dazzled and he will not be able to see anything at all of what are now called realities.

Not all in a moment, he said.   20

He will require to grow accustomed to the sight of the upper   21
world. And first he will see the shadows best, next the reflections of men and other objects in the water, and then the objects themselves; then he will gaze upon the light of the moon and the stars and the spangled heaven; and he will see the sky and the stars by night better than the sun or the light of the sun by day?

Certainly.   22

Last of all he will be able to see the sun, and not mere reflections   23
of him in the water, but he will see him in his own proper place, and not in another; and he will contemplate him as he is.

Certainly.   24

He will then proceed to argue that this is he who gives the season   25
and the years, and is the guardian of all that is in the visible world, and in a certain way the cause of all things which he and his fellows have been accustomed to behold?

Clearly, he said, he would first see the sun and then reason about   26
him.

And when he remembered his old habitation, and the wisdom of   27
the den and his fellow-prisoners, do you not suppose that he would fe-licitate himself on the change, and pity them?

Certainly, he would.   28

And if they were in the habit of conferring honors among them-   29
selves on those who were quickest to observe the passing shadows and to remark which of them went before, and which followed after, and which were together; and who were therefore best able to draw conclusions as to the future, do you think that he would care for such honors and glo-ries, or envy the possessors of them? Would he not say with Homer,

> Better to be the poor servant of a poor master,

and to endure anything, rather than think as they do and live after their manner?

Yes, he said, I think that he would rather suffer anything than en-   30
tertain these false notions and live in this miserable manner.

Imagine once more, I said, such an one coming suddenly out of   31
the sun to be replaced in his old situation; would he not be certain to have his eyes full of darkness?

To be sure, he said. 32

And if there were a contest, and he had to compete in measuring 33 the shadows with the prisoners who had never moved out of the den, while his sight was still weak, and before his eyes had become steady (and the time which would be needed to acquire this new habit of sight might be very considerable) would he not be ridiculous? Men would say of him that up he went and down he came without his eyes; and that it was better not even to think of ascending; and if any one tried to loose another and lead him up to the light, let them only catch the offender, and they would put him to death.

No question, he said. 34

This entire allegory, I said, you may now append, dear Glaucon, 35 to the previous argument; the prison-house is the world of sight, the light of the fire is the sun, and you will not misapprehend me if you interpret the journey upwards to be the ascent of the soul into the intellectual world according to my poor belief, which, at your desire, I have expressed—whether rightly or wrongly God knows. But, whether true or false, my opinion is that in the world of knowledge the idea of good appears last of all, and is seen only with an effort; and, when seen, is also inferred to be the universal author of all things beautiful and right, parent of light and of the lord of light in this visible world, and the immediate source of reason and truth in the intellectual; and that this is the power upon which he who would act rationally either in public or private life must have his eye fixed.

I agree, he said, as far as I am able to understand you. 36

Moreover, I said, you must not wonder that those who attain to 37 this beatific vision are unwilling to descend to human affairs; for their souls are ever hastening into the upper world where they desire to dwell; which desire of theirs is very natural, if our allegory may be trusted.

Yes, very natural. 38

And is there anything surprising in one who passes from divine 39 contemplations to the evil state of man, misbehaving himself in a ridiculous manner; if, while his eyes are blinking and before he has become accustomed to the surrounding darkness, he is compelled to fight in courts of law, or in other places, about the images or the shadows of images of justice, and is endeavouring to meet the conceptions of those who have never yet seen absolute justice?

Anything but surprising, he replied. 40

Any one who has common sense will remember that the bewil- 41 derments of the eyes are of two kinds, and arise from two causes, either from coming out of the light or from going into the light, which is true of the mind's eye, quite as much as of the bodily eye; and he who remembers this when he sees any one whose vision is perplexed and weak, will not be too ready to laugh; he will first ask whether that soul of man has come out of the brighter life, and is unable to see because unaccustomed to the dark, or having turned from darkness to the day is dazzled by excess of light. And he will count the one happy in his condition and state of being, and he will pity the other; or, if he have a mind to laugh at the soul which comes from below into the light, there will be more reason in this than in the laugh which greets him who returns from above out of the light into the den.

That, he said, is a very just distinction. 42

Questions on Meaning

1. An **allegory** or parable is a concrete story on one level and an explication of abstract, moral truths on another. Plato explains at the end what each part of his story **symbolizes** on the moral level. What correspondences does he establish?
2. If we assume that the people in the cave represent humankind, why does Plato call them "prisoners"? Although Plato does not specify who placed the people in chains, who seems to be the jailer when the freed prisoner returns to free the others?
3. Plato equates making the "ascent to see the things in the upper world" on the story level with gaining knowledge on the **abstract** level. Why, instead of making the ascent, would people prefer to remain in the cave with illusions of what is real? Do you agree with Plato's analysis of human nature here? Explain,
4. Plato says of the man who returns to the cave after seeing the sun that if they could lay hands on him they would kill him. Are there historical or contemporary situations that fulfill this prediction?

Questions on Method

1. Plato's essay is presented as a dialogue between teacher and student. What contribution to structure and theme is made by the student's brief comments?
2. Review Plato's concluding paragraph. Is his final comment on the allegory necessary, or would you have been able to fit together his meaning without this ending? Explain.

Writing Topics

1. Write a journal entry agreeing or disagreeing with Plato that human be-ings are often reluctant to confront reality. Cite specific reasons from your point of view.
2. Think of an illustration other than Plato's cave to represent truth versus illusion, and develop it either as an analogy or as an allegory.

The Discus Thrower

Richard Selzer (b. 1928) is a fellow of Ezra Stiles College of Yale University. He teaches surgery at Yale Medical School and is a frequent contributor to Harper's, Esquire, *and* Redbook. *He grew up in Troy, New York, the son of a physician who encouraged him to become a doctor. At the urging of his mother, who wanted him to become a writer, he became a prodigious reader. His medical training was interrupted by military service, but he ultimately became a surgeon. In 1968 he started writing short stories, mainly in the horror genre, which were published in mystery magazines. Nonfiction works on medical topics followed. These included essays published in* Esquire *magazine and several books, including* Mortal Lessons: Notes on the Art of Surgery *(1976), which gained favorable critical attention;* Confessions of a Knife *(1979);* Letters to a Young Doctor *(1982); and* Taking the World in for Repairs *(1986). By 1986 his need to view his medical work dispassionately conflicted with his need to see things with the sensibility of a writer, and he gave up medicine to write full-time. Two autobiographical works followed,* Raising the Dead *(1991) and* Down from Troy: A Doctor Comes of Age *(1993). Despite the honesty, keen insights, and deep compassion for patients, families, and doctors that characterize his work, some of his colleagues have disapproved of his efforts, feeling that he was revealing the secrets of the profession. Selzer is gratified that he has fulfilled the wishes of both his parents in accomplishing two careers.*

I SPY on my patients. Ought not a doctor to observe his patients by any means and from any stance, that he might the more fully assemble evidence? So I stand in the doorways of hospital rooms and gaze. Oh, it is not all that furtive an act. Those in bed need only look up to discover me. But they never do.

From the doorway of Room 542 the man in the bed seems deeply tanned. Blue eyes and close-cropped white hair give him the appearance of vigor and good health. But I know that his skin is not brown from the sun. It is rusted, rather, in the last stage of containing the vile repose within. And the blue eyes are frosted, looking inward like the windows of a snowbound cottage. This man is blind. This man is also legless—the right leg missing from midthigh down, the left from just below the knee. It gives him the look of a bonsai, roots and branches pruned into the dwarfed facsimile of a great tree.

Propped on pillows, he cups his right thigh in both hands. Now 3 and then he shakes his head as though acknowledging the intensity of his suffering. In all of this he makes no sound. Is he mute as well as blind?

The room in which he dwells is empty of all possessions—no get- 4 well cards, small, private caches of food, day-old flowers, slippers, all the usual kickshaws of the sickroom. There is only the bed, a chair, a night-stand, and a tray on wheels that can be swung across his lap for meals.

"What time is it?" he asks. 5

"Three o'clock." 6

"Morning or afternoon?" 7

"Afternoon." 8

He is silent. There is nothing else he wants to know. 9

"How are you?" I say. 10

"Who is it?" he asks. 11

"It's the doctor. How do you feel?" 12

He does not answer right away. 13

"Feel?" he says. 14

"I hope you feel better," I say. 15

I press the button at the side of the bed. 16

"Down you go," I say. 17

"Yes, down," he says. 18

He falls back upon the bed awkwardly. His stumps, unweighted 19 by legs and feet, rise in the air, presenting themselves. I unwrap the bandages from the stumps, and begin to cut away the black scabs and the dead, glazed fat with scissors and forceps. A shard of white bone comes loose. I pick it away. I wash the wounds with disinfectant and redress the stumps. All this while, he does not speak. What is he think-ing behind those lids that do not blink? Is he remembering a time when he was whole? Does he dream of feet? Of when his body was not a rotting log?

He lies solid and inert. In spite of everything, he remains impres- 20 sive, as though he were a sailor standing athwart a slanting deck.

"Anything more I can do for you?" I ask. 21

For a long moment he is silent. 22

"Yes," he says at last and without the least irony. "You can bring 23 me a pair of shoes."

In the corridor, the head nurse is waiting for me. 24

"We have to do something about him," she says. "Every morn- 25
ing he orders scrambled eggs for breakfast, and, instead of eating them,
he picks up the plate and throws it against the wall."

"Throws his plate?" 26

"Nasty. That's what he is. No wonder his family doesn't come to 27
visit. They probably can't stand him any more than we can."

She is waiting for me to do something. 28

"Well?" 29

"We'll see," I say. 30

The next morning I am waiting in the corridor when the kitchen 31
delivers his breakfast. I watch the aide place the tray on the stand and
swing it across his lap. She presses the button to raise the head of the bed.
Then she leaves.

In time the man reaches to find the rim of the tray, then on to 32
find the dome of the covered dish. He lifts off the cover and places it
on the stand. He fingers across the plate until he probes the eggs. He
lifts the plate in both hands, sets it on the palm of his right hand, centers it, balances it. He hefts it up and down slightly, getting the feel of
it. Abruptly, he draws back his right arm as far as he can.

There is the crack of the plate breaking against the wall at the 33
foot of his bed and the small wet sound of the scrambled eggs dropping
to the floor.

And then he laughs. It is a sound you have never heard. It is 34
something new under the sun. It could cure cancer.

Out in the corridor, the eyes of the head nurse narrow. 35

"Laughed, did he?" 36

She writes something down on her clipboard. 37

A second aide arrives, brings a second breakfast tray, puts it on 38
the nightstand, out of his reach. She looks over at me shaking her head
and making her mouth go. I see that we are to be accomplices.

"I've got to feed you," she says to the man. 39

"Oh, no you don't," the man says. 40

"Oh, yes I do," the aide says, "after the way you just did. Nurse 41
says so."

"Get me my shoes," the man says. 42

"Here's oatmeal," the aide says. "Open." And she touches the 43
spoon to his lower lip.

"I ordered scrambled eggs," says the man. 44

"That's right," the aide says. 45

I step forward. 46

"Is there anything I can do?" I say. 47

"Who are you?" the man asks. 48

In the evening I go once more to that ward to make my rounds. 49
The head nurse reports to me that Room 542 is deceased. She has dis-
covered this quite by accident, she says. No, there had been no sound.
Nothing. It's a blessing, she says.

I go into his room, a spy looking for secrets. He is still there in his 50
bed. His face is relaxed, grave, dignified. After a while, I turn to leave.
My gaze sweeps the wall at the foot of the bed, and I see the place
where it has been repeatedly washed, where the wall looks very clean
and very white.

Questions on Meaning

1. Explain the meaning of the title of the essay. Why is the metaphor an appropriate one for this patient?
2. Why does Selzer describe himself as a "spy"? How does his attitude toward the patient compare with the attitude of the nurse or the two aides?
   Is he more or less curious about the patient? Is he more or less emotional
   about him? Explain, citing details.
3. To what extent is the patient really "nasty," as the nurse says? Why, for
   example, does the patient keep asking for a pair of shoes? Why does
   Selzer tell us that the patient asks this "without the least irony"?
4. Why does Selzer in paragraph 19 narrate the process by which he treats
   the patient's legs? Compare this to Selzer's narration in paragraph 32 of
   the process the patient goes through to throw his breakfast against the
   wall. How do such elaborate preparations affect our understanding of
   both men?
5. Discuss the comparison Selzer makes in paragraph 2 between the patient's "frosted" eyes and the windows of a "snowbound" cottage. How
   does Selzer's description in paragraph 4 of the emptiness of the sickroom
   indicate something about his first impression of the patient's mental condition? How does the simile in paragraph 20 that compares the patient to
   "a sailor standing athwart a slanting deck" suggest that Selzer's first impression is beginning to change?
6. In paragraph 11 the patient asks Selzer, "Who is it?" The next morning
   he asks, "Who are you?" Why does he repeat the question?
7. Discuss Selzer's final observation about how "clean" and "white" the wall
   looks after the patient has died. How does Selzer's description of the wall
   symbolize his feelings about both the patient and the treatment the patient
   received?

Questions on Method

1. What does Selzer describe objectively in his essay? What effect do these descriptions have on our understanding of the patient's actions? What spatial arrangements does the author use?
2. How does Selzer's scientific method of gathering "evidence" to reach a conclusion lead to his impression of the patient? What role does description play in this evidence?
3. In paragraph 49 why does the nurse say that "Room 542" is deceased? What does her use of the room number rather than the patient's name indicate about her attitude toward the patient? Why doesn't the patient's name appear at all in the essay?

Writing Topics

1. Have you or has someone you know ever been hospitalized? Describe the character of the treatment received from the hospital staff. Write an essay discussing why people who work in hospitals might often treat patients coldly and distantly.
2. Describe a place where you had an unpleasant experience; use detail sufficient to convey why your surroundings added to the unpleasantness of the experience.
3. Describe a place in such detail that your overall impression of it would be conveyed to a reader. Place your impression at the end of the essay, as does Selzer, rather than at the beginning.

On a Kibbutz

Saul Bellow (b. 1915) is a Jewish American writer who was born in Quebec but has spent most of his life in Chicago. He deals in his novels with "intelligent beings in a complex society struggling with absurdity, meaning, ignominy, while education and abilities multiply, the most vital questions and answers become the internal ones." Bellow believes strongly in the primacy of emotions. A Pulitzer Prize– and Nobel Prize–winning novelist, Saul Bellow has taken a place among the leading figures of twentieth-century American literature. In his writing and teaching, Bellow champions human and moral possibilities in the face of personal and social struggle. His novels include Dangling Man *(1944);* The Victim *(1947);* The Adventures of Augie March *(1953);* Henderson the Rain King *(1956);* Humboldt's Gift *(1975), for which he won a Pulitzer Prize in 1976;* The Dean's December *(1982); and* More Die of Heartbreak *(1987). His collected short stories include* Mosby's Memoirs and Other Stories *(1968) and* Him with His Foot in His Mouth and Other Stories *(1984). Bellow's more recent publications include* It All Adds Up: From the Dim Past to the Uncertain Future: A Nonfiction Collection *(1993) and* The Actual: A Novella. *His awards include the Nobel Prize for Literature (1976). In 1977 he won the Gold Medal from the American Academy of Arts and Letters, the Emerson Thoreau Medal from the Academy of Arts and Sciences, and was honored with the Neil Gunn International fellowship. He won the Brandeis University Creative Arts Award (France) in 1978; the Commander, Legion of Honour (France) in 1983; the Malaporte Prize for Literature (Italy) in 1984; the Commander, Order of Arts and Letters (France) in 1985; and the National Medal of Arts in 1988 for outstanding contributions to the excellence, growth, support, and availability of the arts in the United States.*

ON A KIBBUTZ.

Lucky is Nola's dog. John's dog is Mississippi. But John loves Lucky too, and Nola dotes on Mississippi. And then there are the children— one daughter in the army, and a younger child who still sleeps in the kibbutz dormitory. Lucky is a woolly brown dog, old and nervous. His master was killed in the Golan. When there is a sonic boom over the kibbutz, the dog rushes out, growling. He seems to remember the falling bombs. He is too feeble to bark, too old to run, his teeth are bad, his eyes under the brown fringe are dull, and he is clotted under the tail. Mississippi is a big, long-legged, short-haired, brown-and-white, clever, lively, affectionate, and greedy animal. She is a "child dog"—sits in your lap, puts a paw on your arm when you reach for a tidbit to get it for herself. Since she weighs fifty pounds or more she is not welcome in my lap, but she sits on John and Nola and on the guests—those who permit it. She is winsome but also flatulent. She eats too many sweets but is good company, a wonderful listener and conversationalist; she growls and snuffles when you speak directly to her. She "sings" along with the record player. The Auerbachs are proud of this musical yelping.

In the morning we hear the news in Hebrew and then again on the BBC. We eat an Israeli breakfast of fried eggs, sliced cheese, cucumbers, olives, green onions, tomatoes, and little salt fish. Bread is toasted on the coal-oil heater. The dogs have learned the trick of the door and bang in and out. Between the rows of small kibbutz dwellings the lawns are ragged but very green. Light and warmth come from the sea. Under the kibbutz lie the ruins of Herod's Caesarea. There are Roman fragments everywhere. Marble columns in the grasses. Fallen capitals make garden seats. You have only to prod the ground to find fragments of pottery, bits of statuary, a pair of dancing satyr legs. John's tightly packed bookshelves are fringed with such relics. On the crowded desk stands a framed photograph of the dead son, with a small beard like John's, smiling with John's own warmth. 3

We walk in the citrus groves after breakfast, taking Mississippi with us (John is seldom without her); the soil is kept loose and soft among the trees, the leaves are glossy, the ground itself is fragrant. Many of the trees are still unharvested and bending, tangerines and lemons as dense as stars. "Oh that I were an orange tree/That busie plant!" wrote George Herbert. To put forth such leaves, to be hung with oranges, to be a blessing—one feels the temptation of this on such a morning and I even feel a fibrous woodiness entering my arms as I consider it. You want to take root and stay forever in the most temperate and blue of temperate places. John mourns his son, he always mourns his son, but he is also smiling in the sunlight. 4

In the exporting of oranges there is competition from the North African countries and from Spain. "We are very idealistic here, but when we read about frosts in Spain we're glad as hell," John says. 5

All this was once dune land. Soil had to be carted in and mixed   6
with the sand. Many years of digging and tending made these orchards.
Relaxing, breathing freely, you feel what a wonderful place has been created here, a homeplace for body and soul; then you remember that on
the beaches there are armed patrols. It is always possible that terrorists
may come in rubber dinghies that cannot be detected by radar. They entered Tel Aviv itself in March 1975 and seized a hotel at the seashore.
People were murdered. John keeps an Uzi in his bedroom cupboard.
Nola scoffs at this. "We'd both be dead before you could reach your
gun," she says. Cheerful Nola laughs. An expressive woman—she uses
her forearm to wave away John's preparations. "Sometimes he does the
drill and I time him to see how long it takes to jump out of bed, open
the cupboard, get the gun, put in the clip, and turn around. They'd mow
us down before he could get a foot off the floor."

Mississippi is part of the alarm system. "She'd bark," says John.   7

Just now Mississippi is racing through the orchards, nose to the   8
ground. The air is sweet, and the sun like a mild alcohol makes you
yearn for good things. You rest under a tree and eat tangerines, only
slightly heavyhearted.

From the oranges we go to the banana groves. The green bananas   9
are tied up in plastic tunics. The great banana flower hangs ground-
ward like the sexual organ of a stallion. The long leaves resemble
manes. After two years the ground has to be plowed up and lie fallow.
Groves are planted elsewhere—more hard labor. "You noticed before,"
says John, "that some of the orange trees were withered. Their roots
get into Roman ruins and they die. Some years ago, while we were
plowing, we turned up an entire Roman street."

He takes me to the Herodian Hippodrome. American archeolo-   10
gists have dug out some of the old walls. We look down into the dig-
gings, where labels flutter from every stratum. There are more
potsherds than soil in these bluffs—the broken jugs of the slaves who
raised the walls two thousand years ago. At the center of the Hippodrome, a long, graceful ellipse, is a fallen monolith weighing many
tons. We sit under fig trees on the slope while Mississippi runs through
the high smooth grass. The wind is soft and works the grass gracefully.
It makes white air courses in the green.

Whenever John ships out he takes the dog for company. He had   11
enough of solitude when he sailed on German ships under forged papers. He does not like to be alone. Now and again he was under suspicion. A German officer who sensed that he was Jewish threatened to

turn him in, but one night when the ship was only hours out of Danzig she struck a mine and went down, the officer with her. John himself was pulled from the sea by his mates. Once he waited in a line of nude men whom a German doctor, a woman, was examining for venereal disease. In that lineup he alone was circumcised. He came before the woman and was examined; she looked into his face and she let him live.

John and I go back through the orange groves. There are large weasels living in the bushy growth along the pipeline. We see a pair of them at a distance in the road. They could easily do for Mississippi. She is luckily far off. We sit under a pine on the hilltop and look out to sea where a freighter moves slowly toward Ashkelon. Nearer to shore, a trawler chuffs. The kibbutz does little fishing now. Off the Egyptian coast, John has been shot at, and not long ago several members of the kibbutz were thrown illegally into jail by the Turks, accused of fishing in Turkish waters. Twenty people gave false testimony. They could have had a thousand witnesses. It took three months to get these men released. A lawyer was found who knew the judge. His itemized bill came to ten thousand dollars—five for the judge, five for himself.

Enough of this sweet sun and the transparent blue-green. We turn our backs on it to have a drink before lunch. Kibbutzniks ride by on clumsy old bikes. They wear cloth caps and pedal slowly; their day starts at six. Plain-looking working people from the tile factory and from the barn steer toward the dining hall. The kibbutzniks are a mixed group. There is one lone Orthodox Jew, who has no congregation to pray with. There are several older gentiles, one a Spaniard, one a Scandinavian, who married Jewish women and settled here. The Spaniard, an anarchist, plans to return to Spain now that Franco has died. One member of the kibbutz is a financial wizard, another was a high-ranking army officer who for obscure reasons fell into disgrace. The dusty tarmac path we follow winds through the settlement. Beside the undistinguished houses stand red poinsettias. Here, too, lie Roman relics. Then we come upon a basketball court, and then the rusty tracks of a children's choo-choo, and then the separate quarters for young women of eighteen, and a museum of antiquities, and a recreation hall. A strong odor of cattle comes from the feeding lot. I tell John that Gurdjiev had Katherine Mansfield resting in the stable at Fontainebleau, claiming that the cows' breath would cure her tuberculosis. John loves to hear such bits of literary history. We go into his house and Mississippi climbs into his lap while we drink Russian vodka. "We could live with those bastards if they limited themselves to making this Stolichnaya."

These words put an end to the peaceful morning. At the north   14
there swells up the Russian menace. With arms from Russia and Europe, the PLO and other Arab militants and the right-wing Christians are now destroying Lebanon. The Syrians have involved themselves; in the eyes of the Syrians, Israel is Syrian land. Suddenly this temperate Mediterranean day and the orange groves and the workers steering their bikes and the children's playground flutter like illustrated paper. What is there to keep them from blowing away?

Questions on Meaning

1. What pleasures does life on the kibbutz offer, according to Bellow?
2. How would you characterize John? What sort of a life has he had? How does he feel about his life on the kibbutz?
3. John calls himself and his fellow kibbutzniks "idealistic." What does he mean?
4. How does what Bellow calls "the Russian menace" affect the quality of life on the kibbutz?
5. Bellow tells us that John mourns his son yet smiles in the sunlight. What is Bellow's attitude toward John? How does his attitude toward John reflect his attitude toward the kibbutz in general?

Questions on Method

1. Bellow refers to the Roman ruins twice in the essay. Why are the ruins a significant detail in his description?
2. Why does Bellow tell us about the incident of the Turks' illegally jailing several members of the kibbutz?
3. Why does Bellow begin the essay by describing Lucky and Mississippi? What do the dogs help us to understand about life on the kibbutz?

Writing Topics

1. Places often affect people's behavior. Discuss the influence of the lake and the kibbutz on the characters in White's and Bellow's texts. How might these or similar places affect people in general? How do you think they would affect you?
2. Analyze the responses to nature of White and Bellow. Account as much as possible for the differences in their attitudes.
3. Throughout his sensuous description of his day on the kibbutz, Bellow weaves warnings that this peaceful atmosphere can suddenly be disrupted. If you have had a similar encounter in a place, describe the experience contrasting your physical surroundings and your emotional reactions.

Description
Writing Topics

1. Describe a place as you perceived it when you were feeling particularly romantic, either because you were in love with another person or because you were feeling in love simply with life itself. Redescribe the same place as you perceived it another time, when you were feeling less romantic. Which description is more realistic? How much is a person's perception of nature colored by his or her feelings at a particular moment? Organize your two descriptions so that they illustrate a discussion of this question.

2. Write an essay in which description is used in the service of narration, as Ng, Selzer, or Eiseley use it. Decide first what event you wish to narrate and then what aspects of the event—places, people, objects—the reader must visualize to understand the actions.

3. Describe the flavor of what it is like to live in a certain place so that someone who lives in an entirely different environment can understand your description. To make your essay understandable to such a reader, use metaphors and similes.

4. Write a three-paragraph *objective* description of someone you know well. You might include in your description physical details, personality traits, emotional characteristics, or even a brief narrative describing your subject's behavior. After you have finished, write a three-paragraph *subjective* description about the same person. Compare both descriptions with regard to purpose, meaning, and tone. What general statements can you now make about the nature of objective and subjective description?

5. What is the most important difference between the organization of an effective description and the organization of an effective narration? Illustrate your answer by writing an essay that first describes the details of a place you have visited and then tells a story about something that happened there.

7

Illustration and Example

THE BEST WRITING is vivid writing, and your selection of words sharpens the fine points of your subject. So do examples and illustrations, which support your points and add a vital authenticity to your writing. Clear illustrations and **concrete** examples make your writing alive and fresh. **Illustration and example** are names of two kinds of specifics, an illustration being a longer example with some of the elements of narrative, such as characters and action.

As discussed in Chapter 5, stories are frequently told to illustrate a point, or **generalization;** such stories or illustrations are one kind of "specific," one way to apply a general statement or thesis to a particular set of circumstances. On the other hand, the reader of **exposition** (or nonfiction in general) expects a generalization like "Science has failed us" to be accompanied by a *group* of specifics such as "Science cannot answer moral questions," "Computers can perform only to the level of their programming," and "Technology has bad side effects."

Consider this account of Steve Tesich's wedding ceremony from "An Amateur Marriage."

It was a very hot day in Denver, and I think Becky and I decided to get married because we knew the city hall was air-conditioned. It was a way of hanging around a cool place for a while. I had forgotten to buy a wedding ring, but Becky was still wearing the ring from her previous marriage, so we used that one. It did the job. She had to take it off and then put it back on again, but it didn't seem to bother anyone. The air-conditioners were humming.

I felt no great change take place as I repeated our marriage vows. I did not feel any new rush of "commitment" to the woman who was now my wife, nor did I have any plans to be married to her forever. I did love her, but I saw no reason why I should feel that I had to love her forever. I would love her for as long as I loved her. I assumed she felt the same way. The women I saw on my way out of city hall, a married man, did not look any less beautiful than the women I saw on my way in. It was still hot outside. We walked to our car carrying plastic bags containing little samples of mouth-wash, toothpaste, shampoo and aspirin, gifts from the Chamber of Commerce to all newlyweds.

Tesich uses humor to enhance his meaning. Which examples do you find effective? How does his description of his marriage ceremony contribute to the essay's authenticity?

The purpose of examples and illustrations is to interest the reader, to clarify the major points, and to persuade the reader of the truth of the generalizations. The choice of example varies widely in length, number, specificity, familiarity, and so on, depending on the audience and the writer's purpose. But sooner or later the transition from general to specific (or vice versa) must occur.

There are no rules about the number or **specificity** of examples, but it is probably safe to say the more, the better. Examples, logically, can do no more than indicate a trend or direction (unlike the list of classes in scientific classification, a list of examples need not be exhaustive); but they can also convey the writer's mastery of the subject and sensitivity to the supposed audience and incline the reader to accept the generalizations or conclusions of the essay.

Specificity is relative. The word *specific* is meaningless except in relation to a more inclusive generalization, and what is specific in one context may be general in another. The so-called specific mentioned earlier, "Science cannot answer moral questions," is quite *un*specific when one considers the number of research projects, the number of possible moral questions that societies ask, and the practical implications of both. The writer would probably want to explain *why* science cannot answer moral questions and to give further, more specific examples of scientific research that led to trivial or dangerous results before a convincing level of specificity could be reached.

When writing an essay, in every paragraph you are probably going to be dealing with a topic or subtopic that can be expressed as a general statement **(topic sentence).** You usually have the choice of beginning with either that topic sentence or the specific examples, and there are advantages to both orders. The generalization-first order is clearer and easier to read because the reader knows exactly what each example is supposed to support or prove; everything falls into place. This order is called **deduction.** The examples-first order challenges the reader to try to guess what it all adds up to; this is **induction,** which may make the reader feel included in the thinking process, and it may allow for a dramatic, climactic ending. If your paragraph is long and complex enough, you may want to combine the two orders, beginning with a general statement, going into your examples or illustrations, and returning to a restatement of your topic sentence at the end of the paragraph. Entire essays, as well as single paragraphs, may be developed by both inductive and deductive organization. Whereas many writers begin with an idea and search for examples to support it, other writers, such as scientists, begin with observations of facts (examples) and then formulate a theory about them. As usual, it is helpful to use such transitional words and phrases as "for example" and "finally" to guide the reader.

WRITING WITH ILLUSTRATION AND EXAMPLE

1. Use many examples: the more, the better.
2. Make your examples specific. If possible, make your second and third examples more specific than your first.
3. Experiment with order, choosing from generalization first, examples first, or a combination of the two, depending on your purpose.
4. Use examples and illustrations that are appropriate to your audience.

DAVID GELERNTER

Unplugged

David (Hillel) Gelernter (b. 1955), like his father before him, is a computer scientist/theorist and writer. His father was considered to be a pioneer in the new technology, and David has continued his legacy. He received a B.A. in 1976 from Yale University and attended Yeshiva University for a period before he decided to pursue a career as a computer scientist/theorist as well as writer and academic. In 1982 he was awarded a Ph.D. from State University at Stony Brook. In the early eighties, he joined the faculty as an associate professor at Yale University's Department of Computer Science. He also serves as a consultant for the Scientific Computing Association. He contributed to How to Write Parallel Programs: A First Course, *authored by Nicholas Carriero (1990); co-authored* Programming Linguistics *with Suresh Jagannathan (1990); and edited (with co-editors Alexandru Nicolau and David Padua)* Languages and Compilers for Parallel Computing *(1990). Other publications include* Mirror Worlds *(1991);* The Muse in the Machine: Computerizing the Poetry of Human Thought *(1994), which he admits took him ten years to write; and* 1939: The Lost World of the Fair *(1995). He is also a frequent contributor to periodicals including* New Republic, *the* New York Times, *and the* Washington Post. *He was voted one of the most influential names in computer science in the 1990s.*

OVER THE LAST DECADE an estimated $2 billion has been spent on   1
more than 2 million computers for America's classrooms. That's not
surprising. We constantly hear from Washington that the schools are in
trouble and that computers are a godsend. Within the education establishment, in poor as well as rich schools, the machines are awaited with
nearly religious awe. An inner–city principal bragged to a teacher friend
of mine recently that his school "has a computer in every classroom
…despite being in a bad neighborhood!"

Computers should be in the schools. They have the potential to   2
accomplish great things. With the right software, they could help make
science tangible or teach neglected topics like art and music. They
could help students form a concrete idea of society by displaying on-

screen a version of the city in which they live—a picture that tracks real life moment by moment.

In practice, however, computers make our worst educational nightmares come true. While we bemoan the decline of literacy, computers discount words in favor of pictures and pictures in favor of video. While we fret about the decreasing cogency of public debate, computers dismiss linear argument and promote fast, shallow romps across the information landscape. While we worry about basic skills, we allow into the classroom software that will do a student's arithmetic or correct his spelling. 3

Take multimedia. The idea of multimedia is to combine text, sound and pictures in a single package that you browse on screen. You don't just *read* Shakespeare; you watch actors performing, listen to songs, view Elizabethan buildings. What's wrong with that? By offering children candy-coated books, multimedia is guaranteed to sour them on unsweetened reading. It makes the printed page look even more boring than it used to look. Sure, books will be available in the classroom, too—but they'll have all the appeal of a dusty piano to a teen who has a Walkman handy. 4

So what if the little nippers don't read? If they're watching Olivier instead, what do they lose? The text, the written word along with all of its attendant pleasures. Besides, a book is more portable than a computer, has a higher-resolution display, can be written on and dog-eared and is comparatively dirt cheap. 5

Hypermedia, multimedia's comrade in the struggle for a brave new classroom, is just as troubling. It's a way of presenting documents on screen without imposing a linear start-to-finish order. Disembodied paragraphs are linked by theme; after reading one about the First World War, for example, you might be able to choose another about the technology of battleships, or the life of Woodrow Wilson, or hemlines in the '20s. This is another cute idea that is good in minor ways and terrible in major ones. Teaching children to understand the orderly unfolding of a plot or a logical argument is a crucial part of education. Authors don't merely agglomerate paragraphs; they work hard to make the narrative read a certain way, prove a particular point. To turn a book or a document into hypertext is to invite readers to ignore exactly what counts—the story. 6

The real problem, again, is the accentuation of already bad habits. Dynamiting documents into disjointed paragraphs is one more expression 7 of the sorry fact that sustained argument is not our style. If you're a newspaper or magazine editor and your readership is dwindling, what's the solution? Shorter pieces. If you're a politician and you want to get elected, what do you need? Tasty sound bites. Logical presentation be damned.

Another software species, "allow me" programs, is not much bet-   8
ter. These programs correct spelling and, by applying canned grammatical and stylistic rules, fix prose. In terms of promoting basic skills, though, they have all the virtues of a pocket calculator.

In Kentucky, as *The Wall Street Journal* recently reported, students   9
in grades K–3 are mixed together regardless of age in a relaxed environment. It works great, the *Journal* says. Yes, scores on computation tests have dropped 10 percent at one school, but not to worry: "Drilling addition and subtraction in an age of calculators is a waste of time," the principal reassures us. Meanwhile, a Japanese educator informs University of Wisconsin mathematician Richard Akey that in his country, "calculators are not used in elementary or junior high school because the primary emphasis is on helping students develop their mental abilities." No wonder Japanese kids blow the pants off American kids in math. Do we really think "drilling addition and subtraction in an age of calculators is a waste of time"? If we do, then "drilling reading in an age of multimedia is a waste of time" can't be far behind.

Prose-correcting programs are also a little ghoulish, like asking a   10
computer for tips on improving your personality. On the other hand, I ran this article through a spell-checker, so how can I ban the use of such programs in schools? Because to misspell is human; to have no idea of correct spelling is to be semiliterate.

There's no denying that computers have the potential to perform   11
inspiring feats in the classroom. If we are ever to see that potential realized, however, we ought to agree on three conditions. First, there should be a completely new crop of children's software. Most of today's offerings show no imagination. There are hundreds of similar reading and geography and arithmetic programs, but almost nothing on electricity or physics or architecture. Also, they abuse the technical capacities of new media to glitz up old forms instead of creating new ones. Why not build a time-travel program that gives kids a feel for how history is structured by zooming you backward? A spectrum program that lets users twirl a frequency knob to see what happens?

Second, computers should be used only during recess or relax- 12
ation periods. Treat them as fillips, not as surrogate teachers. When I
was in school in the '60s, we all loved educational films. When we saw
a movie in class, everybody won: teachers didn't have to teach, and pupils didn't have to learn. I suspect that classroom computers are popular
today for the same reasons.

Most important, educators should learn what parents and most 13
teachers already know: you cannot teach a child anything unless you
look him in the face. We should not forget what computers are. Like
books—better in some ways, worse in others—they are devices that
help children mobilize their own resources and learn for themselves.
The computer's potential to do good is modestly greater than a book's
in some areas. Its potential to do harm is vastly greater, across the
board.

Questions on Meaning

1. In paragraph 3, Gelernter states that "computers make our worst educational nightmares come true." What evidence does he offer to support
   his thesis? What role do computers play in your education?
2. How do you respond to paragraphs 4 and 5? Do you agree that computers make books seem boring to students? Why or why not?
3. What is your response to paragraph 9 on the issue of calculators in the
   classroom?

Questions on Method

1. The author uses many illustrations and examples to support his analysis
   on computers in the classroom. Which do you find most convincing?
2. Review Gelernter's introduction and conclusion. How effective are
   they? How do they contribute to his purpose? Is his purpose to inform
   or persuade?

Writing Topics

1. Communication technology has affected the way people live. How have
   answering machines, cellular phones, and beepers affected the way you
   communicate? Can you imagine unplugging yourself from these
   connections?
2. Interview three professors from different disciplines on their experiences
   with computers in the classroom. Did they expand your concept about

computers as teaching tools? How? What specialized vocabulary did you learn during your interviews? Write an article on your findings for the college newspaper.

3. To what extent do your daily activities involve your use of electronic information and technology? Conduct a three-day experiment by recording a journal entry each time you use electronic equipment of any kind. Write an essay summarizing your findings.

Black Men and Public Space

Brent Staples (b. 1951) is from Chester, Pennsylvania. He has a Ph.D. in psychology from the University of Chicago and is currently on the editorial board of the New York Times, *where he writes on culture and politics. His autobiography,* Parallel Time: Growing Up in Black and White, *was published in 1994. His essay "Black Men and Public Space" was published in* Ms. *When asked why he selected* Ms. *for publication of this essay, he responded: "*Ms. *is a women's magazine. Women are more vulnerable to street violence, and judgements about who is safe and who is dangerous is an urgent priority for them."*

MY FIRST VICTIM was a woman—white, well dressed, probably in   1
her early twenties. I came upon her late one evening on a deserted street in Hyde Park, a relatively affluent neighborhood in an otherwise mean, impoverished section of Chicago. As I swung onto the avenue behind her, there seemed to be a discreet, uninflammatory distance between us. Not so. She cast back a worried glance. To her, the youngish black man—a broad six feet two inches with a beard and billowing hair, both hands shoved into the pockets of a bulky military jacket—seemed menacingly close. After a few more quick glimpses, she picked up her pace and was soon running in earnest. Within seconds she disappeared into a cross street.

That was more than a decade ago. I was 22 years old, a graduate   2
student newly arrived at the University of Chicago. It was in the echo of that terrified woman's footfalls that I first began to know the unwieldy inheritance I'd come into—the ability to alter public space in ugly ways. It was clear that she thought herself the quarry of a mugger, a rapist, or worse. Suffering a bout of insomnia, however, I was stalking sleep, not defenseless wayfarers. As a softy who is scarcely able to take a knife to a raw chicken—let alone hold it to a person's throat—I was surprised, embarrassed, and dismayed all at once. Her flight made me feel like an accomplice in tyranny. It also made it clear that I was indistinguishable from the muggers who occasionally seeped into the area from the

surrounding ghetto. That first encounter, and those that followed, signi-
fied that a vast, unnerving gulf lay between nighttime pedestrians—particularly women—and me. And I soon gathered that being perceived as
dangerous is a hazard in itself. I only needed to turn a corner into a dicey
situation, or crowd some frightened, armed person in a foyer somewhere, or make an errant move after being pulled over by a policeman.
Where fear and weapons meet—and they often do in urban America—
there is always the possibility of death.

In that first year, my first away from my hometown, I was to be-   3
come thoroughly familiar with the language of fear. At dark, shadowy
intersections in Chicago, I could cross in front of a car stopped at a
traffic light and elicit the *thunk, thunk, thunk, thunk* of the driver—
black, white, male, or female—hammering down the door locks. On
less traveled streets after dark, I grew accustomed to but never comfortable with people who crossed to the other side of the street rather
than pass me. Then there were the standard unpleasantries with policemen, doormen, bouncers, cab drivers, and others whose business it is
to screen out troublesome individuals *before* there is any nastiness.

I moved to New York nearly two years ago and I have remained   4
an avid night walker. In central Manhattan, the near-constant crowd
cover minimizes tense one-on-one street encounters. Elsewhere—
visiting friends in SoHo, where sidewalks are narrow and tightly
spaced buildings shut out the sky—things can get very taut indeed.

Black men have a firm place in New York mugging literature.   5
Norman Podhoretz in his famed (or infamous) 1963 essay, "My Negro
Problem—And Ours," recalls growing up in terror of black males; they
"were tougher than we were, more ruthless," he writes—and as an
adult on the Upper West Side of Manhattan, he continues, he cannot
constrain his nervousness when he meets black men on certain streets.
Similarly, a decade later, the essayist and novelist Edward Hoagland ex-
tols a New York where once "Negro bitterness bore down mainly on
other Negroes." Where some see mere panhandlers, Hoagland sees "a
mugger who is clearly screwing up his nerve to do more than just *ask*
for money." But Hoagland has "the New Yorker's quick-hunch posture
for broken-field maneuvering," and the bad guy swerves away.

I often witness that "hunch posture," from women after dark on   6
the warrenlike streets of Brooklyn where I live. They seem to set their
faces on neutral and, with their purse straps strung across their chests
bandolier style, they forge ahead as though bracing themselves against
being tackled. I understand, of course, that the danger they perceive is
not a hallucination. Women are particularly vulnerable to street vio-

lence, and young black males are drastically overrepresented among the perpetrators of that violence. Yet these truths are no solace against the kind of alienation that comes of being ever the suspect, against being set apart, a fearsome entity with whom pedestrians avoid making eye contact.

It is not altogether clear to me how I reached the ripe old age of 22 without being conscious of the lethality nighttime pedestrians attributed to me. Perhaps it was because in Chester, Pennsylvania, the small, angry industrial town where I came of age in the 1960s, I was scarcely noticeable against a backdrop of gang warfare, street knifings, and murders. I grew up one of the good boys, had perhaps a half-dozen fist fights. In retrospect, my shyness of combat has clear sources.

Many things go into the making of a young thug. One of those things is the consummation of the male romance with the power to intimidate. An infant discovers that random flailings send the baby bottle flying out of the crib and crashing to the floor. Delighted, the joyful babe repeats those motions again and again, seeking to duplicate the feat. Just so, I recall the points at which some of my boyhood friends were finally seduced by the perception of themselves as tough guys. When a mark cowered and surrendered his money without resistance, myth and reality merged—and paid off. It is, after all, only manly to embrace the power to frighten and intimidate. We, as men, are not supposed to give an inch of our lane on the highway; we are to seize the fighter's edge in work and in play and even in love; we are to be valiant in the face of hostile forces.

Unfortunately, poor and powerless young men seem to take all this nonsense literally. As a boy, I saw countless tough guys locked away; I have since buried several, too. They were babies, really—a teenage cousin, a brother of 22, a childhood friend in his mid-twenties—all gone down in episodes of bravado played out in the streets. I came to doubt the virtues of intimidation early on. I chose, perhaps even unconsciously, to remain a shadow—timid, but a survivor.

The fearsomeness mistakenly attributed to me in public places often has a perilous flavor. The most frightening of these confusions occurred in the late 1970s and early 1980s when I worked as a journalist in Chicago. One day, rushing into the office of a magazine I was writing for with a deadline story in hand, I was mistaken for a burglar. The office manager called security and, with an ad hoc posse, pursued me through the labyrinthine halls, nearly to my editor's door. I had no way of proving who I was. I could only move briskly toward the company of someone who knew me.

Another time I was on assignment for a local paper and killing   11
time before an interview. I entered a jewelry store on the city's affluent
Near North Side. The proprietor excused herself and returned with an
enormous red Doberman pinscher straining at the end of a leash. She
stood, the dog extended toward me, silent to my questions, her eyes
bulging nearly out of her head. I took a cursory look around, nodded,
and bade her good night. Relatively speaking, however, I never fared
as badly as another black male journalist. He went to nearby Wau-
kegan, Illinois, a couple of summers ago to work on a story about a
murderer who was born there. Mistaking the reporter for the killer,
police hauled him from his car at gunpoint and but for his press credentials would probably have tried to book him. Such episodes are not
uncommon. Black men trade tales like this all the time.

In "My Negro Problem—And Ours," Podhoretz writes that the   12
hatred he feels for blacks makes itself known to him through a variety
of avenues—one being his discomfort with that "special brand of paranoid touchiness" to which he says blacks are prone. No doubt he is
speaking here of black men. In time, I learned to smother the rage I
felt at so often being taken for a criminal. Not to do so would surely
have led to madness—via that special "paranoid touchiness" that so annoyed Podhoretz at the time he wrote the essay.

I began to take precautions to make myself less threatening. I   13
move about with care, particularly late in the evening. I give a wide
berth to nervous people on subway platforms during the wee hours,
particularly when I have exchanged business clothes for jeans. If I
happen to be entering a building behind some people who appear
skittish, I may walk by, letting them clear the lobby before I return, so
as not to seem to be following them. I have been calm and extremely
congenial on those rare occasions when I've been pulled over by the
police.

And on late-evening constitutionals along streets less traveled by,   14
I employ what has proved to be an excellent tension-reducing measure: I whistle melodies from Beethoven and Vivaldi and the more
popular classical composers. Even steely New Yorkers hunching toward nighttime destinations seem to relax, and occasionally they even
join in the tune. Virtually everybody seems to sense that a mugger
wouldn't be warbling bright, sunny selections from Vivaldi's *Four Seasons.* It is my equivalent of the cowbell that hikers wear when they
know they are in bear country.

Questions on Meaning

1. As it turns out, the word *victim* in the first sentence doesn't mean what we expect it to mean. Why is it the correct word to use anyway?
2. What is ironic about the word *ability* in the striking phrase "the ability to alter public space in ugly ways."
3. Explain the point that "being perceived as dangerous is a hazard in itself." Is the point important to the essay?
4. Does Staples think there is any justification for New York women's precautions against young African American males?
5. According to Staples, by what steps does a male come to perceive of himself as a tough guy? How does society reinforce this perception?
6. What precautions does Staples take to make himself less threatening? What do you think of Staples's reaction to the problem of "so often being taken for a criminal"? Does he exaggerate the problem? Is there a better solution—or precaution—than this?

Questions on Method

1. Reread the first paragraph of the essay. What makes it an effective introduction? Describe your reaction to the first sentence.
2. Examine the topic sentences in each paragraph. How does the author support them? How do they contribute to the essay's meaning?
3. Staples uses flashbacks several times in the essay. Identify examples and discuss their impact on the meaning and purpose of the essay.
4. Is Staples's tone objective or subjective? In other words, is he merely presenting his point of view, or is he also trying to state publicly acceptable evidence? Is he trying to inform, to persuade, or to do both?
5. Reread the conclusion and analyze the elements that make it effective. Why is the comparison the author makes in the last sentence particularly appropriate? What does it reveal about the author's attitude toward his subject?

Writing Topics

1. Staples cites many examples of unfair treatment to which he and other young African American males have been subjected. Which examples did you find most effective? Write an essay discussing the impressions that his experiences made on you. Cite any ideas you had to modify as a result of reading his essay.
2. Has our society had any success so far in reducing the "touchiness" of African Americans and the fears of whites? What more can be done? Does an essay like this contribute to the solution or to the problem? Do you see any evidence that Staples would like to help solve the problem? Do you see any evidence that he is at least somewhat amused by it?

3. Staples writes that "where fear and weapons meet...there is always the possibility of death." Which—fear or weapons—lies more within the control of society or the individual? Assuming we must start controlling one or the other, with which one do we have the best chance of beginning? Before starting your essay, freewrite about the subject to make sure that your purpose is clear and that you have a specific audience in mind.

Homeless

Anna Quindlen (b. 1953) started her career as a journalist immediately after graduating from Barnard College in New York City. The New York Times *promoted her from general assignments to various columns, culminating in her highly esteemed "Public and Private" column, where she wrote about herself and her family and friends, as well as national and local issues. She won a Pulitzer Prize for her commentaries. In 1994 Quindlen left the New York Times to devote herself to writing novels. Her books to date include two compilations of her columns,* Living Out Loud *(1988) and* Thinking Out Loud *(1993); two novels,* Object Lessons *(1991) and* One True Thing *(1994), which was made into a movie starring Meryl Streep; and a children's book,* The Tree That Came to Stay *(1993). Her most recent book,* How Reading Changed My Life *(1998), reflects the dichotomy of her happy childhood and living in the other world discovered in the books she read. Quindlen's works address universal concerns, treating them in a personal and intimate manner.*

HER NAME WAS ANN, and we met in the Port Authority Bus Terminal several Januarys ago. I was doing a story on homeless people. She said I was wasting my time talking to her; she was just passing through, although she'd been passing through for more than two weeks. To prove to me that this was true, she rummaged through a tote bag and a manila envelope and finally unfolded a sheet of typing paper and brought out her photographs.

They were not pictures of family, or friends, or even a dog or cat, its eyes brown-red in the flashbulb's light. They were pictures of a house. It was like a thousand houses in a hundred towns, not suburb, not city, but somewhere in between, with aluminum siding and a chain-link fence, a narrow driveway running up to a one-car garage and a patch of backyard. The house was yellow. I looked on the back for a date or a name, but neither was there. There was no need for discussion. I knew what she was trying to tell me, for it was something I had often felt. She was not adrift, alone, anonymous, although her bags

and her raincoat with the grime shadowing its creases had made me
believe she was. She had a house, or at least once upon a time had had
one. Inside were curtains, a couch, a stove, potholders. You are where
you live. She was somebody.

I've never been very good at looking at the big picture, taking the   3
global view, and I've always been a person with an overactive sense of
place, the legacy of an Irish grandfather. So it is natural that the thing
that seems most wrong with the world to me right now is that there
are so many people with no homes. I'm not simply talking about shelter from the elements, or three square meals a day or a mailing address
to which the welfare people can send the check—although I know
that all these are important for survival. I'm talking about a home,
about precisely those kinds of feelings that have wound up in cross-
stitch and French knots on samplers over the years.

Home is where the heart is. There's no place like it. I love my   4
home with a ferocity totally out of proportion to its appearance or location. I love dumb things about it: the hot-water heater, the plastic
rack you drain dishes in, the roof over my head, which occasionally
leaks. And yet it is precisely those dumb things that make it what it
is—a place of certainty, stability, predictability, privacy, for me and for
my family. It is where I live. What more can you say about a place than
that? That is everything.

Yet it is something that we have been edging away from gradually   5
during my lifetime and the lifetimes of my parents and grandparents.
There was a time when where you lived often was where you worked
and where you grew the food you ate and even where you were buried. When that era passed, where you lived at least was where your
parents had lived and where you would live with your children when
you became enfeebled. Then, suddenly where you lived was where
you lived for three years, until you could move on to something else
and something else again.

And so we have come to something else again, to children who   6
do not understand what it means to go to their rooms because they
have never had a room, to men and women whose fantasy is a wall
they can paint a color of their own choosing, to old people reduced to
sitting on molded plastic chairs, their skin blue-white in the lights of a
bus station, who pull pictures of house out of their bags. Homes have
stopped being homes. Now they are real estate.

People find it curious that those without homes would rather   7
sleep sitting up on benches or huddled in doorways than go to shelters.

Certainly some prefer to do so because they are emotionally ill, because they have been locked in before and they are damned if they will be locked in again. Others are afraid of the violence and trouble they may find there. But some seem to want something that is not available in shelters, and they will not compromise, not for a cot, or oatmeal, or a shower with special soap that kills the bugs. "One room," a woman with a baby who was sleeping on her sister's floor, once told me, "painted blue." That was the crux of it; not size or location, but pride of ownership. Painted blue.

This is a difficult problem, and some wise and compassionate people are working hard at it. But in the main I think we work around it, just as we walk around it when it is lying on the sidewalk or sitting in the bus terminal—the problem, that is. It has been customary to take people's pain and lessen our own participation in it by turning it into an issue, not a collection of human beings. We turn an adjective into a noun: the poor, not poor people; the homeless, not Ann or the man who lives in the box or the woman who sleeps on the subway grate. 8

Sometimes I think we would be better off if we forgot about the broad strokes and concentrated on the details. Here is a woman without a bureau. There is a man with no mirror, no wall to hang it on. They are not the homeless. They are people who have no homes. No drawer that holds the spoons. No window to look out upon the world. My God. That is everything. 9

Questions on Meaning

1. Characterize your response to the first two paragraphs of Quindlen's essay.
2. "Homes have stopped being homes. Now they are real estate." Which supporting examples do you find most effective? What do they suggest about class differences in the United States?
3. Discuss the difference in implication between the two statements from Quindlen's conclusion: "They are not the homeless. They are people who have no homes."

Questions on Method

1. Are the examples Quindlen cites in this essay meant to inform or persuade her audience? Cite evidence to support your answer.
2. How effective is Quindlen's focusing on her own concept of home in paragraph 4?

Writing Topics

1. Quindlen addresses the contemporary trend of families living in several homes. How might upward mobility affect one's emotional concept of home?
2. Write an essay attacking or defending Quindlen's viewpoint that in making homelessness "into an issue" rather than "a collection of human beings" we become less concerned about the problem.

An Amateur Marriage

Born in Yugoslavia, Steve Tesich (1943–1996) emigrated to the United States when he was fourteen. He frequently contributed articles to the now discontinued "About Men" column in the New York Times Magazine *and often contributed to periodicals. He is best known for the original screenplay* Breaking Away *(1979), for which he won an Academy Award. He also wrote the screenplays* Eyewitness *(1981) and* Four Friends *(1981); many plays for the theater, including* Passing Game *(1977),* The Road *(1978), and* Division Street *(1980); and a novel,* Summer Crossing *(1982). A recurrent theme in Tesich's work is the plight of the outsider.*

EVERYONE TOLD ME that when I turned 16 some great internal change would occur. I truly expected the lights to go down on my former life and come up again on a new, far more enchanting one. It didn't work. Nothing happened. When asked by others, I lied and said that, yes, I did feel a great change had taken place. They lied and told me that they could see it in me. 1

They lied again when I turned 18. There were rumors that I was now a "man." I noticed no difference, but I pretended to have all the rumored symptoms of manhood. Even though these mythical milestones, these rituals of passage, were not working for me, I still clung to the belief that they should, and I lied and said they were. 2

My 21st birthday was the last birthday I celebrated. The rituals weren't working, and I was tired of pretending I was changing. I was merely growing—adding on rooms for all the kids who were still me to live in. At 21, I was single but a family man nevertheless. 3

All these birthday celebrations helped to prepare me for the greatest myth of all: marriage. Marriage comes with more myths attached to it than a six-volume set of ancient Greek history. Fortunately for me, by the time I decided to get married I didn't believe in myths anymore. 4

It was a very hot day in Denver, and I think Becky and I decided to get married because we knew the city hall was air-conditioned. It was a way of hanging around a cool place for a while. I had forgotten 5 to buy a wedding ring, but Becky was still wearing the ring from her previous marriage, so we used that one. It did the job. She had to take it off and then put it back on again, but it didn't seem to bother anyone. The air-conditioners were humming.

I felt no great change take place as I repeated our marriage vows. I did not feel any new rush of "commitment" to the woman who was now my wife, nor did I have any plans to be married to her forever. I did love her, but I saw no reason why I should feel that I had to love her forever. I would love her for as long as I loved her. I assumed she felt the same way. The women I saw on my way out of city hall, a married man, did not look any less beautiful than the women I saw on my way in. It was still hot outside. We walked to our car carrying plastic bags containing little samples of mouthwash, toothpaste, shampoo and aspirin, gifts from the Chamber of Commerce to all newlyweds.   6

And so my marriage began—except that I never really felt the beginning. I had nothing against transforming myself into a married man, but I felt no tidal pull of change. I assumed Becky had married me and not somebody else, so why should I become somebody else? She married a family of kids of various ages, all of them me, and I married a family of kids of various ages, all of them her. At one time or another I assumed some of them were bound to get along.   7

Marriage, I was told, required work. This sounded all wrong to me from the start. I couldn't quite imagine the kind of "work" it required, what the hours were, what the point was. The very idea of walking into my apartment and "working" on my marriage seemed ludicrous. My apartment was a place where I went to get away from work. The rest of life was full of work. If marriage required "work," I would have to get another apartment just for myself where I could go and rest. Since I couldn't afford that at the time, I said nothing to Becky about working on our marriage. She said nothing about it herself. We were either very wise or very lazy.   8

We are led to believe that the harder we try, the better we get. This "aerobic dancing theory" of life may apply to certain things, but I don't think marriage is one of them. You can't go to a gym and pump marriage. It can't be tuned-up like a car. It can't be trained like a dog. In this century of enormous scientific breakthroughs, there have been no major marriage breakthroughs that I know of.   9

Progress junkies find this a frustrating state of affairs. They resist the notion that marriage is essentially an amateur endeavor, not a full-time profession, and they keep trying to work on their marriages and make them better. The only way to do that is to impose a structure on   10 the marriage and then fiddle and improve the structure. But that has nothing to do with the way you feel when the guests have left the house and it's just the two of you again. You are either glad you're there with that person or you're not. I've been both.

This need to improve, the belief that we can improve everything, brings to mind some of my friends who are constantly updating their stereo equipment until, without being aware of it, they wind up listening to the equipment and not to the music. You can do the same thing to friendship, to marriage, to life in general. Let's just say I have chosen to listen to the music, such as it is, on the equipment on hand. 11

The best trips that I have taken were always last-minute affairs, taken as a lark. When I've sent off for brochures and maps, the trips always turned into disappointments. The time I invested in planning fed my expectations, and I traveled to fulfill my expectations rather than just to go somewhere I hadn't been. I consider my marriage one of those trips taken as a lark. I have become rather fond of the sheer aimlessness of the journey. It's a choice. I know full well that people do plan journeys to the Himalayas, they hire guides, they seek advice, and when they get there, instead of being disappointed, they experience a kind of exhilaration that I never will. My kind of marriage will never reach Mount Everest. You just don't go there as a lark, nor do you get there by accident. 12

I'm neither proud nor ashamed of the fact that I've stayed married for 13 years. I don't consider it an accomplishment of any kind. I have changed; my wife has changed. Our marriage, however, for better or worse, is neither better nor worse. It has remained the same. But the climate has changed. 13

I got married on a hot day a long time ago, because it was a way of cooling off for a while. Over the years, it's also become a place where I go to warm up when the world turns cold. 14

Questions on Meaning

1. Why does Tesich begin by mentioning his sixteenth, eighteenth, and twenty-first birthdays?
2. How do you react to his statement that he "saw no reason why I should feel that I had to love her forever"? Is this a cynical or just a realistic view of marriage?
3. Tesich reacts very strongly to society's idea that marriage is work. Are the reasons he offers for resisting this concept convincing? Did he convince you?

4. What are the implications of Tesich's remarks about "progress junkies"? Is he making a point about our society apart from marriage?
5. What point is Tesich making about his marriage by relating it to the fact that the best trips he took were last minute rather than carefully planned?
6. What is the significance of the essay's title?

Questions on Method

1. Tesich's essay was originally published in the "About Men" column of the *New York Times Magazine*. Is his essay one that would appeal primarily to a male audience? Explain your answer.
2. Tesich uses the image of a journey to present his subject. Why is this use of figurative language effective?
3. Tesich's view of marriage is obviously controversial. What was his purpose in writing the essay? Do you think he was only stating his opinion or was he also trying to influence his readers?
4. Tesich arrives at a generalization from his own experience. What other generalizations might he have arrived at? What in his experience could he use to support these other generalizations? Why does he choose this one?

Writing Topics

1. Write an essay responding to Tesich's thesis that "marriage comes with more myths attached to it than a six-volume set of ancient Greek history." Cite as many specific examples as you can.
2. Write an essay in which, like Tesich, you attempt to prove a controversial point through sheer number of examples.
3. Write an essay that **satirizes** the failings of an institution, organization, or system in the United States. Use three or four detailed examples.

Declaration of Sentiments
and Resolutions

Elizabeth Cady Stanton (1815–1902), one of the first activists for women's rights, gained admission to New York's Johnstown Academy, an all-male institution, under special arrangement. She studied law but was denied admission to the New York State Bar because she was female. Profoundly affected by the prejudice by which she was victimized, she dedicated her life to fighting for the abolition of laws that denied women equal opportunity. Stanton and Susan B. Anthony developed a close partnership and together worked to advance the cause of women's suffrage. Stanton's works include A Woman's Bible *(1895), the three-volume* History of Women's Suffrage *(1896), and her autobiographical* Eighty Years and More *(1898).*

WHEN, IN THE COURSE OF HUMAN EVENTS, it becomes necessary for one portion of the family of man to assume among the people of the earth a position different from that which they have hitherto occupied, but one to which the laws of nature and of nature's God entitle them, a decent respect to the opinions of mankind requires that they should declare the causes that impel them to such a course.

We hold these truths to be self-evident: that all men and women are created equal; that they are endowed by their Creator with certain inalienable rights; that among these are life, liberty and the pursuit of happiness; that to secure these rights governments are instituted, deriving their just powers from the consent of the governed. Whenever any form of government becomes destructive of these ends, it is the right of those who suffer from it to refuse allegiance to it, and to insist upon the institution of a new government, laying its foundation on such principles, and organizing its powers in such form, as to them shall seem most likely to effect their safety and happiness. Prudence, indeed, will dictate that governments long established should not be changed for light and transient causes; and accordingly all experience hath shown that mankind are more disposed to suffer, while evils are sufferable, than to right themselves by abolishing the forms to which they were accustomed. But when a long train of abuses and usurpations, pursuing invariably the same object, evinces a design to reduce them under absolute despotism, it is their duty to throw off such government, and to provide new guards for their future security. Such has been the patient sufferance of the women under this government, and such is now the necessity which constrains them to demand the equal station to which they are entitled.

The history of mankind is a history of repeated injuries and usur-   3
pations on the part of man toward woman, having in direct object the establishment of an absolute tyranny over her. To prove this, let facts be submitted to a candid world.

He has never permitted her to exercise her inalienable right to   4
the elective franchise.

He has compelled her to submit to laws, in the formation of   5
which she had no voice.

He has withheld from her rights which are given to the most ig-   6
norant and degraded men—both natives and foreigners.

Having deprived her of this first right of a citizen, the elective   7
franchise, thereby leaving her without representation in the halls of legislation, he has oppressed her on all sides.

He has made her, if married, in the eye of the law, civilly dead.   8

He has taken from her all right in property, even to the wages she   9
earns.

He has made her, morally, an irresponsible being, as she can com-   10
mit many crimes with impunity, provided they be done in the presence of her husband. In the covenant of marriage, she is compelled to promise obedience to her husband, he becoming to all intents and purposes, her master—the law giving him power to deprive her of her liberty, and to administer chastisement.

He has so framed the laws of divorce, as to what shall be the   11
proper causes, and in case of separation, to whom the guardianship of the children shall be given, as to be wholly regardless of the happiness of women—the law, in all cases, going upon a false supposition of the supremacy of man, and giving all power into his hands.

After depriving her of all rights as a married woman, if single, and   12
the owner of property, he has taxed her to support a government which recognizes her only when her property can be made profitable to it.

He has monopolized nearly all the profitable employments, and   13
from those she is permitted to follow, she receives but a scanty remuneration. He closes against her all the avenues to wealth and distinction

which he considers most honorable to himself. As a teacher of theology, medicine, or law, she is not known.

He has denied her the facilities for obtaining a thorough education, all colleges being closed against her. 14

He allows her in Church, as well as State, but a subordinate position, claiming Apostolic authority for her exclusion from the ministry, and, with some exceptions, from any public participation in the affairs of the Church. 15

He has created a false public sentiment by giving to the world a different code of morals for men and women, by which moral delinquencies which exclude women from society, are not only tolerated, but deemed of little account in man. 16

He has usurped the prerogative of Jehovah himself, claiming it as his right to assign for her a sphere of action, when that belongs to her conscience and to her God. 17

He has endeavored, in every way that he could, to destroy her confidence in her own powers, to lessen her self-respect, and to make her willing to lead a dependent and abject life. 18

Now, in view of this entire disfranchisement of one-half the people of this country, their social and religious degradation—in view of the unjust laws above mentioned, and because women do feel themselves aggrieved, oppressed, and fraudulently deprived of their most sacred rights, we insist that they have immediate admission to all the rights and privileges which belong to them as citizens of the United States. 19

In entering upon the great work before us, we anticipate no small amount of misconception, misrepresentation, and ridicule; but we shall use every instrumentality within our power to effect our object. We shall employ agents, circulate tracts, petition the State and National legislatures, and endeavor to enlist the pulpit and the press in our behalf. We hope this Convention will be followed by a series of Conventions embracing every part of the country. 20

[The following resolutions were discussed by Lucretia Mott, Thomas and Mary Ann McClintock, Amy Post, Catharine A. F. Stebbins, and others, and were adopted:]

Whereas, The great precept of nature is conceded to be, that "man shall pursue his own true and substantial happiness." Blackstone in his Commentaries remarks, that this law of Nature being coeval with mankind, and dictated by God himself, is of course superior in 21 obligation to any other. It is binding over all the globe, in all countries, and at all times; no human laws are of any validity if contrary to this, and such of them as are valid, derive all their force, and all their validity, and all their authority, mediately and immediately, from this original; therefore,

Resolved, That such laws as conflict, in any way, with the true and substantial happiness of woman, are contrary to the great precept of nature and of no validity, for this is "superior in obligation to any other." 22

Resolved, That all laws which prevent woman from occupying such a station in society as her conscience shall dictate, or which place her in a position inferior to that of man, are contrary to the great precept of nature, and therefore of no force or authority. 23

Resolved, That woman is man's equal—was intended to be so by the Creator, and the highest good of the race demands that she should be recognized as such. 24

Resolved, That the women of this country ought to be enlightened in regard to the laws under which they live, that they may no longer publish their degradation by declaring themselves satisfied with their present position, nor their ignorance, by asserting that they have all the rights they want. 25

Resolved, That inasmuch as man, while claiming for himself intellectual superiority, does accord to woman moral superiority, it is preeminently his duty to encourage her to speak and teach, as she has an opportunity, in all religious assemblies. 26

Resolved, That the same amount of virtue, delicacy, and refinement of behavior that is required of woman in the social state, should also be required of man, and the same transgressions should be visited with equal severity on both man and woman. 27

Resolved, That the objection of indelicacy and impropriety, which is so often brought against woman when she addresses a public audience, comes with a very ill-grace from those who encourage, by their attendance, her appearance on the stage, in the concert, or in feats of the circus. 28

Resolved, That woman has too long rested satisfied in the circumscribed limits which corrupt customs and a perverted application of the Scriptures have marked out for her, and that it is time she should move in the enlarged sphere which her great Creator has assigned her. 29

Resolved, That it is the duty of the women of this country to secure to themselves their sacred right to the elective franchise. 30

Resolved, That the equality of human rights results necessarily from 31 the fact of the identity of the race in capabilities and responsibilities.

Resolved, therefore, That, being invested by the Creator with the 32 same capabilities, and the same consciousness of responsibility for their exercise, it is demonstrably the right and duty of woman, equally with man, to promote every righteous cause by every righteous means; and especially in regard to the great subjects of morals and religion, it is self-evidently her right to participate with her brother in teaching them, both in private and in public, by writing and by speaking, by any instrumentalities proper to be used, and in any assemblies proper to be held; and this being a self-evident truth growing out of the divinely implanted principles of human nature, any custom or authority adverse to it, whether modern or wearing the hoary sanction of antiquity, is to be regarded as a self-evident falsehood, and at war with mankind.

[At the last session Lucretia Mott offered and spoke to the following resolution:]

Resolved, That the speedy success of our cause depends upon the 33 zealous and untiring efforts of both men and women, for the overthrow of the monopoly of the pulpit, and for the securing to woman an equal participation with men in the various trades, professions, and commerce.

Questions on Meaning

1. Stanton assumes that her audience for "Declaration of Sentiments and Resolutions" is not only familiar with but supports the original Declaration of Independence. How successful is her strategy of writing in a form **parallel** to Jefferson's document?
2. Stanton's declaration was presented in 1848. How many of the rights that she lists have now been granted to women? Which are still unresolved?

Questions on Method

1. What examples among Stanton's list of grievances are most likely to appeal to a contemporary audience? Is there a pattern to her presentation of grievances?
2. Characterize the tone of Stanton's declaration. Does it enhance her purpose? What is her purpose?

Writing Topics

1. Respond to Stanton's statement that men have made women "in the eye of the law, civilly dead."
2. Stanton discusses the role of religious institutions in denying equal rights to women. What examples does she cite? What illustrations would you add to support her argument?
3. Imagine yourself as a member of the audience at Seneca Falls, where this document was presented. Would you have signed the document? Write an essay stating your reasons why you would or would not have appended your signature.

Mall Rats

William Glaberson is a writer for the New York Times. *In January 1998, he covered the Theodore Kaczynski trial. Glaberson's essay "Mall Rats," published in the* New York Times Magazine, *was written after he visited some malls over a period of several weeks and observed the patterns of behavior of the "mall rats"—kids who, like lemmings, flock there regularly whether to buy or not. It's what they do to keep trendy; it's what they do when there's nothing to do.*

IT WAS FRIDAY NIGHT at the mall. Christine Tako, 18 years old, with her straight brown hair falling down over her shoulders, was not sure whether to let the boy with the blue eyes know how much she liked him.   1

The teen-agers were gathering in little groups in the food court near Time Out Amusement, the video arcade that serves as headquarters for what regulars at the Danbury Fair Mall—and malls everywhere—call mall rats, the adolescents who seem to live to go to the mall.   2

Christine Tako kept wavering. She could get hurt again, the way she had in her last mall romance. But, then, there were those blue eyes.   3

She was sure about one thing, though. He would show up sooner or later.   4

"Everybody's a mall rat to an extent," she said. "It's something to do when there is nothing else to do. And there is nothing else to do."   5

Once, it was the malt shop or the diner. These days across the New York region, the mall is the teen-age clubhouse. Sometimes by the hundreds, adolescents meet, mill about, issue dares and join in that ancient teen-age conviction that there is nothing else to do.   6

SHARING "A BORING EMPTINESS"

Some say their time in the shadows of the mall's neon lights leaves them with a hollowness that is deeper than that of former teen-age pastimes. You sit with someone you know and you wait for something to   7 happen, said Brian Fuda, a slight high school graduate with a mustache of fine brown hairs, who dreams of becoming an actor. "You don't become great friends," he said. "You both share that boring emptiness."

But if there is a special starkness in the lives of the mall's teenagers, it is a backdrop to all the usual themes of adolescence. The food court has seen its loves and heartbreaks. It has become the venue for timeless experiments: drugs and liquor can be had for a price.   8

Cars in the mall parking garage are as popular for intimate moments as they have always been. And shoplifting can be a badge of honor for those in search of a rebellious image.   9

Here in Danbury, the tough and the timid come from quiet nearby towns like Brookfield, Bethel and Redding and from comfortable suburbs in Putnam County and northern Westchester, just over the border in New York State. "If you're not here, you're just drawn here," Brian Fuda said.   10

There are the teen-agers flirting with different identities. Nose rings and beepers constitute current chic.   11

There are the picture-perfect suburban youths who seem to have just outfitted at The Gap downstairs and who watch the rougher ones warily.   12

MALL RAT PACK

And then there are the ones whose dress shows their pride in being called mall rats, like Chris Roman, 21, whose hair makes a statement and whose black leather jacket, he said, he bought with a stolen credit card.   13

The afternoon before Christine Tako's night of decision, Chris Roman, known to all the mall rats as Scooby, had been sitting at that same table. He described what he called the dark side of the mall-rat world. His black hair was shoulder length but a three-inch-wide band of white skin showed above his ears where he had shaved it with a straight razor to provide a threatening "heavy metal" look.   14

"I've been smoking pot since I was 12," he said. "I've been drinking since I was 9. I've been hanging out at the mall since it opened." He was 16 then.   15

The nickname came from the inebriated position he was in when he passed out at a party in his early teens, he said. He was entangled with his host's family's dog, and the situation, for some reason, reminded everyone of Scooby Doo, the television cartoon canine.   16

That, Scooby said, was before he was jailed for car theft and be-   17
fore he was arrested for smoking marijuana in the parking garage. It
was back, he said, before the time when he and some of the other mall
rats ran what he called a "black market" in shoplifted items at the mall.

FONZI OF THE FOOD COURT

Scooby's tales and his studied ability to strike a match for his New-   18
port Light cigarettes on the smooth-as-glass surface of the food-court tables have given him a measure of Danbury Fair notoriety. Some say he is
the Fonzi of the food court, their symbol of what it is to be a mall rat.

"Scoob's one of a kind," said Michelle Sell, 17, who had dated   19
Scooby. She seemed proud that her inauguration into mall-rat society
had included a fling with the famous rat.

There were, she said, few rites. Like hundreds of other teen-agers   20
here every year, she got a part-time job in one of the shops that survive
on hourly wage labor. Soon, she said, the mall made its bid even for
her free time.

"When I'm off, I'm at home saying, 'Cool, I have a day off,'" the   21
round-faced teen-ager said. "I'll be watching TV and my friends call
me up and say, 'Michelle, Come and hang out.' And I say, 'Where are
you?' And they say, 'I'm at the mall,' And I say, 'Oh, O.K.' So after a
while, I just became a mall rat."

Scooby said he has had a string of such girlfriends from the mall-   22
rat ranks. At the table that Thursday, Jesse Amila, another young Danbury resident, said that he rarely misses a day outside Time Out and
that some of the newcomers are drawn to veteran rats because they
think they have status.

"We do have status," Scooby answered without a smile. "We   23
own the mall. 'Cause we know so many people—so many mall rats
come around. The more people you know, the more status you have."

A few days after that conversation, Scooby disappeared from his   24
table outside Time Out. Instantly, it seemed, the mall regulars knew
where he was. "When he's not in jail, he's here," said Richard N. De-
Merell, one of the mall's security officers. This time, the charges had to
do with credit-card theft.

"I kind of miss him," said Chris Sullivan, another regular, known   25
as Sully around the food court.

He is a handsome 20-year-old who is never without his red base-   26
ball cap. He says he is an alcoholic, and he often comes to the mall

drunk. Some of the food-court regulars say they surreptitiously add alcohol to their soft-drink cups. Sully's problems with liquor, he said, have contributed to his having been jailed 13 times.

He and Scooby, Sully said, have a lot in common. Scooby's father 27 is a Danbury detective. Sully's is a Fairfield County deputy sheriff.

Quietly, some of the regulars said Scooby and his crew give the 28 other loiterers a bad name. Jon Bourque, who graduated from Danbury High School last year, said he did not like the name mall rat and resented the suggestion that Scooby was the leader. "Not even close," he insisted.

"I don't think there is a mall-rat king," he said. And then he 29 pointed out that he believed he had logged as many hours as anyone outside Time Out. "I'm here every day of the week all day," he said.

At her table in the food court that Friday before Scooby was arrested, Christine Tako made a face at the mention of the full-timers in the food court. Rats like Scooby, she said, are friends. But not her type.

She started coming to the mall after her family moved to this corner of Connecticut in search of safety. They moved from Riverdale in the Bronx for her last year of high school after someone she had never seen before fired a shot in her direction as she walked home from school.

FAITHLESS SUITOR

Her parents wanted to protect her. But there are some hurts, she 32 learned at the mall, for which there is no protection.

Last year, in the Friday night crowd of teen-agers, she met a boy 33 from Brookfield who always wore suits. Not your typical mall rat, she said. For a month and a half, she said, they were together.

And then, as sometimes happens, there was a new group of teen- 34 agers from a high school a few miles into New York State who started to show up and tried to break in to the Connecticut cliques. "They wanted to be a part of it," she said.

One of them, a wiry 14-year-old girl with black hair, seemed to 35 want very badly to be a part of it. Before long, there was talk about her among the teen-agers and how she would do anything to be part of the group. And then one night, when Christine Tako was late for the mall, she said, everyone noticed how the boy in the suit and then the wiry girl slipped away to the mall parking garage.

"People see two people walking out," she said, "and they go to 36 the car and the car doesn't go anywhere. And then they come in."

By the time she got to the mall that night, the news was all over   37
the food court. "I walked into the mall," she said, "and everybody
looked at me because they knew. And once that happened, I knew
everybody knew. It's an odd feeling. Everybody knows what's going
on and either they tell you or they don't and it separates you from
everybody."

At the table in the food court that Friday night, she remembered   38
that she didn't cry until she got home the night she lost the boy in the
suit.

And then she took a deep breath and said her best friend from   39
Danbury High School, who scoops out ice cream at the mall's Häagen
Dazs shop, had warned her that the boy with the blue eyes was the
same kind. "He could ignore me or push me away," she said.

By then, there were more teen-agers filling up the tables in the   40
food court. Someone called to her from over near Time Out Amusement and she stood up. But just at that moment Christine Tako said,
she had decided, "I think I like him enough so I'll just go for it, I
guess," she said.

It was Friday night at the mall. And she disappeared into the   41
crowd.

Questions on Meaning

1. Characterize mall culture according to Glaberson. To what extent does
   his description contrast with your own experience?
2. Is sharing "a boring emptiness" part of the adolescent experience? Has
   the mall, as Glaberson states, become "the backdrop to all the usual
   themes of adolescence"?
3. Characterize Christine. Why do you think the author begins and ends
   his essay with her?
4. What aspects of mall culture does the author discuss with his inclusion of
   "Scooby"? What is your response to him?

Questions on Method

1. Characterize Glaberson's tone. Is it informative, cynical, or ironic? Cite
   examples to support your point of view.
2. Glaberson uses descriptions instead of actual names to introduce mall
   rats. What effect does he achieve through this technique?
3. Focus on paragraph 21. Why does Glaberson include Michelle's direct
   conversation rather than paraphrase it?

Writing Topics

1. Write an essay responding to Christine Tako's statement that "everybody's a mall rat to an extent." Cite examples and illustrations to support your point of view.
2. Speculate as to why the mall has become the hangout of choice for teenagers. You might conduct interviews with several adolescents of both genders and use their responses as a basis for your essay.

Illustration and Example
Writing Topics

1. Write an essay about your favorite sport or hobby. How difficult is it to learn and practice? How expensive is it? Do its difficult or expensive aspects add or detract from your enjoyment of it? Explain with the use of examples.

2. Develop a generalization, or thesis, about your childhood summers, and support it with examples or illustrations.

3. Quindlen and Staples use anecdotes to begin their essays. Write an essay discussing an issue that concerns people today—marriage, homelessness, public space. Begin with an anecdote and provide clear transitions between your examples.

4. How have computers and television affected the role of books in education? Formulate a thesis statement that responds to the question, and write an essay supporting it with as many examples as you can think of from your reading, research, social interactions, and experience.

5. Use one of the following statements, or a similar one, as a thesis for an essay. Before writing, create an outline using examples from your own experience, informal surveys, or current events to illustrate your ideas.
   a. There are times your life depends on keeping your mouth shut.
   b. Participation in a sport tells you a lot about yourself.
   c. Child abuse is not always physical.
   d. Family relationships can often be stressful.

8

Process Analysis

PROCESS ANALYSIS is one of the most common and practical kinds of exposition. It explains how to do something or how something is or was done. It has many purposes; everybody who does anything or tries to teach another person how to do something uses process analysis sooner or later. Success in a profession or career is usually measured by one's success at performing a process or set of processes—a secretary's success at transcribing dictation, a doctor's at diagnosing, a salesperson's at selling. To increase one's proficiency or to teach others, it is usually necessary to analyze this process, dividing it into its constituent steps.

Like narration, process analysis consists of a series of incidents or steps in time, with the difference that "getting there is *not* half the fun"; in process analysis what counts is crossing the finish line, especially in the more practical how-to-do-it (rather than the how-it-was-done) analysis. The how-to-do-it essay is also like cause-and-effect exposition (see Chapter 12) in that it uses a sequence that theoretically can always be repeated to produce the same result.

You have had to learn step by step many processes that you now perform automatically and so take for granted, such as tying your shoes, reading, cooking, swimming, or driving. To analyze these processes so that you can improve your own performance or teach them to another person, you have to try to recover some of your naiveté and relive those learning experiences so that you can divide the process into its simplest steps. That is the pattern for any process analysis. The structure should be chronological where possible, isolating one step from another and isolating smaller processes (driving a car) from larger ones to which they have become attached (maintaining, buying, selling, racing, chauffeuring a car). Later in your essay you can show how the smaller processes link up with the larger ones. Imagine that you are writing one chapter in a textbook and that you will not be on hand to answer your students' questions. Assume an audience of beginners; explain terminology; describe equipment, tools, and parts; include diagrams where appropriate; give a reasonable estimate of the cost in time, training, and money.

Sometimes you may be called on to analyze a set of processes only some of whose components can be explained: There are mysteries to managing an office and writing a novel that cannot be reduced to steps. Isolating the explainable from the unexplainable is an essential step in analysis; admit the limits of your knowledge. The fact that some of the most important processes are complex and imperfectly understood (especially those that involve the human being) has never prevented writers—and should not prevent you—from attempting to analyze them: how to land a job, how to succeed with a relationship, how to invest, how to avoid war, how to lose weight, how to interpret dreams, how to write an essay. Often the analyzer can only give pointers, indicate a direction, and hope that his or her directions find a receptive audience. Suppose, for example, you want to explain how to write an expository essay. You start by dividing the process into steps:

1. Choose a topic.

2. Limit the topic.

3. Make an outline.

4. Write a first draft.

5. Revise what you have written.

You soon find that each step assumes too much knowledge, leaving out too many intervening steps. So you break down these steps into smaller ones. Although each step may seem endlessly divisible, the time comes when you must stop and trust to your reader's good sense.

Make your analysis as specific, practical, and interesting as possible; give a set of clear steps and use other expository modes such as exemplification, definition, and comparison to expand these steps and appeal to the reader's reason, imagination, and ambition to succeed.

WRITING PROCESS ANALYSIS

1. Break down the process into clear, chronological steps.

2. Use transitional words and phrases between steps.

3. Explain unfamiliar terminology or equipment. If you write for a general audience, risk including too much detail rather than too little.

4. If the subject is complex, indicate the time and training necessary to follow your directions.

5. Show how your process links up with others to form a larger process.

Freewriting

Peter Elbow (b. 1935) directs a writing program at the University of Massachusetts at Amherst. He achieved national attention with his book Writing without Teachers *(1973). He published* Writing with Power *in 1981, and his most recent book,* What is English?, *in 1990. While directing the writing program at Stony Brook, Elbow pioneered the use of portfolios for writing assessment. He also coauthored two essays on portfolios in* Portfolios: Process and Product *(1991).*

THE MOST EFFECTIVE WAY I know to improve your writing is to do 1 freewriting exercises regularly. At least three times a week. They are sometimes called "automatic writing," "babbling," or "jabbering" exercises. The idea is simply to write for ten minutes (later on, perhaps fifteen or twenty). Don't stop for anything. Go quickly without rushing. Never stop to look back, to cross something out, to wonder how to spell something, to wonder what word or thought to use, or to think about what you are doing. If you can't think of a word or a spelling, just use a squiggle or else write, "I can't think of it." Just put down something. The easiest thing is just to put down whatever is in your mind. If you get stuck it's fine to write "I can't think what to say, I can't think what to say" as many times as you want; or repeat the last word you wrote over and over again; or anything else. The only requirement is that you *never* stop.

What happens to a freewriting exercise is important. It must be a 2 piece of writing which, even if someone reads it, doesn't send any ripples back to you. It is like writing something and putting it in a bottle in the sea.... Freewritings help you by providing no feedback at all. When I assign one, I invite the writer to let me read it. But also tell him to keep it if he prefers. I read it quickly and make no comments at all and I do not speak with him about it. The main thing is that a freewriting must never be evaluated in any way; in fact there must be no discussion or comment at all.

Here is an example of a fairly coherent exercise (sometimes they   3
are very incoherent, which is fine):

> I think I'll write what's on my mind, but the only thing on my
> mind right now is what to write for ten minutes. I've never done
> this before and I'm not prepared in any way—the sky is cloudy to-
> day, how's that? now I'm afraid I won't be able to think of what to
> write when I get to the end of the sentence—well, here I am at the
> end of the sentence—here I am again, again, again, again, at least
> I'm still writing—Now I ask is there some reason to be happy that
> I'm still writing—ah yes! Here comes the question again—What
> am I getting out of this? What point is there in it? It's almost ob-
> scene to always ask it but I seem to question everything that way
> and I was gonna say something else pertaining to that but I got so
> busy writing down the first part that I forgot what I was leading
> into. This is kind of fun oh don't stop writing—cars and trucks
> speeding by somewhere out the window, pens clittering across
> peoples' papers. The sky is still cloudy—is it symbolic that I should
> be mentioning it? Huh? I dunno. Maybe I should try colors, blue,
> red, dirty words—wait a minute—no can't do that, orange, yellow,
> arm tired, green pink violet magenta lavender red brown black
> green—now that I can't think of any more colors—just about
> done—relief? maybe.

Freewriting may seem crazy but actually it makes simple sense. Think   4
of the difference between speaking and writing. Writing has the advantage of permitting more editing. But that's its downfall too. Almost
everybody interposes a massive and complicated series of editings between the time words start to be born into consciousness and when
they finally come off the end of the pencil or typewriter onto the page.
This is partly because schooling makes us obsessed with the "mistakes"
we make in writing, Many people are constantly thinking about spelling and grammar as they try to write. I am always thinking about the
awkwardness, wordiness, and general mushiness of my natural verbal
product as I try to write down words.

But it's not just "mistakes" or "bad writing" we edit as we write.   5
We also edit unacceptable thoughts and feelings, as we do in speaking.
In writing there is more time to do it so the editing is heavier: when
speaking, there's someone right there waiting for a reply and he'll get
bored or think we're crazy if we don't come out with *something*. Most

of the time in speaking, we settle for the catch-as-catch-can way in which the words tumble out. In writing, however, there's a chance to try to get them right. But the opportunity to get them right is a terrible burden: you can work for two hours trying to get a paragraph "right" and discover it's not right at all. And then give up.

Editing, *in itself,* is not the problem. Editing is usually necessary if 6 we want to end up with something satisfactory. The problem is that editing goes on *at the same time* as producing. The editor is, as it were, constantly looking over the shoulder of the producer and constantly fiddling with what he's doing while he's in the middle of trying to do it. No wonder the producer gets nervous, jumpy, inhibited, and finally can't be coherent. It's an unnecessary burden to try to think of words and also worry at the same time whether they're the right words.

The main thing about freewriting is that it is *nonediting.* It is an 7 exercise in bringing together the process of producing words and putting them down on the page. Practiced regularly, it undoes the ingrained habit of editing at the same time you are trying to produce. It will make writing less blocked because words will come more easily. You will use up more paper, but chew up fewer pencils.

Next time you write, notice how often you stop yourself from 8 writing down something you were going to write down. Or else cross it out after it's written. "Naturally," you say, "it wasn't any good." But think for a moment about the occasions when you spoke well. Seldom was it because you first got the beginning just right. Usually it was a matter of a halting or even garbled beginning, but you kept going and your speech finally became coherent and even powerful. There is a lesson here for writing: trying to get the beginning just right is a formula for failure—and probably a secret tactic to make yourself give up writing. Make some words, whatever they are, and then grab hold of that line and reel in as hard as you can, Afterwards you can throw away lousy beginnings and make new ones. This is the quickest way to get into good writing.

The habit of compulsive, premature editing doesn't just make 9 writing hard. It also makes writing dead. Your voice is damped out by all the interruptions, changes, and hesitations between the consciousness and the page. In your natural way of producing words there is a sound, a texture, a rhythm—a voice—which is the main source of power in your writing. I don't know how it works, but this voice is the force that will make a reader listen to you, the energy that drives the meanings through his thick skull. Maybe you don't *like* your voice;

maybe people have made fun of it. But it's the only voice you've got. It's your only source of power. You better get back into it, no matter what you think of it. If you keep writing in it, it may change into something you like better. But if you abandon it, you'll likely never have a voice and never be heard.

Freewritings are vacuums. Gradually you will begin to carry over   10
into your regular writing some of the voice, force, and connectedness that creep into those vacuums.

Questions on Meaning

1. Define freewriting. What are its advantages according to Elbow?
2. Do you agree with Elbow that much formal writing instruction makes students afraid of making "mistakes"?
3. Explain what Elbow means by "voice" in paragraph 9. How would you characterize your natural writing voice?

Questions on Method

1. Evaluate Elbow's sample of freewriting provided in paragraph 3. Are its characteristics clear? How does it compare with examples of freewriting you have provided?
2. Characterize Elbow's tone. Is it appropriate for his intended audience? Who is that audience?

Writing Topics

1. Freewrite for ten minutes. Next reread what you have written. When you are finished, select only one idea of the many that cropped up in your freewriting and write about it for five more minutes. Use the techniques you learned for freewriting, but this time stick to your single topic as closely as possible.
2. Sit quietly with your eyes closed for three to five minutes. After the time is up, freewrite for fifteen minutes. How did you feel this time when you began writing? Was it helpful to concentrate before beginning to write?
3. Conduct your own experiment with the writing process by writing about anything that comes into your mind—the events of your day, your emotional response to a person or incident, or your thoughts about something you read or saw. Write freely, without stopping, to encourage a flow of ideas and discourage writer's block. What did you learn from this process?

We Kissed the Tomato and Then the Sky

Dana Wehle (b. 1954), born in Queens, New York, now lives in Brooklyn with her husband, Edria Collins. She is a classically trained painter with a B.A. and an M.F.A. The daughter of two Holocaust survivors, her work has been recognized for its effectiveness in communicating the impact of the Holocaust on the second generation. She graduated in May 1999 from the clinically oriented Masters of Social Work program at New York University and hopes to bring her passion for the symbolic as well as expressive nature of art to her work as a clinician.

MY PARENTS' BIG BED was not the kind to take refuge in when I was little. The two twin beds, connected by an elegant walnut headboard, were each clearly assigned. One was his, one was hers. After my father died, my mother made the monumental decision to make his side hers after forty-three years of it being the other way. She defensively explained that her motive was not to help resolve her loss, but simply to be closer to the door. In fact, the increasing number of times she got up during the night became a matter of concern to us all.

When I visited her once she was alone, I knew she would have preferred my sleeping next to her but, always needing my space, I awkwardly told her I preferred to sleep upstairs in my old room. Our love was deep and passionate, but our differences were equally as strong. For years, I had perched on a ledge waiting patiently, and sometimes not so patiently, for an opening for her to let me love her and for her to return that love for an extended period of time without tense interruption. It might have happened that the clock ran out before that opening presented itself. But, like a seagull watching for signs of food, I didn't miss my chance.

Just a year and a half after my father died, as cancer slowed her down and her need to lead was increasingly balanced by her willingness to be led, I cherished sleeping next to her. Two grown women, mother and daughter in corny, flowery nightgowns, filled this once forbidding bed in precious unity. Night after night, our arms stretched across the crack between the beds as our hands warmly joined. With just one reading light easing the darkness, I now viewed the room from her vantage point. In this space that enveloped us both, my mother would share her disbelief at her illness, her increasing symptoms and pains and even her unanswerable questions. I would say, "Pfeh!"; and she would say, "That's right. Pfeh!" Each lying on our own side, we were fully on the same side in sharing the sadness and the anger. We talked about Karl, her first husband, and my father and how blessed she felt for having loved two such loving men. She asked me if I was happy with my husband, and I said "very." We bonded as two women who shared the thankfulness of knowing this type of love.

Once, I crawled on her side and kissed her soft cheek. She gave   4
me her special "Safta"* kiss. I kissed her hand and retreated to my side of the enormous bed. In the middle of the night, I was awakened by her moans of pain, which she did not recall in the morning. Keeping to her routine, I made the bed in just the right way: the bedspread did not touch the floor, the quilts were not bumpy, and the throw pillows were not carelessly placed. In spite of this, she became cold when the temperature was warm; full when she ate only a spoonful; and tired when her day had barely begun.

The big bed, now perfectly made in its flowery pastel-colored   5
spread with matching pillows, holds all these memories plus the last— her lying there no longer able to warmly hold my hand.

★   ★   ★

Who would have believed that in my lifetime I would have got-   6
ten to share meditation space with my mother? But in her last weeks, when the pain of cancer slowed her down, this fast-moving, always self-sufficient woman was too tired to run. She did not stop running all at once, however. It was gradual, more like the increasing presence of the left hand in a piano composition, where the effect of the grave bass notes emerges in time.

For my mother, shopping was once the beginning of a long day   7
that included swimming forty laps, cooking up a storm, writing letters,

---

*"Safta" means grandmother in Hebrew. This kiss had no name when my siblings and I were young but my mother called it "the Safta kiss" with the grandchildren. It can't be described, it has to be experienced.

doing "administrative work," and trying to sit down to write the last essay in a series on her Holocaust experiences. At this time, shopping alone wore her out. As she would say, "she couldn't anymore." How trapped she must have felt. Her survivor instincts told her she had to find new doors. Though she could no longer will her body to do more, she still had command over her mind and soul. At seventy-nine, this Czech Jewish woman who was set in her ways opened herself up to a "New Age" experience.

We meditated in two green-and-white lawn chairs, inhaling and   8 exhaling as we felt the earth's energy travel through our bodies. We visualized ourselves as eagles flying above Floral Park and landing at Jones Beach. We watched the ocean come forward and recede as we observed our breathing doing the same. We felt the rhythm of nature and the universe and experienced ourselves being part of the whole. Guided by ancient wisdom, we tried to find balance within the extremes and centeredness in the moment. After we embraced memories of the past at Jones Beach and absorbed the ocean's lessons, we slowly traveled back to Queens. We landed and gently opened our eyes. My mother and I were sitting in the driveway in the sun, hearing the birds sing, the neighbors rattle their garbage cans, and the dogs bark as we listened to the silence.

One week later, two weeks before her death, we sat in a sculpture   9 park with two dear friends. My mother enthusiastically suggested that she lead us through a meditation. I got to share this sacred space with her; this space she could create only because even at this desperate time, she was open to expansion. I still hear her saying "I feel the wind caressing my face."

★   ★   ★

She sat there with a weak smile on her face as her fading eyes   10 suddenly filled with the recognition of a world once known. Around the large dining room table, my mother, my sisters, and I were assembled. My brother went between this room and another, changing CDs as we all tried to decide which music to play at her funeral. The surrealism of the moment was not lost.

I sat directly across from her and caught the flash of light in her   11 sunken eyes as the Beethoven piece we played at my father's funeral filled the air. I think the others missed this flash as they continued to discuss the options. I requested that we be silent and share the experience.

If music can be worn out, this Beethoven concerto would have   12 been destroyed by how often my mother listened to it after my father's death. After a year or so, however, this same CD became lethal for her as she could no longer bear the pain that it evoked. On this day before her own death and one and a half years after my father's, with fresh ears, she received this music as an offering from heaven.

My mother described our relationship as love/hate. But at that time, 13 when only I seemed to know what filled her heart, I knew what she meant by her last direct words to me: "It always amazed me how you would sometimes know what I was feeling without my saying the words."

Dear Ma, I had a dream a few days after you died and all I re- 14 member is you sitting at the end of the table smiling at me as you knew I knew the profound joy you were feeling at the moment Daddy's music filled your soul.

★   ★   ★

Oddly, my mother's death has given me a sense of completion in 15 a way similar to my finishing a painting. Drawn studies, painted studies, notes, and art materials fill my studio as the residue of final works. Audio tapes and journals crammed with ponderings about my parents' future deaths fill my drawers, which, with my memories, are the stuff of my latest final work. I prepared for the day when I could no longer hear their voices by taping their sweetest answering machine messages. One year after my father's death Ma left these:

> Are you home? Daninko? OK. I just came from the city. I wanted to report to you, OK? Thank you. Bye-bye. (October 1996)

> Hi Dana. Are you there? Are you home? Oh. What a pity. Channel 13. Danny Kaye. So, I thought you would laugh. Anyhow, Bye-bye. (December 1996)

My mother's urgency defined her life-affirming existence, yet it 16 was also a constant reminder to me of her emotional scars. She beat death so many times, from the gas chambers to critical illnesses. She was just beginning to beat her paralyzing grief after my father's death. Now, her obsessive race, which she so ably finessed over her lifetime, was over.

This seventy-nine-year-old woman was a juggler extraordinaire, 17 but a juggler's art is both exhilarating and unsettling to watch. Warding off the sound of shattering plates, my mother looked straight ahead till the very end. One quiet night, however, she did confess that she was not sure whether she or the cancer was in control. When the terror of death found its way through her thick defenses, my mother found solace in knowing she would be with my father when she died.

The last of her messages was left thirty-four days before her end,   18
and it went like this:

> Hi Dana. I am just reporting. I am chewing my breakfast very slowly. I came from swimming…and will rest…and then I will go to get the drug. And I had a very good, peaceful night. And also Dr. Li called me, how I am feeling after that tea. So, that was very nice. I hope you are fine. I am just reporting. Bye-bye. (May 1997)

I suppose it's because she had no regrets, and because I now have   19
many answers to questions that occupied me since I was young, that I feel some sense of completion. Both finishing a painting and saying goodbye to someone you love require time to reflect upon moments that are just right as well as unanswered questions.

> Hello? Dani? Are you home? That's Ma. Are you there? Dana? OK, so I just wanted to know what is going on. I didn't hear from you, so I wanted to make sure that you are OK. So call me if you feel up to it. OK? Bye-bye. (March 1997)

> Ma. I'm here. Where are you?

★   ★   ★

The house is still intact; the pillows on the couch are still   20
scrunched from someone's weight; the flowers in the vases are still more alive than dead; the mail is still coming to a woman who was alive less than a month ago and to a man long gone. My home. My house where I grew up. My parents' house. My mother's house.

Soon my mother's beloved tomato plants, still green, will bear the   21
red harvest that she knew she would not live to see. The piano, which once eloquently spoke for my father through his strong fingers and passionate heart, will be among the things removed. The smell of cardboard boxes mingling with the sight of frenzied dust particles will signal that the pain of saying goodbye is near.

I comfort myself by knowing that my mother's refined artistic   22
sensibility will filter into my home when some of her artwork and belongings will become my own. I look forward to honoring my promise to my father to organize "the stuff downstairs" into an archive. This

stuff (rare, browning photographs and documents from before the war; my parents' published writings as witnesses to the Holocaust; materials from my father's years as administrative head of the Jewish Community in Prague, hospital administrator, and Czech Jewish historian; as well as newer family memorabilia) has always been, and will always be, a defiant symbol of their survival. I feel calmed by the honor of this task.

Though the breakdown has not yet started, I have already felt 23 compelled to rescue a remnant of my mother's favorite shirt from being used simply as a rag. The familiar battle between a need to hold on and a voice that says let go has begun. I guess that saying goodbye to her, to him again, and to the house will mean separating from the rags. I guess that the struggle itself will bestow honor upon them and the home they created.

★   ★   ★

Today is September 4, 1997, and always counting the time since 24 my father died, I just realized that today is exactly one year and ten months since his death. Ma died on June 11 and I now count both their days, though hers is still counted only in months. The house has been totally dismantled, and its stark emptiness is especially pronounced when strangers come to check out whether they want to make it their home. Like the sound of a wailing Greek chorus, the lamenting of old neighbors, family, and dear friends counters the silent indifference of those who pass through with no feeling. A sweet, subtle reminder of the way Ma sounded when she answered the phone by one of those who loved her the most brings it all back.

Last week, my husband and I picked a juicy red tomato off the 25 stem. Holding each other tightly, we kissed this symbol of life, each other, and then the sky. Our hands could not part. This was our goodbye. Later on, my sister and I held each other. We cried. We prayed. We laughed in our childhood bedroom, as we got one last touch of the textured linoleum tiles that used to bruise our hands while we endlessly practiced to be in the "Jacks Olympics." Filled with the joy of sharing, we said our goodbye.

While pouring through my files to hear their voices again, I stum- 26 bled upon the last birthday card that my mother gave to me, in which she wrote, "so read carefully the words in this card and put them in your 'archive' so that whenever need will be, you will remember how much I love you!" I then found a gem my father wrote almost twenty years ago: "Schnupsinko, you must feel great that the undergraduate school is nearly over and that you made it in good time and that you really learned and achieved a lot. One does not measure these years by the doors they open for the future, but by the knowledge and insight they provide to a student's searching mind and soul. In this respect you can count yourself fortunate for the tremendous intellectual and artistic growth you experienced through these years. And the future for you will be bright, I do not doubt one moment. Love and kisses, Dad."

I feel the wind caressing my face.   27

Questions on Meaning

1. The author refers several times to her mother's urgency. Does this word also describe the author? What examples can you cite? What is the underlying reason for Wehle's urgency?
2. Characterize Wehle's relationship with her mother. What different aspects of this relationship does she portray in the essay?
3. Analyze her father's role in the essay. What symbols does the author associate with him? How do these add unity to the memoir?

Questions on Method

1. Time is an important theme in this essay. What direct and indirect techniques does Wehle use to suggest the passing of time?
2. Wehle uses many literary techniques to enhance theme. Cite examples of foreshadowing, similes, and metaphors. To what senses do they appeal? Are there examples that indicate Wehle's interest in the visual arts? Why does she end her essay with a line that occurs earlier? How has its meaning changed?
3. Trace the process of Wehle's coming to terms with her mother's death intellectually and emotionally.

Writing Topics

1. Wehle describes the stages of her emotional and intellectual responses to her mother's death. In an essay, analyze her responses and the insights she gained as a result. How did her experience affect you?
2. Have you, like Wehle, gone through a rite of passage? Write an essay describing this process as you experienced it.
3. Write an essay that describes an educational process to which you were subjected as a child and toward which your feelings have changed, either positively or negatively, now that you are older.

Becoming American, by Degrees

Jim Fusilli (b. 1953) has written for a variety of publications, most notably the Wall Street Journal. *He says he particularly enjoys writing personal essays. "When I get to write about things that allow me to examine my childhood, it gives me a new opportunity to see how it affected me. It either reinforces my perspective or gives me a new one. That's pretty healthful, I think."*

I'VE RECENTLY come to realize that, for a native, an understanding 1 of what it means to be an American isn't so much a matter of heritage as a matter of consciousness. It's a matter of awareness that comes in degrees, sometimes slowly, if at all.

For me, this consciousness, this awareness, began when I started to 2 travel often outside the U.S., a fairly recent activity for me. I imagine for a young child who is well traveled from birth, toted along with the luggage, it may occur on a subconscious level, like the awareness of race, class and organized religion (though faced with bigotry these deeply rooted identities surface to the conscious level with the power of a thunderbolt). For me, whose idea of an adventure in travel as a child was a 25-cent bus ride to an adjoining town, there was no such opportunity.

We lived in an immigrant community, within sight of the Statue of 3 Liberty and Ellis Island; a steady flow of imposing ships brought European immigrants to the piers at the other end of our mile-square town. If memory serves, in kindergarten I had classmates whose parents had recently come from Italy, Germany, the Netherlands and Yugoslavia.

But if this was a form of training for life in a multinational envi- 4 ronment, I was unaware of it. It seemed to me these families were remarkably similar, sharing the same basic characteristics: They worked hard and aspired to assimilate. A few remnants of their native culture remained—music and food, in particular—but they came to America to be American.

At the same time, though, the seeds of my American identity 5 were sown: I was part of something others aspired to. But this wasn't an active thought by any means—I was not yet old enough to have active thoughts about much of anything—but, I see now, it's in there. Fortunately, it appears to manifest itself as a kind of quiet self-confidence rather than ugly American arrogance. I've come to see that I'm lucky that way.

As a boy, I struggled with national identity. My Irish-American mother had married a second-generation Italian, and they drew, if not the wrath, a level of scorn from her family, though not so much as to cause her to actively side with her husband. In fact, we lived among my mother's family, and they never ceased to remind me that I was an outsider. Something stubborn within me made me emphasize what was the other in me; and I still look at life as not what I ought to be, not what I am being coaxed to be, but what I am and what I can be, and that too gives me self-confidence, though as a boy I very often felt isolated and had to learn to thrive by myself. (This, I think, is the shared, fundamental characteristic of all writers: the ability to live comfortably, at times preferably, in a world of our own creation. But, another time for that.)

The idea of an American character came to me as it did to most people my age: through the mass media. Of course, in school we learned of Thomas Paine and John Adams and Abraham Lincoln and Woodrow Wilson. But, so upstanding were they, and completely without human foibles, they might as well have been literary devices to advance a fictional story of a country of gods. But, via mass media—glimmering images at the Fabian Theater, our only movie house; the flopping picture on our black-and-white TV; New York City's myriad newspapers, all available at nearby candy stores—I learned of the American character: Jimmy Stewart as good, honest, self-sacrificing George Bailey in "It's a Wonderful Life"; the steel-jawed determination of Robert Ryan in "The Longest Day"; James Cagney as George M. Cohan, "a real live nephew of my Uncle Sam, born on the Fourth of July"; clean-cut John Glenn orbiting the earth in *Friendship* 7; Leonard Bernstein, patiently teaching us the joys of Copland; and Superman, "who, disguised as Clark Kent, mild-mannered reporter for a great metropolitan newspaper, fights a never-ending battle for truth, justice and the American Way."

Frankly, at that age, with the exception of Superman, it was impossible to tell who was real and who was fictional, for they shared one absolute: They did, or were doing, the right thing for us, the Americans. Even John Wayne, who massacred Indians in the promotion of our standard, had God on his side.

I must confess that as a boy I had no real heroes, besides the almost-mandatory sports idols. Men in the neighborhood had served and had been wounded in the second World War, but, seeing them every day, they hardly seemed heroic. Sadly, through drink and intolerance, some seemed smaller, not larger, than life. My father adored Frank Sinatra, a native of our town, but he made my skin crawl with his ring-a-ding-ding, booze-and-broads routine. To my grandfather's peers, men who had come from Italy to establish a new life in America, Joe DiMaggio was an idol: Joe D, a man of enormous dignity, a baseball legend *and* husband to Marilyn Monroe. (Madonna mio! *That's* assimilation.) I thought Joe Namath was pretty neat, and since he had dark hair and a kind of appealing, post-Sinatra swagger, I imagined he might have some Italian blood in him. Maybe he too was a half-breed.

The idea of what is the American character, what are the inherent   10
characteristics of an American, began to be challenged during the Vietnam War–era by hippies, assertive feminists, pop psychologists, contrarians of all kinds, and I had the best view of this debate: a tad too young to have to serve in the war, a bit too young to have to deal with assertive women, often alone, willingly assaulted by media, and interested enough to observe. Perhaps confused by all of it—there really was nobody to root for then, save slaughtered saints like Martin Luther King and the impenetrables like Bob Dylan and Miles Davis; and so many loathsome worms like the crook Nixon and his subordinates—I withdrew, thus avoiding the subject of what it really means to be an American.

Avoidance, to be frank, was easy. My experiences in college were   11
extremely limited: I attended a college to which virtually everyone commuted from nearby communities, and in my class were at least a dozen people with whom I'd gone to high school. I had a full-time night job, so I stayed pretty close to home. I'd joined the college newspaper and began interviewing people from different backgrounds, which was somewhat enlightening: only somewhat, because most of my subjects were Anglo-Saxon musicians, a narrowly focused group, I can assure you. So insulated was I that as I spoke with the Grateful Dead's Jerry Garcia I remember thinking that he was the first person I'd ever met from California.

My exposure to the other began in earnest about five years after   12
graduation when I fell into the company of world–class journalists at a major daily newspaper, people who had dodged the Khmer Rouge, been detained by the KGB, conversed with Castro, Deng, Khomeini, walked the streets of Baghdad, Palestine, Johannesburg. They had been eyewitnesses to every historic event of the past 20 years and knew how to relate their experiences with vivid color and nuance, even over cof-

fee or a quick lunch. And among these reporters were men and women born in Taiwan, Egypt and Japan as well as all parts of the English-speaking world. They had an entirely different perspective on things, and it was enlightening to try to see as they did. When a question was raised, it was impossible to anticipate what the answer could be, and when the topic was an event occurring in America—be it political, economic, social, the arts—I soon realized they weren't merely addressing the subject, they were talking about America and its nature.

And this was a revelation to me. Despite attempts to avoid it, I'd   13
heard echoes of the public debate on the American character, and knew it had degenerated into diatribes shouted from the polar fringes, with all forms of recrimination and bilge replacing thoughtful analysis. Remember, this was the era of family values promoted by men and women who couldn't keep their own families together, and the whining of the well-off who demanded more personal liberties without a shred of discussion about community and responsibility. Had I not been privy to the considered comments of those editors and reporters, I would've come to believe self-indulgence, insincerity and intolerance were our defining features now. But, no, they knew this was all so much babble, and that real issues could be solved, or at least prudently addressed, by a people who were better than their leaders, either elected or self-appointed. They knew quality when they saw it.

After leaving the company of those journalists, I began working for   14
an organization with headquarters in Paris, France, and offices in more than 100 countries. I suddenly found myself a part of a global team with members from each country in Western Europe as well as Hungary and several countries in South America, all of whom spoke, in addition to their native language, French and, thankfully, English. With these people, I had no identity other than American. They didn't much care that I was from New Jersey (which they knew was close to New York City) or that I considered myself an Italian-American. "My grandfather is from Foggia," I told my colleague from Milan. She replied, "Ah, you speak Italian?" "No," I admitted. At that moment, I lost my hyphen.

It was early in my tenure that I first heard the expression "You   15
Americans." While traveling across the south of France, a British colleague who was based in Brazil tapped me on the shoulder and said, "Say, James, where do you stand on the issue of the coloreds?"

"What?" I was hoping I misunderstood.   16

"Well, I know you Americans are of two minds on this issue—"   17

"I'm not," I snapped.   18

(An imperial bore on many issues, he was fired shortly thereafter.)   19

But most allusions to "you Americans" were complimentary; in   20
fact, some were over the top. I was riding in a New York City subway
with a colleague from Paris, and the crowded car was filled with a tension typical of certain lines at certain times of the day. After we surfaced,
he asked me if I was afraid on the train. No, I replied, and that was true:
I took that line every day for several years. "Yes," he said, "you Americans are never afraid." Too many John Wayne movies, I thought.

As I became integrated into the team, my opinion was sought, per-   21
haps more often than that of others with more experience than I. "Let's
get the American viewpoint" was how it was often presented. And I
gave the American viewpoint, as if there was such a thing, and I tried to
be as humble and unobtrusive as possible: I was new, still, and I understood that these people were accommodating me by conducting meet-
ings in English. I did know enough French to overhear one colleague
say, "He's not a typical American" as I quietly acquiesced to some now-
forgotten scheme. I wasn't sure what she meant, but I took the comment
as a mild insult and determined to be a bit more assertive. Maybe a bit
more daring and steel-jawed determination, and a little less self-sacrifice.

Once the team became comfortable with me, and I with them,   22
we found common ground on subjects that transcended nationality
and language. I knew at least a little about Stendhal and Baudelaire,
Manet and Seurat, Truffault and Godard, and they knew rock 'n' roll
and American movies and much more. I was sitting in a cafe by the
water in Stockholm with a colleague who spoke no English. The ships
in the harbor reminded me of my hometown and I suddenly felt compelled to tell her about my childhood. In carefully crafted French, I
asked her if she ever saw a movie called "On the Waterfront" with
Marlon Brando, Eva Marie Saint, Lee J. Cobb and Rod Steiger. She
brightened and nodded. "Ma ville," I said proudly.

These relationships have become precious. People from many   23
countries know my family and me, and I know some of their children.
My Italian colleague has researched my grandfather's hometown and
presented me with her findings. The daughters of my German colleague wear Oshkosh jeans I purchased at Macy's. My wife, daughter
and I saw "Turnadot" performed at the Acropolis, and when I ranted
about the experience at a team meeting the next morning, these people
looked at me with benign bemusement: They liked it that the American was pleased. The goodwill continues: Diet Coke is kept in the refrigerator at headquarters in Paris. My colleagues wear baseball caps.

Meanwhile, back at home, I've become irrationally proud of   24
American things: geysers in Yellowstone National Park. Pathfinder on
the surface of Mars. A New England clam bake. Walt Whitman. David
Mamet. Thelonious Monk....

Questions on Meaning

1. How did Fusilli's cultural encounters as a child in his neighborhood
   shape his awareness of what it means to be an American?
2. "As a boy, I struggled with national identity." What role did his family
   play in this process?
3. Fusilli examines at some length the extent to which figures from mass
   media helped form his generation's ideas about American culture. With
   how many of the people he mentions are you familiar?

Questions on Method

1. Trace the various stages involved in Fusilli's becoming an American.
2. In "Becoming American, by Degrees," Fusilli also uses contrast and
   comparison to illustrate how travel and being part of an international
   group of professionals changed his concept of being an American. What
   examples impressed you most?
3. What is Fusilli's purpose? Is he mainly informing his audience, or does
   he also wish to persuade? Cite evidence for your point of view.

Writing Topics

1. Fusilli lists movie stars and sports figures who influenced his generation.
   Update that list for your generation. How have these celebrities shaped
   your ideas of what being an American means?
2. Have you, like Fusilli, had an experience that transcended language and
   culture? What insight did you gain from it? Write an essay recounting
   your thoughts about yourself.

Finding a Wife

Gary Soto (b. 1952) was born in California's San Joaquin Valley to a family of migrant workers who toiled in the fruit and vegetable fields. Often the theme of his fiction, poetry, and nonfiction is the plight of the poor, especially Mexican Americans who have endured despite social inequities. He now teaches at the University of California. Living Up the Street *received the 1985 Before Columbus Foundation's America Book Award. Among his other works are* The Elements of San Joaquin *(1977),* Father Is a Pillow Tied to a Broom *(1980),* Small Faces *(1986),* Who Will Know Us? *(1990),* Home Course in Religion *(1991), and* New and Selected Poems *(1995).*

IT'S EASY to find a wife, I told my students. Pick anybody, I said, and they chuckled and fidgeted in their chairs. I laughed a delayed laugh, feeling hearty and foolish as a pup among these young men who were in my house to talk poetry and books. We talked, occasionally making sense, and drank cup after cup of coffee until we were so wired we had to stand up and walk around the block to shake out our nerves.

When they left I tried to write a letter, grade papers, and finally nap on the couch. My mind kept turning to how simple it is to find a wife; that we can easily say after a brief two- or three-week courtship, "I want to marry you."

When I was twenty, in college and living on a street that was a row of broken apartment buildings, my brother and I returned to our apartment from a game of racquetball to sit in the living room and argue whether we should buy a quart of beer. We were college poor, living off the cheap blessings of rice, raisins, and eggs that I took from our mom's refrigerator when Rick called her into the back yard about a missing sock from his laundry—a ploy from the start.

"Rick, I only got a dollar," I told him. He slapped his thigh and told me to wake up. It was almost the end of the month. And he was right. In two days our paychecks from Zak's Car Wash would burn like good report cards in our pockets. So I gave in. I took the fifteen cents—a dime and five pennies—he had plucked from the ashtray of loose change in his bedroom, and went downstairs, across the street and the two blocks to Scott's Liquor. While I was returning home, swinging the quart of beer like a lantern, I saw the Japanese woman who was my neighbor, cracking walnuts on her front porch. I walked slowly so that she looked up, smiling. I smiled, said hello, and continued walking to the rhythm of her hammer rising and filling.

In the apartment I opened the beer and raised it like a chalice before we measured it in glasses, each of us suspicious that the other would get more. I rattled sunflower seeds onto a plate, and we pinched fingersful, the beer in our hands cutting loose a curtain of bubbles. We were at a party with no music, no host, no girls. Our cat, Mensa, dawdled in, blinking from the dull smoke of a sleepy afternoon. She looked at us, and we looked at her. Rick flicked a seed at her and said, "That's what we need—a woman!"

I didn't say anything. I closed my eyes, legs shot out in a V from the couch, and thought of that girl on the porch, the rise and fill of her hammer, and the walnuts cracking open like hearts.

I got up and peeked from our two-story window that looked out onto a lawn and her apartment. No one. A wicker chair, potted plants, and a pile of old newspapers. I looked until she came out with a broom to clean up the shells. "Ah, my little witch," I thought, and raced my heart downstairs, but stopped short of her house because I didn't know what to say or do. I stayed behind the hedge that separated our yards and listened to her broom swish across the porch, then start up the walk to the curb. It was then that I started to walk casually from behind the hedge and, when she looked at me with a quick grin, I said a hearty hello and walked past her without stopping to talk. I made my way to the end of the block where I stood behind another hedge, feeling foolish, I should have said something. "Do you like walnuts," I could have said, or maybe, "Nice day to sweep, isn't it?"—anything that would have my mouth going.

I waited behind that hedge, troubled by my indecision. I started back up the street and found her bending over a potted geranium, a jar of cloudy water in her hand. Lucky guy, I thought, to be fed by her.

I smiled as I passed, and she smiled back. I returned to the apartment and my bedroom where I stared at my homework and occasionally looked out the window to see if she was busy on the porch. But she wasn't there. Only the wicker chair, the plants, the pile of newspapers.

The days passed, white as clouds. I passed her house so often that   10
we began to talk, sit together on the porch, and eventually snack on
sandwiches that were thick as Bibles, with tumblers of milk to wash
down her baked sweet bread flecked with tiny crushed walnuts.

After the first time I ate at her house, I hurried to the apartment   11
to brag about my lunch to my brother who was in the kitchen sprinkling raisins on his rice. Sandwiches, I screamed, milk, cold cuts, choc-
olate ice cream! I spoke about her cupboards, creaking like ships
weighed down with a cargo of rich food, and about her, that woman
who came up to my shoulder. I was in love and didn't know where to
go from there.

As the weeks passed, still white as clouds, we saw more of each   12
other. Then it happened. On another Saturday, after browsing at a
thrift shop among gooseneck lamps and couches as jolly as fat men, we
went to the west side of Fresno for Mexican food—menudo for me
and burritos for her, with two beers clunked down on our table. When
we finished eating and were ready to go, I wiped my mouth and
plucked my sole five-dollar bill from my wallet as I walked to the cashier. It was all the big money I had. I paid and left the restaurant as if it
were nothing, as if I spent such money every day. But inside I was
thinking, "What am I going to do?"

Scared as I was, I took Carolyn's hand into mine as we walked to   13
the car. I released it to open the door for her. We drove and drove, past
thrift shops she longed to browse through, but I didn't want to stop because I was scared I would want to hold her hand again. After turning
corners aimlessly, I drove back to her house where we sat together on
the front porch, not touching. I was shivering, almost noticeably. But
after a while, I did take her hand into mine and that space between us
closed. We held hands, little tents opening and closing, and soon I nuz-
zled my face into her neck to find a place to kiss.

I married this one Carolyn Oda, a woman I found cracking wal-   14
nuts on an afternoon. It was a chance meeting: I was walking past
when she looked up to smile. It could have been somebody else, a girl
drying persimmons on a line, or one hosing down her car, and I might
have married another and been unhappy. But it was Carolyn, daughter
of hard workers, whom I found cracking walnuts. She stirred them
into dough that she shaped into loaves, baked in the oven, and set before me so that my mouth would keep talking in its search of the words
to make me stay.

Questions on Meaning

1. "It's easy to find a wife," Soto tells his students. What did his process involve? Was it as easy as he first implies?
2. What portrait of Soto emerges from the essay? What does the last paragraph suggest about his values? To what extent do you agree with his thoughts about "chance"?

Questions On Method

1. Outline the various stages in Soto's "finding a wife."
2. Comment on Soto's use of figurative language in his essay. Which metaphors and similes are most vivid?
3. Review Soto's introductory paragraph. Is it effective? Why or why not? Does Soto use irony in his introduction? How does his conclusion reinforce his first paragraph?

Writing Topics

1. Write an essay in which you compare different techniques used to attain the same general results, such as the different ways that women try to pick up men (or vice versa).
2. Describe the process you went through to find a job.
3. Write down the lines you remember from your favorite love song or love poem. Then develop inductively a thesis about love implicitly and explicitly suggested by the lyric or poem.

Dancing in the Cracks between Worlds

Tom Daly earned both a B.S. in zoology and botany and an M.S. in counseling and psychology at the University of Colorado. He also received a Ph.D. in fine arts and men's studies from The Union Institute in Cincinnati, Ohio. Daly is the founder and director of The Living Arts Foundation and Men's Council Project, both headquartered in Boulder, Colorado. He has led men's groups since 1971, has taught classes from junior high to postgraduate levels, and has written articles for such publications as Harper's, Edges, *and* Man! *Daly travels around North America helping men to form men's councils, create male initiations, and transmit rituals such as drum-dancing and the sweat lodge. In 1992 he published an anthology of writing by men about men, entitled* Wingspan: Inside the Men's Movement.

LIKE MOST OF THE BOYS in the neighborhood I loved to hang out in   1
the vacant lots nearby. The lots represented a natural wilderness, a place where the kids could get together to practice a kind of instinctive alchemy. We could transform thrown-away lumber into airplanes and swords, turn dogs and cats into jungle beasts and dragons, and make cardboard boxes and dirt mounds into forts and battleships. Behind the wall of lush weeds and grasses, we created a mythic realm where the forces of good and evil could play themselves out with wild abandon. For me, it was a place of fundamental sacredness. Rooted in rich Nebraska earth and my fertile imagination, I made up chants and spells, swore oaths, created and inscribed runes, and evoked the gods. This was the happiest and healthiest period of my life.

About the time I left the primary grades, things began to change.   2
I learned that the sacred belonged in church, that stories of mythic heroes and fabulous quests weren't for real, and that magic and witchcraft were bad. I learned that being dirty and sweaty and loud and passionate weren't okay. And all this at a time when my hormones were really beginning to kick in. I began a period of profound confusion and self-consciousness that lasted well into manhood.

Somehow I made it through the usual rites of passage into manhood. I came to live in a man's body and have a man's name. I got good at sports and drank beer with the guys. I did the mandatory flirting with death by climbing mountains in Colorado and driving like a madman. I learned to hide my feelings and act as though I knew what I was doing at all times, especially around women. I fathered two children, paid taxes, voted, and had a decent job. I was miserable.

Something was missing, and I had no idea what it was. I felt a deep longing, but I was so busy making a living and being a nice guy that I couldn't really touch some essential part of myself. In fact, I had been trained not to. The world was pulling too hard on the outside for me to notice the inside. I had to find out from others what I really wanted. My family and friends, the advertisers and authorities were more than happy to tell me. I needed "stuff," endless stuff, that I had to work my ass off to get, to keep, and to maintain. I needed to follow a lot of written and often unwritten rules if I wanted to be really successful. And it was totally my fault if I didn't make it.

I was convinced that there weren't any other guys like me out there. I never heard other guys expressing personal doubts about themselves, only complaining about their wives or girlfriends, talking sports, or expressing frustration about their jobs. I couldn't trust men; they were the competition. I found, however, that I could confide in certain women; they could understand my feelings. They could cry or express uncertainties. A deep part of me wanted that. I had been bonded to my mom; she had been my source of nourishment both physically and emotionally. I couldn't go to Dad for that stuff. If he and I talked at all, it was about how I was doing in school or at work and arguing about politics. So I found myself dependent on women for emotional needs, not really as adults, more as substitute mothers. I came to judge my manhood by comparison. All the cues about manhood were outside me, separate from my deeper self. With both men and women there was a constant need to keep checking. I felt manly if I could compete successfully with men and if I was very different from women.

I knew things weren't working, yet I kept trying to do more, and bigger, and better. Nothing seemed to be enough. After a divorce and a series of deadend relationships with women, in desperation I reached out to a couple of men I knew at work. Slowly, but surely, I started to get the feeling that maybe there were other men like me and that I could talk to them about how I really felt. I began to trust those men more deeply and in the process started to trust myself more. I dropped some of my walls and the struggle to measure myself against others.

I read the works of Carlos Castaneda and Joseph Campbell and an interview with Robert Bly titled "What Do Men Really Want?" Something began to come alive in me: A more primitive, younger, and wilder side that had been man. And I find that I am not alone. Most of my Council brothers are also questers and wild men and warriors and pilgrims, spiraling in and out of a great labyrinth. We are meeting and exploring ways to connect with our deepest selves and the earth, to bring that into our communities and to create a sustainable culture.

As we men gather to live out the truths of ourselves, we discover the value of our secular rites of passage and we cocreate new sacred ones that honor our manhood. Only when we have accepted ourselves and our brothers as men can we become fully humanized adults. This is not a one-time process. Nor can it be in this age. We are not conforming to a set of traditional beliefs or established doctrines. We are living in the mystery of what we will become. To do this, we need all our brothers. We must use the grief, the anger, the fear, and the wildness to take us down into our souls.

One of the beauties for me in this self-reclamation project is that I am now defining myself more from an internal place and can meet both men and women out of shared interest and not so much out of competition and dependency. Everything I do, be it writing for this book, changing my godson's diapers, or putting a supportive arm around a brother, is manly and comes more from myself. I can see the world with more clarity now, and paradoxically that makes the world far more mysterious. This awareness has a price. I feel the pain in others and in the earth. My choices seem infinitely more complex and difficult. Being adult and male is a huge responsibility. Fortunately, I now understand that this is not to be done alone. I have Council brothers and many sisters who enjoy this serious and blissful business of dancing in the cracks between worlds.

Questions on Meaning

1. Why did Daly as a boy love "to hang out in the vacant lots nearby"? What are his associations with these places? How do they change as he grows older? (Paragraph 2)
2. Why did Daly feel he could not trust other men? What made it possible for him to confide in women?

3. Explain the last paragraph of the essay. To what extent do you agree with Daly about the price of awareness?

Questions on Method

1. Reevaluating his manhood involves Daly in the process of confronting stereotypes that he was expected as a male to embrace or reject. List some of these.
2. Review Daly's introduction and conclusion and cite examples of his effective use of detail.

Writing Topics

1. Write an essay on the thematic significance of Daly's title and its relation to the process he describes in his essay.
2. Write an essay that describes the process by which you taught someone to do or understand something new to him or her.
3. Daly writes: "Somehow I made it through the usual rites of passage into manhood." Describe the process you went through to reach manhood or womanhood, including the extent to which it was similar to or different from Daly's experience.

On Transcendental Metaworry (TMW)

Lewis Thomas (1913–1993), born in Flushing, New York, attended Prince-
ton University and Harvard Medical School. He held teaching, research, and
administrative positions at several medical schools and hospitals including
Johns Hopkins, Cornell, Harvard, and Massachusetts General. Although he
had a distinguished career in medicine, he is more widely known for his es-
says, which are often poetic, personal, and philosophical. He began to write a
monthly column for the New England Journal of Medicine *in 1971,*
which is when he came to the attention of the reading public. His books in-
clude Lives of a Cell *(1974), for which he won a National Book Award,*
The Medusa and the Snail *(1979),* Late Night Thoughts on Listening to Mahler's Ninth Symphony *(1983), and* Etcetera, Etcetera
(1990), all essay collections; and The Young Science *(1983), a memoir*
about becoming a doctor.

IT IS SAID that modern, industrialized, civilized human beings are uniquely nervous and jumpy, unprecedentedly disturbed by the future, despaired by the present, sleepless at memories of the recent past, all because of the technological complexity and noisiness of the machinery by which we are surrounded, and the rigidified apparatus of cold steel and plastic which we have constructed between ourselves and the earth. Incessant worry, according to this view, is a modern invention. To turn it off, all we need do is turn off the engines and climb down into the countryside. Primitive man, rose-garlanded, slept well. 1

I doubt this. Man has always been a specifically anxious creature with an almost untapped capacity for worry; it is a gift that distinguishes him from other forms of life. There is undoubtedly a neural center deep in the human brain for mediating this function, like the centers for hunger or sleep. 2

Prehistoric man, without tools or fire to be thinking about, must have been the most anxious of us all. Fumbling about in dimly lit caves, trying to figure out what he ought really to be doing, sensing the awesome responsibilities for toolmaking just ahead, he must have 3 spent a lot of time contemplating his thumbs and fretting about them. I can imagine him staring at his hands, apposing thumbtips to each fingertip in amazement, thinking, By God, that's something to set us apart from the animals—and then the grinding thought, What on earth are they for? There must have been many long, sleepless nights, his mind all thumbs.

It would not surprise me to learn that there were ancient prefire committees, convened to argue that thumbs might be taking us too far, that we'd have been better off with simply another finger of the usual sort.   4

Worrying is the most natural and spontaneous of all human functions. It is time to acknowledge this, perhaps even to learn to do it better. Man is the Worrying Animal. It is a trait needing further development, awaiting perfection. Most of us tend to neglect the activity, living precariously out on the thin edge of anxiety but never plunging in.   5

For total immersion in the experience of pure, illuminating harassment, I can recommend a modification of the technique of Transcendental Meditation, which I stumbled across after reading an article on the practice in a scholarly magazine and then trying it on myself, sitting on an overturned, stove-in canoe under a beech tree in my backyard. Following closely the instructions, I relaxed, eyes closed, breathing regularly, repeating a recommended mantra, in this instance the word "oom," over and over. The conditions were suitable for withdrawal and detachment; my consciousness, which normally spends its time clutching for any possible handhold, was prepared to cut adrift. Then, suddenly, the telephone began to ring inside the house, rang several times between breathed "oom"s, and stopped. In the instant, I discovered Transcendental Worry.   6

Transcendental Worry can be engaged in at any time, by anyone, regardless of age, sex, or occupation, and in almost any circumstance. For beginners, I advise twenty-minute sessions, in the morning before work and late in the evening just before insomnia.   7

What you do is sit down someplace, preferably by yourself, and tense all muscles. If you make yourself reasonably uncomfortable at the outset, by sitting on a canoe bottom, say, the tension will come naturally. Now close the eyes, concentrate on this until the effort causes a slight tremor of the eyelids. Now breathe, thinking analytically about the muscular effort involved; it is useful to attempt breathing through one nostril at a time, alternating sides.   8

Now, the mantra. The word "worry," repeated quite rapidly, is   9
itself effective, because of the allusive cognates in its history. Thus, in-
truding into the recitation of the mantra comes the recollection that it
derives from the Indo-European root *wer,* meaning to turn or bend in
the sense of evading, which became *wyrgan* in Old English, meaning to
kill by strangling, with close relatives "weird," "writhe," "wriggle,"
"wrestle," and "wrong." "Wrong" is an equally useful mantra, for
symmetrical reasons.

Next, try to float your consciousness free. You will feel some-   10
thing like this happening after about three minutes, and, almost simultaneously with the floating, yawing and sinking will begin. This
complex of conjoined sensations becomes an awareness of concentrated, irreversible trouble.

Finally you will begin to hear the *zing,* if you are successful. This   11
is a distant, rhythmic sound, not timed with either the breathing or the
mantra. After several minutes, you will discover by taking your pulse
that the *zing* is synchronous, and originates somewhere in the lower
part of the head or perhaps high up in the neck, presumably due to
turbulence at the bend of an artery, maybe even the vibration of a small
plaque. Now you are In Touch.

Nothing remains but to allow the intensification of Transcen-   12
dental Worry to proceed spontaneously to the next stage, termed the
Primal Wince. En route, you pass through an almost confluent series
of pictures, random and transient, jerky and running at overspeed like
an old movie, many of them seemingly trivial but each associated
with a sense of dropping abruptly through space (it is useful, here, to
recall that "vertigo" also derives from *wer*). You may suddenly see,
darting across the mind like a shrieking plumed bird, a current
electric-light bill, or the vision of numbers whirring too fast to read
on a gasoline pump, or the last surviving humpback whale, singing a
final song into empty underseas, or simply the television newscast an-
nouncing that détente now signifies a Soviet-American Artificial-
Heart Project. Or late bulletins from science concerning the pulsing
showers of neutrino particles, aimed personally by collapsing stars,
which cannot be escaped from even at the bottom of salt mines in
South Dakota. Watergate, of course. The music of John Cage. The ascending slopes of chalked curves on academic blackboards, inter-
changeably predicting the future population of pet dogs in America,
rats in Harlem, nuclear explosions overhead and down in salt mines,
suicides in Norway, crop failures in India, the number of people at

large. The thought of moon gravity as a cause of baldness. The unpreventability of continental drift. The electronic guitar. The slipping away of things, the feel of rugs sliding out from under everywhere. These images become confluent and then amorphous, melting together into a solid, gelatinous thought of skewness. When this happens, you will be entering the last stage, which is pure worry about pure worry. This is the essence of the Wisdom of the West, and I shall call it Transcendental Metaworry (TMW).

Now, as to the usefulness of TMW. First of all, it tends to fill the mind completely at times when it would otherwise be empty. Instead of worrying at random, continually and subliminally, wondering always what it is that you've forgotten and ought to be worrying about, you get the full experience, all in a rush, on a schedule which you arrange for yourself. 13

Secondly, it makes the times of the day when there is really nothing to worry about intensely pleasurable, because of the contrast. 14

Thirdly, I have forgotten the third advantage, which is itself one less thing to worry about. 15

There are, of course, certain disadvantages, which must be faced up to. TMW is, admittedly, a surrogate experience, a substitute for the real thing, and in this sense there is always the danger of overdoing it. Another obvious danger is the likely entry of technology into the field. I have no doubt that there will soon be advertisements in the back pages of small literary magazines, offering for sale, money back if dissatisfied (or satisfied), electronic devices encased in black plastic boxes with dials, cathode screens, earphones with simulated sonic booms, and terminals to be affixed at various areas of the scalp so that brain waves associated with pure TMW can be identified and volitionally selected. These will be marketed under attractive trade names, like the Angst Amplifier or the Artificial Heartsink. The thought of such things is something else to worry about, but perhaps not much worse than the average car radio. 16

Questions on Meaning

1. According to Thomas, why is it said that worry is "a modern invention"? Why does Thomas disagree?
2. How did Thomas stumble across the technique of Transcendental Metaworry? Why does he recommend such a "total immersion in the experience of pure, illuminating harassment"?

3. What steps must one perform before hearing what Thomas refers to in paragraph 11 as "the *zing*"? Once one is "In Touch," what sort of thoughts and images are experienced en route to entering "the last stage"? What happens during this last stage?
4. In what ways, according to Thomas, is TMW useful? What are its disadvantages?

Questions on Method

1. "On Transcendental Metaworry" is a **parody.** What sort of serious process analysis is Thomas mocking in his essay?
2. A parody's humor often derives from the way the parodist undercuts or reverses our usual expectations and standards of judgment. How does Thomas's parody do this?
3. In paragraph 12, Thomas offers a long list of examples of thoughts and images that dart across the mind as one slips into a state of pure TMW. How satirical are these examples? Where else does the humor of the essay become satirical?

Writing Topics

1. How seriously do you take the worry about life that Thomas expresses? Is it possible that worrying can be beneficial at times? Write an essay that describes seriously a way to use worry to one's benefit.
2. Try writing a parody of some process that you think people perform either too seriously or not seriously enough.
3. Write a process analysis that instructs the reader how to do something you do well. Attempt to dramatize your essay in a step-by-step sequence and still make it clear when more than one step must be performed at the same time.

Process Analysis — *Writing Topics*

1. Write an essay in which you narrate a step-by-step process you perform regularly; include descriptions of how you feel and what you think about as you perform each step.

2. Analyze the thought process you went through in making an important decision. Explain how and why one step or thought led to the next and so on until you reached your final decision. Did this process lead to a repeatable or teachable method? Explain it. What audience might find this method useful? Try to appeal to this audience.

3. Write an essay in which you describe a process that you perform in order to relax. Does the way in which you relax reveal anything about your philosophy of life, about what things in life you consider important and valuable?

4. Describe the process you went through to find a summer job. Be as practical as possible, use a tone that is matter of fact, and include the chronology of each step in your process.

5. Describe how you were taught to write in high school and college. Use your description as part of an essay that explains what you think would be the most effective way to learn how to write well.

9

Classification

CLASSIFICATION, LIKE SORTING CLOTHES or silverware, is an act of organizing. The Yellow Pages, classified ads, and catalogs and indexes of all kinds use classification to bring order to a subject or a set of things by showing the relationship of parts to the whole and to one another. Classification is one of the best ways to understand and explain a subject.

When making a classification, you are asking the question "What kinds of *x* are there?" and are grouping these kinds on the basis of resemblances and differences. Classification, indeed, can be viewed as a special application of comparison and contrast. For example, in the system devised by the botanist Charles Linnaeus all plants and animals have two names, the first being the name of the genus; the second, of the species. Thus similarity gives to all carnations the common name *Dianthus,* and the differences among carnations are accounted for by the names *Dianthus prolifer, Dianthus barbatus, Dianthus deltoides,* and many more. (A good classification would never include the phrase "and many more" or the abbreviation "etc.," for a classification must be a complete list of classes.) The members of a class, therefore, are all alike in some one way, and that way (or basis of classification) must be applied throughout the system. If you have a choice of several bases of classification, choose the one that fits your purpose for making a classification. Linnaeus's basis—structure or morphology rather than, say, appearance—allows for the widest application to a continually growing field of knowledge, which was his main purpose. But plants can also be classified according to their food value, their medical use, their scent, their environment, their mythological associations, and so on.

Suppose your purpose—more modest than Linnaeus's—is to persuade the local school board to spend more money on certain sports. You might begin by classifying them, using as your basis of classification the objective you want to promote. Some possible bases might be (a) popularity with townspeople and alumni, (b) local traditions, (c) age at which the sport can be played, (d) number of players required, and (e) cost. You can see what a different classification each basis would produce. Your choice would finally have to depend on your purpose for making the classification—for example, to convince the board to budget more money for lifelong sports like tennis and swimming. Having chosen the basis, you would include every sport that fits your classes and exclude all others; you would choose and label your classes so that a sport fits into only one class. You could not divide sports into the categories of soccer, basketball, and tennis because your system would be incomplete. You could not divide sports into winter, summer, and team because some sports would fit into two classes, making the division meaningless.

Not every subject can be easily classified, and many bases of classification do not provide clear-cut classes. One of the bases for classifying sports noted above, cost, will not provide clear-cut classes: Is a sport that uses $100 worth of equipment different in kind from one that uses $101 worth? The color red shades imperceptibly into reddish orange; the compass direction west into west-northwest and northwest; and middle class, into lower middle class. In a continuum or spectrum, the basis of classification becomes more important than the classes because, instead of absolute and fixed classes, we have trends or tendencies toward one or the other end of the spectrum. More of our classes than we often realize are arbitrary points on a continuum—"the Middle Ages," "animal," "person." If you find it difficult to answer the question "What kinds of person are there?" you may have to settle for a spectrum on which people "tend" toward one pole or the other rather than for a set of absolute classes into which they fit. Even so, if you can devise such a spectrum, you will have brought some order to the subject.

Having devised a system, use other expository modes to develop it, such as explaining your purpose and the basis of classification, defining class names, and perhaps comparing your system with less adequate ones. Narration and description may also come to your aid.

WRITING CLASSIFICATION

1. Choose a basis of classification that serves your purpose.
2. Provide only one class for every part.
3. Develop your outline with examples, description, definition, process analysis, or cause and effect.

ANNE NORTON

The Signs of Shopping

We are not only what we eat but what we wear and buy. Shopping malls, cat-
alogs, and home shopping networks influence our identities and may even af-
fect how we act. Anne Norton (b. 1954), a political science professor at the
University of Pennsylvania, investigates the profound effect such seemingly
innocent cultural entities may have on our lives in a selection from her book
The Republic of Signs *(1993). She has also written* Alternative Amer-
icas *(1986) and* Reflections on Political Identity *(1988).*

SHOPPING AT THE MALL

THE MALL has been the subject of innumerable debates. Created   1
out of the modernist impulse for planning and the centralization of
public activity, the mall has become the distinguishing sign of suburban
decentralization, springing up in unplanned profusion. Intended to restore something of the lost unity of city life to the suburbs, the mall has
come to export styles and strategies to stores at the urban center. De-
plored by modernists, it is regarded with affection only by their postmodern foes. Ruled more by their content than by their creators'
avowed intent, the once sleek futurist shells have taken on a certain
aura of postmodern playfulness and popular glitz.

The mall is a favorite subject for the laments of cultural conserva-   2
tives and others critical of the culture of consumption. It is indisput-
ably the cultural locus of commodity fetishism. It has been noticed,
however, by others of a less condemnatory disposition that the mall has
something of the mercado, or the agora, about it. It is both a place of
meeting for the young and one of the rare places where young and old
go together. People of different races and classes, different occupations,
different levels of education meet there. As M. Pressdee and John Fiske
note, however, though the mall appears to be a public place, it is not.
Neither freedom of speech nor freedom of assembly is permitted there.
Those who own and manage malls restrict what comes within their

confines. Controversial displays, by stores or customers or the plethora
of organizations and agencies that present themselves in the open
spaces of the mall, are not permitted. These seemingly public spaces
conceal a pervasive private authority.

The mall exercises its thorough and discreet authority not only in   3
the regulation of behavior but in the constitution of our visible, inau-
dible, public discourse. It is the source of those commodities through
which we speak of our identities, our opinions, our desires. It is a focus
for the discussion of style among peripheral consumers. Adolescents,
particularly female adolescents, are inclined to spend a good deal of
time at the mall. They spend, indeed, more time than money. They
acquire not simple commodities (they may come home with many,
few, or none) but a well-developed sense of the significance of those
commodities. In prowling the mall they embed themselves in a lexicon
of American culture. They find themselves walking through a dictionary. Stores hang a variety of identities on their racks and mannequins.
Their window displays provide elaborate scenarios conveying not only
what the garment is but what the garment means.

A display in the window of Polo provides an embarrassment of   4
semiotic riches. Everyone, from the architecture critic at the *New York
Times* to kids in the hall of a Montana high school, knows what *Ralph
Lauren* means. The polo mallet and the saddle, horses and dogs, the
broad lawns of Newport, Kennebunkport, old photographs in silver
frames, the evocation of age, of ancestry and Anglophilia, of indolence
and the Ivy League, evoke the upper class. Indian blankets and buffalo
plaids, cowboy hats and Western saddles, evoke a past distinct from England, but nevertheless determinedly Anglo. The supposedly arcane
and suspect arts of deconstruction are deployed easily, effortlessly, by
the readers of these cultural texts.

Walking from one window to another, observing one another,   5
shoppers, especially the astute and observant adolescents, acquire a fa-
cility with the language of commodities. They learn not only words
but a grammar. Shop windows employ elements of sarcasm and irony,
strategies of inversion and allusion. They provide models of elegant,
economical, florid, and prosaic expression. They teach composition.

The practice of shopping is, however, more than instructive. It   6
has long been the occasion for women to escape the confines of their
homes and enjoy the companionship of other women. The construction of woman's role as one of provision for the needs of the family le-
gitimated her exit. It provided an occasion for women to spend long
stretches of time in the company of their friends, without the presence

of their husbands. They could exchange information and reflections, ask advice, and receive support. As their daughters grew, they would be brought increasingly within this circle, included in shopping trips and lunches with their mothers. These would form, reproduce, and restructure communities of taste.

The construction of identity and the enjoyment of friendship outside the presence of men was thus effected through a practice that constructed women as consumers and subjected them to the conventions of the marketplace. Insofar as they were dependent on their husbands for money, they were dependent on their husbands for the means to the construction of their identities. They could not represent themselves through commodities without the funds men provided, nor could they, without money, participate in the community of women that was realized in "going shopping." Their identities were made contingent not only on the possession of property but on the recognition of dependence.

Insofar as shopping obliges dependent women to recognize their dependence, it also opens up the possibility of subversion.[1] The housewife who shops for pleasure takes time away from her husband, her family, and her house and claims it for herself. Constantly taught that social order and her private happiness depend on intercourse between men and women, she chooses the company of women instead. She engages with women in an activity marked as feminine, and she enjoys it. When she spends money, she exercises an authority over property that law and custom may deny her. If she has no resources independent of her husband, this may be the only authority over property she is able to exercise. When she buys things her husband does not approve—or does not know—of she further subverts an order that leaves control over property in her husband's hands.[2]

Her choice of feminine company and a feminine pursuit may involve additional subversions. As Fiske and Pressdee recognize, shopping without buying and shopping for bargains have a subversive quality. This is revealed, in a form that gives it additional significance, when a saleswoman leans forward and tells a shopper, "Don't buy that

7

8

9

---

[1]Nuanced and amusing accounts of shopping as subversion are provided in John Fiske's analyses of popular culture, particularly *Reading the Popular* (Boston: Unwin Hyman [now Routledge], 1989), pp. 13–42.

[2]See R. Bowlby, *Just Looking: Consumer Culture in Dreiser, Gissing, and Zola* (London: Methuen, 1985), p. 22, for another discussion and for an example of the recommendation of this strategy by Elizabeth Cady Stanton in the 1850s.

today, it will be on sale on Thursday." Here solidarity of gender (and
often of class) overcome, however partially and briefly, the imperatives
of the economic order.

Shoppers who look, as most shoppers do, for bargains, and sales-   10
people who warn shoppers of impending sales, see choices between
commodities as something other than the evidence and the exercise of
freedom. They see covert direction and exploitation; they see the
withholding of information and the manipulation of knowledge. They
recognize that they are on enemy terrain and that their shopping can
be, in Michel de Certeau's term, a "guerrilla raid." This recognition in
practice of the presence of coercion in choice challenges the liberal
conflation of choice and consent.

SHOPPING AT HOME

Shopping is an activity that has overcome its geographic limits.   11
One need no longer go to the store to shop. Direct mail catalogues,
with their twenty-four-hour phone numbers for ordering, permit
people to shop where and when they please. An activity that once
obliged one to go out into the public sphere, with its diverse array of
semiotic messages, can now be done at home. An activity that once
obliged one to be in company, if not in conversation, with one's com-
patriots can now be conducted in solitude.

The activity of catalogue shopping, and the pursuit of individuality,   12
are not, however, wholly solitary. The catalogues invest their commodities with vivid historical and social references. The J. Peterman catalogue, for example, constructs the reader as a man of rugged outdoor
interests, taste, and money.[3] He wears "The Owner's Hat" or "Heming-
way's Cap," a leather flight jacket or the "Horseman's Duster," and various other garments identified with the military, athletes, and European
imperialism. The copy for "The Owner's Hat" naturalizes class distinctions and, covertly, racism:

---

[3]I have read several of these. I cite *The J. Peterman Company Owner's Manual No. 5,*
from the J. Peterman Company, 2444 Palumbo Drive, Lexington, Ky. 40509.

[4]Ibid., p. 5. The hat is also identified with the Canal Zone, "successfully bidding at
Beaulieu," intimidation, and LBOs. Quite a hat. It might be argued against my
reading that the J. Peterman Company also offers the "Coal Miner's Bag" and a
mailbag. However, since the descriptive points of reference on color and texture and
experience for these bags are such things as the leather seats of Jaguars, and driving
home in a Bentley, I feel fairly confident in my reading.

Some of us work on the plantation.
Some of us own the plantation.
Facts are facts.
This hat is for those who own the plantation.[4]

Gender roles are strictly delineated. The copy for a skirt captioned
"Women's Legs" provides a striking instance of the construction of the
gaze as male, of women as the object of the gaze:

> just when you think you see something, a shape you think you rec-
> ognize, it's gone and then it begins to return and then it's gone and
> of course you can't take your eyes off it.
>
> Yes, the long slow motion of women's legs. Whatever hap-
> pened to those things at carnivals that blew air up into girls' skirts
> and you could spend hours watching.[5]

"You," of course, are male. There is also the lace blouse captioned
"Mystery": "lace says yes at the same time it says no."[6] Finally, there
are notes of imperialist nostalgia: the Sheapherd's Hotel (Cairo) bath-
robe and white pants for "the bush" and "the humid hell-holes of
Bombay and Calcutta."[7]

> It may no longer be unforgivable to say that the British left a
> few good things behind in India and in Kenya, Singapore, Borneo,
> etc., not the least of which was their Englishness.[8]

As Paul Smith observes, in his reading of their catalogues, the *Ba-* 13
nana Republic has also made capital out of imperial nostalgia.[9]

The communities catalogues create are reinforced by shared mail- 14
ing lists. The constructed identities are reified and elaborated in an array of semiotically related catalogues. One who orders a spade or a
packet of seed will be constructed as a gardener and receive a deluge of
catalogues from plant and garden companies. The companies themselves may expand their commodities to appeal to different manifesta-
tions of the identities they respond to and construct. Smith and

[5]Ibid., p. 3. See also pp. 15 and 17 for instances of women as objects of the male gaze.
The identification of the gaze with male sexuality is unambiguous here as well.

[6]Ibid., p. 17.

[7]Ibid., pp. 7, 16, 20, 21, 37, and 50.

[8]Ibid., p 20.

[9]Paul Smith, "Visiting the Banana Republic," in *Universal Abandon?* ed. Andrew Ross
for Social Text (Minneapolis: University of Minnesota Press, 1988), pp. 128–48.

Hawken, a company that sells gardening supplies with an emphasis on aesthetics and environmental concern, puts out a catalogue in which a group of people diverse in age and in their ethnicity wear the marketed clothes while gardening, painting, or throwing pots. Williams–Sonoma presents its catalogue not as a catalogue of things for cooking but as "A Catalogue for Cooks." The catalogue speaks not to need but to the construction of identity.

The Nature Company dedicates its spring 1990 catalogue "to   15 trees," endorses Earth Day, and continues to link itself to *The Nature Conservancy* through posters and a program in which you buy a tree for a forest restoration project. Here, a not-for-profit agency is itself commodified, adding to the value of the commodities offered in the catalogue.[10] In this catalogue, consumption is not merely a means for the construction and representation of the self, it is also a means for political action. Several commodities are offered as "A Few Things You Can Do" to save the earth: a string shopping bag, a solar battery recharger, a home newspaper recycler. Socially conscious shopping is a liberal practice in every sense. It construes shopping as a form of election, in which one votes for good commodities or refuses one's vote to candidates whose practices are ethically suspect. In this respect, it reveals its adherence to the same ideological presuppositions that structure television's Home Shopping Network and other cable television sales shows.

Both politically informed purchasing and television sales conflate   16 the free market and the electoral process. Dollars are identified with votes, purchases with endorsements. Both offer those who engage in them the possibility to "talk back" to manufacturers. In television sales shows this ability to talk back is both more thoroughly elaborated and more thoroughly exploited. Like the "elections" on MTV that invite viewers to vote for their favorite video by calling a number on their telephones, they permit those who watch to respond, to speak, and to be heard by the television. Their votes, of course, cost money. On MTV, as in the stores, you can buy as much speech as you can afford. On the Home Shopping Network, the purchase of speech becomes complicated by multiple layers and inversions.

Each commodity is introduced. It is invested by the announcer   17 with a number of desirable qualities. The value of these descriptions of

---

[10] *The Nature Company Catalog,* The Nature Company, P.O. Box 2310, Berkeley, Calif. 94702, Spring 990. See pp. 1–2 and order form insert between pp. 18 and 19. Note also the entailed donation to Designs for Conservation on p. 18.

the commodities is enhanced by the construction of the announcer as a mediator not only between the commodity and the consumer but between the salespeople and the consumer. The announcer is not, the format suggests, a salesperson (though of course the announcer is). He or she is an announcer, describing goods that others have offered for sale. Television claims to distinguish itself by making objects visible to the eyes, but it is largely through the ears that these commodities are constructed. The consumer, in purchasing the commodity, purchases the commodity, what the commodity signifies, and, as we say, "buys the salesperson's line." The consumer may also acquire the ability to speak on television. Each purchase is recorded and figures as a vote in a rough plebiscite, confirming the desirability of the object. Although the purchase figures are announced as if they were confirming votes, it is, of course, impossible to register one's rejection of the commodity. Certain consumers get a little more (or rather less) for their money. They are invited to explain the virtue of the commodity—and their purchase—to the announcer and the audience. The process of production, of both the consumers and that which they consume, continues in this apology for consumption.

The semiotic identification of consumption as an American activity, indeed, a patriotic one, is made with crude enthusiasm on the Home Shopping Network and other video sales shows. Red, white, and blue figure prominently in set designs and borders framing the television screen. The Home Shopping Network presents its authorities in an office conspicuously adorned with a picture of the Statue of Liberty.[11] Yet the messages that the Home Shopping Network sends its customers—that you can buy as much speech as you can afford, that you are recognized by others in accordance with your capacity to consume—do much to subvert the connection between capitalism and democracy on which this semiotic identification depends.   18

Questions on Meaning

1. At the end of paragraph 2, Norton writes of shopping malls that "these seemingly public spaces conceal a pervasive private authority." What does she mean? What evidence does she cite?

[11]This moment from the Home Shopping Network was generously brought to my attention, on videotape, by Peter Bregman, a student in my American Studies class of fall 1988, at Princeton University.

2. Do you agree with Norton that shopping in the mall teaches familiarity with "the language of communities"? What examples would you add?
3. How, according to Norton, has shopping affected women's identities, including their relationships? Do you agree with her gender analysis? Why or why not?

Questions on Method

1. Norton claims that the language of mail-order catalogs exhibits a sophisticated awareness of audience. What examples does she cite to support her thesis?
2. What evidence does Norton offer to persuade her audience that the Home Shopping Network presents "consumption" as a "patriotic" activity?

Writing Topics

1. Test Norton's thesis on the targeting of window displays to a particular audience by visiting a shopping mall and focusing on one or two displays. Pay attention to specific details and write an analysis of how effectively they appeal to their intended audience.
2. Browse through several mail-order catalogs and analyze their consumer appeal. Who is the intended audience? Is there a pitch for gender and ethnicity? What other classifications do you discern?

ANNA LISA RAYA

It's Hard Enough Being Me

Anna Lisa Raya was born in the United States of a second-generation Mexican American father and a Puerto Rican mother. Raya grew up in a Mexican neighborhood of Los Angeles. Although she saw herself as part of Los Angeles's multicultural majority, she was unprepared for the identity problems she would encounter as a multicultural American in the academic environment of Columbia University in New York City, where she majored in English and was a member of the Columbia College class of 1995. She contributed articles to Columbia College Today *in which she looked at ethnic labeling. Raya's frustrations, although focused on her attempts to define a multicultural self, are also universal, directed as they are at reconciling our views of ourselves with the images that are often imposed from the outside.*

WHEN I ENTERED COLLEGE, I *discovered* I was Latina. Until then, I had never questioned who I was or where I was from: My father is a second-generation Mexican-American, born and raised in Los Angeles, and my mother was born in Puerto Rico and raised in Compton, Calif. My home is El Sereno, a predominantly Mexican neighborhood in L.A. Every close friend I have back home is Mexican. So I was always just Mexican. Though sometimes I was just Puerto Rican—like when we would visit Mamo (my grandma) or hang out with my Aunt Titi.

Upon arriving in New York as a first-year student, 3000 miles from home, I not only experienced extreme culture shock, but for the first time I had to define myself according to the broad term "Latina." Although culture shock and identity crisis are common for the newly minted collegian who goes away to school, my experience as a newly minted Latina was, and still is, even more complicating. In El Sereno, I felt like I was part of a majority, whereas at the College I am a minority.

I've discovered that many Latinos like myself have undergone similar experiences. We face discrimination for being a minority in this country while also facing criticism for being "whitewashed" or "sellouts" in the countries of our heritage. But as an ethnic group in college, we are forced to define ourselves according to some vague, generalized Latino experience. This requires us to know our history, our language, our music, and our religion. I can't even be a content "Puerto Mexican" because I have to be a politically-and-socially-aware-Latina-with-a-chip-on-my-shoulder-because-of-how-repressed-I-am-in-this-country.

I am none of the above. I am the quintessential imperfect Latina. 4
I can't dance salsa to save my life, I learned about Montezuma and the Aztecs in sixth grade, and I haven't prayed to the *Virgen de Guadalupe* in years.

Apparently I don't even look Latina. I can't count how many 5
times people have just assumed that I'm white or asked me if I'm Asian. True, my friends back home call me *güera* ("whitey") because I have green eyes and pale skin, but that was as bad as it got. I never thought I would wish my skin were a darker shade or my hair a curlier texture, but since I've been in college, I have—many times.

Another thing: my Spanish is terrible. Every time I call home, I be- 6
rate my mama for not teaching me Spanish when I was a child. In fact, not knowing how to speak the language of my home countries is the biggest problem that I have encountered, as have many Latinos. In Mexico there is a term, *pocha,* which is used by native Mexicans to ridicule Mexican-Americans. It expresses a deep-rooted antagonism and dislike for those of us who were raised on the other side of the border. Our failed attempts to speak pure, Mexican Spanish are largely responsible for the dislike. Other Latin American natives have this same attitude. No matter how well a Latino speaks Spanish, it can never be good enough.

Yet Latinos can't even speak Spanish in the U.S. without running 7
the risk of being called "spic" or "wetback." That is precisely why my mother refused to teach me Spanish when I was a child. The fact that she spoke Spanish was constantly used against her: It prevented her from getting good jobs, and it would have placed me in bilingual education—a construct of the Los Angeles public school system that has proved to be more of a hindrance to intellectual development than a help.

To be fully Latina in college, however, I *must* know Spanish. I 8
must satisfy the equation: Latina = Spanish-speaking.

So I'm stuck in this black hole of an identity crisis, and college 9
isn't making my life any easier, as I thought it would. In high school, I was being prepared for an adulthood in which I would be an individual, in which I wouldn't have to wear a Catholic school uniform anymore. But though I led an anonymous adolescence, I knew who I was. I knew I was different from white, black, or Asian people. I knew there

was a language other than English that I could call my own if I only knew how to speak it better. I knew there were historical reasons why I was in this country, distinct reasons that make my existence here easier or more difficult than other people's existence. Ultimately, I was content.

Now I feel pushed into a corner, always defining, defending, and 10 proving myself to classmates, professors, or employers. Trying to understand who and why I am, while understanding Plato or Homer, is a lot to ask of myself.

A month ago, I heard three Nuyorican (Puerto Ricans born and 11 raised in New York) writers discuss how New York City has influenced their writing. One problem I have faced as a young writer is finding a voice that is true to my community. I was surprised and reassured to discover that as Latinos, these writers had faced similar pressures and conflicts as myself; some weren't even taught Spanish in childhood. I will never forget the advice that one of them gave me that evening: She said that I need to be true to myself. "Because people will always complain about what you are doing—you're a 'gringa' or a 'spic' no matter what," she explained. "So you might as well do things for yourself and not for them."

I don't know why it has taken 20 years to hear this advice, but 12 I'm going to give it a try. *Soy yo* and no one else. *Punto.*★

Questions on Meaning

1. "When I entered college, I *discovered* I was Latina." How does this experience affect Raya? Give examples.
2. Why does Raya criticize her mother for not teaching her Spanish as a child?
3. What is her attitude toward bilingual education? How does it compare with yours?

Questions on Method

1. Comment on Raya's use of minority and majority in the essay. In what classification process does she become involved as a "Latina"?
2. Create a profile of the audience most likely to respond to Raya's essay. How do you respond?

★*soy yo:* (Spanish) I am myself; *punto:* (Spanish) period, final.

Writing Topics

1. Describe the process Raya undergoes as she reclassifies herself from being "just Mexican" to "Latina."
2. Although the United States is supposed to be a melting pot, its people are divided into social classes. Write an essay in which you identify different types of Americans according to social class.

The Men We Carry in Our Minds

Scott Russell Sanders (b. 1945), born in Memphis, Tennessee, is currently a professor of English at Indiana University. After receiving a summa cum laude B.A. from Brown University, he went on to earn a Ph.D. at Cambridge University in England in 1971. Sanders, a prolific writer, has an impressive list of publications to his credit. He has written science fiction, realistic fiction, children's stories, literary criticism, historical novels, folktales, and essays. His published books include D. H. Lawrence: The World of Novels *(1974),* Wilderness Plots: Tales about the Settlement of the American Land *(1983),* Fetching the Dead: Stories *(1984),* Stone County *(1985),* Hear the Wind Blow: American Folksongs Retold *(1985), and* The Paradise of Bombs *(1987). He is the recipient of several grants and awards, including a Woodrow Wilson fellowship, a Marshall scholarship, and a Bennett fellowship in creative writing. In his work, Sanders explores the ways in which human beings come to terms with the political problems of living on a planet and interacting with nature and communities and expresses an interest in the lives people make together in marriage and family and towns.*

THE FIRST MEN, besides my father, I remember seeing were black convicts and white guards, in the cotton field across the road from our farm on the outskirts of Memphis. I must have been three or four. The prisoners wore dingy gray–and–black zebra suits, heavy as canvas, sodden with sweat. Hatless, stooped, they chopped weeds in the fierce heat, row after row, breathing the acrid dust of boll-weevil poison. The overseers wore dazzling white shirts and broad shadowy hats. The oiled barrels of their shotguns flashed in the sunlight. Their faces in memory are utterly blank. Of course those men, white and black, have become for me an emblem of racial hatred. But they have also come to stand for the twin poles of my early vision of manhood—the brute toiling animal and the boss. 1

When I was a boy, the men I knew labored with their bodies. They were marginal farmers, just scraping by, or welders, steelworkers, 2 carpenters; they swept floors, dug ditches, mined coal, or drove trucks, their forearms ropy with muscle; they trained horses, stoked furnaces, built fires, stood on assembly lines wrestling parts onto cars and refrigerators. They got up before light, worked all day long whatever the weather, and when they came home at night they looked as though somebody had been whipping them. In the evenings and on weekends they worked on their own places, tilling gardens that were lumpy with clay, fixing broken-down cars, hammering on houses that were always too drafty, too leaky, too small.

The bodies of the men I knew were twisted and maimed in ways   3
visible and invisible. The nails of their hands were black and split, the hands tattooed with scars. Some had lost fingers. Heavy lifting had given many of them finicky backs and guts weak from hernias. Racing against conveyor belts had given them ulcers. Their ankles and knees ached from years of standing on concrete. Anyone who had worked for long around machines was hard of hearing. They squinted, and the skin of their faces was creased like the leather of old work gloves. There were times, studying them, when I dreaded growing up. Most of them coughed, from dust or cigarettes, and most of them drank cheap wine or whisky, so their eyes looked bloodshot and bruised. The fathers of my friends always seemed older than the mothers. Men wore out sooner. Only women lived into old age.

As a boy I also knew another sort of men, who did not sweat and   4
break down like mules. They were soldiers, and so far as I could tell they scarcely worked at all. During my early school years we lived on a military base, an arsenal in Ohio, and every day I saw GIs in the guard shacks, on the stoops of barracks, at the wheels of olive drab Chevrolets. The chief fact of their lives was boredom. Long after I left the Arsenal I came to recognize the sour smell the soldiers gave off as that of souls in limbo. They were all waiting—for wars, for transfers, for leaves, for promotions, for the end of their hitch—like so many braves waiting for the hunt to begin. Unlike the warriors of older tribes, however, they would have no say about when the battle would start or how it would be waged. Their waiting was broken only when they practiced for war. They fired guns at targets, drove tanks across the churned-up fields of the military reservation, set off bombs in the wrecks of old fighter planes. I knew this was all play. But I also felt certain that when the hour for killing arrived, they would kill. When the real shooting started, many of them would die. This was what soldiers were *for*, just as a hammer was for driving nails.

Warriors and toilers: those seemed, in my boyhood vision, to be   5
the chief destinies for men. They weren't the only destinies, as I
learned from having a few male teachers, from reading books, and
from watching television. But the men on television—the politicians,
the astronauts, the generals, the savvy lawyers, the philosophical doctors, the bosses who gave orders to both soldiers and laborers—seemed
as removed and unreal to me as the figures in tapestries. I could no
more imagine growing up to become one of these cool, potent creatures than I could imagine becoming a prince.

A nearer and more hopeful example was that of my father, who   6
had escaped from a red-dirt farm to a tire factory, and from the assembly line to the front office. Eventually he dressed in a white shirt and
tie. He carried himself as if he had been born to work with his mind.
But his body, remembering the earlier years of slogging work, began to
give out on him in his fifties, and it quit on him entirely before he
turned sixty-five. Even such a partial escape from man's fate as he had
accomplished did not seem possible for most of the boys I knew. They
joined the Army, stood in line for jobs in the smoky plants, helped
build highways. They were bound to work as their fathers had worked,
killing themselves or preparing to kill others.

A scholarship enabled me not only to attend college, a rare   7
enough feat in my circle, but even to study in a university meant for
the children of the rich. Here I met for the first time young men who
had assumed from birth that they would lead lives of comfort and
power. And for the first time I met women who told me that men
were guilty of having kept all the joys and privileges of the earth for
themselves. I was baffled. What privileges? What joys? I thought about
the maimed, dismal lives of most of the men back home. What had
they stolen from their wives and daughters? The right to go five days a
week, twelve months a year, for thirty or forty years to a steel mill or a
coal mine? The right to drop bombs and die in war? The right to feel
every leak in the roof, every gap in the fence, every cough in the engine, as a wound they must mend? The right to feel, when the lay-off
comes or the plant shuts down, not only afraid but ashamed?

I was slow to understand the deep grievances of women. This   8
was because, as a boy, I had envied them. Before college, the only people I had ever known who were interested in art or music or literature,
the only ones who read books, the only ones who ever seemed to enjoy a sense of ease and grace were the mothers and daughters. Like the
menfolk, they fretted about money, they scrimped and made-do. But,

when the pay stopped coming in, they were not the ones who had failed. Nor did they have to go to war, and that seemed to me a blessed fact. By comparison with the narrow, ironclad days of fathers, there was an expansiveness, I thought, in the days of mothers. They went to see neighbors, to shop in town, to run errands at school, at the library, at church. No doubt, had I looked harder at their lives, I would have envied them less. It was not my fate to become a woman, so it was easier for me to see the graces. Few of them held jobs outside the home, and those who did filled thankless roles as clerks and waitresses. I didn't see, then, what a prison a house could be, since houses seemed to me brighter, handsomer places than any factory. I did not realize—because such things were never spoken of—how often women suffered from men's bullying. I did learn about the wretchedness of abandoned wives, single mothers, widows; but I also learned about the wretchedness of lone men. Even then I could see how exhausting it was for a mother to cater all day to the needs of young children. But if I had been asked, as a boy, to choose between tending a baby and tending a machine, I think I would have chosen the baby. (Having now tended both, I know I would choose the baby.)

So I was baffled when the women at college accused me and my sex of having cornered the world's pleasures. I think something like my bafflement has been felt by other boys (and girls as well) who grew up in dirt-poor farm country, in mining country, in black ghettos, in Hispanic barrios, in the shadows of factories, in Third World nations— any place where the fate of men is as grim and bleak as the fate of women. Toilers and warriors. I realize now how ancient these identities are, how deep the tug they exert on men, the undertow of a thousand generations. The miseries I saw, as a boy, in the lives of nearly all men I continue to see in the lives of many—the body-breaking toil, the tedium, the call to be tough, the humiliating powerlessness, the battle for a living and for territory.

When the women I met at college thought about the joys and privileges of men, they did not carry in their minds the sort of men I had known in my childhood. They thought of their fathers, who were bankers, physicians, architects, stockbrokers, the big wheels of the big cities. These fathers rode the train to work or drove cars that cost more than any of my childhood houses. They were attended from morning to night by female helpers, wives and nurses and secretaries. They were never laid off, never short of cash at month's end, never lined up for welfare. These fathers made decisions that mattered. They ran the world.

The daughters of such men wanted to share in this power, this   11
glory. So did I. They yearned for a say over their future, for jobs worthy of their abilities, for the right to live at peace, unmolested, whole.
Yes, I thought, yes yes. The difference between me and these daughters was that they saw me, because of my sex, as destined from birth to
become like their fathers, and therefore as an enemy to their desires. I
was an ally. If I had known, then, how to tell them so, would they have
believed me? Would they now?

Questions on Meaning

1. Sanders thought of the men he grew up with as people who endured
   physical hardships or soldiers trained to kill. How are the men you "carried in your mind" similar to or different from them?
2. Later in life, Sanders became aware of men who had power and didn't do
   physical labor. How did he feel toward them?
3. Why was Sanders "slow to understand the deep grievances of women"?
   For what reason as a young boy would he have preferred to be a woman?

Questions on Method

1. Sanders classifies men as warriors or workers. What other categories
   would you add?
2. Review Sanders's conclusion. Is it effective? Why does he end with two
   questions? How would you answer them?

Writing Topics

1. Sanders considers social class a major determinant in life. Do you agree
   that class is more influential than gender or race in shaping one's destiny?
   Cite examples from your experience.
2. Are men more powerful than women, or is the reverse true? How would
   you classify gender power? Is having power based on other factors besides
   gender? Explain.

Of Studies

Francis Bacon (1561–1626) was an English philosopher, statesman, and essayist. One of the finest legal minds of his day, he is the symbol of Elizabethan greatness. Although he spent many years in public service, Bacon's activity in literature and philosophy was prodigious. His goal was to lift humankind out of a state of despair and into the modern scientific movement of Bacon's vision chiefly through his literature. In 1597 he published his first Essays, *which were expanded and revised in later editions.* Advancement of Learning, *which appeared in 1605, is a preliminary survey of the ground that he proposed to conquer in his projected* Instauratio Magna, *which was to be the complete exposition of his philosophy. Unfortunately, this work was never finished. Although his essays proved to be revolutionary for his time, his fable,* The New Atlantis, *published in 1629, probably reached the greatest audience.*

STUDIES SERVE FOR DELIGHT, for ornament, for ability. Their chief use for delight is in privateness and retiring; for ornament, is in discourse; and for ability, is in the judgment and disposition of business; for expert[1] men can execute, and perhaps judge of particulars, one by one; but the general counsels, and the plots and marshaling of affairs come best from those that are learned. To spend too much time in studies is sloth; to use them too much for ornament is affectation; to make judgment wholly by their rules is the humor[2] of a scholar. They perfect nature, and are perfected by experience; for natural abilities are like natural plants, that need pruning by study; and studies themselves do give forth directions too much at large,[3] except they be bounded in by experience. Crafty men condemn studies, simple men admire them, and wise men use them; for they teach not their own use; but that is a wisdom without them and above them, won by observation.

[1]Experienced.
[2]Inclination.
[3]Too general.

Read not to contradict and confute, nor to believe and take for granted, nor to find talk and discourse, but to weigh and consider. Some books are to be tasted, others to be swallowed, and some few to be chewed and digested; that is, some books are to be read only in parts; others to be read but not curiously, and some few to be read wholly, and with diligence and attention. Some books also may be read by deputy, and extracts made of them by others; but that would be only in the less important arguments and the meaner sort of books; else distilled books are, like common distilled waters, flashy[4] things. Reading maketh a full man; conference a ready man; and writing an exact man. And, therefore, if a man write little, he had need have a great memory; if he confer little, he had need have a present wit; and if he read little, he had need have much cunning, to seem to know that he doth not. Histories make men wise; poets, witty; the mathematics, subtle; natural philosophy, deep; moral, grave; logic and rhetoric, able to contend: *Abeunt studia in mores!*[5] Nay, there is no stand[6] or impediment in the wit but may be wrought out by fit studies; like as diseases of the body may have appropriate exercises. Bowling is good for the stone and reins,[7] shooting for the lungs and breast, gentle walking for the stomach, riding for the head, and the like. So if a man's wit be wandering, let him study the mathematics; for in demonstrations, if his wit be called away never so little, he must begin again. If his wit be not apt to distinguish or find differences, let him study the schoolmen; for they are *cymini sectores!*[8] If he be not apt to beat over[9] matters, and to call up one thing to prove and illustrate another, let him study the lawyers' cases. So every defect of the mind may have a special receipt.

Questions on Meaning

1. What, according to Bacon, are the three reasons that people study? What are the three reasons that some spend more time studying than they should?

[4]Tasteless, flat.

[5]"Studies develop into habits."

[6]Obstacles.

[7]Testicles and kidneys.

[8]Hairsplitters.

[9]Thrash.

2. Explain Bacon's observation that studies "perfect nature, and are perfected by experience." What is the relationship, as Bacon develops it, between the knowledge that someone gains from study and the knowledge that someone gains from experience?
3. What are the reasons Bacon gives for reading? What general effect does reading have on a person compared with the general effect of conference or writing? How does Bacon classify the different types of effect that different types of reading have?

Questions on Method

1. An **epigram** is a witty, terse saying. List the epigrams you find in this classification. How many of them come in threes? What percentage of this classification consists of epigrams? Is this a convincing method of classifying?
2. Why does Bacon first classify books according to how they should be read, then according to why they should be read?

Writing Topics

1. Bacon says, "*Abeunt studia in mores,*" that is, "Studies develop into habits." Do you agree with Bacon's theory that different classes of study help us develop or train different mental habits or skills? Write an essay in which you classify different subjects you have studied according to the type of mental skill each subject stressed.
2. How would you classify American attitudes toward study today? Do Americans tend to view study too pragmatically, simply as a means to a practical or useful end? Discuss this issue in an essay that classifies various attitudes one might take toward one's studies.
3. Write an essay in which you classify different types of wisdom or knowledge according to the way such knowledge is learned or used.

Growing Up Asian in America

Kesaya E. Noda (b. 1950) was born in California and raised in rural New Hampshire. After high school graduation, she learned Japanese while studying in Japan. Following college, she researched and wrote The Yamato Colony *(1981), a history of the California community where her grandparents settled and her parents were raised. Noda earned a master's degree from Harvard Divinity School and now teaches at Lesley College in Cambridge, Massachusetts.*

SOMETIMES WHEN I WAS GROWING UP, my identity seemed to hurtle toward me and paste itself right to my face. I felt that way, encountering the stereotypes of my race perpetuated by non-Japanese people (primarily white) who may or may not have had contact with other Japanese in America. "You don't like cheese, do you?" someone would ask. "I know your people don't like cheese." Sometimes questions came making allusions to history. That was another aspect of the identity. Events that had happened quite apart from the me who stood silent in that moment connected my face with an incomprehensible past. "Your parents were in California? Were they in those camps during the war?" And sometimes there were phrases or nicknames: "Lotus Blossom." I was sometimes addressed or referred to as racially Japanese, sometimes as Japanese-American, and sometimes as an Asian woman. Confusions and distortions abounded.

How is one to know and define oneself? From the inside—within a context that is self-defined, from a grounding in community and a connection with culture and history that are comfortably accepted? Or from the outside—in terms of messages received from the media and people who are often ignorant? Even as an adult I can still see two sides of my face and past. I can see from the inside out, in freedom. And I can see from the outside in, driven by the old voices of childhood and lost in anger and fear.

I Am Racially Japanese

A voice from my childhood says: "You are other. You are less 3
than. You are unalterably alien." This voice has its own history. We
have indeed been seen as other and alien since the early years of our
arrival in the United States. The very first immigrants were welcomed
and sought as laborers to replace the dwindling numbers of Chinese,
whose influx had been cut off by the Chinese Exclusion Act of 1882.
The Japanese fell natural heir to the same anti-Asian prejudice that had
arisen against the Chinese. As soon as they began striking for better
wages, they were no longer welcomed.

I can see myself today as a person historically defined by law and 4
custom as being forever alien. Being neither "free white," nor "African," our people in California were deemed "aliens, ineligible for citizenship," no matter how long they intended to stay here. Aliens
ineligible for citizenship were prohibited from owning, buying, or leas-
ing land. They did not and could not belong here. The voice in me remembers that I am always a *Japanese*-American in the eyes of many. A
third-generation German-American is an American. A third-generation
Japanese-American is a Japanese-American. Being Japanese means being
a danger to the country during the war and knowing how to use chop-
sticks. I wear this history on my face.

I move to the other side. I see a different light and claim a differ- 5
ent context. My race is a line that stretches across ocean and time to
link me to the shrine where my grandmother was raised. Two high,
white banners lift in the wind at the top of the stone steps leading to
the shrine. It is time for the summer festival. Black characters are written against the sky as boldly as the clouds, as lightly as kites, as sharply
as the big black crows I used to see above the fields in New Hampshire.
At festival time there is liquor and food, ritual, discipline, and abandonment. There is music and drunkenness and invocation. There is
hope. Another season has come. Another season has gone.

I am racially Japanese. I have a certain claim to this crazy place 6
where the prayers intoned by a neighboring Shinto priest (standing in
for my grandmother's nephew who is sick) are drowned out by the re-
hearsals for the pop singing contest in which most of the villagers will
compete later that night. The village elders, the priest, and I stand respectfully upon the immaculate, shining wooden floor of the outer
shrine, bowing our heads before the hidden powers. During the
patchy intervals when I can hear him, I notice the priest has a stutter.

His voice flutters up to my ears only occasionally because two men and a women are singing gustily into a microphone in the compound, testing the sound system. A prerecorded tape of guitars, samisens, and drums accompanies them. Rock music and Shinto prayers. That night, to loud applause and cheers, a young man is given the award for the most *netsuretsu*—passionate, burning—rendition of a song. We roar our approval of the reward. Never mind that his voice had wandered and slid, now slightly above, now slightly below the given line of the melody. Netsuretsu. Netsuretsu.

In the morning, my grandmother's sister kneels at the foot of the stone stairs to offer her morning prayers. She is too crippled to climb the stairs, so each morning she kneels here upon the path. She shuts her eyes for a few seconds, her motions as matter of fact as when she washes rice. I linger longer than she does, so reluctant to leave, savoring the connection I feel with my grandmother in America, the past, and the power that lives and shines in the morning sun.

Our family has served this shrine for generations. The family's need to protect this claim to identity and place outweighs any individual claim to any individual hope. I am Japanese.

I Am a Japanese-American

"Weak." I hear the voice from my childhood years. "Passive," I hear. Our parents and grandparents were the ones who were put into those camps. They went without resistance; they offered cooperation as proof of loyalty to America. "Victim," I hear. And, "Silent."

Our parents are painted as hard workers who were socially uncomfortable and had difficulty expressing even the smallest opinion. Clean, quiet, motivated, and determined to match the American way; that is us, and that is the story of our time here.

"Why did you go into those camps?" I raged at my parents, frightened by my own inner silence and timidity. "Why didn't you do anything to resist? Why didn't you name it the injustice it was?" Couldn't our parents even think? Couldn't they? Why were we so passive?

I shift my vision and my stance. I am in California. My uncle is in the midst of the sweet potato harvest. He is pressed, trying to get the harvesting crews onto the field as quickly as possible, worried about the flow of equipment and people. His big pickup is pulled off to the side, motor running, door ajar. I see two tractors in the yard in front of an old shed; the flatbed harvesting platform on which the workers will stand has already been brought over from the other field. It's early morning. The workers stand loosely grouped and at ease, but my uncle looks as harried and tense as a police officer trying to unsnarl a New York City traffic jam. Driving toward the shed, I pull my car off the road to make way for an approaching tractor. The front wheels of the car sink luxuriously into the soft, white sand by the roadside and the car slides to a dreamy halt, tail still on the road. I try to move forward. I try to move back. The front bites contentedly into the sand, the back lifts itself at a jaunty angle. My uncle sees me and storms down the road, running. He is shouting before he is even near me.

"What's the matter with you?" he screams. "What the hell are   13
you doing?" In his frenzy, he grabs his hat off his head and slashes it through the air across his knee. He is beside himself. "Don't you know how to drive in sand? What's the matter with you? You've blocked the whole roadway. How am I supposed to get my tractors out of here? Can't you use your head? You've cut off the whole roadway, and we've got to get out of here."

I stand on the road before him helplessly thinking, "No, I don't   14
know how to drive in sand. I've never driven in sand."

"I'm sorry, uncle," I say, burying a smile beneath a look of sin-   15
cere apology. I notice my deep amusement and my affection for him with great curiosity. I am usually devastated by anger. Not this time.

During the several years that follow I learn about the people and   16
the place, and much more about what has happened in this California village where my parents grew up. The issei, our grandparents, made this settlement in the desert. Their first crops were eaten by rabbits and ravaged by insects. The land was so barren that men walking from house to house sometimes got lost. Women came here too. They bore children in 114-degree heat, then carried the babies with them into the fields to nurse when they reached the end of each row of grapes or other truck-farm crops.

I had had no idea what it meant to buy this kind of land and make   17
it grow green. Or how, when the war came, there was no space at all for the subtlety of being who we were—Japanese-Americans. Either/or was the way. I hadn't understood that people were literally afraid for their lives then, that their money had been frozen in banks; that there was a five-mile travel limit; that when the early evening curfew came and they were inside their houses, some of them watched helplessly as people they knew went into their barns to steal their belongings. The police were

patrolling the road, interested only in violators of curfew. There was no help for them in the face of thievery. I had not been able to imagine before what it must have felt like to be an American—to know absolutely that one is an American—and yet to have almost everyone else deny it. Not only deny it, but challenge that identity with machine guns and troops of white American soldiers. In those circumstances it was difficult to say, "I'm a Japanese-American." "American" had to do.

But now I can say that I am a Japanese-American. It means I have   18
a place here in this country, too. I have a place here on the East Coast, where our neighbor is so much a part of our family that my mother never passes her house at night without glancing at the lights to see if she is home and safe; where my parents have hauled hundreds of pounds of rocks from fields and arduously planted Christmas trees and blueberries, lilacs, asparagus, and crab apples; where my father still dreams of angling a stream to a new bed so that he can dig a pond in the field and fill it with water and fish. "The neighbors already came for their Christmas tree?" he asks in December. "Did they like it? Did they like it?"

I have a place on the West Coast where my relatives still farm,   19
where I heard the stories of feuds and backbiting, and where I saw that people survived and flourished because fundamentally they trusted and relied upon one another. A death in the family is not just a death in a family; it is a death in the community. I saw people help each other with money, materials, labor, attention, and time. I saw men gather once a year, without fail, to clean the grounds of a ninety-year-old woman who had helped the community before, during, and after the war. I saw her remembering them with birthday cards sent to each of their children.

I come from a people with a long memory and a distinctive grace.   20
We live our thanks. And we are Americans. Japanese-Americans.

I AM A JAPANESE-AMERICAN WOMAN

Woman. The last piece of my identity. It has been easier by far for   21
me to know myself in Japan and to see my place in America than it has been to accept my line of connection with my own mother. She was my dark self, a figure in whom I thought I saw all that I feared most in myself. Growing into womanhood and looking for some model of strength. I turned away from her. Of course, I could not find what I sought. I was looking for a black feminist or a white feminist. My mother is neither white nor black.

My mother is a woman who speaks with her life as much as with   22
her tongue. I think of her with her own mother. Grandmother had
Parkinson's disease and it had frozen her gait and set her fingers,
tongue, and feet jerking and trembling in a terrible dance. My aunts
and uncles wanted her to be able to live in her own home. They fed
her, bathed her, dressed her, awoke at midnight to take her for one last
trip to the bathroom. My aunts (her daughters-in-law) did most of the
care, but my mother went from New Hampshire to California each
summer to spend a month living with Grandmother, because she
wanted to and because she wanted to give my aunts at least a small rest.
During those hot summer days, mother lay on the couch watching the
television or reading, cooking foods that Grandmother liked, and
speaking little. Grandmother thrived under her care.

The time finally came when it was too dangerous for Grand-   23
mother to live alone. My relatives kept finding her on the floor beside
her bed when they went to wake her in the mornings. My mother
flew to California to help clean the house and make arrangements for
Grandmother to enter a local nursing home. On her last day at home,
while Grandmother was sitting in her big, overstuffed armchair, hair
combed and wearing a green summer dress, my mother went to her
and knelt at her feet. "Here, Mamma," she said. "I've polished your
shoes." She lifted Grandmother's legs and helped her into the shiny
black shoes. My Grandmother looked down and smiled slightly. She
left her house walking, supported by her children, carrying her pocket
book, and wearing her polished black shoes. "Look, Mamma," my
mom had said, kneeling. "I've polished your shoes."

Just the other day, my mother came to Boston to visit. She had   24
recently lost a lot of weight and was pleased with her new shape and
her feeling of good health. "Look at me, Kes," she exclaimed, turning
toward me, front and back, as naked as the day she was born. I saw her
small breasts and the wide, brown scar, belly button to pubic hair, that
marked her because my brother and I were both born by Caesarean
section. Her hips were small. I was not a large baby, but there was so
little room for me in her that when she was carrying me she could not
even begin to bend over toward the floor. She hated it, she said.

"Don't I look good? Don't you think I look good?"   25

I looked at my mother, smiling and as happy as she, thinking of   26
all the times I have seen her naked. I have seen both my parents naked
throughout my life, as they have seen me. From childhood through

adulthood we've had our naked moments, sharing baths, idle conversations picked up as we moved between showers and closets, hurried moments at the beginning of days, quiet moments at the end of days.

I know this to be Japanese, this ease with the physical, and it   27
makes me think of an old Japanese folk song. A young nursemaid, a fifteen-year-old girl, is singing a lullaby to a baby who is strapped to her back. The nursemaid has been sent as a servant to a place far from her own home. "We're the beggars," she says, "and they are the nice people. Nice people wear fine sashes. Nice clothes."

> If I should drop dead,
> bury me by the roadside!
> I'll give a flower
> to everyone who passes.
>
> What kind of flower?
> The cam-cam-camellia [*tsun-tsun-tsubaki*]
> watered by Heaven:
> alms water.

The nursemaid is the intersection of heaven and earth, the inter-   28
section of the human, the natural world, the body, and the soul. In this song, with clear eyes, she looks steadily at life, which is sometimes so very terrible and sad. I think of her while looking at my mother, who is standing on the red and purple carpet before me, laughing, without any clothes.

I am my mother's daughter. And I am myself.   29
I am a Japanese-American woman.   30

EPILOGUE

I recently heard a man from West Africa share some memories of   31
his childhood. He was raised Muslim, but when he was a young man, he found himself deeply drawn to Christianity. He struggled against his inner impulse for years, trying to avoid the church yet feeling pushed to return to it again and again. "I would have done *anything* to avoid the change," he said. At last, he became Christian. Afterwards he was afraid to go home, fearing that he would not be accepted. The fear was groundless, he discovered, when at last he returned—he had separated

himself, but his family and friends (all Muslim) had not separated themselves from him.

The man, who is now a professor of religion, said that in the Africa he knew as a child and a young man, pluralism was embraced rather than feared. There was "a kind of tolerance that did not deny your particularity," he said. He alluded to zestful, spontaneous debates that would sometimes loudly erupt between Muslims and Christians in the village's public spaces. His memories of an atheist who harangued the villagers when he came to visit them once a week moved me deeply. Perhaps the man was an agricultural advisor or inspector. He harassed the women. He would say: "Don't go to the fields! Don't even bother to go to the fields. Let God take care of you. He'll send you the food. If you believe in God, why do you need to work? You don't need to work! Let God put the seeds in the ground. Stay home." 32

The professor said, "The women laughed, you know? They just laughed. Their attitude was, 'Here is a child of God. When will he come home?'" 33

The storyteller, the professor of religion, smiled a most fantastic tender smile as he told this story, "In my country, there is a deep affirmation of the oneness of God," he said. "The atheist and the women were having quite different experiences in their encounter, though the atheist did not know this. He saw himself as quite separate from the women. But the women did not see themselves as being separate from him. 'Here is a child of God,' they said. 'When will he come home?'" 34

Questions on Meaning

1. Respond to Noda's question "How is one to know and define oneself?"
2. Noda hears a voice from her childhood say: "You are other. You are less than. You are unalterably alien." What evidence does she cite in this section of her essay that addresses the issue of being "historically defined"?
3. To what extent do you agree with the sentiments of the epilogue about the unity of all things?

Questions on Method

1. Noda uses classification to organize her essay on identity. What factors are involved in being a Japanese American according to Noda? Which images are most effective? Is there a recurring motif? Cite evidence.

2. What stages does Noda go through, particularly with her mother, as she shapes her identity as a Japanese American woman? What use does she make of contrast and comparison in this section of her essay?

Writing Topics

1. To what extent is it possible in the United States to embrace rather than fear pluralism? What is involved in fostering a tolerance that does not deny the particularity of the individual?
2. Discuss the link between perception of race and presentation of the self in the struggle to achieve ethnic identity.
3. How important is it to understand your ethnic and/or cultural heritage? Write an essay describing how your ethnic and/or cultural background has affected your concept of yourself.

The Terrible Twenties

Daniel Smith-Rowsey majored in politics and filmmaking at the University of California, Santa Cruz. He is from the "twentysomething" generation. He was brought up in a culture of MTV, Nintendo, latchkey freedom, cellular phones, BMWs, and sprawling malls. But as an adult he questions the values and resources he and his indulged generation inherited from their parents. "You never taught us to be smart—you only taught us to be young." With skyrocketing costs and unemployment and a college degree that no longer guarantees a good job, he wonders if today's twentysomethings have the wherewithal to survive a future rushing down on them.

SOMETIMES I WONDER what it would be like to have been 20, my age, in the '60s. Back when you could grow up, count on a career and maybe think about buying a house. When one person could expect to be the wage earner for a household.

In the space of one generation those dreams have died. The cost of living has skyrocketed, unemployment has gone up, going to college doesn't guarantee you can get a good job. And no one seems to care. Maybe it's because the only people my age you older people have heard from are those who *do* make a lot of money: investment bankers, athletes, musicians, actors. But more and more of us twentysomethings are underachievers who loaf around the house until well past our college years.

This is an open letter to the baby boomers from the *next* generation. I think it's time we did a little hitting back. Aside from the wealthy, none of you ever told your children, "Someday this will all be yours," and you're the first middle class to fail that way. Did you think we wouldn't care? Thanks a lot. But the real danger lies in the way we've been taught to deal with failure: gloss over and pretend the problem doesn't exist. It's evidence you never taught us to be smart— you only taught us to be young.

We are the stupidest generation in American history, we 20-year-olds. You already know that. We really do get lower SAT scores than our parents. Our knowledge of geography is pathetic, as is our ability with foreign languages and even basic math. We don't read books like you did. We care only about image. We love fads. Talk to college professors, and they'll tell you they don't get intelligent responses like they used to, when you were in school. We're perfectly mush-headed.

You did this to us. You prized your youth so much you made sure   5
ours would be carefree. It's not that you didn't love us; you loved us so much you pushed us to follow your idea of what you were—or would like to have been—instead of teaching us to be responsible. After legitimizing youthful rebellion you never let us have our own innocence— perhaps because Vietnam and Watergate shattered yours. That's why we're already mature enough to understand and worry about racism, the environment, abortion, the homeless, nuclear policy. But we also were fed on the video culture you created to idealize your own irresponsible days of youth. Your slim-and-trim MTV bimbos, fleshy beer commercials and racy TV shows presented adolescence as a time only for fun and sex. Why should we be expected to work at learning anything?

Not that we're not smart—in some ways. We're street smart, David   6
Letterman clever, whizzes at Nintendo. We can name more beers than presidents. Pop culture is, to us, more attractive than education.

I really don't think we can do this dance much longer. Not a sin-   7
gle industrialized country has survived since 1945 without a major re-evaluation of its identity except ours. That's what you thought you were doing in the '60s, but soon you gave way to chasing the dreams of the Donald Trump–Michael Milken get-rich-quick ethos—and all you had left for us was a bankrupt economy. The latchkey lifestyle you gave us in the name of your own "freedom" has made us a generation with missing parents and broken homes. And what about the gays and blacks and Hispanics and Asians and women who you pretended to care so much about, and then forgot? It's not that I'm angry at you for selling out to the system. It's that there won't be a system. It's that there won't be a system for *me* to sell out to, if I want to. The money isn't there anymore because you spent it all.

To be honest, I can't blame you for all that's happened. The pre-   8
eminence of new technologies and the turn toward cutthroat capitalism over the past two decades would have happened with or without the peculiarities of your generation. If I had been born in the '50s, I too would have been angry at racism and the war in Vietnam. But that's not the same thing as allowing the system to unravel out of my own greed.

Don't say you didn't start the fire of selfishness and indulgence, building it up until every need or desire was immediately appeased. Cable TV, BMWs, cellular phones, the whole mall culture has reduced us all to 12-year-olds who want everything *now*. I'm not in love with everything your parents did, but at least they gave you a chance. As Billy Joel said, "Every child had a pretty good shot to get at least as far as their old man got." For most of us, all we've been left with are the erotic fantasies, aggressive tendencies and evanescent funds of youth. Pretty soon we won't have youth *or* money, and that's when we may get a little angry.

Or maybe we won't. Perhaps you really have created a nation of 9 mush-heads who will always prefer style over substance, conservative politics and reading lessons. If that's so, the culture can survive, as it seems to be doing with the bright smile of optimism breaking through the clouds of decaying American institutions. And then you really will be the last modern smart generation because our kids will be even dumber, poorer and more violent than us. You guys will be like the old mule at the end of Orwell's "Animal Farm," thinking about how great things used to be when you were kids. You will differ from your own parents in that you will have missed your chance to change the world and robbed us of the skills and money to do it ourselves. If there's any part of you left that still loves us enough to help us, we could really use it. And it's not just your last chance. It's our only one.

Questions on Meaning

1. How does the author classify twentysomethings? To what extent do you agree with his characterizations?
2. In paragraph 6, Smith-Rowsey states, "Pop culture is, to us, more attractive than education." Do you share his points of view? Are education and pop culture mutually exclusive? Explain your answer.
3. Is the future of twentysomethings as bleak as the author implies? What examples can you think of to modify his point of view?

Questions on Method

1. In paragraph 7, the author refers to a "latchkey lifestyle." How would you classify that lifestyle? What other products of contemporary culture does he cite? What would you add?
2. Characterize Smith-Rowsey's tone. Is it informative, critical, angry? Is it convincing? Why or why not?

Writing Topics

1. Write an essay refuting the author's classifications of your generation or that of your parents.
2. Write an essay in which you classify the influence of MTV, Nintendo, cellular phones, and shopping malls on your generation.

Classification
Writing Topics

1. How much does the act of classification require the ability to contrast and compare? Devise a system for classifying something with which you are familiar—the compact discs in your collection, for example—then write an essay that explains what sort of contrast and comparison you made to devise your system.

2. A gourmand might well devise a different system for classifying restaurants than would a dieter or a business executive. Pick a subject about which people with differing interests are likely to have differing views, then write an essay that describes the systems that might be devised to classify the subject.

3. Devise a system for classifying the teachers at your school, a system that would help students decide whether to take a course with a particular teacher. Write an essay that explains how your system would work.

4. Select a word with which you have strong associations such as anxiety, stress, charm, success, failure, or jealousy, and write an essay in which you classify its various types. Use a dictionary and a thesaurus to find words with similar meanings.

5. For a day or two keep a record of all the bumper stickers you see. Then classify them into several categories—comic, serious, political, erotic, or religious, for example. Write an essay classifying your information about bumper stickers. Focus on your introductory paragraph and experiment with creative ways to introduce your favorite, most unusual, or most outrageous sticker.

10

Definition

To DEFINE IS TO SET LIMITS or boundaries and thereby to give shape or meaning. With words, we usually depend on a dictionary to set these limits and provide these meanings, and the basic **definition** of a word is called a dictionary or formal definition. How does the dictionary define? Here is a dictionary definition of "jujitsu":

> A Japanese art of self-defense or hand-to-hand combat based on set maneuvers that force an opponent to use his weight and strength against himself.

As usual, this dictionary definition falls into two parts: placement in a class (or genus) and the differentiation from other members of the same genus. Here the genus is "art of self-defense"; the differentiation is the rest of the definition: "based on set maneuvers that force an opponent to use his weight and strength against himself." **Synonyms** are another standard feature of dictionary definitions, and derivations from other languages (etymologies) are often included: "ju" derives from the ancient Chinese for "soft" and "yielding," and "jitsu" derives from the ancient Chinese for "art"—we can see just how literal the translation is from Chinese to Japanese to English. Some dictionaries also list **antonyms,** which define by excluding, or telling what a word does *not* mean. (Jujitsu is *not* karate or judo.) Any formal definition you might write could use any or all of these techniques—putting the word into a genus and differentiating it from other members of the genus and giving synonyms, antonyms, or etymologies. But the use of dictionary definitions is limited for expository purposes because these definitions tend to be objective, short, and noncontroversial and because readers may be insulted or bored if they read definitions of words they already know or can easily look up in a dictionary.

But there are several classes of words—technical, philosophical, scientific, **slang,** newly coined—whose definition cannot be left to lexicographers; these are words whose definitions are often controversial and must be attempted generation after generation and extended beyond a mere recital of synonyms and etymology. Such words require different, extended definition.

The purpose of extended definition is to carry "limit setting" into the area of explanation or argument; in fact such discussions, although they may begin with the definition of a key word, usually move quickly to a critique of what is defined. Any extended definition of, say, "liberty," "justice," or "love" soon leaves the dictionary and its methods far behind. Words about which people care deeply (many of them are related to ethics, esthetics, psychology, religion, and politics) invite extended definition. "Superstition" is such a word and such a concept, a touchstone for a worldview, around which entire essays might be organized. Other types of words that may require extended definition are coined (or new) words, such as "dystopia" and "freewriting"; words whose meanings have changed, such as "hangout" and "holocaust"; and technical words, such as "cyberspace."

Extended definition frequently begins with the dictionary definition and expands both the genus (What is an art? Is self-defense an art?) and the differentiation (Is jujitsu superior to karate? Is it superior to Chinese or European forms of self-defense? How can the opponent's strength be used against him- or herself? What are the various holds or stances? How was jujitsu developed?). These expansions require the use of other expository techniques; the questions listed here require contrast, process analysis, description, exemplification, and narration, respectively. An essay on jujitsu might expand to a consideration of many related issues—Japanese character, physical fitness, crime, comparative sociology, history, and so on, using dictionary definition merely as a starting point.

WRITING EXTENDED DEFINITION

1. Use extended definition for technical, scientific, philosophical, slang, or newly coined words.
2. Begin with a dictionary definition (classification, synonyms, antonyms, etymology).
3. Extend your definition by using other expository modes such as contrast, exemplification, and description.

The Holocaust

Bruno Bettelheim (1903–1990) was born in Austria and emigrated to Chicago in 1939. As a young man, he became interested in psychoanalysis and trained as a psychologist at the University of Vienna. The Nazis imprisoned him in the Buchenwald and Dachau concentration camps; he was released due to American intervention in 1939. Bettelheim was a professor of psychology at the University of Chicago until he retired in 1973, and he also headed the Sonia Shankman Orthogenic School in Chicago. Well known for his sensitive approach to childhood schizophrenia and autism, he was also a gifted and sensitive writer who wrote about puberty rites, the dynamics of racial prejudice, and the determinants of concentration camp survival. His best-known book, The Informed Heart *(1960), is about the loss of self in modern society. In his collection of essays,* Surviving and Other Essays *(1979), Bettelheim examines his and others' experiences in the Nazi concentration camps. Many of his books were on children, and they include* Love is Not Enough *(1950),* Truants from Life *(1955),* The Children of the Dream *(1969), and* The Uses of Enchantment *(1976).*

To BEGIN WITH, it was not the hapless victims of the Nazis who named their incomprehensible and totally unmasterable fate the "holocaust." It was the Americans who applied this artificial and highly technical term to the Nazi extermination of the European Jews. But while the event when named as mass murder most foul evokes the most immediate, most powerful revulsion, when it is designated by a rare technical term, we must first in our minds translate it back into emotionally meaningful language. Using technical or specially created terms instead of words from our common vocabulary is one of the best-known and most widely used distancing devices, separating the intellectual from the emotional experience. Talking about "the holocaust" permits us to manage it intellectually where the raw facts, when given their ordinary names, would overwhelm us emotionally—because it was catastrophe beyond comprehension, beyond the limits of our imagination, unless we force ourselves against our desire to extend it to encompass these terrible events.[1]

This linguistic circumlocution began while it all was only in the planning stage. Even the Nazis—usually given to grossness in language and action—shied away from facing openly what they were up to and called this vile mass murder "the final solution of the Jewish problem." After all, solving a problem can be made to appear like an honorable enterprise, as long as we are not forced to recognize that the solution we are about to embark on consists of the completely unprovoked, vicious murder of millions of helpless men, women, and children. The Nuremberg judges of these Nazi criminals followed their example of circumlocution by coining a neologism out of one Greek and one Latin root: genocide. These artificially created technical terms fail to connect with our strongest feelings. The horror of murder is part of our most common human heritage. From earliest infancy on, it arouses violent abhorrence in us. Therefore in whatever form it appears we should give such an act its true designation and not hide it behind polite, erudite terms created out of classical words.

2

To call this vile mass murder "the holocaust" is not to give it a special name emphasizing its uniqueness which would permit, over time, the word becoming invested with feelings germane to the event it refers to. The correct definition of *holocaust* is "burnt offering." As such, it is part of the language of the psalmist, a meaningful word to all who have some acquaintance with the Bible, full of the richest emotional connotations. By using the term "holocaust," entirely false associations are established through conscious and unconscious connotations between the most vicious of mass murders and ancient rituals of a deeply religious nature.

3

Using a word with such strong unconscious religious connotations when speaking of the murder of millions of Jews robs the victims of this abominable mass murder of the only thing left to them: their

4

---

[1]Between the years 1941–45 the Nazi regime planned and executed the unique mass murder of European Jewry. This political ideological task was in accordance with Hitler's orders for the "final solution of the Jewish question"—that is, the elimination of the Jewish people from the European community through a systematic program of murder. Special crematories with gas chambers were erected for the systematic extermination throughout Germany, Poland, and other European countries, where 6 million Jews were gassed.

uniqueness. Calling the most callous, most brutal, most horrid, most heinous mass murder a burnt offering is a sacrilege, a profanation of God and man.

Martyrdom is part of our religious heritage. A martyr, burned at the stake, is a burnt offering to his god. And it is true that after the Jews were asphyxiated, the victims' corpses were burned. But I believe we fool ourselves if we think we are honoring the victims of systematic murder by using this term, which has the highest moral connotations. By doing so, we connect for our own psychological reasons what happened in the extermination camps with historical events we deeply regret, but also greatly admire. We do so because this makes it easier for us to cope; only in doing so we cope with our distorted image of what happened, not with the events the way they did happen.

By calling the victims of the Nazis martyrs, we falsify their fate. The true meaning of *martyr* is: "One who voluntarily undergoes the penalty of death for refusing to renounce his faith" (*Oxford English Dictionary*). The Nazis made sure that nobody could mistakenly think that their victims were murdered for their religious beliefs. Renouncing their faith would have saved none of them. Those who had converted to Christianity were gassed, as were those who were atheists, and those who were deeply religious Jews.[2] They did not die for any conviction, and certainly not out of choice.

Millions of Jews were systematically slaughtered, as were untold other "undesirables," not for any convictions of theirs, but only because they stood in the way of the realization of an illusion. They neither died for their convictions, nor were they slaughtered because of their convictions, but only in consequence of the Nazis' delusional belief about what was required to protect the purity of their assumed superior racial endowment, and what they thought necessary to guarantee them the living space they believed they needed and were entitled to. Thus while these millions were slaughtered for an idea, they did not die for one.

Millions—men, women, and children—were processed after they had been utterly brutalized, their humanity destroyed, their clothes torn from their bodies. Naked, they were sorted into those who were

[2]To specify the "undesirable" Jews—or in German terminology, the non-Aryan—a decree was promulgated in 1933 according to which anyone descending from non-Aryan parents or grandparents (even if only one parent or grandparent was non-Aryan) was considered a Jew. The Nazi definition simply meant that a Jew is a Jew is a Jew—that is, down to the third generation—and eligible for racial persecution.

destined to be murdered immediately, and those others who had a short-term usefulness as slave labor. But after a brief interval they, too, were to be herded into the same gas chambers into which the others were immediately piled, there to be asphyxiated so that, in their last moments, they could not prevent themselves from fighting each other in vain for a last breath of air.

To call these most wretched victims of a murderous delusion, of destructive drives run rampant, martyrs or a burnt offering is a distortion invented for our comfort, small as it may be. It pretends that this most vicious of mass murders had some deeper meaning; that in some fashion the victims either offered themselves or at least became sacrifices to a higher cause. It robs them of the last recognition which could be theirs, denies them the last dignity we could accord them: to face and accept what their death was all about, not embellishing it for the small psychological relief this may give us.   9

We could feel so much better if the victims had acted out of choice. For our emotional relief, therefore, we dwell on the tiny minority who did exercise some choice: the resistance fighters of the Warsaw ghetto, for example, and others like them. We are ready to overlook the fact that these people fought back only at a time when everything was lost, when the overwhelming majority of those who had been forced into the ghettos had already been exterminated without resisting. Certainly those few who finally fought for their survival and their convictions, risking and losing their lives in doing so, deserve our admiration; their deeds give us a moral lift. But the more we dwell on these few, the more unfair are we to the memory of the millions who were slaughtered—who gave in, did not fight back—because we deny them the only thing which up to the very end remained uniquely their own: their fate.   10

Questions on Meaning

1. Why does Bettelheim object to the word *holocaust* as a definition of the "mass murder" of Jews by the Nazis? Is it true, as he asserts in paragraph 1, that whereas the phrase "mass murder most foul" makes us feel an immediate and powerful revulsion, the term *holocaust* is a distancing device used to separate "the intellectual from the emotional experience"? Are there really any words that might make us feel the true horror of the Nazi extermination of European Jews?

2. Discuss the comparison Bettelheim offers in paragraph 2 between the use of the word *holocaust* by Americans and the examples of such

"linguistic circumlocution" used by the Nazis and by the Nuremberg judges. How does his example of the Nazi use of the phrase "the final solution of the Jewish problem" help us understand the definition of "linguistic circumlocution"?

3. How fair is it of Bettelheim to apply the phrase "linguistic circumlocution" to the American use of the word *holocaust*? Why, according to Bettelheim, do we use the word *holocaust*?

4. What, according to the third paragraph, are the actual emotional connotations of the word *holocaust*? Why do these connotations lead us to view the European Jews as martyrs?

5. Why is it inappropriate, so far as Bettelheim is concerned, to define the European Jews as martyrs? How does the analysis of why and the description of how the Jews were slaughtered that Bettelheim offers in paragraphs 7 through 9 clarify his objections to the word *martyr*?

Questions on Method

1. Although Bettelheim's essay is concerned with what he feels is the inappropriate use of a particular word, what broader meaning does it imply about the difficulties of definition in general? What general conclusions might you draw from Bettelheim's specific example about the limitations of using any single word to define a complex idea or experience?

2. In paragraph 3, Bettelheim suggests that the act of definition involves giving a "special name" that, over time, becomes "invested with feelings germane to the event it refers to." In what sense is the act of definition as much an act of identifying the definer's subjective thoughts and feelings about something as it is an act of identifying the objective meaning of something? To what extent does this subjective definition apply to the word *holocaust* itself?

3. Might you argue that as Bettelheim differentiates between what *holocaust* actually does and does not mean, and as he discusses the background of the word, he in effect redefines the word so that it begins to represent what he thinks is the true meaning of the event it is supposed to name?

Writing Topics

1. In paragraph 2, Bettelheim says that "the horror of murder" is something that arouses "violent abhorrence" in us from earliest infancy, yet his main point is that society conditions us to accept certain kinds of murder. In what ways does such social conditioning involve inappropriately defining certain acts of murder as something else so that we feel them to be less horrible than they actually are? Write an essay in which you discuss the different definitions society gives to murder.

2. What expressions of contemporary jargon—the jargon of commercials, for example, or of slang that is popular among young people today—might you classify as being linguistic circumlocutions? Develop your essay by defining the words and phrases you choose as examples.
3. Write an essay in which you use illustrative examples to define the word *genocide*. Does your use of such examples help translate this word into what Bettelheim calls "emotionally meaningful language"?

Anatomy and Destiny

Perri Klass (b. 1958) was born in Tunapuna, Trinidad, to a family of writers. Her father, Morton, is an anthropologist; her mother, Sheila, is a writer and English professor; and her brother, David, is also a writer. Klass earned an A.B. at Harvard University and attended the University of California in Berkeley from 1979 to 1981. In 1986 she received her M.D. from Harvard University. She served as a resident in pediatrics at Boston's Children's Hospital in Boston, Massachusetts, in 1986. Her publications include a novel, Recombinations *(1985); a collection of short stories,* I Am Having An Adventure *(1986); and* A Not Entirely Benign Procedure: Four Years as a Medical Student *(1987). In 1984 she authored the "Hers" column for the* New York Times *and is the author of the monthly column "Vital Signs" in* Discover *magazine. She also contributes articles and short stories to a number of periodicals, which include the* Boston Globe, *the* New York Times, Vogue, Esquire, Ms., Massachusetts Medicine, Self, Mademoiselle, Berkeley, *and* The Fiction Review. *She received the Le Baron Russell Briggs Prize from Harvard University in 1978 for "Two New Jersey Stories," the Elizabeth Mills Crothers Award from the University of California, Berkeley, in 1980 for "Style and Substance" and in 1981 for "A Gift of Sweet Mustard," and the O'Henry Award in 1983 for "The Secret Life of Dieters" and in 1984 for "Not a Good Girl."*

WHEN I WAS A MEDICAL STUDENT, writing about being a medical 1 student, I had two different editors ask me whether professors had taught anatomy with *Playboy* pinups instead of diagrams, or lecturers had made offensive jokes about women. There seemed to be a sort of common knowledge about the medical school experience that my articles didn't incorporate. In fact, I went through medical school without encountering that sort of nonsense, and if a lecturer did occasionally try a would-be witty, would-be provocative remark about women, he got roundly hissed for his trouble—it's very satisfying to hiss a lecturer, and few of them keep their composure well during the process.

There were, however, other, more subtle, ways in which medical 2 school made me aware that I and my kind were newcomers. There was, above all, the unending parade of male lecturers. There was the pervasive (and almost unconscious) practice of using the generic *he* for the doctor in any clinical anecdote and the generic *she* for the patient (provided it wasn't prostate trouble, of course). I can still remember a day when one of our rare female lecturers said to us something on the order of, "So one day someone will come in with these symptoms, and you'll get an orthopedist to look at the patient with you, and she'll tell you such and such," and the women in the audience burst into applause.

So we hissed sexist jokes and we applauded the use of the female 3 pronoun. Did that mean that the women with whom I went to medical school considered themselves feminists? I can't say, but I do know this: many of us felt poised, as women entering a traditionally (and sometimes militantly) male profession, between gratitude to the women who had fought their way through before us on the one hand and a desire to identify with our new brotherhood on the other.

Most people who go to medical school want very badly to be 4 doctors. It takes a great deal of effort to get to medical school, let alone to get through. Wanting to be a doctor means identifying with the people up ahead of you, the group you are trying to join, and up until very recently, that group has been a brotherhood, in every sense of the word. For some women, the word *feminist* may have been unwelcome, a reminder that they might never be fully accepted into that brotherhood, an awkward and public attempt to make an ideology out of a fact of life. And yet, I think my class was still close enough to the pioneers who had gone before for us to understand that we owed our opportunity, our comparatively easy path, entirely to those resolute embattled pioneers. The graffiti in the women's bathroom in the dormitory at my medical school read, "Every time you sit down here, thank the women who have come before you."

I have taken for granted that I was a feminist ever since I was in 5 junior high school, but I have never seen myself as a banner-carrier. Certainly in college and in graduate school there were women who would have considered me a fellow traveler at best: because I did not live a truly politically correct life, because I was not more active in women's causes. I never minded this and it never kept me from considering myself a feminist; others could carry the banners, but I would march; I would acknowledge the debt I owed to other women and to the Women's Movement. I was a feminist, but I was not The Feminist.

When I got to medical school, I discovered that I was a radical feminist. By medical school standards I was in fact The Feminist or one of them. It didn't take much; there was almost no one person, and certainly no group, to carry the banner or smile patronizingly at my lack of seriousness. I found myself running the medical school women's association, along with a friend. Our activities were far short of revolutionary; we used to invite speakers to come and talk once a week. We covered topics of obvious relevance to women—battered women, midwifery—and also medical topics that we thought might be relevant—alcoholism, child abuse—and we also invited a number of women physicians to come talk about their training and their lives. The talks were generally very well attended, by both female and male students, and they were fun, but not particularly radical. Still, one day when I and a couple of other women from our class were talking to the women who had directed the organization before us about possible speakers and other activities (Develop a women's medical directory of the area? Get involved with a study that was being done of the medical school's failure to give tenure to women?), one of my classmates said abruptly that she didn't want to help run the organization since it was clear that the group was going to be headed by some radical people. It wasn't that I minded the label. I was vaguely thrilled to find myself finally something other than a weak-minded fellow traveler. But it was disconcerting not to know when I was doing something "extreme."

I was once called to the office of the director of medical school admissions along with the heads of some other student groups to discuss his concern because the women's organization was writing to female applicants, offering encouragement and information, even offering to put them up when they came for interviews. He pointed out that the Hispanic and black student groups were making similar offers to their constituents, and he wanted to put a stop to all these separate letters. Among other things, he said, it just wasn't fair—no one was writing to the white men. There was a pause, and then I said, in unison with one of the other students present, "And yet, somehow they keep coming!" The lesson, in the end, was that medicine is fundamentally a conservative world, that medical students as a group are a far more conservative context for any kind of political thinking than college students or graduate students.

Most female medical students, as I remember, were highly aware 8 of the sex ratios on the hospital teams on which they worked. And I remember a sense of betrayal when a female resident or attending physician proved ineffective, unpleasant, uninspiring. I also remember how different it felt the first time I was ever in an operating room with an all-female group: the orthopedic resident, the surgical intern, the medical student (me), the scrub nurse, *and* the patient. And in fact it was nothing like the usual, operating room drama; there was less yelling, more courtesy, more collegiality, and less strict hierarchy. That distinction has held up in a fair number of operating rooms since then.

You can't help feeling these differences, whatever the association 9 you choose to claim with feminism. However wary you may be of the word, medical school is an educational experience, and one of the courses everyone gets, like it or not, is an introduction to sexual politics. Many of the men, of course, don't quite realize it's going on.

Now I am doing a residency in pediatrics, a field that has tradi- 10 tionally had a relatively high percentage of women. In my own program there are many female residents. When the list of interns came out for next year, several of us reviewed with fascination the list of the people who would take over our position at the very bottom of the totem pole. Only later did we realize that none of us had thought to count how many of the new interns were male and how many female—the most striking evidence, we all agreed, that we are in a situation where that really isn't an issue. When half or more of the residents are female, a female resident doesn't feel she is by definition on probation. Polarizations of male and female doctor styles are acknowledged; residents are regularly twitted for being macho.

Many of the young female doctors I work with today would call 11 themselves feminists. Their feminism involves a sense of entitlement, and that is also valuable. In a way the victory is the sense of entitlement, the feeling that you belong.

You need both—you need a balance of a rock-hard confidence 12 that you belong in medicine, and also an awareness that you only got there because the women ahead of you battered down the doors. With that confidence and that awareness, the hope is you can enjoy your position, preserve it for those who will come next, and also preserve the challenge to the traditional style that is one of the greatest contributions women bring to medicine.

Questions on Meaning

1. What does Klass suggest about sexism in medical school in the first paragraph? How does she elaborate on this subject in her second paragraph?
2. Klass's definition of feminism changes throughout the essay. Identify these changes and the reasons for them. Do you consider yourself a feminist or someone sympathetic to the ideals of feminism? Why or why not?
3. Explain the thematic significance of Klass's title.

Questions on Method

1. How does Klass define sexism? Are her examples convincing? How does her definition of sexism compare with yours?
2. Klass originally published her essay in *Ms.* magazine. How might her intended audience have influenced her tone and purpose? Characterize her tone and explain her purpose in this essay.

Writing Topics

1. Klass discusses sexism in the context of medical school. Are there other professions in which you or someone you know has experienced sexism? Write an essay defining the instances of sexism that took place.
2. In paragraph 8, Klass focuses on gender behavior in the operating room. What points does she make? What is your experience of gender behavior in the workplace? Write an essay comparing and contrasting your observations with those of Klass.
3. Write an essay in which you define a word or phrase both by offering examples that enumerate its characteristics and by differentiating it from other, similar terms.

The Cult of Busyness

Barbara Ehrenreich (b. 1941) has a Ph.D. in biology. She was an early critic of the health care system in the United States as well as a social critic. She has also written about globalism, welfare, sexism, and war and is an active member of the Democratic Socialists of America. Ehrenreich is a regular columnist for Time *and a regular contributor to other publications such as* The Nation, Mother Jones, *and the* New York Times Magazine. *She often writes about social and political issues. Her books include* For Her Own Good: One Hundred and Fifty Years of the Experts' Advice to Women *(1978);* Witches, Midwives, and Nurses: A History of Women Healers, *coauthored with Deirdre English (1973);* The Hearts of Men: American Dreams and the Flight from Commitment *(1983);* Fear of Falling: The Inner Life of the Middle Class *(1989);* The Worst Years of Our Lives: Irreverent Notes from a Decade of Greed *(1990), about the 1980s; and* Blood Rites: Origins and History of the Passion of War *(1997).*

NOT TOO LONG AGO a former friend and soon-to-be acquaintance called me up to tell me how busy she was. A major report, upon which her professional future depended, was due in three days; her secretary was on strike; her housekeeper had fallen into the hands of the Immigration Department; she had two hours to prepare a dinner party for eight; and she was late for her time-management class. Stress was taking its toll, she told me: her children resented the fact that she sometimes got their names mixed up, and she had taken to abusing white wine. 1

All this put me at a distinct disadvantage, since the only thing I was doing at the time was holding the phone with one hand and attempting to touch the opposite toe with the other hand, a pastime that I had perfected during previous telephone monologues. Not that I'm not busy too: as I listened to her, I was on the alert for the moment the dryer would shut itself off and I would have to rush to fold the clothes before they settled into a mass of incorrigible wrinkles. But if I mentioned this little deadline of mine, she might think I wasn't busy 2 enough to need a housekeeper, so I kept on patiently saying "Hmm" until she got to her parting line: "Look, this isn't a good time for me to talk, I've got to go now."

I don't know when the cult of conspicuous busyness began, but it has swept up almost all the upwardly mobile, professional women I know. Already, it is getting hard to recall the days when, for example "Let's have lunch" meant something other than "I've got more important things to do than talk to you right now." There was even a time when people used to get together without the excuse of needing something to eat—when, in fact, it was considered rude to talk with your mouth full. In the old days, hardly anybody had an appointment book, and when people wanted to know what the day held in store for them, they consulted a horoscope.

It's not only women, of course; for both sexes, busyness has become an important insignia of upper-middle-class status. Nobody, these days, admits to having a hobby, although two or more careers— say, neurosurgery and an art dealership—is not uncommon, and I am sure we will soon be hearing more about the tribulations of the four-paycheck couple. Even those who can manage only one occupation at a time would be embarrassed to be caught doing only one *thing* at a time. Those young men who jog with their headsets on are not, as you might innocently guess, rocking out, but are absorbing the principles of international finance law or a lecture on one-minute management. Even eating, I read recently, is giving way to "grazing"—the conscious ingestion of unidentified foods while drafting a legal brief, cajoling a client on the phone, and, in ambitious cases, doing calf-toning exercises under the desk.

But for women, there's more at stake than conforming to another upscale standard. If you want to attract men, for example, it no longer helps to be a bimbo with time on your hands. Upscale young men seem to go for the kind of woman who plays with a full deck of credit cards who won't cry when she's knocked to the ground while trying to board the six o'clock Eastern shuttle, and whose schedule doesn't allow for a sexual encounter lasting more than twelve minutes. Then there is the economic reality: any woman who doesn't want to wind up a case study in the feminization of poverty has to be successful at something more demanding than fingernail maintenance or come-hither looks. Hence all the bustle, my busy friends would explain—they want to succeed.

But if success is the goal, it seems clear to me that the fast track is   6
headed the wrong way. Think of the people who are genuinely
successful—path-breaking scientists, best-selling novelists, and design-
ers of major new software. They are not, on the whole, the kind of
people who keep glancing shiftily at their watches or making small lists
entitled "To Do." On the contrary, many of these people appear to be
in a daze, like the distinguished professor I once had who, in the middle of a lecture on electron spin, became so fascinated by the dispersion
properties of chalk dust that he could not go on. These truly successful
people are childlike, easily distractable, fey sorts, whose usual demeanor resembles that of a recently fed hobo on a warm summer
evening.

The secret of the truly successful, I believe, is that they learned   7
very early in life how *not* to be busy. They saw through that adage, repeated to me so often in childhood, that anything worth doing is worth
doing well. The trouble is, many things are worth doing only in the
most slovenly, halfhearted fashion possible, and many other things are
not worth doing at all. Balancing a checkbook, for example. For some
reason, in our culture, this dreary exercise is regarded as the supreme
test of personal maturity, business acumen, and the ability to cope with
math anxiety. Yet it is a form of busyness which is exceeded in futility
only by going to the additional trouble of computerizing one's checking account—and that, in turn, is only slightly less silly than taking the
time to discuss, with anyone, what brand of personal computer one
owns, or is thinking of buying, or has heard of others using.

If the truly successful manage never to be busy, it is also true that   8
many of the busiest people will never be successful. I know this firsthand from my experience, many years ago, as a waitress. Any executive
who thinks the ultimate in busyness consists of having two important
phone calls on hold and a major deadline in twenty minutes, should try
facing six tablefuls of clients simultaneously demanding that you give
them their checks, fresh coffee, a baby seat, and a warm, spontaneous
smile. Even when she's not busy, a waitress has to look busy—refilling
the salt shakers and polishing all the chrome in sight—but the only reward is the minimum wage and any change that gets left on the tables.
Much the same is true of other high-stress jobs, like working as a telephone operator, or doing data entry on one of the new machines that
monitors your speed as you work: "success" means surviving the shift.

Although busyness does not lead to success, I am willing to be-   9
lieve that success—especially when visited on the unprepared—can

cause busyness. Anyone who has invented a better mousetrap, or the contemporary equivalent, can expect to be harassed by strangers demanding that you read their unpublished manuscripts or undergo the humiliation of public speaking, usually on remote Midwestern campuses. But if it is true that success leads to more busyness and less time for worthwhile activities—like talking (and listening) to friends, reading novels, or putting in some volunteer time for a good cause—then who needs it? It would be sad to have come so far—or at least to have run so hard—only to lose each other.

Questions on Meaning

1. Explain the thematic significance of the essay's title, focusing primarily on the definition of the term *cult*.
2. "It's not only women, of course, for both sexes, busyness has become an important insignia of upper-middle-class status." What evidence does the author provide to support her thesis?
3. To what extent do you agree or disagree with Ehrenreich's point of view that "the fast track is headed the wrong way"? (Paragraph 6)

Questions on Method

1. How effective is Ehrenreich's choice of an anecdote to introduce her essay? Was her story convincing? Why or why not?
2. How does Ehrenreich define "success" and "busyness" in paragraphs 6–9? What would you add to her definitions?
3. Review the author's conclusion. How effective is it? To what extent does it contribute to the essay's **coherence?**

Writing Topics

1. The author focuses primarily on professionals in the workplace. Might her essay apply also to college students? Have you observed a "cult of busyness" in the lives of your fellow students or in your own daily experiences?
2. Ehrenreich distinguishes between activities she considers "worthwhile" and those she thinks contribute mainly to busyness. Write an essay defining your concept of a "worthwhile" activity citing specific examples.
3. Write an essay in which you define a word whose meaning has changed for you over a period of time by differentiating between what that word means to you now and what it meant at an earlier period. What does your changing definition reflect about your own growth?

What's in a Name?

Gloria Naylor (b. 1950) was born in New York City, where she did mis-
sionary work for the Jehovah's Witnesses for several years. She later worked
in a hotel while attending Brooklyn College of the City University of New
York. She earned a bachelor's degree and then went on to pursue graduate
work in African American studies at Yale University. Her first novel, The
Women of Brewster Place, *published in 1982, won the American Award*
for fiction and was later made into a movie for television. Her other works in-
clude Linden Hills *(1985),* Mama Day *(1988), and* Bailey's Café
(1992). The author has also edited the 1995 anthology Children of the
Night: The Best Stories by Black Writers, '67 to the Present *and has*
published a number of essays.

LANGUAGE IS THE SUBJECT. It is the written form with which I've 1
managed to keep the wolf away from the door and, in diaries, to keep
my sanity. In spite of this, I consider the written word inferior to the
spoken, and much of the frustration experienced by novelists is the
awareness that whatever we manage to capture in even the most transcendent passages falls far short of the richness of life. Dialogue
achieves its power in the dynamics of a fleeting moment of sight,
sound, smell and touch.

I'm not going to enter the debate here about whether it is lan- 2
guage that shapes reality or vice versa. That battle is doomed to be
waged whenever we seek intermittent reprieve from the chicken and
egg dispute. I will simply take the position that the spoken word, like
the written word, amounts to a nonsensical arrangement of sounds or
letters without a consensus that assigns "meaning." And building from
the meanings of what we hear, we order reality. Words themselves are
innocuous; it is the consensus that gives them true power.

I remember the first time I heard the word nigger. In my third- 3
grade class, our math tests were being passed down the rows, and as I
handed the papers to a little boy in back of me, I remarked that once

again he had received a much lower mark than I did. He snatched his test from me and spit out that word. Had he called me a nymphomaniac or a necrophiliac, I couldn't have been more puzzled. I didn't know what a nigger was, but I knew that whatever it meant, it was something he shouldn't have called me. This was verified when I raised my hand, and in a loud voice repeated what he had said and watched the teacher scold him for using a "bad" word. I was later to go home and ask the inevitable question that every black parent must face— "Mommy, what does 'nigger' mean?"

And what exactly did it mean? Thinking back, I realize that this 4 could not have been the first time the word was used in my presence. I was part of a large extended family that had migrated from the rural South after World War II and formed a close-knit network that gravitated around my maternal grandparents. Their ground-floor apartment in one of the buildings they owned in Harlem was a weekend mecca for my immediate family, along with countless aunts, uncles and cousins who brought along assorted friends. It was a bustling and open house with assorted neighbors and tenants popping in and out to exchange bits of gossip, pick up an old quarrel or referee the ongoing checkers game in which my grandmother cheated shamelessly. They were all there to let down their hair and put up their feet after a week of labor in the factories, laundries and shipyards of New York.

Amid the clamor, which could reach deafening proportions— 5 two or three conversations going on simultaneously, punctuated by the sound of a baby's crying somewhere in the back rooms or out on the street—there was still a rigid set of rules about what was said and how. Older children were sent out of the living room when it was time to get into the juicy details about "you-know-who" up on the third floor who had gone and gotten herself "p-r-e-g-n-a-n-t!" But my parents, knowing that I could spell well beyond my years, always demanded that I follow the others out to play. Beyond sexual misconduct and death, everything else was considered harmless for our young ears. And so among the anecdotes of the triumphs and disappointments in the various workings of their lives, the word nigger was used in my presence, but it was set within contexts and inflections that caused it to register in my mind as something else.

In the singular, the word was always applied to a man who had 6 distinguished himself in some situation that brought their approval for his strength, intelligence or drive:

"Did Johnny *really* do that?"   7

"I'm telling you, that nigger pulled in $6,000 of overtime last 8
year. Said he got enough for a down payment on a house."

When used with a possessive adjective by a woman—"my 9
nigger"—it became a term of endearment for husband or boyfriend.
But it could be more than just a term applied to a man. In their
mouths it became the pure essence of manhood—a disembodied force
that channeled their past history of struggle and present survival against
the odds into a victorious statement of being: "Yeah, that old foreman
found out quick enough—you don't mess with a nigger."

In the plural, it became a description of some group within the 10
community that had overstepped the bounds of decency as my family
defined it: Parents who neglected their children, a drunken couple
who fought in public, people who simply refused to look for work,
those with excessively dirty mouths or unkempt households were all
"trifling niggers." This particular circle could forgive hard times, unemployment, the occasional bout of depression—they had gone
through all of that themselves—but the unforgivable sin was a lack of
self-respect.

A woman could never be a "nigger" in the singular, with its con- 11
notation of confirming worth. The noun girl was its closest equivalent
in that sense, but only when used in direct address and regardless of the
gender doing the addressing. "Girl" was a token of respect for a
woman. The one-syllable word was drawn out to sound like three in
recognition of the extra ounce of wit, nerve or daring that the woman
had shown in the situation under discussion.

"G-i-r-l, stop. You mean you said that to his face?" 12

But if the word was used in a third-person reference or shortened 13
so that it almost snapped out of the mouth, it always involved some element of communal disapproval. And age became an important factor
in these exchanges. It was only between individuals of the same generation, or from an older person to a younger (but never the other way
around), that "girl" would be considered a compliment.

I don't agree with the argument that use of the word nigger at 14
this social stratum of the black community was an internalization of
racism. The dynamics were the exact opposite: the people in my
grandmother's living room took a word that whites used to signify
worthlessness or degradation and rendered it impotent. Gathering
there together, they transformed "nigger" to signify the varied and
complex human beings they knew themselves to be. If the word was to

dissappear totally from the mouths of even the most liberal of white society, no one in that room was naïve enough to believe it would disappear from white minds. Meeting the word head-on, they proved it had absolutely nothing to do with the way they were determined to live their lives.

So there must have been dozens of times that the word "nigger"   15
was spoken in front of me before I reached the third grade. But I didn't "hear" it until it was said by a small pair of lips that had already learned it could be a way to humiliate me. That was the word I went home and asked my mother about. And since she knew that I had to grow up in America, she took me in her lap and explained.

Questions on Meaning

1. What is Naylor saying about language in the first two paragraphs of the essay?
2. What do we learn about Naylor's family? Why does she include them?
3. What distinctions does Naylor go on to make about the differences in the connotations of *nigger* in black and white culture? Is the word always used favorably within black culture? Explain your answer.
4. What point does Naylor make about *nigger* in paragraph 14? Describe your reaction to it.
5. What is the meaning of the concluding paragraph? What does Naylor imply about America in her last sentence?
6. Is Naylor's experience one with which you can empathize? Why or why not?

Questions on Method

1. Naylor begins her essay with the generalization "Language is the subject." What technique does she then use to get to her major generalization as thesis statement in paragraph 3? Would her essay have been more effective had she reversed paragraphs 1 and 3? Why or why not?
2. What is the tone of Naylor's essay? Neutral? Angry? Sad? Does it remain consistent throughout? If it changes, where and how does it change?
3. Discuss Naylor's purpose in writing this essay. Is she merely informing or is she also trying to persuade her readers? How in general did the essay affect you?
4. Does Naylor give credence to her definition of *nigger* by using examples from her own family, or does this method make her essay too subjective? Why or why not?

Writing Topics

1. Reread Naylor's essay and write your reaction to the statement that "words themselves are innocuous; it is the consensus that gives them true power." Using a word that has powerful emotional connotations for you, write an essay defining that word as consensus has defined it and analyzing your emotional reactions to it.

2. In defining the word *nigger,* Naylor asks a series of questions. Identify these questions. What other questions did she ask herself about the subject as she wrote the essay? How does she arrange her answers?

3. Naylor writes about racial prejudice. If you have personally been the victim of prejudice, define the nature of the prejudice and analyze the emotions that were part of this experience.

Simplicity

Henry David Thoreau (1817–1862) was an American essayist and poet who was part of the American romantic literary movement. In 1845 he built a cabin at Walden Pond in Massachusetts, where he lived for the next two years. In Walden *(1854), he describes his daily experiences. A nonconformist, Thoreau was imprisoned for failing to pay his taxes and recorded the episode in his essay "Civil Disobedience." He is recognized today not only for his prose style but also for his individualism, which not only challenged the social status quo of his contemporaries but challenges ours today as well. His belief in passive resistance influenced Mahatma Gandhi and Martin Luther King Jr.*

I WENT TO THE WOODS because I wished to live deliberately, to 1
front only the essential facts of life, and see if I could not learn what it
had to teach, and not, when I came to die, discover that I had not
lived. I did not wish to live what was not life, living is so dear; nor did
I wish to practice resignation, unless it was quite necessary. I wanted to
live deep and suck out all the marrow of life, to live so sturdily and
Spartan-like as to put to rout all that was not life, to cut a broad swath
and shave close, to drive life into a corner, and reduce it to its lowest
terms, and, if it proved to be mean, why then to get the whole and
genuine meanness of it, and publish its meanness to the world; or if it
were sublime, to know it by experience, and be able to give a true account of it in my next excursion. For most men, it appears to me, are
in a strange uncertainty about it, whether it is of the devil or of God,
and have *somewhat hastily* concluded that it is the chief end of man here
to "glorify God and enjoy him forever."

Still we live meanly, like ants; though the fable tells us that we 2
were long ago changed into men; like pygmies we fight with cranes;[1]
it is error upon error, and clout upon clout, and our best virtue has for

[1]In an ancient Greek fable, the god Zeus transformed ants into men to populate a kingdom. In the Greek epic poem *The Illiad,* the poet Homer compares the Trojan army with cranes fighting against pygmies.

its occasion a superfluous and evitable wretchedness. Our life is frittered away by detail. An honest man has hardly need to count more than his ten fingers, or in extreme cases he may add his ten toes, and lump the rest. Simplicity, simplicity, simplicity! I say, let your affairs be as two or three, and not a hundred or a thousand; instead of a million count half a dozen, and keep your accounts on your thumb nail. In the midst of this chopping sea of civilized life, such are the clouds and storms and quicksands and thousand-and-one items to be allowed for, that a man has to live, if he would not founder and go to the bottom and not make his port at all, by dead reckoning, and he must be a great calculator indeed who succeeds. Simplify, simplify. Instead of three meals a day, if it be necessary eat but one; instead of a hundred dishes, five; and reduce other things in proportion.

Our life is like a German Confederacy,[2] made up of petty states, with its boundary forever fluctuating, so that even a German cannot tell you how it is bounded at any moment. The nation itself, with all its so-called internal improvements, which, by the way are all external and superficial, is just such an unwieldy and overgrown establishment, cluttered with furniture and tripped up by its own traps, ruined by luxury and heedless expense, by want of calculation and a worthy aim, as the million households in the land; and the only cure for it as for them is in a rigid economy, a stern and more than Spartan simplicity of life and elevation of purpose. It lives too fast. Men think that it is essential that the *Nation* have commerce, and export ice, and talk through a telegraph, and ride thirty miles an hour, without a doubt, whether *they* do or not; but whether we should live like baboons or like men, is a little uncertain. If we do not get our sleepers, and forge rails, and devote days and nights to the work, but go to tinkering upon our *lives* to improve *them,* who will build railroads? And if railroads are not built, how shall we get to heaven in season? But if we stay at home and mind our business, who will want railroads? We do not ride on the railroad; it rides upon us. Did you ever think what those sleepers are that underlie the railroad? Each one is a man, an Irishman, or a Yankee man. The rails are laid on them, and they are covered with sand, and the cars run smoothly over them. They are sound sleepers, I assure you. And every few years a new lot is laid down and run over; so that, if some have the pleasure of riding on a rail, others have the misfortune to be ridden upon. And when they run over a man that is walking in his

3

[2]At the time Thoreau wrote, Germany consisted of many different kingdoms.

sleep, a supernumerary sleeper in the wrong position, and wake him up, they suddenly stop the cars, and make a hue and cry about it, as if this were an exception. I am glad to know that it takes a gang of men for every five miles to keep the sleepers down and level in their beds as it is, for this is a sign that they may sometime get up again.

Why should we live with such hurry and waste of life? We are de-   4
termined to be starved before we are hungry. Men say that a stitch in time saves nine, and so they take a thousand stitches to-day to save nine to-morrow. As for *work,* we haven't any of any consequence. We have the Saint Vitus' dance, and cannot possibly keep our heads still. If I should only give a few pulls at the parish bell-rope, as for a fire, that is, without setting the bell, there is hardly a man on his farm in the outskirts of Concord, notwithstanding that press of engagements which was his excuse so many times this morning, nor a boy, nor a woman, I might al-most say, but would forsake all and follow that sound, not mainly to save property from the flames, but, if we will confess the truth, much more to see it burn, since burn it must, and we, be it known, did not set it on fire,—or to see it put out, and have a hand in it, if that is done as hand-somely; yes, even if it were the parish church itself. Hardly a man takes a half hour's nap after dinner, but when he wakes he holds up his head and asks, "What's the news?" as if the rest of mankind had stood his sentinels. Some give directions to be waked every half hour, doubtless for no other purpose; and then, to pay for it, they tell what they have dreamed. After a night's sleep the news is as indispensable as the breakfast. "Pray tell me anything new that has happened to a man anywhere on this globe,"— and he reads it over his coffee and rolls, that a man has had his eyes gouged out this morning on the Wachito River;[3] never dreaming the while that he lives in the dark unfathomed mammoth cave of this world, and has but the rudiment of an eye himself.

For my part, I could easily do without the post-office. I think   5
that there are very few important communications made through it. To speak critically, I never received more than one or two letters in my life—I wrote this some years ago—that were worth the postage. The penny-post is, commonly, an institution through which you seriously offer a man that penny for his thoughts which is so often safely offered in jest. And I am sure that I never read any memorable news in a news-paper. If we read of one man robbed, or murdered, or killed by acci-dent, or one house burned, or one vessel wrecked, or one steamboat

---

[3]A river in Arkansas.

blown up, or one cow run over on the Western Railroad, or one mad dog killed, or one lot of grasshoppers in the winter,—we never need read of another. One is enough. If you are acquainted with the principle, what do you care for a myriad of instances and applications? To a philosopher all *news,* as it is called, is gossip, and they who edit and read it are old women over their tea. Yet not a few are greedy after this gossip. There was such a rush, as I hear, the other day at one of the offices to learn the foreign news by the last arrival, that several large squares of plate glass belonging to the establishment were broken by the pressure,—news which I seriously think a ready wit might write a twelvemonth or twelve years beforehand with sufficient accuracy. As for Spain, for instance, if you know how to throw in Don Carlos and the Infanta, and Don Pedro and Seville and Granada, from time to time in the right proportions,—they may have changed the names a little since I saw the papers,—and serve up a bull-fight when other entertainments fail, it will be true to the letter, and give us as good an idea of the exact state or ruin of things in Spain as the most succinct and lucid reports under this head in the newspapers: and as for England, almost the last significant scrap of news from that quarter was the revolution of 1649;[4] and if you have learned the history of her crops for an average year, you never need attend to that thing again, unless your speculations are of a merely pecuniary character. If one may judge who rarely looks into the newspapers, nothing new does ever happen in foreign parts, a French revolution not excepted.[5]

What news! How much more important to know what that is which was never old! "Kieou-he-yu (great dignitary of the state of Wei) sent a man to Khoung-tseu to know his news. Khoung-tseu caused the messenger to be seated near him, and questioned him in these terms: What is your master doing? The messenger answered with respect: My master desires to diminish the number of his faults, but he cannot come to the end of them. The messenger being gone, the philosopher remarked: What a worthy messenger! What a worthy messenger!"[6] The preacher, instead of vexing the ears of drowsy farmers

6

---

[4]When King Charles I was beheaded and the Puritans under Oliver Cromwell assumed control of the government.

[5]Several French revolutions had occurred in the sixty years before Thoreau wrote: 1789, 1830, and 1848, the latter while Thoreau was writing *Walden,* the book in which this essay appeared.

[6]Quoted from Confucius, *Analects,* XIV.

on their day of rest at the end of the week,—for Sunday is the fit conclusion of an ill-spent week, and not the fresh and brave beginning of
a new one,—with this one other draggle-tail of a sermon, should
shout with thundering voice,—"Pause! Avast! Why so seeming fast,
but deadly slow?"

Shams and delusions are esteemed for soundest truths, while real-   7
ity is fabulous. If men would steadily observe realities only, and not allow themselves to be deluded, life, to compare it with such things as
we know, would be like a fairy tale and the Arabian Nights' Entertainments.[7] If we respected only what is inevitable and has a right to be,
music and poetry would resound along the streets. When we are un-
hurried and wise, we perceive that only great and worthy things have
any permanent and absolute existence,—that petty fears and petty
pleasures are but the shadow of the reality. This is always exhilarating
and sublime. By closing the eyes and slumbering, and consenting to be
deceived by shows, men establish and confirm their daily life of routine
and habit everywhere, which still is built on purely illusory foundations. Children, who play life, discern its true law and relations more
clearly than men, who fail to live it worthily, but who think that they
are wiser by experience, that is, by failure. I have read in a Hindoo
book, that "there was a king's son, who, being expelled in infancy
from his native city, was brought up by a forester, and, growing up to
maturity in that state, imagined himself to belong to the barbarous race
with which he lived. One of his father's ministers having discovered
him, revealed to him what he was, and the misconception of his character was removed, and he knew himself to be a prince. So soul," continues the Hindoo philosopher, "from the circumstances in which it is
placed, mistakes its own character, until the truth is revealed to it by
some holy teacher, and then it knows itself to be *Brahme*."[8] I perceive
that we inhabitants of New England live this mean life that we do because our vision does not penetrate the surface of things. We think that
that *is* which *appears* to be. If a man should walk through this town and
see only the reality, where, think you, would the "Milldam"[9] go to? If
he should give us an account of the realities he beheld there, we should
not recognize the place in his description. Look at a meeting-house, or

[7] *The Thousand and One Nights,* a collection of exotic stories including those about
Sindbad the Sailor and Ali Baba and the Forty Thieves.
[8] The soul (after Brahma, the Hindu god).
[9] Main street in Concord, Thoreau's hometown.

a courthouse, or a jail, or a shop, or a dwelling-house, and say what that thing really is before a true gaze, and they would all go to pieces in your account of them. Men esteem truth remote, in the outskirts of the system, behind the farthest star, before Adam and after the last man. In eternity there is indeed something true and sublime. But all these times and places and occasions are now and here. God himself culminates in the present moment, and will never be more divine in the lapse of all the ages. And we are enabled to apprehend at all what is sublime and noble only by the perpetual instilling and drenching of the reality that surrounds us. The universe constantly and obediently answers to our conceptions; whether we travel fast or slow, the track is laid for us. Let us spend our lives in conceiving then. The poet or the artist never yet had so fair and noble a design but some of his posterity at least could accomplish it.

8   Let us spend one day as deliberately as Nature, and not be thrown off the track by every nutshell and mosquito's wing that falls on the rails. Let us rise early and fast, or break fast, gently and without perturbation; let company come and let company go, let the bells ring and the children cry,—determined to make a day of it. Why should we knock under and go with the stream? Let us not be upset and overwhelmed in that terrible rapid and whirlpool called a dinner, situated in the meridian shallows. Weather this danger and you are safe, for the rest of the way is down hill. With unrelaxed nerves, with morning vigor, sail by it, looking another way, tied to the mast like Ulysses.[10] If the engine whistles, let it whistle till it is hoarse for its pains. If the bell rings, why should we run? We will consider what kind of music they are like.

9   Let us settle ourselves, and work and wedge our feet downward through the mud and slush of opinion, and prejudice, and tradition, and delusion, and appearance, that alluvion which covers the globe, through Paris and London, through New York and Boston and Concord, through church and state, through poetry and philosophy and religion, till we come to a hard bottom and rocks in place, which we can call *reality,* and say, This is, and no mistake; and then begin, having a *point d'appui,*[11] below freshet and frost and fire, a place where you

---

[10]Ulysses, the hero of Homer's other epic poem, *The Odyssey,* ties himself to the mast of his ship rather than respond to the alluring song of the Sirens, for to do so would send him to his death. Thoreau compares eating dinner to responding to the Sirens.

[11]French expression meaning "point of support" or foundation.

might found a wall or a state, or set a lamppost safely, or perhaps a gauge, not a Nilometer,[12] but a Realometer, that future ages might know how deep a freshet of shams and appearances had gathered from time to time. If you stand right fronting and face to face to a fact, you will see the sun glimmer on both its surfaces, as if it were a cimeter,[13] and feel its sweet edge dividing you through the heart and marrow, and so you will happily conclude your mortal career. Be it life or death, we crave only reality. If we are really dying, let us hear the rattle in our throats and feel cold in the extremities; if we are alive, let us go about our business.

Time is but the stream I go a-fishing in. I drink at it; but while I drink I see the sandy bottom and detect how shallow it is. Its thin current slides away, but eternity remains. I would drink deeper; fish in the sky, whose bottom is pebbly with stars. I cannot count one. I know not the first letter of the alphabet. I have always been regretting that I was not as wise as the day I was born. The intellect is a cleaver; it discerns and rifts its way into the secret of things. I do not wish to be any more busy with my hands than is necessary. My head is hands and feet. I feel all my best faculties concentrated in it. My instinct tells me that my head is an organ for burrowing, as some creatures use their snout and forepaws, and with it I would mine and burrow my way through these hills. I think that the richest vein is somewhere hereabouts; so by the divining rod and thin rising vapors I judge; and here I will begin to mine.

Questions on Meaning

1. What is Thoreau's definition of simplicity?
2. What is Thoreau criticizing in the third paragraph? Why does he dislike railroads? Do you think his point of view is reactionary? Why or why not?
3. "Why should we live with such hurry and waste of life?" What examples does Thoreau cite? What additional instances would you offer?
4. Thoreau thinks that being preoccupied with news is a form of distraction. What is your reaction to his point of view? Is it practical for today's world? Why or why not?
5. Why does Thoreau quote from Confucius? Does he make his point of view more convincing as a result? Why or why not?

---

[12]A gauge used in ancient Egypt for measuring the depth of the Nile.

[13]A scimitar, a curved sword used by Arabs and Turks.

Questions on Method

1. For what audience is Thoreau writing? What is the significance of his beginning and ending the essay with "I," and then changing to "we" and "you" in the middle part?
2. How would you characterize the tone of this essay? Notice that it changes in the first and last paragraphs. How do these changes affect the meaning of the essay?
3. What is Thoreau's purpose in writing "Simplicity"? Is he seeking to inform his readers, or does he want to influence them? Give evidence for your point of view.

Writing Topics

1. Thoreau feels very strongly about the negative aspects of complicating one's life. Write an essay analyzing the choices you would have to make to simplify your life, including your attitude toward having to make them.
2. Write an extended definition of one of the following concepts: freedom, character, friendship, parenthood, honesty, or marriage. Prepare a profile of your intended audience, and clarify your definition with concrete examples.

New Superstitions for Old

Margaret Mead (1901–1978) was among the most widely recognized of American anthropologists. She won early and immediate acclaim for her study of the transition from adolescence to adulthood in Coming of Age in Samoa *(1928). She also taught for many years at Columbia University and wrote more than twenty books, including* Culture and Commitment *(1970) and* Blackberry Winter: A Memoir *(1972). In the following essay, she defines various kinds of superstitions.*

ONCE IN A WHILE there is a day when everything seems to run smoothly and even the riskiest venture comes out exactly right. You exclaim, "This is my lucky day!" Then as an afterthought you say, "Knock on wood!" Of course, you do not really believe that knocking on wood will ward off danger. Still, boasting about your own good luck gives you a slightly uneasy feeling—and you carry out the little protective ritual. If someone challenged you at that moment, you would probably say, "Oh, that's nothing. Just an old superstition."

But when you come to think about it, what is a superstition?

In the contemporary world most people treat old folk beliefs as superstitions—the belief, for instance, that there are lucky and unlucky days or numbers, that future events can be read from omens, that there are protective charms or that what happens can be influenced by casting spells. We have excluded magic from our current world view, for we know that natural events have natural causes.

In a religious context, where truths cannot be demonstrated, we accept them as a matter of faith. Superstitions, however, belong to the category of beliefs, practices and ways of thinking that have been discarded because they are inconsistent with scientific knowledge. It is easy to say that other people are superstitious because they believe what we regard to be untrue. "Superstition" used in that sense is a derogatory term for the beliefs of other people that we do not share. But there is more to it than that. For superstitions lead a kind of half life in a twilight world where, sometimes, we partly suspend our disbelief and act as if magic worked.

Actually, almost every day, even in the most sophisticated home, something is likely to happen that evokes the memory of some old folk belief. The salt spills. A knife falls to the floor. Your nose tickles. Then perhaps, with a slightly embarrassed smile, the person who spilled the salt tosses a pinch over his left shoulder. Or someone recites the old rhyme, "Knife falls, gentleman calls." Or as you rub your nose you think, That means a letter. I wonder who's writing? No one takes these small responses very seriously or gives them more than a passing thought. Sometimes people will preface one of these ritual acts—walking around instead of under a ladder or hastily closing an umbrella that has been opened inside a house—with such a remark as "I remember my great-aunt used to..." or "Germans used to say you ought not..." And then, having placed the belief at some distance away in time or space, they carry out the ritual.

Everyone also remembers a few of the observances of childhood—wishing on the first star; looking at the new moon over the right shoulder; avoiding the cracks in the sidewalk on the way to school while chanting, "Step on a crack, break your mother's back"; wishing on white horses, on loads of hay, on covered bridges, on red cars; saying quickly, "Bread-and-butter" when a post or a tree separated you from the friend you were walking with. The adult may not actually recite the formula "Star light, star bright..." and may not quite turn to look at the new moon, but his mood is tempered by a little of the old thrill that came when the observance was still freighted with magic.

Superstition can also be used with another meaning. When I discuss the religious beliefs of other peoples, especially primitive peoples, I am often asked, "Do they really have a religion, or is it all just superstition?" The point of contrast here is not between a scientific and magical view of the world but between the clear, theologically defensible religious beliefs of members of civilized societies and what we regard as the false and childish views of the heathen who "bow down to wood and stone." Within the civilized religions, however, where membership includes believers who are educated and urbane and others who are ignorant and simple, one always finds traditions and practices that the more sophisticated will dismiss offhand as "just superstition" but that guide the steps of those who live by older ways. Mostly these are very ancient beliefs, some handed on from one religion to another and carried from country to country around the world.

Very commonly, people associate superstition with the past, with very old ways of thinking that have been supplanted by modern knowledge. But new superstitions are continually coming into being and flourishing in our society. Listening to mothers in the parks in the 1930's, one heard them say, "Now, don't you run out into the sun, or Polio will get you." In the 1940's elderly people explained to one another in tones of resignation, "It was the Virus that got him down." And every year the cosmetics industry offers us new magic—cures for baldness, lotions that will give every woman radiant skin, hair coloring that will restore to the middle-aged the charm and romance of youth—results that are promised if we will just follow the simple directions. Families and individuals also have their cherished, private superstitions. You must leave by the back door when you are going on a journey, or you must wear a green dress when you are taking an examination. It is a kind of joke, of course, but it makes you feel safe.

These old half-beliefs and new half-beliefs reflect the keenness of our wish to have something come true or to prevent something bad from happening. We do not always recognize new superstitions for what they are, and we still follow the old ones because someone's faith long ago matches our contemporary hopes and fears. In the past people "knew" that a black cat crossing one's path was a bad omen, and they turned back home. Today we are fearful of taking a journey and would give anything to turn back—and then we notice a black cat running across the road in front of us.

Child psychologists recognize the value of the toy a child holds in his hand at bedtime. It is different from his thumb, with which he can close himself in from the rest of the world, and it is different from the real world, to which he is learning to relate himself. Psychologists call these toys—these furry animals and old, cozy baby blankets—"transitional objects"; that is, objects that help the child move back and forth between the exactions of everyday life and the world of wish and dream.

Superstitions have some of the qualities of these transitional objects. They help people pass between the areas of life where what happens has to be accepted without proof and the areas where sequences of events are explicable in terms of cause and effect, based on knowledge. Bacteria and viruses that cause sickness have been identified; the cause of symptoms can be diagnosed and a rational course of treatment prescribed. Magical charms no longer are needed to treat the sick; modern medicine has brought the whole sequence of events into the secular world. But people often act as if this change had not taken place. Laymen still treat germs as if they were invisible, malign spirits, and physicians sometimes prescribe antibiotics as if they were magic substances.

Over time, more and more of life has become subject to the controls of knowledge. However, this is never a one-way process. Scientific investigation is continually increasing our knowledge. But if we are to make good use of this knowledge, we must not only rid our minds of old, superseded beliefs and fragments of magical practice, but also recognize new superstitions for what they are. Both are generated by our wishes, our fears and our feelings of helplessness in difficult situations.

Civilized peoples are not alone in having grasped the idea of superstitions—beliefs and practices that are superseded but that still may evoke compliance. The idea is one that is familiar to every people, however primitive, that I have ever known. Every society has a core of transcendent beliefs—beliefs about the nature of the universe, the world and man—that no one doubts or questions. Every society also has a fund of knowledge related to practical life—about the succession of day and night and of the seasons; about correct ways of planting seeds so that they will germinate and grow; about the processes involved in making dyes or the steps necessary to remove the deadly poison from manioc roots so they become edible. Island peoples know how the winds shift and they know the star toward which they must point the prow of the canoe exactly so that as the sun rises they will see the first fringing palms on the shore toward which they are sailing.

This knowledge, based on repeated observations of reliable sequences, leads to ideas and hypotheses of the kind that underlie scientific thinking. And gradually as scientific knowledge, once developed without conscious plan, has become a great self-corrective system and the foundation for rational planning and action, old magical beliefs and observances have had to be discarded.

But it takes time for new ways of thinking to take hold, and often the transition is only partial. Older, more direct beliefs live on in the hearts and minds of elderly people. And they are learned by children who, generation after generation, start out life as hopefully and fearfully as their forebears did. Taking their first step away from home, children use the old rituals and invent new ones to protect themselves against the strangeness of the world into which they are venturing.

So whatever has been rejected as no longer true, as limited, provincial and idolatrous, still leads a half life. People may say, "It's just a superstition," but they continue to invoke the ritual's protection or potency. In this transitional, twilight state such beliefs come to resemble dreaming. In the dream world a thing can be either good or bad; a cause can be an effect and an effect can be a cause. Do warts come from touching toads, or does touching a toad cure the wart? Is sneezing a good omen or a bad omen? You can have it either way—or both ways at once. In the same sense, the half-acceptance and half-denial accorded superstitions give us the best of both worlds.

Superstitions are sometimes smiled at and sometimes frowned upon as observances characteristic of the old-fashioned, the unenlightened, children, peasants, servants, immigrants, foreigners or backwoods people. Nevertheless, they give all of us ways of moving back and forth among the different worlds in which we live—the sacred, the secular and the scientific. They allow us to keep a private world also, where, smiling a little, we can banish danger with a gesture and summon luck with a rhyme, make the sun shine in spite of storm clouds, force the stranger to do our bidding, keep an enemy at bay and straighten the paths of those we love. 17

Questions on Meaning

1. In paragraph 4, Mead says that superstitions "belong to the category of beliefs, practices and ways of thinking that have been discarded because they are inconsistent with scientific knowledge." How do the examples she offers of such superstitions help us understand why they are inconsistent with scientific knowledge? Discuss the definitions of *scientific knowledge* that Mead offers in paragraphs 11 and 14.
2. In paragraph 7, Mead says that the word *superstition* also is applied to the religious beliefs of uncivilized peoples. Does the use of *superstition* in such cases trivialize these beliefs? Discuss.
3. Why, according to Mead, might even the most civilized person continue to practice some superstitions as if they were what she calls in paragraph 9 "half-beliefs"? In what ways are these half-beliefs comparable to childhood toys or to dreams? What does Mead mean when she says in paragraph 17 that such half-beliefs "give all of us ways of moving back and forth among the different worlds in which we live—the sacred, the secular and the scientific"?

Questions on Method

1. How effectively does Mead use the technique of defining a word by differentiating between what it does and does not mean? Is she right in sug-

gesting in paragraph 1 that people tend to misuse the word *superstition* as a way to avoid admitting how superstitious they really are?

2. How complex is Mead's use of the technique of contrast and comparison? How, for example, does her distinguishing in paragraphs 13 through 15 of a primitive society's "transcendent beliefs," "scientific knowledge," and "old magical beliefs" from one another help us understand that a primitive society is not necessarily classifiable as one that is more superstitious than a developed society?

3. How does Mead's process analysis in paragraph 15 of the way superstitions get carried on from generation to generation help us understand a key value of superstition in even the most advanced society?

4. How accurate is Mead's definition in paragraph 16 of the "world of dreams" as a world where "a cause can be an effect and an effect can be a cause"? Which of her examples makes clear that this unsciencific mix-up of cause and effect is also a chief characteristic of superstitions?

Writing Topics

1. Write an essay in which you discuss the superstitious qualities of some contemporary ritual, such as a sporting event, a high school prom, or a political election. Do the superstitions associated with such events make these events any less sophisticated or complex? Explain.

2. Mead says in paragraph 9 that we do not always recognize "new superstitions" for what they are. Write an essay in which you identify some examples of such new superstitions.

3. What "private superstitions" (paragraph 8) do you practice? Write an essay that discusses why such private superstitions are important or helpful to you.

Definition
Writing Topics

1. Many of the authors in this section seem to take an almost superstitious view of the act of definition, regarding a word like "holocaust" as almost magical in its capacity to protect us from understanding or feeling the most uncomfortable and upsetting truths. How magical is the act of defining or naming? Discuss the extent to which one of the following words or phrases is a "magical" definition or, in Bettelheim's phrase, a linguistic circumlocution: euthanasia, nuclear incident, enemy, sacrifice, hero, law and order, survivor.

2. Write an essay in which you define a word whose meaning has changed for you over a period of time, by differentiating between what that word means to you now and what it meant to you at the earlier period. What does your changing definition reflect about your own growth? Does the word "freedom," for example, have a different meaning to you now than it had when you were 15?

3. Is the act of definition less a matter of finding the right synonym for a word than it is a matter of offering one's opinion on some subject associated with the word? Discuss this question in an essay that evaluates how opinionated one of the definitions offered in this section is.

4. The fields of medicine, psychology, and sociology are constantly adding new words to the common vocabulary. Choose a new scientific word with which you are familiar, define it, and discuss the effect the word and its definition have had on society.

5. Some words—liberty, justice, and love, for example—have emotional meanings, meanings beyond the dictionary definition, that may change from century to century. Discuss the current definition of one of these words in an extended definition in which you also contrast its definition today with that of a past age.

11

Comparison and Contrast

COMPARISON IS THE EXAMINATION of two or more subjects for the purpose of noting similarities and differences. In expository comparison, specific likenesses and differences are usually examined in detail with the view to making both subjects better known. Comparison is an especially useful mode of organizing expository writing, as it can be adapted to long or short paragraphs or essays. **Contrast** is a special kind of comparison in which only differences are noted. (Examples of expository comparison are by no means confined to this chapter, but are liberally scattered throughout the book.)

A comparison that discusses only similarities is simpler to organize than a comparison that examines both similarities *and* differences. If you write about similarities, you will find yourself using a lot of *both*s: Both Grant and Lee were expert generals; both Grant and Lee were representative of their region; both Grant and Lee were forgiving to their enemies.

If you want to point out both similarities and differences, it is best to separate the two, for when you come to the differences you will find you have two options: (a) organize the material subject by subject,

263

finishing with *x* before moving on to *y,* or (b) organize point by point, switching back and forth between *x* and *y* even within the same paragraph. If your composition is divided into many subtopics or if you are dealing with both similarities and differences, the point-by-point method is probably better. Arthur L. Campa's introductory paragraph to "Anglo vs. Chicano: Why?" explains the purpose of his comparison, which is a good way to begin. He then uses paragraph division to show his numerous points of comparison—differences between the mother countries Spain and England, attitudes toward values, motives for colonization, effects of the horse, and so on. The following outlines show at a glance the two ways of organizing Campa's material, the one on the left being his actual choice:

Point by Point	*Subject by Subject*
I. Introduction	I. Introduction
II. Body	II. Body
A. Differences between	A. Anglo
mother countries	B. Chicano
1. Spain	III. Conclusion
2. England	
B. Different attitudes	
toward values	
1. Spanish	
2. English	
C. Different motives	
for colonization	
1. Spanish	
2. English	
D. Different effects of the horse	
⋮	
III. Conclusion	

Note that for every "Chicano point" Campa has an "Anglo point" and that the order of the points remains the same, Spanish (or Chicano) then English (or Anglo). The subject-by-subject method also requires equal and corresponding points for each subject, and consistent ordering of your points is even more important, because the points may be widely separated as they are in the selection from Aristotle's writing.

    In "Youth and Old Age," Aristotle juxtaposes two portraits—one of youth, the other of old age—and lets the reader infer most of the differences; he is concerned almost wholly with one point, emotional and mental attitude, so his subject-by-subject method works well.

There is a special kind of comparison called **analogy,** in which *x* and *y* are necessarily unequal in both interest and importance. An analogy compares a well-known *x* with a less well-known *y*, with the sole purpose of teaching what *y* is. Once the reader understands *y*, *x* can be forgotten. C. G. Jung, for example, compares the psyche to an oil well that penetrates stratum after stratum of different rocks and minerals. He is using an analogy to teach, not because he considers the psyche and the oil well to be really comparable, but because he wants to give a picture of the psyche, and he believes that most of his readers would know what a geological cross section looks like.

Most important of all, comparison and contrast can be useful only if you know and tell why you are using it. Why compare? Why contrast? *Listing* similarities and differences is not sufficient to command someone's interest; make it clear to your reader *why* you are comparing *x* with *y*. Aristotle presents his contrast as a lesson about oration; by understanding youth and old age, "we can now see how to compose our speeches so as to adapt both them and ourselves to our audience."

Transitional words and phrases are especially necessary in writing contrast, because you are continually alternating between points or subjects; get used to providing signals like "yet," "on the other hand," and "finally."

WRITING COMPARISON

1. Explain the purpose of your comparison in your introduction.
2. Decide, primarily by considering the length and complexity of the material, which pattern is clearest, subject by subject or point by point.
3. Choose subjects for comparison that are from the same general class.
4. Use comparison of a well-known subject and an unfamiliar subject (analogy) as a teaching device.
5. Use transitions.

Anglo vs. Chicano: Why?

American-born Arthur L. Campa (b. 1905) lives in Mexico. He graduated from Columbia University with a doctorate in Spanish and has taught at several universities, including the University of Mexico and the University of Colorado at Denver. He was a cultural attaché at the U.S. Embassy in Lima, Peru, from 1955 to 1957. His publications include several Spanish textbooks as well as more than seventy monographs, bulletins, and articles on folklore. His writing often reflects his interest in cultural interrelationships.

THE CULTURAL DIFFERENCES between Hispanic and Anglo–American people have been dwelt upon by so many writers that we should all be well informed about the values of both. But audiences are usually of the same persuasion as the speakers, and those who consult published works are for the most part specialists looking for affirmation of what they believe. So, let us consider the same subject, exploring briefly some of the basic cultural differences that cause conflict in the Southwest, where Hispanic and Anglo–American cultures meet.

Cultural differences are implicit in the conceptual content of the languages of these two civilizations, and their value systems stem from a long series of historical circumstances. Therefore, it may be well to consider some of the English and Spanish cultural configurations before these Europeans set foot on American soil. English culture was basically insular, geographically and ideologically; was more integrated on the whole, except for some strong theological differences; and was particularly zealous of its racial purity. Spanish culture was peninsular, a geographical circumstance that made it a catchall of Mediterranean, central European and north African peoples. The composite nature of the population produced a market regionalism that prevented close integration, except for religion, and led to a strong sense of individualism. These differences were reflected in the colonizing enterprise of the two cultures. The English isolated themselves from the Indians physically and culturally; the Spanish, who had strong notions about *pureza de sangre* [purity of blood] among the nobility, were not collectively averse to adding one more strain to their racial cocktail. Cortés led the way by siring the first *mestizo* in North America, and the rest of the conquistadores followed suit. The ultimate products of these two orientations meet today in the Southwest.

Anglo-American culture was absolutist at the onset; that is, all the dominant values were considered identical for all, regardless of time and place. Such values as justice, charity, honesty were considered the superior social order for all men and were later embodied in the American Constitution. The Spaniard brought with him a relativistic viewpoint and saw fewer moral implications in man's actions. Values were looked upon as the result of social and economic conditions.

The motives that brought Spaniards and Englishmen to America also differed. The former came on an enterprise of discovery, searching for a new route to India initially, and later for new lands to conquer, the fountain of youth, minerals, the Seven Cities of Cíbola and, in the case of the missionaries, new souls to win for the Kingdom of Heaven. The English came to escape religious persecution, and once having found a haven, they settled down to cultivate the soil and establish their homes. Since the Spaniards were not seeking a refuge or running away from anything, they continued their explorations and circled the globe 25 years after the discovery of the New World.

This peripatetic tendency of the Spaniard may be accounted for in part by the fact that he was the product of an equestrian culture. Men on foot do not venture far into the unknown. It was almost a century after the landing on Plymouth Rock that Governor Alexander Spotswood of Virginia crossed the Blue Ridge Mountains, and it was not until the nineteenth century that the Anglo-Americans began to move west of the Mississippi.

The Spaniard's equestrian role meant that he was not close to the soil, as was the Anglo-American pioneer, who tilled the land and built the greatest agricultural industry in history. The Spaniard cultivated the land only when he had Indians available to do it for him. The uses to which the horse was put also varied. The Spanish horse was essentially a mount, while the more robust English horse was used in cultivating the soil. It is therefore not surprising that the viewpoints of these two cultures should differ when we consider that the pioneer is looking at the world at the level of his eyes while the *caballero* [horseman] is looking beyond and down at the rest of the world.

One of the most commonly quoted, and often misinterpreted, characteristics of Hispanic peoples is the deeply ingrained individualism

in all walks of life. Hispanic individualism is a revolt against the incursion of collectivity, strongly asserted when it is felt that the ego is being
fenced in. This attitude leads to a deficiency in those social qualities
based on collective standards, an attitude that Hispanos do not consider
negative because it manifests a measure of individual freedom. Naturally, such an attitude has no *reglas fijas* [fixed rules].

Anglo-Americans who achieve a measure of success and security   8
through institutional guidance not only do not mind a few fixed rules
but demand them. The lack of a concerted plan of action, whether in
business or in politics, appears unreasonable to Anglo-Americans.
They have a sense of individualism, but they achieve it through action
and self-determination. Spanish individualism is based on feeling, on
something that is the result not of rules and collective standards but of
a person's momentary, emotional reaction. And it is subject to change
when the mood changes. In contrast to Spanish emotional individualism, the Anglo-American strives for objectivity when choosing a
course of action or making a decision.

The Southwestern Hispanos voiced strong objections to the lack   9
of courtesy of the Anglo-Americans when they first met them in the
early days of the Sante Fe trade. The same accusation is leveled at the
Americanos today in many quarters of the Hispanic world. Some of this
results from their different conceptions of polite behavior. Here too
one can say that the Spanish have no *reglas fijas* because for them courtesy is simply an expression of the way one person feels toward another. To some they extend the hand, to some they bow and for the
more *íntimos* there is the well-known *abrazo*. The concepts of "good or
bad" or "right and wrong" in polite behavior are moral considerations
of an absolutist culture.

Another cultural contrast appears in the way both cultures share   10
part of their material substance with others. The pragmatic Anglo-
American contributes regularly to such institutions as the Red Cross,
the United Fund and a myriad of associations. He also establishes
foundations and quite often leaves millions to such institutions. The
Hispano prefers to give his contribution directly to the recipient so he
can see the person he is helping.

A century of association has inevitably acculturated both Hispanos   11
and Anglo-Americans to some extent, but there still persist a number of
culture traits that neither group has relinquished altogether. Nothing is
more disquieting to an Anglo-American who believes that time is
money than the time perspective of Hispanos. They usually refer to this

attitude as the "*mañana* psychology." Actually, it is more of a "today psychology," because Hispanos cultivate the present to the exclusion of the future; because the latter has not arrived yet, it is not a reality. They are reluctant to relinquish the present, so they hold on to it until it becomes the past. To an Hispano, nine is nine until it is ten, so when he arrives at nine-thirty, he jubilantly exclaims: "¡Justo!" [right on time]. This may be why the clock is slowed down to a walk in Spanish while in English it runs. In the United States, our future-oriented civilization plans our lives so far in advance that the present loses its meaning. January magazine issues [including ID's] are out in December; 1973 cars have been out since October; cemetery plots and even funeral arrangements are bought on the installment plan. To a person engrossed in living today the very idea of planning his funeral sounds like the tolling of the bells.

It is a natural corollary that a person who is present oriented 12
should be compensated by being good at improvising. An Anglo-American is told in advance to prepare for an "impromptu speech," but an Hispano usually can improvise a speech because "*Nosotros lo improvisamos todo*" [we improvise everything].

Another source of cultural conflict arises from the difference 13
between *being* and *doing*. Even when trying to be individualistic, the Anglo-American achieves it by what he does. Today's younger generation decided to be themselves, to get away from standardization, so they let their hair grow, wore ragged clothes and even went barefoot in order to be different from the Establishment. As a result they all ended up doing the same things and created another stereotype. The freedom enjoyed by the individuality of *being* makes it unnecessary for Hispanos to strive to be different.

In 1963 a team of psychologists from the University of Guadalajara 14
in Mexico and the University of Michigan compared 74 upper-middle-class students from each university. Individualism and personalism were found to be central values for the Mexican students. This was explained by saying that a Mexican's value as a person lies in his *being* rather than, as is the case of the Anglo-Americans, in concrete accomplishments. Efficiency and accomplishments are derived characteristics that do not affect worthiness in the Mexican, whereas in the American it is equated with success, a value of highest priority in the American culture. Hispanic people disassociate themselves from material things or from actions that may impugn a person's sense of being, but the Anglo-American shows great concern for material things and assumes responsibility for his actions. This is expressed in the language of each culture. In Spanish one

says, *"Se me cayó la taza"* [the cup fell away from me] instead of "I dropped the cup."

In English, one speaks of money, cash and all related transactions 15 with frankness because material things of this high order do not trouble Anglo-Americans. In Spanish such materialistic concepts are circumvented by referring to cash as *efectivo* [effective] and when buying or selling as something *al contado* [counted out], and when without it by saying *No tengo fondos* [I have no funds]. This disassociation from material things is what produces *sobriedad* [sobriety] in the Spaniard according to Miguel de Unamuno, but in the Southwest the disassociation from materialism leads to *dejadez* [lassitude] and *desprendimiento* [disinterestedness]. A man may lose his life defending his honor but is unconcerned about the lack of material things. *Desprendimiento* causes a man to spend his last cent on a friend, which when added to lack of concern for the future may mean that tomorrow he will eat beans as a result of today's binge.

The implicit differences in words that appear to be identical in 16 meaning are astonishing. Versatile is a compliment in English and an insult in Spanish. An Hispano student who is told to apologize cannot do it, because the word doesn't exist in Spanish. *Apologia* means words in praise of a person. The Anglo-American either apologizes, which is a form of retraction abhorrent in Spanish, or compromises, another concept foreign to Hispanic culture. *Compromiso* means a date, not a compromise. In colonial Mexico City, two hidalgos once entered a narrow street from opposite sides, and when they could not go around, they sat in their coaches for three days until the viceroy ordered them to back out. All this because they could not work out a compromise.

It was that way then and to some extent now. Many of today's 1: conflicts in the Southwest have their roots in polarized cultural differences, which need not be irreconcilable when approached with mutual respect and understanding.

Questions on Meaning

1. What historical differences between England and Spain, according to Campa, account for the differences today between Anglo American and Hispanic American cultures?
2. How does the difference that Campa points out in paragraphs 5 and 6 between the English pioneer and the Spanish horseman prepare us to understand the difference between Anglo American and Hispanic American concepts of individualism?

3. Why, according to Campa, are Anglo Americans more "pragmatic" than Hispanic Americans? How is this difference reflected in each culture's attitude toward time?

4. What is the difference Campa points out in paragraph 13 between "being" and "doing"? What effect does the Hispanic emphasis on being have on Hispanic attitudes toward material success?

5. In paragraph 2, Campa states, "Cultural differences are implicit in the conceptual content of the languages of these two civilizations." In what way is Campa's discussion in paragraph 16 of "implicit differences in words that appear to be identical in meaning" an effective summary of the major cultural differences between Anglos and Hispanos? How would you summarize the essential differences between these two groups of people? Do you agree with Campa's conclusion that these differences "need not be irreconcilable"?

Questions on Method

1. How effective is Campa's organizational method?

2. Although Campa compares characteristics of each culture, he devotes many more words to explaining Hispanic characteristics than he does to explaining Anglo characteristics. How can you account for this emphasis?

3. How logical and reasonable is Campa's tone? Do you think that his essay would convince both an Anglo American and a Hispanic American that their cultural characteristics, however different, deserve "mutual respect and understanding"? Are there characteristics of either culture that, as Campa presents them, you find unreasonable and difficult to understand?

Writing Topics

1. Campa's essay focuses on the contrasting values of two of the European-based cultures that meet in the United States. Write an essay on the contrasting values of some of the other cultures in this country. How are the contrasts between Anglos and Hispanos comparable to contrasts that you can point out between Americans from other cultures?

2. In paragraph 11, Campa argues that in America "our future-oriented civilization plans our lives so far in advance that the present loses its meaning." Write an essay in which you compare specific examples of American attitudes toward the past, the present, and the future.

3. One theme of Campa's essay is that the language we use reveals a good deal about the values we live by. Write an essay in which you discuss what the specialized language of a particular cultural activity in America reveals about American values in general. What, for example, does the language of American sportscasters, disc jockeys, or movie heroes reveal about our present-day values?

Youth and Old Age

Aristotle (384–322 B.C.E.) was a Greek philosopher who defined much of the content of Western thought. He spent twenty years at Plato's Athenian academy and in later life established his own institution, the Lyceum, which became a center for research into every field of inquiry. Of his numerous works, forty-seven remain, primarily in the form of notes used in his Lyceum lectures. In the following essay, he draws many contrasts between youth and age that are still pertinent today.

YOUNG MEN have strong passions, and tend to gratify them indis-   1
criminately. Of the bodily desires, it is the sexual by which they are
most swayed and in which they show absence of self-control. They are
changeable and fickle in their desires, which are violent while they last,
but quickly over: their impulses are keen but not deep-rooted, and are
like sick people's attacks of hunger and thirst. They are hot-tempered
and quick-tempered, and apt to give way to their anger; bad temper often gets the better of them, for owing to their love of honor they cannot bear being slighted, and are indignant if they imagine themselves
unfairly treated. While they love honor, they love victory still more; for
youth is eager for superiority over others, and victory is one form of
this. They love both more than they love money, which indeed they
love very little, not having yet learnt what it means to be without it—
this is the point of Pittacus' remark about Amphiaraus.[1] They look at
the good side rather than the bad, not having yet witnessed many instances of wickedness. They trust others readily, because they have not
often been cheated. They are sanguine; nature warms their blood as
though with excess of wine; and besides that, they have as yet met with
few disappointments. Their lives are mainly spent not in memory but in
expectation; for expectation refers to the future, memory to the past,
and youth has a long future before it and a short past behind it: on the
first day of one's life one has nothing at all to remember, and can only

---

[1]Reference unknown.

look forward. They are easily cheated, owing to the sanguine disposition just mentioned. Their hot tempers and hopeful dispositions make them more courageous than older men are; the hot temper prevents fear, and the hopeful disposition creates confidence; we cannot feel fear so long as we are feeling angry, and any expectation of good makes us confident. They are shy, accepting the rules of society in which they have been trained, and not yet believing in any other standard of honor. They have exalted notions, because they have not yet been humbled by life or learnt its necessary limitations; moreover, their hopeful disposition makes them think themselves equal to great things—and that means having exalted notions. They would always rather do noble deeds than useful ones: their lives are regulated more by moral feeling than by reasoning; and whereas reasoning leads us to choose what is useful, moral goodness leads us to choose what is noble. They are fonder of their friends, intimates, and companions than older men are, because they like spending their days in the company of others, and have not yet come to value either their friends or anything else by their usefulness to themselves. All their mistakes are in the direction of doing things excessively and vehemently. They disobey Chilon's precept[2] by overdoing everything; they love too much and hate too much, and the same with everything else. They think they know everything, and are always quite sure about it; this, in fact, is why they overdo everything. If they do wrong to others, it is because they mean to insult them, not to do them actual harm. They are ready to pity others, because they think every one an honest man, or anyhow better than he is: they judge their neighbour by their own harmless natures, and so cannot think he deserves to be treated in that way. They are fond of fun and therefore witty, wit being well-bred insolence.

Such, then, is the character of the Young. The character of Elderly Men—men who are past their prime—may be said to be formed for the most part of elements that are the contrary of all these. They have lived many years; they have often been taken in, and often made mistakes; and life on the whole is a bad business. The result is that they are sure about nothing and *under-do* everything. They 'think,' but they never 'know'; and because of their hesitation they always add a 'possibly' or a 'perhaps,' putting everything this way and nothing positively. They are cynical; that is, they tend to put the worse construction on everything. Further, their experience makes them distrustful and

___

[2]"(Do) nothing in excess."

therefore suspicious of evil. Consequently they neither love warmly nor hate bitterly, but following the hint of Bias they love as though they will some day hate and hate as though they will some day love.[3] They are small-minded, because they have been humbled by life: their desires are set upon nothing more exalted or unusual than what will help them to keep alive. They are not generous, because money is one of the things they must have, and at the same time their experience has taught them how hard it is to get and how easy to lose. They are cowardly, and are always anticipating danger; unlike that of the young, who are warm-blooded, their temperament is chilly; old age has paved the way for cowardice; fear is, in fact, a form of chill. They love life; and all the more when their last day has come, because the object of all desire is something we have not got, and also because we desire most strongly that which we need most urgently. They are too fond of themselves; this is one form that small-mindedness takes. Because of this, they guide their lives too much by considerations of what is useful and too little by what is noble—for the useful is what is good for oneself, and the noble what is good absolutely. They are not shy, but shameless rather; caring less for what is noble than for what is useful, they feel contempt for what people may think of them. They lack confidence in the future; partly through experience—for most things go wrong, or anyhow turn out worse than one expects; and partly because of their cowardice. They live by memory rather than by hope; for what is left to them of life is but little as compared with the long past; and hope is of the future, memory of the past. This, again, is the cause of their loquacity; they are continually talking of the past, because they enjoy remembering it. Their fits of anger are sudden but feeble. Their sensual passions have either altogether gone or have lost their vigour: consequently they do not feel their passions much, and their actions are inspired less by what they do feel than by the love of gain. Hence men at this time of life are often supposed to have a self-controlled character; the fact is that their passions have slackened, and they are slaves to the love of gain. They guide their lives by reasoning more than by moral feeling; reasoning being directed to utility and moral feeling to moral goodness. If they wrong others, they mean to injure them, not to insult them. Old men may feel pity, as well as young men, but not for the same reason. Young men feel it out of kindness; old men out of weak-

---

[3]Bias of Priene; "they treat their friends as probable future enemies and their enemies as probable future friends."

ness, imagining that anything that befalls any one else might easily happen to them, which, as we saw, is a thought that excites pity. Hence they are querulous, and not disposed to jesting or laughter—the love of laughter being the very opposite of querulousness.

Such are the characters of Young Men and Elderly Men. People always think well of speeches adapted to, and reflecting, their own character; and we can now see how to compose our speeches so as to adapt both them and ourselves to our audiences. 3

Questions on Meaning

1. According to Aristotle, what are the basic character traits of youth? Why do young men overdo everything?
2. What does Aristotle mean when he says that the lives of young men "are regulated more by moral feeling than by reasoning"?
3. What are the basic character traits of old age as Aristotle defines them? Why do elderly men underdo everything?
4. What does Aristotle mean when he says that elderly men "love as though they will some day hate and hate as though they will some day love"?
5. In what ways are elderly men more selfish than young men? Why is the pity that old men feel less kind than the pity that young men feel?
6. Why, according to Aristotle, are elderly men "supposed to have a self-controlled character" in contrast to young men? In what way are elderly men, in your opinion, as lacking in self-control as young men?

Questions on Method

1. Aristotle offers one long paragraph that describes numerous characteristics of young men, then a second long paragraph that describes the contrasting characteristics of old men. What effect might Aristotle have gained had he instead organized a series of short paragraphs in each of which he contrasted one character trait of youth with one corresponding trait of old age?
2. How effectively does Aristotle employ cause-and-effect analysis to explain the differences between youth and old age?
3. Discuss Aristotle's use of the simile of sickness in his third sentence. Where does he make use of this image later in the essay?
4. While Aristotle's overall purpose is to compare young men and elderly men, he also devotes a good deal of the essay to comparisons between the respective characteristics of each age class. Where do you find a "bad" trait canceling out a "good" trait, or vice versa? Which subject is left with more "good" traits, the young or the old?

Writing Topics

1. How fair do you think Aristotle's characterization of youth or old age is? How would you characterize them? Write an essay comparing your characterization of either youth or old age with Aristotle's.

2. Do you agree with Aristotle when he says that "we desire most strongly that which we need most urgently"? Write an essay in which you compare your desires with your needs.

3. Aristotle tells us experience teaches old men that "most things go wrong, or anyhow turn out worse than one expects." Write an essay in which you compare the validity of such a suspicious or "cynical" view of life to the validity of what Aristotle calls youth's "sanguine" or optimistic view.

Sex, Lies and Conversation: Why Is It So Hard for Men and Women to Talk to Each Other?

Deborah Tannen (b. 1945) has written many articles and books on linguistics that are easily accessible to the general public. You Just Don't Understand: Women and Men in Conversation *(1990);* That's Not What I Meant: How Conversational Style Makes or Breaks Your Relations with Others *(1986);* Gender and Discourse *(1994); and* Talking from 9 to 5: How Women's and Men's Conversational Styles Affect Who Gets Heard, Who Gets Credit, and What Gets Done at Work *(1994) are her most well known. As a professor of linguistics at Georgetown University, she has also written scholarly works such as* Framing in Discourse *(1993) and* Linguistics in Context *(1988).*

I WAS ADDRESSING a small gathering in a suburban Virginia living room—a women's group that had invited men to join them. Throughout the evening, one man had been particularly talkative, frequently offering ideas and anecdotes, while his wife sat silently beside him on the couch. Toward the end of the evening, I commented that women frequently complain that their husbands don't talk to them. This man quickly concurred. He gestured toward his wife and said, "She's the talker in our family." The room burst into laughter; the man looked puzzled and hurt. "It's true," he explained. "When I come home from work I have nothing to say. If she didn't keep the conversation going, we'd spend the whole evening in silence."

This episode crystallizes the irony that although American men tend to talk more than women in public situations, they often talk less at home. And this pattern is wreaking havoc with marriage.

The pattern was observed by political scientist Andrew Hacker in the late '70s. Sociologist Catherine Kohler Riessman reports in her new book *Divorce Talk* that most of the women she interviewed—but

only a few of the men—gave lack of communication as the reason for
their divorces. Given the current divorce rate of nearly 50 percent, that
amounts to millions of cases in the United States every year—a virtual
epidemic of failed conversation.

In my own research, complaints from women about their husbands   4
most often focused not on tangible inequities such as having given up
the chance for a career to accompany a husband to his, or doing far more
than their share of daily life-support work like cleaning, cooking, social
arrangements and errands. Instead, they focused on communication:
"He doesn't listen to me," "He doesn't talk to me." I found, as Hacker
observed years before, that most wives want their husbands to be, first
and foremost, conversational partners, but few husbands share this expectation of their wives.

In short, the image that best represents the current crisis is the   5
stereotypical cartoon scene of a man sitting at the breakfast table with
a newspaper held up in front of his face, while a woman glares at the
back of it, wanting to talk.

LINGUISTIC BATTLE OF THE SEXES

How can women and men have such different impressions of   6
communication in marriage? Why the widespread imbalance in their
interests and expectations?

In the April [1990] issue of *American Psychologist,* Stanford Uni-   7
versity's Eleanor Maccoby reports the results of her own and others'
research showing that children's development is most influenced by the
social structure of peer interactions. Boys and girls tend to play with
children of their own gender, and their sex-separate groups have different organizational structures and interactive norms.

I believe these systematic differences in childhood socialization   8
make talk between women and men like cross-cultural communication, heir to all the attraction and pitfalls of that enticing but difficult
enterprise. My research on men's and women's conversations uncov-
ered patterns similar to those described for children's groups.

For women, as for girls, intimacy is the fabric of relationships,   9
and talk is the thread from which it is woven. Little girls create and
maintain friendships by exchanging secrets; similarly, women regard
conversation as the cornerstone of friendship. So a woman expects her
husband to be a new and improved version of a best friend. What is
important is not the individual subjects that are discussed but the sense

of closeness, of a life shared, that emerges when people tell their thoughts, feelings, and impressions.

Bonds between boys can be as intense as girls', but they are based   10
less on talking, more on doing things together. Since they don't assume talk is the cement that binds a relationship, men don't know what kind of talk women want, and they don't miss it when it isn't there.

Boy's groups are larger, more inclusive, and more hierarchical, so   11
boys must struggle to avoid the subordinate position in the group. This may play a role in women's complaints that men don't listen to them. Some men really don't like to listen, because being the listener makes them feel one-down, like a child listening to adults or an employee to a boss.

But often when women tell men, "You aren't listening," and the   12
men protest, "I am," the men are right. The impression of not listening results from misalignment in the mechanics of conversation. The misalignment begins as soon as a man and a woman take physical positions. This became clear when I studied videotapes made by psychologist Paul Dorval of children and adults talking to their same-sex best friends. I found that at every age, the girls and women faced each other directly, their eyes anchored on each other's faces. At every age, the boys and men sat at angles to each other and looked elsewhere in the room, periodically glancing at each other. They were obviously attuned to each other, often mirroring each other's movements. But the tendency of men to face away can give women the impression they aren't listening even when they are. A young woman in college was frustrated: Whenever she told her boyfriend she wanted to talk to him, he would lie down on the floor, close his eyes, and put his arm over his face. This signaled to her, "He's taking a nap." But he insisted he was listening extra hard. Normally, he looks around the room, so he is easily distracted. Lying down and covering his eyes helped him concentrate on what she was saying.

Analogous to the physical alignment that women and men take in   13
conversation is their topical alignment. The girls in my study tended to talk at length about one topic, but the boys tended to jump from topic to topic. The second-grade girls exchanged stories about people they knew. The second-grade boys teased, told jokes, noticed things in the room and talked about finding games to play. The sixth-grade girls talked about problems with a mutual friend. The sixth-grade boys talked about 55 different topics, none of which extended over more than a few turns.

LISTENING TO BODY LANGUAGE

Switching topics is another habit that gives women the impres-   14
sion men aren't listening, especially if they switch to a topic about
themselves. But the evidence of the 10th-grade boys in my study indicates otherwise. The 10th-grade boys sprawled across their chairs with
bodies parallel and eyes straight ahead, rarely looking at each other.
They looked as if they were riding in a car, staring out the windshield.
But they were talking about their feelings. One boy was upset because
a girl had told him he had a drinking problem, and the other was feeling alienated from all his friends.

Now, when a girl told a friend about a problem, the friend re-   15
sponded by asking probing questions and expressing agreement and
understanding. But the boys dismissed each other's problems. Todd assured Richard that his drinking was "no big problem" because "sometimes you're funny when you're off your butt." And when Todd said
he felt left out, Richard responded, "Why should you? You know
more people than me."

Women perceive such responses as belittling and unsupportive.   16
But the boys seemed satisfied with them. Whereas women reassure
each other by implying, "You shouldn't feel bad because I've had similar experiences," men do so by implying, "You shouldn't feel bad because your problems aren't so bad."

There are even simpler reasons for women's impression that men   17
don't listen. Linguist Lynette Hirschman found that women make
more listener-noise, such as "mhm," "uhuh," and "yeah," to show
"I'm with you." Men, she found, more often give silent attention.
Women who expect a stream of listener-noise interpret silent attention
as no attention at all.

Women's conversational habits are as frustrating to men as men's   18
are to women. Men who expect silent attention interpret a stream of
listener-noise as overreaction or impatience. Also, when women talk to
each other in a close, comfortable setting, they often overlap, finish each
other's sentences and anticipate what the other is about to say. This
practice, which I call "participatory listenership," is often perceived by
men as interruption, intrusion and lack of attention.

A parallel difference caused a man to complain about his wife,   19
"She just wants to talk about her own point of view. If I show her another view, she gets mad at me." When most women talk to each
other, they assume a conversationalist's job is to express agreement and

support. But many men see their conversational duty as pointing out the other side of an argument. This is heard as disloyalty by women, and refusal to offer the requisite support. It is not that women don't want to see other points of view, but that they prefer them phrased as suggestions and inquiries rather than as direct challenges.

In his book *Fighting for Life,* Walter Ong points out that men use   20 "agonistic" or warlike, oppositional formats to do almost anything; thus discussion becomes debate, and conversation a competitive sport. In contrast, women see conversation as a ritual means of establishing rapport. If Jane tells a problem and June says she has a similar one, they walk away feeling closer to each other. But this attempt at establishing rapport can backfire when used with men. Men take too literally women's ritual "troubles talk," just as women mistake men's ritual challenges for real attack.

THE SOUNDS OF SILENCE

These differences begin to clarify why women and men have   21 such different expectations about communication in marriage. For women, talk creates intimacy. Marriage is an orgy of closeness: you can tell your feelings and thoughts, and still be loved. Their greatest fear is being pushed away. But men live in a hierarchical world, where talk maintains independence and status. They are on guard to protect themselves from being put down and pushed around.

This explains the paradox of the talkative man who said of his si-   22 lent wife, "She's the talker." In the public setting of a guest lecture, he felt challenged to show his intelligence and display his understanding of the lecture. But at home, where he has nothing to prove and no one to defend against, he is free to remain silent. For his wife, being home means she is free from the worry that something she says might offend someone, or spark disagreement, or appear to be showing off; at home she is free to talk.

The communication problems that endanger marriage can't be   23 fixed by mechanical engineering. They require a new conceptual framework about the role of talk in human relationships. Many of the psychological explanations that have become second nature may not be helpful, because they tend to blame either women (for not being as-sertive enough) or men (for not being in touch with their feelings). A sociolinguistic approach by which male-female conversation is seen as cross-cultural communication allows us to understand the problem and forge solutions without blaming either party.

Once the problem is understood, improvement comes naturally,   24 as it did to the young woman and her boyfriend who seemed to go to sleep when she wanted to talk. Previously, she had accused him of not listening, and he had refused to change his behavior, since that would be admitting fault. But then she learned about and explained to him the differences in women's and men's habitual ways of aligning themselves in conversation. The next time she told him she wanted to talk, he began, as usual, by lying down and covering his eyes. When the familiar negative reaction bubbled up, she reassured herself that he really was listening. But then he sat up and looked at her. Thrilled she asked why. He said, "You like me to look at you when we talk, so I'll try to do it." Once he saw their differences as cross-cultural rather than right and wrong, he independently altered his behavior.

Women who feel abandoned and deprived when their husbands   25 won't listen to or report daily news may be happy to discover their husbands trying to adapt once they understand the place of small talk in women's relationships. But if their husbands don't adapt, the women may still be comforted that for men, this is not a failure of intimacy. Accepting the difference, the wives may look to their friends or family for that kind of talk. And husbands who can't provide it shouldn't feel their wives have made unreasonable demands. Some couples will still decide to divorce, but at least their decisions will be based on realistic expectations.

In these times of resurgent ethnic conflicts, the world desperately   2ℓ needs cross-cultural understanding. Like charity, successful cross-cultural communication should begin at home.

Questions on Meaning

1. According to Tannen, the causes of difficulties in communication between men and women are rooted in childhood patterns of socialization. What evidence does she provide to support her thesis? How accurately does it reflect your own experience as a child and as an adult?
2. "Women's conversational habits are as frustrating to men as men's are to women." To what extent do you agree or disagree with Tannen? What examples did you find most convincing?
3. What "solutions" does Tannen offer to improve communication between men and women? What is your interpretation of and response to "cross-cultural communication"?

Questions on Method

1. What contrast/comparison method does Tannen use to develop her subject?
2. Is Tannen's purpose to inform, or does she also wish to persuade her readers? How do style and tone contribute to her purpose?

Writing Topics

1. Review Tannen's title and analyze carefully the components of sex, lies, and conversation. How do your responses compare with those of the generation cited in Tannen's research? How do you account for differences that exist?
2. Conduct an informal survey among your peers or coworkers on the role of communication in their sexual and nonsexual relationships. How do they differ? Write a brief report on your findings for your college newspaper.
3. To construct a contemporary profile of gender images in our culture, select several issues of magazines targeted at men only and women only, and compare and contrast the advertisements in each. What techniques did these magazines use to reflect and influence their readership? What is the profile of their intended audiences?

from *Hunger of Memory*

The child of Spanish-speaking Mexican immigrants, Richard Rodriguez (b. 1944) grew up in California. Entering school with little knowledge of English, he later studied at Stanford University, Columbia University, and earned his Ph.D. in literature from the University of California at Berkeley, where he now teaches. In addition to writing essays, he has published the autobiographical Hunger of Memory: The Education of Richard Rodriguez *(1982), which received critical acclaim, and* Days of Obligation: An Argument with My Mexican Father *(1992).*

I REMEMBER TO START with that day in Sacramento—a California now nearly thirty years past—when I first entered a classroom, able to understand some fifty stray English words.

The third of four children, I had been preceded to a neighborhood Roman Catholic school by an older brother and sister. But neither of them had revealed very much about their classroom experiences. Each afternoon they returned, as they left in the morning, always together, speaking in Spanish as they climbed the five steps of the porch. And their mysterious books, wrapped in shopping-bag paper, remained on the table next to the door, closed firmly behind them.

An accident of geography sent me to a school where all my classmates were white, many the children of doctors and lawyers and business executives. All my classmates certainly must have been uneasy on that first day of school—as most children are uneasy—to find themselves apart from their families in the first institution of their lives. But I was astonished.

The nun said, in a friendly but oddly impersonal voice, "Boys and girls, this is Richard Rodriguez," (I heard her sound out: *Rich-heard Road-ree-guess.*) It was the first time I had heard anyone name me in English. "Richard," the nun repeated more slowly, writing my name down in her black leather book. Quickly I turned to see my mother's face dissolve in a watery blur behind the pebbled glass door.

Many years later there is something called bilingual education—a scheme proposed in the late 1960s by Hispanic-American social activists, later endorsed by a congressional vote. It is a program that seeks to permit non-English-speaking children, many from lower-class homes, to use their family language as the language of school. (Such is the goal its supporters announce.) I hear them and am forced to say no: it is not possible for a child—any child—ever to use his family's language in school. Not to understand this is to misunderstand the public uses of schooling and to trivialize the nature of intimate life—a family's "language."

Memory teaches me what I know of these matters; the boy reminds the adult. I was a bilingual child, a certain kind—socially disadvantaged—the son of working-class parents, both Mexican immigrants.

In the early years of my boyhood, my parents coped very well in America. My father had steady work. My mother managed at home. They were nobody's victims. Optimism and ambition led them to a house (our home) many blocks from the Mexican south side of town. We lived among *gringos* and only a block from the biggest, whitest houses. It never occurred to my parents that they couldn't live wherever they chose. Nor was the Sacramento of the fifties bent on teaching them a contrary lesson. My mother and father were more annoyed than intimidated by those two or three neighbors who tried initially to make us unwelcome. ("Keep your brats away from my sidewalk!") But despite all they achieved, perhaps because they had so much to achieve, any deep feeling of ease, the confidence of "belonging" in public was withheld from them both. They regarded the people at work, the faces in crowds, as very distant from us. They were the others, *los gringos.* That term was interchangeable in their speech with another, even more telling, *los americanos.*

I grew up in a house where the only regular guests were my relations. For one day, enormous families of relatives would visit and there would be so many people that the noise and the bodies would spill out to the backyard and front porch. Then, for weeks, no one came by. (It was usually a salesman who rang the doorbell.) Our house stood apart. A gaudy yellow in a row of white bungalows. We were the people with the noisy dog. The people who raised pigeons and chickens. We were the foreigners on the block. A few neighbors smiled and waved. We waved back. But no one in the family knew the names of the old couple who lived next door; until I was seven years old, I did not know the names of the kids who lived across the street.

In public, my father and mother spoke a hesitant, accented, not   9
always grammatical English. And they would have to strain—their
bodies tense—to catch the sense of what was rapidly said by *los gringos.*
At home they spoke Spanish. The language of their Mexican past
sounded in counterpoint to the English of public society. The words
would come quickly, with ease. Conveyed through those sounds was
the pleasing, soothing, consoling reminder of being at home.

During those years when I was first conscious of hearing, my   10
mother and father addressed me only in Spanish; in Spanish I learned
to reply. By contrast, English (*inglés*), rarely heard in the house, was the
language I came to associate with *gringos.* I learned my first words of
English overhearing my parents speak to strangers. At five years of age,
I knew just enough English for my mother to trust me on errands to
stores one block away. No more.

I was a listening child, careful to hear the very different sounds of   11
Spanish and English. Wide-eyed with hearing, I'd listen to sounds more
than words. First, there were English (*gringos*) sounds. So many words
were still unknown that when the butcher or the lady at the drugstore
said something to me, exotic polysyllabic sounds would bloom in the
midst of their sentences. Often, the speech of people in public seemed
to me very loud, booming with confidence. The man behind the
counter would literally ask, "What can I do for you?" But by being so
firm and so clear, the sound of his voice said that he was a *gringo;* he belonged in public society.

I would also hear then the high nasal notes of middle-class Amer-   12
ican speech. The air stirred with sound. Sometimes, even now, when I
have been traveling abroad for several weeks, I will hear what I heard as
a boy. In hotel lobbies or airports, in Turkey or Brazil, some Americans
will pass, and suddenly I will hear it again—the high sound of American voices. For a few seconds I will hear it with pleasure, for it is now
the sound of *my* society—a reminder of home. But inevitably—already
on the flight headed for home, the sound fades with repetition. I will
be unable to hear it anymore.

When I was a boy, things were different. The accent of *los gringos*   1
was never pleasing nor was it hard to hear. Crowds at Safeway or at bus
stops would be noisy with sound. And I would be forced to edge away
from the chirping chatter above me.

I was unable to hear my own sounds, but I knew very well that I   1
spoke English poorly. My words could not stretch far enough to form
complete thoughts. And the words I did speak I didn't know well

enough to make into distinct sounds. (Listeners would usually lower their heads, better to hear what I was trying to say.) But it was one thing for *me* to speak English with difficulty. It was more troubling for me to hear my parents speak in public: their high-whining vowels and guttural consonants; their sentences that got stuck with "eh" and "ah" sounds; the confused syntax; the hesitant rhythm of sounds so different from the way *gringos* spoke. I'd notice, moreover, that my parents' voices were softer than those of *gringos* we'd meet.

I am tempted now to say that none of this mattered. In adulthood 15 I am embarrassed by childhood fears. And, in a way, it didn't matter very much that my parents could not speak English with ease. Their linguistic difficulties had no serious consequences. My mother and father made themselves understood at the county hospital clinic and at government offices. And yet, in another way, it mattered very much—it was unsettling to hear my parents struggle with English. Hearing them, I'd grow nervous, my clutching trust in their protection and power weakened.

There were many times like the night at a brightly lit gasoline 16 station (a blaring white memory) when I stood uneasily, hearing my father. He was talking to a teenaged attendant. I do not recall what they were saying, but I cannot forget the sounds my father made as he spoke. At one point his words slid together to form one word—sounds as confused as the threads of blue and green oil in the puddle next to my shoes. His voice rushed through what he had left to say. And, toward the end, reached falsetto notes, appealing to his listener's understanding. I looked away to the lights of passing automobiles. I tried not to hear anymore. But I heard only too well the calm, easy tone in the attendant's reply. Shortly afterward, walking toward home with my father, I shivered when he put his hand on my shoulder. The very first chance that I got, I evaded his grasp and ran on ahead into the dark, skipping with feigned boyish exuberance.

But then there was Spanish. *Español:* my family's language. *Es-* 17 *pañol:* the language that seemed to me a private language. I'd hear strangers on the radio and in the Mexican Catholic church across town speaking in Spanish, but I couldn't really believe that Spanish was a public language, like English. Spanish speakers, rather, seemed related to me, for I sensed that we shared—through our language—the experience of feeling apart from *los gringos.* It was thus a ghetto Spanish that I heard and I spoke. Like those whose lives are bound by a barrio, I was reminded by Spanish of my separateness from *los otros, los gringos* in power. But more intensely than for most barrio children—because I

did not live in a barrio—Spanish seemed to me the language of home.
(Most days it was only at home that I'd hear it.) It became the language
of joyful return.

A family member would say something to me and I would feel   18
myself specially recognized. My parents would say something to me
and I would feel embraced by the sounds of their words. Those sounds
said: *I am speaking with ease in Spanish. I am addressing you in words I never
use with* los gringos. *I recognize you as someone special, close, like no one
outside. You belong with us. In the family.*

(*Ricardo.*)

At the age of five, six, well past the time when most other chil-   19
dren no longer easily notice the difference between sounds uttered at
home and words spoken in public, I had a different experience. I lived
in a world magically compounded of sounds. I remained a child longer
than most; I lingered too long, poised at the end of language—often
frightened by the sounds of *los gringos,* delighted by the sounds of
Spanish at home, I shared with my family a language that was star-
tlingly different from that used in the great city around us.

For me there were none of the gradations between public and   20
private society so normal to a maturing child. Outside the house was
public society; inside the house was private. Just opening or closing the
screen door behind me was an important experience. I'd rarely leave
home all alone or without reluctance. Walking down the sidewalk, under the canopy of tall trees, I'd warily notice the—suddenly—silent
neighborhood kids who stood warily watching me. Nervously, I'd arrive at the grocery store to hear there the sounds of the *gringo*—foreign
to me—reminding me that in this world so big, I was a foreigner. But
then I'd return. Walking back toward our house, climbing the steps
from the sidewalk, when the front door was open in summer, I'd hear
voices beyond the screen door talking in Spanish. For a second or two,
I'd stay, linger there, listening. Smiling, I'd hear my mother call out,
saying in Spanish (words): "Is that you, Richard?" All the while her
sounds would assure me: *You are home now; come closer; inside. With us.*

"*Sí,*" I'd reply.   21

Once more inside the house I would resume (assume) my place   22
in the family. The sounds would dim, grow harder to hear. Once more
at home, I would grow less aware of that fact. It required, however, no
more than the blurt of the doorbell to alert me to listen to sounds all
over again. The house would turn instantly still while my mother went
to the door. I'd hear her hard English sounds. I'd wait to hear her voice

return to soft-sounding Spanish, which assured me, as surely as did the clicking tongue of the lock on the door, that the stranger was gone.

Plainly, it is not healthy to hear such sounds so often. It is not healthy to distinguish public words from private sounds so easily. I remained cloistered by sounds, timid and shy in public, too dependent on voices at home. And yet it needs to be emphasized: I was an extremely happy child at home. I remember many nights when my father would come back from work, and I'd hear him call out to my mother in Spanish, sounding relieved. In Spanish, he'd sound light and free notes he never could manage in English. Some nights I'd jump up just at hearing his voice. With *mis hermanos* I would come running into the room where he was with my mother. Our laughing (so deep was the pleasure!) became screaming. Like others who know the pain of public alienation, we transformed the knowledge of our public separateness and made it consoling—the reminder of intimacy. Excited, we joined our voices in a celebration of sounds. *We are speaking now the way we never speak out in public. We are alone—together,* voices sounded, surrounded to tell me. Some nights, no one seemed willing to loosen the hold sounds had on us. At dinner, we invented new words. (Ours sounded Spanish, but made sense only to us.) We pieced together new words by taking, say, an English verb and giving it Spanish endings. My mother's instructions at bedtime would be lacquered with mock-urgent tones. Or a word like *sí* would become, in several notes, able to convey added measures of feeling. Tongues explored the edges of words, especially the fat vowels. And we happily sounded that military drum roll, the twirling roar of the Spanish *r.* Family language: my family's sounds. The voices of my parents and sisters and brother. Their voices insisting: *You belong here. We are family members. Related. Special to one another. Listen!* Voices singing and sighing, rising, straining, then surging, teeming with pleasure that burst syllables into fragments of laughter. At times it seemed there was steady quiet only when, from another room, the rustling whispers of my parents faded and I moved closer to sleep.

Questions on Meaning

1. Rodriguez says that he was "a listening child." What does he mean?
2. How did Rodriguez feel about the sounds of English when he was a boy? How have his feelings changed now that he is grown?
3. What effect did his parents' halting English have on Rodriguez when he was a boy?

4. Why did Spanish seem "a private language" to Rodriguez? What negative effects did his early feelings about Spanish have on him? What were the positive effects?

5. Do you get a sense from this short excerpt why Rodriguez is opposed to bilingual education?

Questions on Method

1. Rodriguez compares the way he felt about English as a child to the way he felt about Spanish. To what extent does he organize his comparison by focusing first on English, then on Spanish? What more specific comparisons does he draw in the essay?

2. Rodriguez begins the essay by recalling how, on his first day in public school, he watched his mother's face "dissolve in a watery blur behind the pebbled glass door." In what sense is the image of the door symbolic? Where else in the essay is the image of a door important? What other images does Rodriguez employ to symbolize his thoughts and feelings?

3. What effect does the repeated use of the Spanish word *gringos* have on a reader? What other Spanish words does Rodriguez introduce into the essay, and to what effect?

Writing Topics

1. How does "Hunger of Memory" dramatize the relationship between social pressures and natural instincts?

2. How important is the difference between our private and public worlds? Why is it necessary to have a private life? To what extent is it harmful to withdraw into a private world? Compare the contrasts drawn between public and private life in Rodriguez's essay.

3. In order to express the strong, contrasting emotions that English and Spanish awoke in him as a child, Rodriguez has chosen his vocabulary carefully. Write an essay comparing and contrasting his descriptions of what Americans sounded like to him, what the efforts of his family to learn English sounded like, and what the sounds of their family language, Spanish, conveyed.

Grant and Lee: A Study in Contrasts

Bruce Catton (1899–1978), a native of Michigan who attended Oberlin College, was a former newspaper reporter, a one-time editor of American Heritage, *and a noted historian of the Civil War.* A Stillness at Appomattox *(1953) won both the Pulitzer Prize and the National Book Award for history in 1954. It was not, said Catton, "the strategy or political meanings" that fascinated him but the "almost incomprehensible emotional experience which this war brought to our country." Among Catton's many other books are* This Hallowed Ground *(1956),* The Coming Fury *(1961),* The Army of the Potomac *(1962),* Grant Takes Command *(1969), and* Michigan: A Bicentennial History *(1976).*

WHEN ULYSSES S. GRANT and Robert E. Lee met in the parlor of a modest house at Appomattox Court House, Virginia, on April 9, 1865, to work out the terms for the surrender of Lee's Army of Northern Virginia, a great chapter in American life came to a close, and a great new chapter began. 1

These men were bringing the Civil War to its virtual finish. To be sure, other armies had yet to surrender, and for a few days the fugitive Confederate government would struggle desperately and vainly, trying to find some way to go on living now that its chief support was gone. But in effect it was all over when Grant and Lee signed the papers. And the little room where they wrote out the terms was the scene of one of the poignant, dramatic contrasts in American history. 2

They were two strong men, these oddly different generals, and they represented the strengths of two conflicting currents that, through them, had come into final collision. 3

Back of Robert E. Lee was the notion that the old aristocratic concept might somehow survive and be dominant in American life. 4

Lee was tidewater Virginia, and in his background were family, culture, and tradition...the age of chivalry transplanted to a New World which was making its own legends and its own myths. He embodied a way of life that had come down through the age of knighthood and the 5

English country squire. America was a land that was beginning all over again, dedicated to nothing much more complicated than the rather hazy belief that all men had equal rights and should have an equal chance in the world. In such a land Lee stood for the feeling that it was somehow of advantage to human society to have a pronounced inequality in the social structure. There should be a leisure class, backed by ownership of land; in turn, society itself should be keyed to the land as the chief source of wealth and influence. It would bring forth (according to this ideal) a class of men with a strong sense of obligation to the community; men who lived not to gain advantage for themselves, but to meet the solemn obligations which had been laid on them by the very fact that they were privileged. From them the country would get its leadership; to them it could look for the higher values—of thought, of conduct, of personal deportment—to give it strength and virtue.

Lee embodied the noblest elements of this aristocratic ideal.   6
Through him, the landed nobility justified itself. For four years, the Southern states had fought a desperate war to uphold the ideals for which Lee stood. In the end, it almost seemed as if the Confederacy fought for Lee; as if he himself was the Confederacy...the best thing that the way of life for which the Confederacy stood could ever have to offer. He had passed into legend before Appomattox. Thousands of tired, underfed, poorly clothed Confederate soldiers, long since past the simple enthusiasm of the early days of the struggle, somehow considered Lee the symbol of everything for which they had been willing to die. But they could not quite put this feeling into words. If the Lost Cause, sanctified by so much heroism and so many deaths, had a living justification, its justification was General Lee.

Grant, the son of a tanner on the Western frontier, was every-   7
thing Lee was not. He had come up the hard way and embodied nothing in particular except the eternal toughness and sinewy fiber of the men who grew up beyond the mountains. He was one of a body of men who owed reverence and obeisance to no one, who were self-reliant to a fault, who cared hardly anything for the past but who had a sharp eye for the future.

These frontier men were the precise opposites of the tidewater   8
aristocrats. Back of them, in the great surge that had taken people over the Alleghenies and into the opening Western country, there was a deep, implicit dissatisfaction with a past that had settled into grooves. They stood for democracy, not from any reasoned conclusion about the proper ordering of human society, but simply because they had

grown up in the middle of democracy and knew how it worked. Their society might have privileges, but they would be privileges each man had won for himself. Forms and patterns meant nothing. No man was born to anything, except perhaps to a chance to show how far he could rise. Life was competition.

Yet along with this feeling had come a deep sense of belonging to a national community. The Westerner who developed a farm, opened a shop, or set up in business as a trader, could hope to prosper only as his own community prospered—and his community ran from the Atlantic to the Pacific and from Canada down to Mexico. If the land was settled, with towns and highways and accessible markets, he could better himself. He saw his fate in terms of the nation's own destiny. As its horizons expanded, so did his. He had, in other words, an acute dollars-and-cents stake in the continued growth and development of his country.

And that, perhaps, is where the contrast between Grant and Lee becomes most striking. The Virginia aristocrat, inevitably, saw himself in relation to his own region. He lived in a static society which could endure almost anything except change. Instinctively, his first loyalty would go to the locality in which that society existed. He would fight to the limit of endurance to defend it, because in defending it he was defending everything that gave his own life its deepest meaning.

The Westerner, on the other hand, would fight with an equal tenacity for the broader concept of society. He fought so because everything he lived by was tied to growth, expansion, and a constantly widening horizon. What he lived by would survive or fall with the nation itself. He could not possibly stand by unmoved in the face of an attempt to destroy the Union. He would combat it with everything he had, because he could only see it as an effort to cut the ground out from under his feet.

So Grant and Lee were in complete contrast, representing two diametrically opposed elements in American life. Grant was the modern man emerging; beyond him, ready to come on the stage, was the great age of steel and machinery, of crowded cities and a restless burgeoning vitality. Lee might have ridden down from the old age of chivalry, lance in hand, silken banner fluttering over his head. Each man was the perfect champion of his cause, drawing both his strengths and his weaknesses from the people he led.

Yet it was not all contrast, after all. Different as they were—in background, in personality, in underlying aspiration—these two great soldiers had much in common. Under everything else, they were marvelous fighters. Furthermore, their fighting qualities were really very much alike.

Each man had, to begin with, the great virtue of utter tenacity   14
and fidelity. Grant fought his way down the Mississippi Valley in spite of acute personal discouragement and profound military handicaps. Lee hung on in the trenches at Petersburg after hope itself had died. In each man there was an indomitable quality...the born fighter's refusal to give up as long as he can still remain on his feet and lift his two fists.

Daring and resourcefulness they had, too; the ability to think   15
faster and move faster than the enemy. These were the qualities which gave Lee the dazzling campaigns of Second Manassas and Chancellorsville and won Vicksburg for Grant.

Lastly, and perhaps greatest of all, there was the ability, at the end,   16
to turn quickly from war to peace once the fighting was over. Out of the way these two men behaved at Appomattox came the possibility of a peace of reconciliation. It was a possibility not wholly realized, in the years to come, but which did, in the end, help the two sections to become one nation again...after a war whose bitterness might have seemed to make such a reunion wholly impossible. No part of either man's life became him more than the part he played in this brief meeting in the McLean house at Appomattox. Their behavior there put all succeeding generations of Americans in their debt. Two great Americans, Grant and Lee—very different, yet under everything very much alike. Their encounter at Appomattox was one of the great moments of American history.

Questions on Meaning

1. According to Catton, Grant and Lee had contrasting attitudes toward the past. What were they?
2. Create a character profile of both men. With whose ideals do you empathize?
3. Focus on paragraphs 10 and 12. What is implicit in the author's associating Lee with a "static" society as opposed to Grant's concept of a "restless burgeoning vitality"?
4. In the latter part of the essay, Catton focuses on the similarities between the two men. Why does he state that their conduct was crucial to "all succeeding generations"?

Questions on Method

1. Focus on paragraphs 3–13 and create an outline of Catton's rhetorical pattern of organization. Does he focus equally on contrasts between the two men? Where does he contrast both in the same paragraph?
2. In paragraphs 13–16, Catton presents similarities between the two men. List them. Does the author remain objective throughout this comparison? Explain.
3. How do Catton's introduction and conclusion contribute to the essay's unity?

Writing Topics

1. Catton describes Lee as an aristocrat who believed in differences in social classes, whereas Grant embodied the ideal that America "was a land that was beginning all over again." With whose attitude do you agree? Are the values of both men implicit in your concept of the American dream?
2. Catton believes that history is shaped to a great extent by the personalities who dominate particular historical events. To what extent do you agree with his point of view?
3. How much education goes on outside as opposed to inside the classroom? Compare two educational experiences that you have had, one inside the classroom or library, one outside.

My People

Chief Seattle (c. 1786–1866), born near the city that now bears his name, was chief of the Squamish and allied Indian tribes in the 1800s. He saw the influx of settlers that poured into the Pacific Northwest region and, fearing that conflicts could cause wars between them and his tribes, encouraged friendship and trading relations with the newcomers. Seattle managed to maintain peace until 1854, when the governor of the Washington Territories proposed buying two million acres of tribal land. The selection included here is the chief's reply, and it reflects his fears about the future. In the following year, treaty agreements were breached, and Seattle chose not to fight in the Yakima War. Instead he consented to relocating his tribes to a reservation. When the city of Seattle was named for him, he objected, believing that after death his spirit would be troubled each time his name was spoken.

YONDER SKY that has wept tears upon my people for centuries untold, and which to us appears changeless and eternal, may change. Today is fair. Tomorrow may be overcast with clouds. My words are like the stars that never change. Whatever Seattle says the great chief at Washington can rely upon with as much certainty as he can upon the return of the sun or the seasons. The White Chief says that Big Chief at Washington sends us greetings of friendship and goodwill. That is kind of him for we know he has little need of our friendship in return. His people are many. They are like the grass that covers vast prairies. My people are few. They resemble the scattering trees of a storm-swept plain. The great, and—I presume—good, White Chief sends us word that he wishes to buy our lands but is willing to allow us enough to live comfortably. This indeed appears just, even generous, for the Red Man no longer has rights that he need respect, and the offer may be wise also, as we are no longer in need of an extensive country.... I will not dwell on, nor mourn over, our untimely decay, nor reproach our paleface brothers with hastening it, as we too may have been somewhat to blame.

Youth is impulsive. When our young men grow angry at some 2
real or imaginary wrong, and disfigure their faces with black paint, it
denotes that their hearts are black, and then they are often cruel and
relentless, and our old men and old women are unable to restrain
them. Thus it has ever been. Thus it was when the white men first began to push our forefathers further westward. But let us hope that the
hostilities between us may never return. We would have everything to
lose and nothing to gain. Revenge by young men is considered gain,
even at the cost of their own lives, but old men who stay at home in
times of war, and mothers who have sons to lose, know better.

Our good father at Washington—for I presume he is now our fa- 3
ther as well as yours, since King George has moved his boundaries further north—our great good father, I say, sends us word that if we do as
he desires he will protect us. His brave warriors will be to us a bristling
wall of strength, and his wonderful ships of war will fill our harbors so
that our ancient enemies far to the northward—the Hydas and Tsim-
psians—will cease to frighten our women, children, and old men. Then
in reality will he be our father and we his children. But can that ever be?
Your God is not our God! Your God loves your people and hates mine.
He folds his strong and protecting arms lovingly about the paleface and
leads him by the hand as a father leads his infant son—but He has forsaken His red children—if they really are His. Our God, the Great
Spirit, seems also to have forsaken us. Your God makes your people wax
strong every day. Soon they will fill the land. Our people are ebbing
away like a rapidly receding tide that will never return. The white man's
God cannot love our people or He would protect them. They seem to
be orphans who can look nowhere for help. How then can we be
brothers? How can your God become our God and renew our prosperity and awaken in us dreams of returning greatness? If we have a common heavenly father He must be partial—for He came to His paleface
children. We never saw Him. He gave you laws but He had no word for
His red children whose teeming multitudes once filled this vast continent as stars fill the firmament. No; we are two distinct races with
separate origins and separate destinies. There is little in common between us.

To us the ashes of our ancestors are sacred and their resting place 4
is hallowed ground. You wander far from the graves of your ancestors
and seemingly without regret. Your religion was written upon tables of
stone by the iron finger of your God so that you could not forget. The

Red Man could never comprehend nor remember it. Our religion is the traditions of our ancestors—the dreams of our old men, given them in solemn hours of night by the Great Spirit; and the visions of our sachems,* and it is written in the hearts of our people.

Your dead cease to love you and the land of their nativity as soon   5
as they pass the portals of the tomb and wander way beyond the stars. They are soon forgotten and never return. Our dead never forget the beautiful world that gave them being.

Day and night cannot dwell together. The Red Man has ever fled   6
the approach of the White Man, as the morning mist flees before the morning sun. However, your proposition seems fair and I think that my people will accept it and will retire to the reservation you offer them. Then we will dwell apart in peace, for the words of the Great White Chief seem to be the words of nature speaking to my people out of dense darkness.

It matters little where we pass the remnant of our days. They will   7
not be many. A few more moons; a few more winters—and not one of the descendants of the mighty hosts that once moved over this broad land or lived in happy homes, protected by the Great Spirit, will remain to mourn over the graves of a people once more powerful and hopeful than yours. But why should I mourn at the untimely fate of my people? Tribe follows tribe, and nation follows nation, like the waves of the sea. It is the order of nature, and regret is useless. Your time of decay may be distant, but it will surely come, for even the White Man whose God walked and talked with him as friend with friend, cannot be exempt from the common destiny. We may be brothers after all. We will see.

We will ponder your proposition, and when we decide we will   8
let you know. But should we accept it, I here and now, make this condition that we will not be denied the privilege without molestation of visiting at any time the tombs of our ancestors, friends and children. Every part of this soil is sacred in the estimation of my people. Every hillside, every valley, every plain and grove, has been hallowed by some sad or happy event in days long vanished.... The very dust upon which you now stand responds more lovingly to their footsteps than to yours, because it is rich with the blood of our ancestors and our bare feet are conscious of the sympathetic touch.... Even the little children who lived here and rejoiced here for a brief season will love these somber

---

*Tribal chiefs.

solitudes and at eventide they greet shadowy returning spirits. And when the last Red Man shall have perished, and the memory of my tribe shall have become a myth among the White Men, these shores will swarm with the invisible dead of my tribe, and when your children's children think themselves alone in the field, the store, the shop, upon the highway, or in the silence of the pathless woods, they will not be alone.... At night when the streets of your cities and villages are silent and you think them deserted, they will throng with the returning hosts that once filled and still love this beautiful land. The White Man will never be alone.

Let him be just and deal kindly with my people, for the dead are   9
not powerless. Dead, did I say? There is not death, only a change of worlds.

Questions on Meaning

1. Chief Seattle chooses compromise rather than confrontation in his dealings with the United States government. Which aspects of his traditional beliefs might account for his choice?
2. "There is not death, only a change of worlds." To what extent do you agree with this attitude toward death?

Questions on Method

1. Chief Seattle's speech contains many effective examples of figurative language. What metaphors and similes can you identify?
2. Speculate about Chief Seattle's purpose in this address. Who is his intended audience?
3. Chief Seattle uses contrast and comparison at several points in his speech. What differences between the traditions of his people and those of the settlers are highlighted by this technique?

Writing Topics

1. Write a journal entry responding to Chief Seattle's comparisons of youth and age.
2. Write an essay in which you contrast the settlers' relationship to nature with that of the Native American according to Chief Seattle. To what extent do you agree with his characterizations?

Comparison and Contrast
Writing Topics

1. Which of the authors in this chapter do you find to be the most objective in comparing the relative attributes of two different points of view? Which do you find to be the least objective, the most slanted, or biased? Write an essay that explains your answer.

2. Write an essay comparing two important stages of your life: childhood and adolescence or adolescence and adulthood. Highlight a specific experience through which you explain the similarities and differences.

3. Write an essay that compares the views that two people who differ in age, personality, or background take toward a controversial subject.

4. What is the difference between being educated and being intelligent? Write an essay comparing these two concepts, making sure that you clearly define what you mean by both terms.

5. Select two reviews of a controversial movie you have seen, one from a very liberal newspaper and one from a more conservative source. Write an essay comparing and contrasting the targeted audience for each review.

12

Cause and Effect

CAUSE-AND-EFFECT EXPOSITION is often used in argumentation and persuasion because it can support a logical appeal. The structure of **cause and effect,** like that of narration, is a series of events or conditions, the last of which, the effect, could not occur without the preceding one(s). The immediately preceding events or conditions are the "immediate" causes; if *one* immediate cause can alone produce the effect, it is called the "sufficient" cause. When scientists discovered that tuberculosis was caused by the tubercle bacillus and nothing else, they had found the sufficient cause of tuberculosis; they could stop prescribing mountain air, close the sanitariums, and practically eliminate occurrence of the disease.

How do we know the constituents of this series of events? It's not always easy to identify them; in fact causes are harder to identify than effects. One of the fallacies of causal thinking is the *non sequitur* (Latin for "it doesn't follow"), which is ascribing an effect to the wrong cause. For example, a character in Frank O'Connor's story "Guests of the Nation" says,

> Mr. Hawkins, you can say what you like about the war [World War I], and think you'll deceive me because I'm only a simple poor countrywoman, but I know what started the war. It was the Italian Count that stole the heathen divinity out of the temple in Japan.

We have all seen the damage done by this kind of "simple" fallacy; we should watch for it in our own and our opponents' arguments.

Another fallacy of causal thinking is to *assume* that an event is in the series of events. Just because event A happened before event B is no guarantee that A and B are in series, with A causing B. To make this assumption without evidence is to commit the fallacy called *post hoc, ergo propter hoc* (Latin for "after this, therefore, on account of this"). For example, Mary Smith wins the lottery. John Russell then proposes marriage to her. To say the former caused the latter is an example of the *post hoc, ergo propter hoc* fallacy and an injustice to a couple who may be in love.

In answering the question "What caused the burglary?" you would look for a series of earlier events or conditions among which might be poorly lighted streets and yards, unlocked doors or windows, accessible fire escapes, an ineffective police and court system, high unemployment, drug use, and so on, some of which may have been recently aggravated or exacerbated, and you would certainty hope to find an immediate cause called "the perpetrator." But where you begin in this series will surely depend on your purpose in asking the question. You might also ask yourself the practical question "What had to happen before this particular burglary could occur?" For example, it is probably starting too far back in the series to say the burglary was caused by World War II, which deprived the burglar of a father, who might have made an honest man of his son. Conversely, to avoid beginning too *late* in your series (oversimplification again), remember that the causes may be numerous and various. Again, depending on your purpose, it is probably an oversimplification to say the burglary was caused by the burglar.

Cause-and-effect exposition can answer the corollary question "What is the effect of X?" You can ask, "What is the *effect* of the burglary?" (or, what amounts to the same thing, "What did the burglary cause?"). Now the series begins with burglary and ends with later events or conditions: fear, anger, increased insurance costs, purchase of a burglar alarm, deterioration of a neighborhood, and so on. To keep the series from growing unmanageably long, keep in mind the practical question "What would not have happened if the robbery had not happened?"

Cause-and-effect exposition requires rigorous thinking and an awareness of the pitfalls and possibilities of **diction.** It is often useful in argumentation or persuasion, whether the goal of changing belief and behavior is acknowledged. For example, in "Kids in the Mall: Growing Up Controlled," William Severini Kowinski draws on surveys, quotations from authorities, and comments from teenagers to answer the question of whether teenagers are being harmed by the mall. In presenting your case for cause and effect, support your conclusions with proof or evidence. Use statistics, reports, your own experience, and that of others. Don't expect readers to believe you merely because you say something is the cause: Proof is the writer's job. Use any of the other expository modes, and narration and description, to help you present your case. After writing your essay, vigorously reexamine the methods you have used to arrive at your conclusions. Make sure that generalizations are true, that conclusions are valid, and that effects are in fact derived from their proper causes.

WRITING CAUSE-AND-EFFECT EXPOSITION

1. Distinguish between causality and mere sequence.
2. Avoid the causal fallacies of hasty generalization: oversimplification; *non sequitur;* and *post hoc, ergo propter hoc.*
3. Identify various kinds of cause: sufficient, immediate, contributing, remote.
4. Use narration, description, and expository methods to support your appeal.
5. Provide sufficient evidence for your inductive conclusion. The burden of proof is on you.

E. M. FORSTER

My Wood

E. M. Forster (1879–1970) was an English novelist, short-story writer, and essayist. He wrote six novels, all of which deal with the class concerns of his era. In the early 1900s, Forster lived in Greece and Italy, and during these years, he wrote his first four novels: Where Angels Fear to Tread (1905), The Longest Journey (1907), A Room with a View (1908), and Howards End (1910). After World War I, Forster moved to India where he wrote his best-known novel, A Passage to India (1924), which exemplifies the liberal humanism so pervasive in his work and so much a part of his philosophy. A Passage to India exposes the prejudices and injustices that existed under British domination in colonial India. With subtle irony, he reveals the moral and emotional emptiness of British middle-class life. He believed that the bourgeoisie buries their capacity for passion and has to recapture those qualities for their lives to have meaning. Forster also wrote seven books of literary criticism, and in 1951 he published a collection of sociological essays entitled Two Cheers for Democracy.

A FEW YEARS AGO I wrote a book which dealt in part with the difficulties of the English in India. Feeling that they would have no difficulties in India themselves, the Americans read the book freely. The more they read it the better it made them feel, and a cheque to the author was the result. I bought a wood with the cheque. It is not a large wood—it contains scarcely any trees, and it is intersected, blast it, by a public footpath. Still, it is the first property that I have owned, so it is right that other people should participate in my shame, and should ask themselves, in accents that will vary in horror, this very important question: What is the effect of property upon the character? Don't let's touch economics; the effect of private ownership upon the community as a whole is another question—a more important question, perhaps, but another one. Let's keep to psychology. If you own things, what's their effect on you? What's the effect on me of my wood?

In the first place, it makes me feel heavy. Property does have this effect. Property produces men of weight, and it was a man of weight who failed to get into the Kingdom of Heaven. He was not wicked, the unfortunate millionaire in the parable, he was only stout; he stuck out in front, not to mention behind, and as he wedged himself this way and that in the crystalline entrance and bruised his well-fed flanks, he saw beneath him a comparatively slim camel passing through the eye of a needle and being woven into the robe of God. The Gospels all through couple stoutness and slowness. They point out what is perfectly obvious, yet seldom realized: that if you have a lot of things you cannot move about a lot, that furniture requires dusting, dusters require servants, servants require insurance stamps, and the whole tangle of them makes you think twice before you accept an invitation to dinner or go for a bathe in the Jordan. Sometimes the Gospels proceed further and say with Tolstoy that property is sinful; they approach the difficult ground of asceticism here, where I cannot follow them. But as to the immediate effects of property on people, they just show straightforward logic. It produces men of weight. Men of weight cannot, by definition, move like the lightning from the East unto the West, and the ascent of a fourteen-stone bishop into a pulpit is thus the exact antithesis of the coming of the Son of Man. My wood makes me feel heavy.

In the second place, it makes me feel it ought to be larger. 3

The other day I heard a twig snap in it. I was annoyed at first, for 4 I thought that someone was blackberrying, and depreciating the value of the undergrowth. On coming nearer, I saw it was not a man who had trodden on the twig and snapped it, but a bird, and I felt pleased. My bird. The bird was not equally pleased. Ignoring the relation between us, it took fright as soon as it saw the shape of my face, and flew straight over the boundary hedge into a field, the property of Mrs. Henessy, where it sat down with a loud squawk. It had become Mrs. Henessy's bird. Something seemed grossly amiss here, something that would not have occurred had the wood been larger. I could not afford to buy Mrs. Henessy out, I dared not murder her, and limitations of this sort beset me on every side. Ahab did not want that vineyard—he only needed it to round off his property, preparatory to plotting a new curve—and all the land around my wood has become necessary to me in order to round off the wood. A boundary protects. But—poor little thing—the boundary ought in its turn to be protected. Noises on the edge of it. Children throw stones. A little more, and then a little more, until we reach the sea. Happy Canute! Happier Alexander! And after all, why should even the world be the limit of possession? A rocket containing a Union Jack, will, it is hoped, be shortly fired at the moon.

Mars. Sirius. Beyond which…But these immensities ended by saddening me. I could not suppose that my wood was the destined nucleus of universal dominion—it is so very small and contains no mineral wealth beyond the blackberries. Nor was I comforted when Mrs. Henessey's bird took alarm for the second time and flew clean away from us all, under the belief that it belonged to itself.

In the third place, property makes its owner feel that he ought to do something to it. Yet he isn't sure what. A restlessness comes over him, a vague sense that he has a personality to express—the same sense which, without any vagueness, leads the artist to an act of creation. Sometimes I think I will cut down such trees as remain in the wood, at other times I want to fill up the gaps between them with new trees. Both impulses are pretentious and empty. They are not honest movements towards money-making or beauty. They spring from a foolish desire to express myself and from an inability to enjoy what I have got. Creation, property, enjoyment form a sinister trinity in the human mind. Creation and enjoyment are both very, very good, yet they are often unattainable without a material basis, and at such moments property pushes itself in as a substitute, saying, "Accept me instead—I'm good enough for all three." It is not enough. It is, as Shakespeare said of lust, "The expense of spirit in a waste of shame"; it is "Before, a joy proposed; behind, a dream." Yet we don't know how to shun it. It is forced on us by our economic system as the alternative to starvation. It is also forced on us by an internal defect in the soul, by the feeling that in property may lie the germs of self-development and of exquisite or heroic deeds. Our life on earth is, and ought to be, material and carnal. But we have not yet learned to manage our materialism and carnality properly; they are still entangled with the desire for ownership, where (in the words of Dante) "Possession is one with loss."

And this brings us to our fourth and final point: the blackberries.

Blackberries are not plentiful in this meagre grove, but they are easily seen from the public footpath which traverses it, and all too easily gathered. Foxgloves, too—people will pull up the foxgloves, and ladies of an educational tendency even grub for toadstools to show them on the Monday in class. Other ladies, less educated, roll down the bracken in the arms of their gentlemen friends. There is paper, there are tins. Pray, does my wood belong to me or doesn't it? And, if it does, should I not own it best by allowing no one else to walk there? There is a wood near Lyme Regis, also cursed by a public footpath, where the owner has not hesitated on this point. He has built high stone walls each side of the path, and has spanned it by bridges, so that the public circulate like termites while he gorges on the blackberries unseen. He really does own his wood, this able chap. Dives in Hell did pretty well, but the gulf dividing him from Lazarus could be traversed by vision, and nothing traverses it here. And perhaps I shall come to this in time. I shall wall in and fence out until I really taste the sweets of property. Enormously stout, endlessly avaricious, pseudo-creative, intensely selfish, I shall weave upon my forehead the quadruple crown of possession until those nasty Bolshies come and take it off again and thrust me aside into the outer darkness.

Questions on Meaning

1. Why does Forster say that the effect of private ownership on the community is another, perhaps more important, issue than is its effect on character?
2. How do the examples Forster uses in his second paragraph illustrate the first effect of property on character? Do you agree that property produces men or women of weight? Are people more virtuous if they have fewer possessions?
3. Who are Ahab, Canute, and Alexander? From what you know or can learn about their lives, why are they good examples of Forster's second effect? Does ownership always make one more greedy?
4. What effect does the last sentence in paragraph 4 have on the meaning of the paragraph?
5. "Creation, property, enjoyment form a sinister trinity in the human mind." What does Forster mean by this statement? What examples does he give to explain it? What examples can you add of your own? Is property in your opinion a substitute for creativity?
6. What point does Forster make with the example of the blackberries? Do you agree that property generally has this effect?
7. Who are the "nasty Bolshies" mentioned in the last paragraph? What does this sentence contribute to the essay?

Questions on Method

1. Forster leads into his introduction by commenting that Americans provided him with the money to purchase his wood. For what reason does Forster mention Americans in an introduction to an essay on materialism? What attitude does he have toward them?
2. What attitude toward his wood does Forster have? Do the words *shame* and *horror* used in paragraph 1 describe his tone in any way? How does the last sentence of the essay contribute to tone?

3. Forster's organization is perfectly clear. What devices does he use to convey the movement of the essay? Is this device effective? Why don't all writers mark each section of their essays as clearly?
4. What would the essay have been like without all the examples Forster uses? Would it have been as effective?

Writing Topics

1. Property "makes me feel heavy" writes Forster in "My Wood." Write an essay analyzing the causes and effects of materialism according to Forster.
2. Write an essay explaining Dante's words, "Possession is one with loss."
3. Recall an experience that caused you to feel a singularly strong emotion. Pick one word that denotes this emotion, then make use of as many synonyms for this word as you can think of in the course of describing the experience and its effect on you. Once the essay is written, replace those synonyms that seem repetitious with whatever metaphors the details of your description suggest might better symbolize the emotion.

The Fear of Being Alone

Anne Taylor Fleming began her writing career shortly after she graduated from the University of California at Santa Cruz in 1971 with Highest Honors in Political Philosophy. Her freelance career began after returning to her native Los Angeles. She wrote several "My Turn" essays for News-week. *She writes regularly for the* New York Times Magazine, *does weekly radio commentary for CBS, and contributes essays to* The News-Hour with Jim Lehrer.

AT THE END of this past summer I had plans to go away for a week, simply a week, without my husband. It was the first time in three years that I was making such a solo pilgrimage, and I was frightened. As I walked down the long corridor to the plane, I looked straight ahead, turning a bottle of tranquilizers over and over in my pocket. I felt like a child lost in a department store; my palms were sweaty and my face was flushed. I tried to remember other solitary departures when I had been similarly discomfited: the walk to the first day of school; the bus ride to Girl Scout camp when I was 9 and my sister, who was also on the bus, was 10 and suddenly wanted nothing to do with me; the first midnight jet to college.

Of what was I so afraid? I was afraid of being by myself, of being wholly quiet, of being with people who did not know my name and did not care. I was afraid of being liked by strangers and of not being liked by strangers. Mostly I was afraid of being alone again, even for so short a time. After four and a half years of marriage I had simply lost the habit.

Marriage is not the culprit, though it is an obvious protective mantle against aloneness. The fear of being alone is not reserved for the married just as it is not reserved for women. I have heard stories like mine from young boys and have seen the same childlike fear in the faces of middle-aged men. Nor is this fear the special property of Americans. But we seem, in this country, to fan the fear of being alone. We are raised and in turn raise our children in clumps, in groups, in auditoriums and car pools and locker rooms and scout dens. Great emphasis is placed on how sociable we are as children, on how popular we are with our peers. Great emphasis is also placed on how well children mix in their own families. Despite the alleged falling apart of the American family, the dialogue about familial relations is constant, binding. If only in talk, parents and children do not leave each other much alone. Great nostalgic emphasis is still placed on the ritual togetherness of the family meal. A solitary eater, anytime, anywhere, conjures up one of those sad, empty, too well-lighted diners of an Edward Hopper painting.

And when for children there is no meal to attend, no group activity, no distraction planned by a weekend father, there is the constant company of the people on TV. A child need never be alone, need never know silence except when asleep. Even then, for urban and suburban children, there are the nonceasing nighttime noises of cars, of neighbors, of arguing or partying parents. To be away from the noise, away from the group—parents or peers—becomes a scary thing and aloneness becomes confused and synonymous with loneliness.   4

I used to think that the worst thing I could say to my husband when lying next to him was, "I'm lonely." That, I thought, was very wounding, a reflection on his inability to be company to me. I think now that it's a reflection on me, on my inability to be gracefully alone even in the presence of someone I love. We all marry, in part, to avoid being alone; many of us divorce when we find we can be just as alone in marriage as before, and sometimes more so. Often, women in crumbling marriages conceive babies not to try to hold a man, as the cliché goes, but to guarantee themselves some company—even that of an infant— when that man is gone. After the divorce, for a man or woman, comes the frantic search for a replacement, a new lover, a dog, a singles club, a stronger drink or drug. Waking next to strangers in strange beds—surely, the loneliest habit—is considered preferable to being alone.   5

Of this random bedding there has been much written lately, especially by a handful of philosopher-journalists who blame such "promiscuity" on what they call the New Narcissism, the inward-turning, selfish, self-absorption of the American people. Each one of us, their lament goes, is "into" his or her own jollies—the pursuit of happiness having become the pursuit of hedonism—our faces resolutely turned away from the world and its problems. But this is the oddest of narcissisms then, the insecure narcissism of people who do not like to be alone. The anti-narcissists point to the prodigious number and variety of soul searchers—est devotees, Aricans, Moonies, meditators and Rolfers—as proof of the neurotic self-celebration of Americans. But even these soul searchings go on in huge groups; they are orgies of   6 mass psyche scratching. Hundreds of people writhe together on auditorium floors in an attempt to soothe their individual wounds. They jog together and ride bicycles together and walk the most beautiful country roads together in an effort to slim their individual thighs.

So even if Americans are involved in a manic and somewhat self-   7
ish pursuit of psychic and physical fitness, it is a collective not a private pursuit. Everyone is holding hands; they're one long daisy chain of self-improvement. This is, at best, a symbiotic narcissism, the narcissism of people very dependent on one another, of people afraid or bored to be alone, of people homogenizing into one sex—it is less scary and less lonely, perhaps, to bed with a body that looks and feels more like one's own—of people who need to see reflected in the water not only their own faces but countless other faces as well.

I do not mean to advertise the advantages of being alone. Many   8
have done that with more conviction than I could. I regard aloneness not as a pleasure so much as an accident that, if one is to be at all happy, must be survived. Nor do I mean to put down narcissism. On the contrary, I find no fault with a certain healthy narcissism. Few among us would undertake the saving of other souls until we first have a stab of saving our own.

The point is simply that narcissism is not the point and that in   9
many ways it's a misnomer. A true narcissist is a true loner and most of us, raised as we are, make lousy loners. We share each other's beds somewhat freely not out of boldness but out of timidity, out of the fear of being alone. We hunt for gurus not out of self-love, or narcissism, but out of self-doubt. If we are to be even mildly happy and therefore generous of spirit—as the anti-narcissists would have us be—then what we need is more narcissism, more privatism, not less. What we need instead of soul-searching sessions are classes on how to be alone: Aloneness 1A, Intermediary Aloneness, Advanced Aloneness. The great joy of these new classes is that attendance would not only not be required, it would be forbidden.

Questions on Meaning

1. According to Fleming, what causes Americans to fear being alone? What effects does this fear have on them?
2. What is the "New Narcissism" to which Fleming refers in paragraph 6? Why does she think it is incorrect to blame the "promiscuity" of contemporary American life on narcissism?

3. In what way, according to Fleming, might learning to cope better with being alone improve the quality of life in America? Do you agree with her analysis?

Questions on Method

1. List the effects of loneliness Fleming describes in paragraphs 1 and 2. How does her consideration, then rejection, of two alleged causes of loneliness strengthen her analysis when she later reveals the "real" cause?
2. What is the evidence Fleming produces to prove that Americans are trained to regard aloneness as loneliness?
3. How well does Fleming use cause-and-effect analysis to support her thesis? Can you point out other prose patterns that she depends on to make her point?
4. In what sense is Fleming's conclusion paradoxical or ironic? Can you point out other examples of paradox or irony in the essay?

Writing Topics

1. Write an essay in which you argue, against Fleming, that Americans are skilled at the art of being alone.
2. Fleming mentions the "alleged" falling apart of the American family. Is family life falling apart in America? Write an essay that analyzes the causes behind either the weakness or the strength of American family life.
3. To what extent do you identify with Fleming's opening description of one of her "solitary departures"? Recall a similar experience you had, either as a child or as an adult. Offer your own analysis of the emotional effect such a solitary departure produced in you.

Death in the Open

Lewis Thomas (1913–1993), born in Flushing, New York, attended Prince-
ton University and Harvard Medical School. He held teaching, research, and
administrative positions at several medical schools and hospitals including
Johns Hopkins, Cornell, Harvard, and Massachusetts General. Although he
had a distinguished career in medicine, he is more widely known for his es-
says, which are often poetic, personal, and philosophical. He began to write a
monthly column for the New England Journal of Medicine *in 1971,*
which is when he came to the attention of the reading public. His books in-
clude Lives of a Cell *(1974), for which he won a National Book Award,*
The Medusa and the Snail *(1979),* Late Night Thoughts on Listening to Mahler's Ninth Symphony *(1983), and* Etcetera, Etcetera
(1990), all essay collections; and The Young Science *(1983), a memoir*
about becoming a doctor.

MOST OF THE DEAD ANIMALS you see on highways near the cities are 1
dogs, a few cats. Out in the countryside, the forms and coloring of the
dead are strange; these are the wild creatures. Seen from a car window
they appear as fragments, evoking memories of woodchucks, badgers,
skunks, voles, snakes, sometimes the mysterious wreckage of a deer.

It is always a queer shock, part a sudden upwelling of grief, part 2
unaccountable amazement. It is simply astounding to see an animal
dead on a highway. The outrage is more than just the location; it is the
impropriety of such visible death, anywhere. You do not expect to see
dead animals in the open. It is the nature of animals to die alone, off
somewhere, hidden. It is wrong to see them lying out on the highway;
it is wrong to see them anywhere.

Everything in the world dies, but we only know about it as a kind 3
of abstraction. If you stand in a meadow, at the edge of a hillside, and
look around carefully, almost everything you can catch sight of is in the
process of dying, and most things will be dead long before you are. If it
were not for the constant renewal and replacement going on before your
eyes, the whole place would turn to stone and sand under your feet.

There are some creatures that do not seem to die at all; they sim- 4
ply vanish totally into their own progeny. Single cells do this. The cell
becomes two, then four, and so on, and after a while the last trace is
gone. It cannot be seen as death; barring mutation, the descendants are
simply the first cell, living all over again. The cycles of the slime mold
have episodes that seem as conclusive as death, but the withered slug,
with its stalk and fruiting body, is plainly the transient tissue of a developing animal; the free-swimming amebocytes use this organ collectively in order to produce more of themselves.

There are said to be a billion billion insects on the earth at any 5
moment, most of them with very short life expectancies by our standards. Someone has estimated that there are 25 million assorted insects
hanging in the air over every temperate square mile, in a column ex-
tending upward for thousands of feet, drifting through the layers of the
atmosphere like plankton. They are dying steadily, some by being
eaten, some just dropping in their tracks, tons of them around the
earth, disintegrating as they die, invisibly.

Who ever sees dead birds, in anything like the huge numbers 6
stipulated by the certainty of the death of all birds? A dead bird is an
incongruity, more startling than an unexpected live bird, sure evidence to the human mind that something has gone wrong. Birds do
their dying off somewhere, behind things, under things, never on the
wing.

Animals seem to have an instinct for performing death alone, hid- 7
den. Even the largest, most conspicuous ones find ways to conceal
themselves in time. If an elephant missteps and dies in an open place,
the herd will not leave him there; the others will pick him up and carry
the body from place to place, finally putting it down in some inexplica-
bly suitable location. When elephants encounter the skeleton of an elephant out in the open, they methodically take up each of the bones and
distribute them, in a ponderous ceremony, over neighboring acres.

It is a natural marvel. All of the life of the earth dies, all of the 8
time, in the same volume as the new life that dazzles us each morning,
each spring. All we see of this is the odd stump, the fly struggling on
the porch floor of the summer house in October, the fragment on the
highway. I have lived all my life with an embarrassment of squirrels in
my backyard, they are all over the place, all year long, and I have never
seen, anywhere, a dead squirrel.

I suppose it is just as well. If the earth were otherwise, and all the
dying were done in the open, with the dead there to be looked at, we

would never have it out of our minds. We can forget about it much of
the time, or think of it as an accident to be avoided, somehow. But it
does make the process of dying seem more exceptional than it really is,
and harder to engage in at the times when we must ourselves engage.

In our way, we conform as best we can to the rest of nature. The   10
obituary pages tell us of the news that we are dying away, while the
birth announcements in finer print, off at the side of the page, inform
us of our replacements, but we get no grasp from this of the enormity
of scale. There are 3 billion of us on the earth, and all 3 billion must be
dead, on a schedule, within this lifetime. The vast mortality, involving
something over 50 million of us each year, takes place in relative se-
crecy. We can only really know of the deaths in our households, or
among our friends. These, detached in our minds from all the rest, we
take to be unnatural events, anomalies, outrages. We speak of our own
dead in low voices; struck down, we say, as though visible death can
only occur for cause, by disease or violence, avoidably. We send off for
flowers, grieve, make ceremonies, scatter bones, unaware of the rest of
the 3 billion on the same schedule. All of that immense mass of flesh
and bone and consciousness will disappear by absorption into the
earth, without recognition by the transient survivors.

Less than a half century from now, our replacements will have   11
more than doubled the numbers. It is hard to see how we can continue
to keep the secret, with such multitudes doing the dying. We will have
to give up the notion that death is catastrophe, or detestable, or avoidable, or even strange. We will need to learn more about the cycling of
life in the rest of the system, and about our connection to the process.
Everything that comes alive seems to be in trade for something that
dies, cell for cell. There might be some comfort in the recognition of
synchrony, in the formation that we all go down together, in the best
of company.

Questions on Meaning

1. Why, according to Thomas, do we feel shocked by the body of a dead
   animal on a highway?
2. What effects does the animal world's "instinct for performing death
   alone" have on human beings? How do humans express this instinct?
3. Why does Thomas feel that we will have to give up the notion that death
   is "catastrophe, or detestable, or avoidable, or even strange"? What effect
   might giving up this notion have on us?

Questions on Method

1. Is there a logic to the order in which Thomas offers examples of how animals perform death alone? What effect does he achieve by pointing to insects, then birds, then elephants? Why does he mention squirrels last?
2. How scientific is the cause-and-effect analysis offered by Thomas? To what degree would you describe his tone as argumentative?
3. For what audience is Thomas writing?

Writing Topics

1. Thomas writes about the effects of confronting death. Discuss the different emotions that he suggests are aroused when a person confronts the reality of death and dying. To what extent do you share his point of view?
2. Write an essay attempting to evaluate a highly emotional issue from a detached, objective, analytical point of view.
3. Describe something you disliked as a child about which your feelings changed as you grew older, such as a place you visited or an activity you engaged in. What caused your feelings to change? What lesson can you draw from your analysis of how and why your feelings changed?

In Ethnic America

Michael Novak (b. 1933), from Johnstown, Pennsylvania, is an American of Slovak descent. A distinguished scholar, he has earned several degrees, including an M.A. (1966) from Harvard University. His teaching career has spanned a number of prestigious universities, and he is currently a Professor of American Studies at the University of Notre Dame. Novak has authored numerous books, including Naked I Leave (1970), The Rise of the Unmeltable Ethnics (1972), Confession of a Catholic (1983), and Human Rights and the New Realism (1986).

GROWING UP in America has been an assault upon my sense of   1
worthiness. It has also been a kind of liberation and delight.

There must be countless women in America who have known   2
for years that something is peculiarly unfair, yet who only recently
have found it possible, because of Women's Liberation, to give tongue
to their pain. In recent months I have experienced a similar inner thaw,
a gradual relaxation, a willingness to think about feelings heretofore
shepherded out of sight.

I am born of PIGS—those Poles, Italians, Greeks, and Slavs,   3
those non–English-speaking immigrants numbered so heavily among
the workingmen of this nation. Not particularly liberal or radical; born
into a history not white Anglo-Saxon and not Jewish; born outside
what, in America, is considered the intellectual mainstream—and thus
privy to neither power nor status nor intellectual voice.

Those Poles of Buffalo and Milwaukee—so notoriously taciturn,   4
sullen, nearly speechless. Who has ever understood them? It is not that
Poles do not feel emotion—what is their history if not dark passion, ro-
manticism, betrayal, courage, blood? But where in America is there
anywhere a language for voicing what a Christian Pole in this nation
feels? He has no Polish culture left him, no Polish tongue. Yet Polish
feelings do not go easily into the idiom of happy America, the America
of the Anglo-Saxons and yes, in the arts, the Jews. (The Jews have long
been a culture of the word, accustomed to exile, skilled in scholarship

317

and in reflection. The Christian Poles are largely of peasant origin, free men for hardly more than a hundred years.) Of what shall the young man of Lackawanna think on his way to work in the mills, departing his relatively dreary home and street? What roots does he have? What language of the heart is available to him?

The PIGS are not silent willingly. The silence burns like hidden coals in the chest.

All four of my grandparents, unknown to one another, arrived in America from the same county in Slovakia. My grandfather had a small farm in Pennsylvania; his wife died in a wagon accident. Meanwhile, Johanna, fifteen, arrived on Ellis Island, dizzy from witnessing births and deaths and illnesses aboard the crowded ship. She had a sign around her neck lettered PASSAIC. There an aunt told her of a man who had lost his wife in Pennsylvania. She went. They were married. She inherited his three children.

Each year for five years Grandma had a child of her own. She was among the lucky; only one died. When she was twenty-two and the mother of seven (my father was the last), her husband died. "Grandma Novak," as I came to know her many years later, resumed the work she had begun in Slovakia at the town home of a man known to my father only as "the Professor"; she housecleaned and she laundered.

I heard this story only weeks ago. Strange that I had not asked insistently before. Odd that I should have such shallow knowledge of my roots. Amazing to me that I do not know what my family suffered, endured, learned, and hoped these last six or seven generations. It is as if there were no project in which we all have been involved, as if history in some way began with my father and with me.

The estrangement I have come to feel derives not only from lack of family history. Early in life, I was made to feel a slight uneasiness when I said my name. When I was very young, the "American" kids still made something out of names unlike their own, and their earnest, ambitious mothers thought long thoughts when I introduced myself.

Under challenge in grammar school concerning my nationality, I had been instructed by my father to announce proudly: "American." When my family moved from the Slovak ghetto of Johnstown to the WASP suburb on the hill, my mother impressed upon us how well we must be dressed, and show good manners, and behave—people think of us as "different" and we mustn't give them any cause. "Whatever you do, marry a Slovak girl," was other advice to a similar end: "They cook. They clean. They take good care of you. For your own good." I was taught to be proud of being Slovak, but to recognize that others wouldn't know what it meant, or care.

Nowhere in my schooling do I recall any attempt to put me in touch with my own history. The strategy was clearly to make an American of me. English literature, American literature, and even the history books, as I recall them, were peopled mainly by Anglo-Saxons from Boston (where most historians seemed to live). Not even my native Pennsylvania, let alone my Slovak forebears, counted for very many paragraphs. (We did have something called "Pennsylvania History" somewhere; I seem to remember its puffs for industry.) It could have been written by a Mellon. I don't remember feeling envy or regret: a feeling, perhaps, of unimportance, of remoteness, of not having heft enough to count.

The fact that I was born a Catholic also complicated life. What is a Catholic but what everybody else is in reaction against? Protestants reformed "the whore of Babylon." Others were "enlightened" from it, and Jews had reason to help Catholicism and the social structure it was rooted in fall apart. The history books and the whole of education hummed in upon that point (for during crucial years I attended a public school): to be modern is decidedly not to be medieval; to be reasonable is not to be dogmatic; to be free is clearly not to live under ecclesiastical authority; to be scientific is not to attend ancient rituals, cherish irrational symbols, indulge in mythic practices. It is hard to grow up Catholic in America without becoming defensive, perhaps a little paranoid, feeling forced to divide the world between "us" and "them."

We had a special language all our own, our own pronunciation for words we shared in common with others (Augústine, contémplative), sights and sounds and smells in which few others participated (incense at Benediction of the Most Blessed Sacrament, Forty Hours, wakes, and altar bells at the silent consecration of the Host); and we had our own politics and slant on world affairs. Since earliest childhood, I have known about a "power elite" that runs America: the boys from the Ivy League in the State Department as opposed to the Catholic boys in Hoover's FBI who (as Daniel Moynihan once put it), keep watch on them. And on a whole host of issues, my people have been, though largely Democratic, conservative: on censorship, on communism, on abortion, on religious schools, etc. "Harvard" and "Yale" long meant "them" to us.

We did not feel this country belonged to us. We felt fierce pride in it, more loyalty than anyone could know. But we felt blocked at every turn. There were not many intellectuals among us, not even very many professional men. Laborers mostly. Small businessmen, agents for corporations perhaps. Content with a little, yes, modest in expectation, and content. But somehow feeling cheated. For a thousand years the Slovaks survived Hungarian hegemony and our strategy here remained the same: endurance and steady work. Slowly, one day, we would overcome.

A special word is required about a complicated symbol: sex. To   15
this day my mother finds it hard to spell the word intact, preferring to write "s——." Not that much was made of sex in our environment. And that's the point: silence. Demonstrative affection, emotive dances, an exuberance Anglo-Saxons seldom seem to share; but on the realities of sex, discretion. Reverence, perhaps; seriousness, surely. On intimacies, it was as though our tongues had been stolen, as though in peasant life for a thousand years—as in the novels of Tolstoi, Sholokhov, and even Kosinski—the context had been otherwise. Passion, certainly; romance, yes; family and children, certainly; but sex rather a minor if explosive part of life.

Imagine, then, the conflict in the generation of my brothers, sis-   16
ter, and myself. Suddenly, what for a thousand years was minor becomes an all-absorbing investigation. Some view it as a drama of "liberation" when the ruling classes (subscribers to the *New Yorker,* I suppose) move progressively, generation by generation since Sigmund Freud, toward concentration upon genital stimulation, and latterly toward consciousness-raising sessions in Clit. Lib. But it is rather a different drama when we stumble suddenly upon mores staggering any expectation our grandparents ever cherished.

Yet more significant in the ethnic experience in America is the   17
intellectual world one meets: the definition of values, ideas, and purposes emanating from universities, books, magazines, radio, and television. One hears one's own voice echoed back neither by spokesmen of "middle America" (so complacent, smug, nativist, and Protestant), nor by the "intellectuals." Almost unavoidably, perhaps, education in America leads the student who entrusts his soul to it in a direction which, lacking a better word, we might call liberal: respect for individual conscience, a sense of social responsibility, trust in the free exchange of ideas and procedures of dissent, a certain confidence in the ability of men to "reason together" and adjudicate their differences, a frank recognition of the vitality of the unconscious, a willingness to protect workers and the poor against the vast economic power of industrial corporations, and the like.

On the other hand, the liberal imagination has appeared to be as-   18
tonishingly universalist and relentlessly missionary. Perhaps the metaphor "enlightenment" offers a key. One is *initiated into light*. Liberal
education tends to separate children from their parents, from their roots,
from their history, in the cause of a universal and superior religion.

In particular, I have regretted and keenly felt the absence of that   19
sympathy for PIGS which simple human feeling might have prodded
intelligence to muster, that same sympathy which the educated find so
easy to conjure up for black culture, Chicano culture, Indian culture,
and other cultures of the poor. In such cases one finds the universalist
pretensions of liberal culture suspended; some groups, at least, are entitled to be both different and respected. Why do the educated classes
find it so difficult to want to understand the man who drives a beer
truck, or the fellow with a helmet working on a site across the street
with plumbers and electricians, while their sensitivities race easily to
Mississippi or even Bedford-Stuyvesant?

There are deep secrets here, no doubt, unvoiced fantasies and   20
scarcely admitted historical resentments. Few persons in describing
"middle Americans," "the silent majority," or Scammon and Watten-
berg's "typical American voter" distinguish clearly enough between
the nativist American and the ethnic American. The first is likely to be
Protestant, the second Catholic. Both may be, in various ways, conservative, loyalist, and unenlightened. Each has his own agonies, fears, be-
trayed expectations. Neither is ready, quite, to become an ally of the
other. Neither has the same history behind him here. Neither has the
same hopes. Neither lives out the same psychic voyage, shares the same
symbols, has the same sense of reality. The rhetoric and metaphors
proper to each differ from those of the other.

There is overlap, of course. But country music is not a polka; a   21
successful politician in a Chicago ward needs a very different "common
touch" from the one needed by the county clerk in Normal. The urban
experience of immigration lacks that mellifluous, optimistic, biblical vision of the good America which springs naturally to the lips of politicians from the Bible Belt. The nativist tends to believe with Richard
Nixon that he "knows America, and the American heart is good." The
ethnic tends to believe that every American who preceded him has an
angle, and that he, by God, will some day find one, too. (Often, ethnics
complain that by working hard, obeying the law, trusting their political
leaders, and relying upon the American dream, they now have only
their own naiveté to blame for rising no higher than they have.)

Unfortunately, it seems, the ethnics erred in attempting to Amer- 22
icanize themselves before clearing the project with the educated
classes. They learned to wave the flag and to send their sons to war.
They learned to support their President—an easy task, after all, for
those accustomed to obeying authority. And where would they have
been if Franklin Roosevelt had not sided with them against established
interests? They knew a little about communism—the radicals among
them in one way, and by far the larger number of conservatives in another. To this day not a few exchange letters with cousins and uncles
who did not leave for America when they might have, whose lot is demonstrably harder than their own and less than free.

Finally, the ethnics do not like, or trust, or even understand the in- 23
tellectuals. It is not easy to feel uncomplicated affection for those who
call you "pig," "fascist," "racist." One had not yet grown accustomed to
not hearing "hunkie," "Polack," "spic," "mick," "dago," and the rest.

At no little sacrifice, one had apologized for foods that smelled too 24
strong for Anglo-Saxon noses; moderated the wide swings of Slavic and
Italian emotion; learned decorum; given oneself to education, American style; tried to learn tolerance and assimilation. Each generation criticized the earlier for its authoritarian and European and old-fashioned
ways. "Up-to-date" was a moral lever. And now when the process
nears completion, when a generation appears that speaks without accent and goes to college, still you are considered "pigs," "fascists," and
"racists." Racists? Our ancestors owned no slaves. Most of us ceased being serfs only in the last two hundred years—the Russians in 1861....

Whereas the Anglo-Saxon model appears to be a system of 25
atomic individuals and high mobility, our model has tended to stress
communities of our own, attachment to family and relatives, stability,
and roots. Ethnics tend to have a fierce sense of attachment to their
homes, having been homeowners for less than three generations: a
home is almost fulfillment enough for one man's life. Some groups save
arduously in a passion to *own;* others rent. We have most ambivalent
feelings about suburban assimilation and mobility. The melting pot is a
kind of homogenized soup, and its mores only partly appeal to ethnics:
to some, yes, and to others, no.

It must be said that ethnics think they are better people than the 2
blacks. Smarter, tougher, harder working, stronger in their families.
But maybe many are not sure. Maybe many are uneasy. Emotions here
are delicate; one can understand the immensely more difficult circumstances under which the blacks have suffered; and one is not unaware

of peculiar forms of fear, envy, and suspicion across color lines. How much of this we learned in America by being made conscious of our olive skin, brawny backs, accents, names, and cultural quirks is not plain to us. Racism is not our invention; we did not bring it with us; we had prejudices enough and would gladly have been spared new ones. Especially regarding people who suffer more than we.

Questions on Meaning

1. Novak says that his "estrangement" resulted from lack of knowledge of his family's history and from his sense—symbolized in his name—of being different and not understood. Is not knowing one's family history a common condition among immigrants? What else contributed to Novak's sense of alienation?
2. Those who lived through the 1988 presidential campaign have become very conscious of the word *liberal*. Examine Novak's extended definition of this word and evaluate it. How does it compare with yours?
3. "Nowhere in my schooling do I recall any attempt to put me in touch with my own history. The strategy was clearly to make an American out of me." Should such a "strategy" be the purpose of American education? Why or why not?

Questions on Method

1. The first two sentences of this essay serve as a striking introduction; they grab the reader's interest. Do they also state the main point (thesis) of the essay? Is each sentence equally important to the thesis?
2. Why do you think Novak wrote this essay? What was his purpose?
3. What reason does Novak give to support his thesis that the educated classes are more likely to sympathize with African Americans than with Slovaks, Poles, Italians, or Greeks? If you agree, why do you? Cite supporting evidence.

Writing Topics

1. "We did not feel this country belonged to us" reflects not only Novak's point of view but that of many other immigrants. To whom, then, does America belong?
2. "The ethnics do not like, or trust, or even understand the intellectuals." Why not? What characteristics do the ethnics associate with intellectuals? What is your definition of an intellectual? How does it compare with Novak's? What interactions can you imagine taking place between ethnics

and intellectuals that would contribute to better personal and cultural understanding?

3. "Growing up in America has been an assault upon my sense of worthiness. It has also been a kind of liberation and delight." What causes and effects does Novak cite in his essay to support this thesis?

Kids in the Mall:
Growing Up Controlled

William Severini Kowinski (b. 1946) was raised in Greensburg, Pennsylvania, and studied at Knox College in Illinois and at the fiction and poetry workshops at the University of Iowa. He has published articles in the Boston Phoenix, Esquire, *the* New York Times, *and the* New York Times Magazine. *He began thinking about the impact malls have had on American values and behavior as a youth in Greensburg. His book,* The Malling of America: An Inside Look at the Great Consumer Paradise *(1985), considers why and how teenagers spend so much time in the shopping malls.*

Butch heaved himself up and loomed over the group. "Like it was different for me," he piped. "My folks used to drop me off at the shopping mall every morning and leave me all day. It was like a big free baby-sitter, you know? One night they never came back for me. Maybe they moved away. Maybe there's some kind of a Bureau of Missing Parents I could check with."

—RICHARD PECK, *Secrets of the Shopping Mall,* a novel for teenagers

FROM HIS SISTER at Swarthmore, I'd heard about a kid in Florida whose mother picked him up after school every day, drove him straight to the mall, and left him there until it closed—all at his insistence. I'd heard about a boy in Washington who, when his family moved from one suburb to another, pedaled his bicycle five miles every day to get back to his old mall, where he once belonged.

These stories aren't unusual. The mall is a common experience for the majority of American youth; they have probably been going there all their lives. Some ran within their first large open space, saw their first fountain, bought their first toy, and read their first book in a mall. They may have smoked their first cigarette or first joint or turned them down, had their first kiss or lost their virginity in the mall parking lot. Teenagers in America now spend more time in the mall than anywhere else but home and school. Mostly it is their choice, but some of that mall time is put in as the result of two-paycheck and single-parent households, and the lack of other viable alternatives. But are these kids being harmed by the mall?

I wondered first of all what difference it makes for adolescents to   3
experience so many important moments in the mall. They are, after all, at play in the fields of its little world and they learn its ways; they adapt to it and make it adapt to them. It's here that these kids get their street sense, only it's mall sense. They are learning the ways of a large-scale artificial environment: its subtleties and flexibilities, its particular pleasures and resonances, and the attitudes it fosters.

The presence of so many teenagers for so much time was not   4
something mall developers planned on. In fact, it came as a big surprise. But kids became a fact of mall life very early, and the International Council of Shopping Centers found it necessary to commission a study, which they published along with a guide to mall managers on how to handle the teenage incursion.

The study found that "teenagers in suburban centers are bored   5
and come to the shopping centers mainly as a place to go. Teenagers in suburban centers spent more time fighting, drinking, littering, and walking than did their urban counterparts, but presented fewer overall problems." The report observed that "adolescents congregated in groups of two to four and predominantly at locations selected by them rather than management." This probably had something to do with the decision to install game arcades, which allow management to channel these restless adolescents into naturally contained areas away from major traffic points of adult shoppers.

The guide concluded that mall management should tolerate and   6
even encourage the teenage presence because, in the words of the report, "The vast majority support the same set of values as does shopping center management." *The same set of values* means simply that mall kids are already preprogrammed to be consumers and that the mall can put the finishing touches to them as hard-core, lifelong shoppers just like everybody else. That, after all, is what the mall is about. So it shouldn't be surprising that in spending a lot of time there, adolescents find little that challenges the assumption that the goal of life is to make money and buy products, or that just about everything else in life is to be used to serve those ends.

Growing up in a high-consumption society already adds inestima-   7
ble pressure to kids' lives. Clothes consciousness has invaded the grade

schools, and popularity is linked with having the best, newest clothes in the currently acceptable styles. Even what they read has been affected. "Miss [Nancy] Drew wasn't obsessed with her wardrobe, " noted *The Wall Street Journal*. "But today the mystery in teen fiction for girls is what outfit the heroine will wear next." Shopping has become a survival skill and there is certainly no better place to learn it than the mall, where its importance is powerfully reinforced and certainly never questioned.

The mall as a university of suburban materialism, where Valley Girls and Boys from coast to coast are educated in consumption, has its other lessons in this era of change in family life and sexual mores and their economic and social ramifications. The plethora of products in the mall, plus the pressure on teens to buy them, may contribute to the phenomenon that psychologist David Elkind calls "the hurried child": kids who are exposed to too much of the adult world too quickly, and must respond with a sophistication that belies their still-tender emotional development. Certainly the adult products marketed for children—form-fitting designer jeans, sexy tops for preteen girls—add to the social pressure to look like an adult, along with the homegrown need to understand adult finances (why mothers must work) and adult emotions (when parents divorce).

Kids spend so much time at the mall partly because their parents allow it and even encourage it. The mall is safe, it doesn't seem to harbor any unsavory activities, and there is adult supervision; it is, after all, a controlled environment. So the temptation, especially for working parents, is to let the mall be their babysitter. At least the kids aren't watching TV. But the mall's role as a surrogate mother may be more extensive and more profound.

Karen Lansky, a writer living in Los Angeles, has looked into the subject and she told me some of her conclusions about the effects on its teenaged denizens of the mall's controlled and controlling environment. "Structure is the dominant idea, since true 'mall rats' lack just that in their home lives," she said, "and adolescents about to make the big leap into growing up crave more structure than our modern society cares to acknowledge." Karen pointed out some of the elements malls supply that kids used to get from their families, like warmth (Strawberry Shortcake dolls and similar cute and cuddly merchandise), old-fashioned mothering ("We do it all for you," the fast-food slogan), and even home cooking (the "homemade" treats at the food court).

The problem in all this, as Karen Lansky sees it, is that while families nurture children by encouraging growth through the assumption of responsibility and then by letting them rest in the bosom of the family from the rigors of growing up, the mall as a structural mother encourages passivity and consumption, as long as the kid doesn't make trouble. Therefore all they learn about becoming adults is how to act and how to consume.

Kids are in the mall not only in the passive role of shoppers—they   12
also work there, especially as fast-food outlets infiltrate the mall's enclosure. There they learn how to hold a job and take responsibility, but still within the same value context. When *CBS Reports* went to Oak Park Mall in suburban Kansas City, Kansas, to tape part of their hourlong consideration of malls, "After the Dream Comes True," they interviewed a teenaged girl who worked in a fast-food outlet there. In a sequence that didn't make the final program, she described the major goal of her present life, which was to perfect the curl on top of the ice-cream cones that were her store's specialty. If she could do that, she would be moved from the lowly soft-drink dispenser to the more prestigious ice-cream division, the curl on top of the status ladder at her restaurant. These are the achievements that are important at the mall.

Other benefits of such jobs may also be overrated, according to   13
Laurence D. Steinberg of the University of California at Irvine's social ecology department, who did a study on teenage employment. Their jobs, he found, are generally simple, mindlessly repetitive, and boring. They don't really learn anything, and the jobs don't lead anywhere. Teenagers also work primarily with other teenagers; even their supervisors are often just a little older than they are. "Kids need to spend time with adults," Steinberg told me. "Although they get benefits from peer relationships, without parents and other adults it's one-sided socialization. They hang out with each other, have age-segregated jobs, and watch TV."

Perhaps much of this is not so terrible or even so terribly differ-   14
ent. Now that they have so much more to contend with in their lives, adolescents probably need more time to spend with other adolescents without adult impositions, just to sort things out. Though it is more concentrated in the mall (and therefore perhaps a clearer target), the value system there is really the dominant one of the whole society. Attitudes about curiosity, initiative, self-expression, empathy, and disinterested learning aren't necessarily made in the mall; they are mirrored there, perhaps a bit more intensely—as through a glass brightly.

Besides, the mall is not without its educational opportunities.   1
There are bookstores, where there is at least a short shelf of classics at great prices, and other books from which it is possible to learn more than how to do sit-ups. There are tools, from hammers to VCRs, and

products, from clothes to records, that can help the young find and express themselves. There are older people with stories, and places to be alone or to talk one-on-one with a kindred spirit. And there is always the passing show.

The mall itself may very well be an education about the future. I 16 was struck with the realization, as early as my first forays into Greengate [Mall], that the mall is only one of a number of enclosed and controlled environments that are part of the lives of today's young. The mall is just an extension, say of those large suburban schools—only there's Karmelkorn instead of chem lab, the ice rink instead of the gym: It's high school without the impertinence of classes.

Growing up, moving from home to school to the mall—from en- 17 closure to enclosure, transported in cars—is a curiously continuous process, without much in the way of contrast or contact with unenclosed reality. Places must tend to blur into one another. But whatever differences and dangers there are in this, the skills these adolescents are learning may turn out to be useful in their later lives. For we seem to be moving inexorably into an age of preplanned and regulated environments, and this is the world they will inherit.

Still, it might be better if they had more of a choice. One teen- 18 aged girl confessed to *CBS Reports* that she sometimes felt she was missing something by hanging out at the mall so much. "But I'm here," she said, "and this is what I have."

Questions on Meaning

1. What is your response to Kowinski's question that concludes paragraph 3?
2. Do you agree that parents permit teenagers to spend too much time in the mall? Review paragraphs 2 and 10 before responding.
3. "Growing up in a high-consumption society already adds inestimable pressure to kids' lives." What supporting evidence does Kowinski provide? To what extent do you find it convincing?
4. Kowinski points out the "educational opportunities" available at the mall. Do they outweigh the negative aspects of "hanging out" there? Why or why not?

Questions on Method

1. How does the author's use of studies from experts and interviews with teenagers contribute to his essay's validity? Which data do you find supports his point of view? What is his purpose?

2. Select five of Kowinski's topic sentences, and list the supporting evidence he provides.
3. Review the first two and last two paragraphs of Kowinski's essay. Do they support or undermine the author's purpose? What is his purpose?

Writing Topics

1. Write an essay on the significance of Kowinski's title, including an analysis of the effects it strives for that justify it.
2. Visit your local mall and interview personnel such as shop owners, shoppers, and security guards on their impressions of how teenagers affect life at the mall. Using their responses, write an essay analyzing the effects of their presence on the mall's social and economic environment.
3. Why do people go to a hangout? Why do you? Spend a night at your favorite hangout, and write an essay based on your observations that explains why people enjoy spending time there.

A Peaceful Woman Explains Why She Carries a Pistol

Linda Hasselstrom lives and ranches in western South Dakota. She is an essayist, poet, and writer. Her writing often reflects her interest in the environment, and her books include Caught by One Wing *(1984) and* Roadkill *(1987), both poetry; and* Windbreak: A Woman Rancher on the Northern Plains *(1987). In 1987 she published her journals in* Going over East *and in 1991 her essays and poetry in* Land Circle: Writings Collected from the Land. *She has contributed essays to such magazines as* High Country News, Northern Lights, North American Review, Working Parents, Iowa Woman, Whole Earth Review, *and* Utne Reader. *She also contributes articles and essays to the* Los Angeles Times *and the* Christian Science Monitor.

I AM A PEACE-LOVING WOMAN. But several events in the past 10 years have convinced me I'm safer when I carry a pistol. This was a personal decision, but because handgun possession is a controversial subject, perhaps my reasoning will interest others.

I live in western South Dakota on a ranch 25 miles from the nearest large town; for several years I spent winters alone here. As a free-lance writer, I travel alone a lot—more than 100,000 miles by car in the last four years. With women freer than ever before to travel alone, the odds of our encountering trouble seem to have risen. And help, in the West, can be hours away. Distances are great, roads are deserted, and the terrain is often too exposed to offer hiding places.

A woman who travels alone is advised, usually by men, to protect herself by avoiding bars and other "dangerous situations," by approaching her car like an Indian scout, by locking doors and windows. But these precautions aren't always enough. I spent years following them and still found myself in dangerous situations. I began to resent the idea that just because I am female, I have to be extra careful.

A few years ago, with another woman, I camped for several   4
weeks in the West. We discussed self-defense, but neither of us had
taken a course in it. She was against firearms, and local police told us
Mace was illegal. So we armed ourselves with spray cans of deodorant
tucked into our sleeping bags. We never used our improvised Mace because we were lucky enough to camp beside people who came to our
aid when men harassed us. But on one occasion we visited a national
park where our assigned space was less than 15 feet from other campers. When we returned from a walk, we found that our closest neighbors were two young men. As we gathered our cooking gear, they
drank beer and loudly discussed what they would do to us after dark.
Nearby campers, even families, ignored them; rangers strolled past, unconcerned. When we asked the rangers point-blank if they would protect us, one of them patted my shoulder and said, "Don't worry, girls.
They're just kidding." At dusk we drove out of the park and hid our
camp in the woods a few miles away. The illegal spot was lovely, but
our enjoyment of that park was ruined. I returned from the trip determined to reconsider the options available for protecting myself.

At that time, I lived alone on the ranch and taught night classes in   ﹖
town. Along a city street I often traveled, a woman had a flat tire, called
for help on her CB radio, and got a rapist who left her beaten. She was
afraid to call for help again and stayed in her car until morning. For that
reason, as well as because CBs work best along line-of-sight, which
wouldn't help much in the rolling hills where I live, I ruled out a CB.

As I drove home one night, a car followed me. It passed me on a
narrow bridge while a passenger flashed a blinding spotlight in my face.
I braked sharply. The car stopped, angled across the bridge, and four men
jumped out. I realized the locked doors were useless if they broke the
windows of my pickup. I started forward, hoping to knock their car aside
so I could pass. Just then another car appeared, and the men hastily got
back in their car. They continued to follow me, passing and repassing. I
dared not go home because no one else was there. I passed no lighted
houses. Finally they pulled over to the roadside, and I decided to use their
tactic: fear. Speeding, the pickup horn blaring, I swerved as close to them
as I dared as I roared past. It worked; they turned off the highway. But I
was frightened and angry. Even in my vehicle I was too vulnerable.

Other incidents occurred over the years. One day I glanced out
at a field below my house and saw a man with a shotgun walking toward a pond full of ducks. I drove down and explained that the land
was posted. I politely asked him to leave. He stared at me, and the

muzzle of the shotgun began to rise. In a moment of utter clarity I realized that I was alone on the ranch, and that he could shoot me and simply drive away. The moment passed; the man left.

One night, I returned home from teaching a class to find deep 8 tire ruts in the wet ground of my yard, garbage in the driveway, and a large gas tank empty. A light shone in the house; I couldn't remember leaving it on. I was too embarrassed to drive to a neighboring ranch and wake someone up. An hour of cautious exploration convinced me the house was safe, but once inside, with the doors locked, I was still afraid. I kept thinking of how vulnerable I felt, prowling around my own house in the dark.

My first positive step was to take a kung fu class, which teaches 9 evasive or protective action when someone enters your space without permission. I learned to move confidently, scanning for possible attackers. I learned how to assess danger and techniques for avoiding it without combat.

I also learned that one must practice several hours every day to be 10 good at kung fu. By that time I had married George; when I practiced with him, I learned how *close* you must be to your attacker to use martial arts, and decided a 120-pound woman dare not let a six-foot, 220-pound attacker get that close unless she is very, very good at self-defense. I have since read articles by several women who were extremely well trained in the martial arts, but were raped and beaten anyway.

I thought back over the times in my life when I had been at- 11 tacked or threatened and tried to be realistic about my own behavior, searching for anything that had allowed me to become a victim. Overall, I was convinced that I had not been at fault. I don't believe myself to be either paranoid or a risk-taker, but wanted more protection.

With some reluctance I decided to try carrying a pistol. George 12 had always carried one, despite his size and his training in martial arts. I practiced shooting until I was sure I could hit an attacker who moved close enough to endanger me. Then I bought a license from the county sheriff, making it legal for me to carry the gun concealed.

But I was not yet ready to defend myself. George taught me that 13 the most important preparation was mental: convincing myself I could actually *shoot a person.* Few of us wish to hurt or kill another human being. But there is no point in having a gun—in fact, gun possession might increase your danger—unless you know you can use it. I got in the habit of rehearsing, as I drove or walked, the precise conditions that would be required before I would shoot someone.

People who have not grown up with the idea that they are capa-   14
ble of protecting themselves—in other words, most women—might
have to work hard to convince themselves of their ability, and of the
necessity. Handgun ownership need not turn us into gunslingers, but it
can be part of believing in, and relying on, *ourselves* for protection.

To be useful, a pistol had to be available. In my car, it's within in-   15
stant reach. When I enter a deserted rest stop at night, it's in my purse,
with my hand on the grip. When I walk from a dark parking lot into a
motel, it's in my hand, under a coat. At home, it's on the headboard. In
short, I take it with me almost everywhere I go alone.

Just carrying a pistol is not protection; avoidance is still the best   16
approach to trouble. Subconsciously watching for signs of danger, I believe I've become more alert. Handgun use, not unlike driving, becomes instinctive. Each time I've drawn my gun—I have never fired it
at another human being—I've simply found it in my hand.

I was driving the half-mile to the highway mailbox one day when   1
I saw a vehicle parked about midway down the road. Several men were
standing in the ditch, relieving themselves. I have no objection to
emergency urination, but I noticed they'd dumped several dozen beer
cans in the road. Besides being ugly, cans can slash a cow's feet or
stomach.

The men noticed me before they finished and made quite a per-   1
formance out of zipping their trousers while walking toward me. All
four of them gathered around my small foreign car, and one of them
demanded what the hell I wanted.

"This is private land. I'd appreciate it if you'd pick up the beer   1
cans."

"What beer cans?" said the belligerent one, putting both hands   2
on the car door and leaning in my window. His face was inches from
mine, and the beer fumes were strong. The others laughed. One tried
the passenger door, locked; another put his foot on the hood and
rocked the car. They circled, lightly thumping the roof, discussing my
good fortune in meeting them and the benefits they were likely to bestow upon me. I felt very small and very trapped and they knew it.

"The ones you just threw out," I said politely.

"I don't see no beer cans. Why don't you get out here and show
them to me, honey?" said the belligerent one, reaching for the handle
inside my door.

"Right over there," I said, still being polite, "—there, and over
there." I pointed with the pistol, which I'd slipped under my thigh.

Within one minute the cans and the men were back in the car and headed down the road.

I believe this incident illustrates several important principles. The men were trespassing and knew it; their judgment may have been impaired by alcohol. Their response to the polite request of a woman alone was to use their size, numbers, and sex to inspire fear. The pistol was a response in the same language. Politeness didn't work; I couldn't match them in size or number. Out of the car, I'd have been more vulnerable. The pistol just changed the balance of power. It worked again recently when I was driving in a desolate part of Wyoming. A man played cat-and-mouse with me for 30 miles, ultimately trying to run me off the road. When his car passed mine with only two inches to spare, I showed him my pistol, and he disappeared. 24

When I got my pistol, I told my husband, revising the old Colt slogan, "God made men *and women,* but Sam Colt made them equal." Recently I have seen a gunmaker's ad with a similar sentiment. Perhaps this is an idea whose time has come, though the pacifist inside me will be saddened if the only way women can achieve equality is by carrying weapons. 25

We must treat a firearm's power with caution. "Power tends to corrupt, and absolute power corrupts absolutely," as a man (Lord Acton) once said. A pistol is not the only way to avoid being raped or murdered in today's world, but, intelligently wielded, it can shift the balance of power and provide a measure of safety. 26

Questions on Meaning

1. In paragraphs 1–8, Hasselstrom cites examples from her own experience to justify buying a pistol. How effective is this strategy? Cite examples you found convincing.
2. What role does gender play in her decision to carry a gun?
3. What is your attitude toward gun ownership? To what extent did Hasselstrom's essay affect your point of view on this issue?

Questions on Method

1. Hasselstrom uses several rhetorical strategies in her essay. How effective is her use of contrast and comparison in paragraphs 9–11? Where does she use cause and effect?
2. For what audience is the author writing? What attitude toward gun ownership does she assume her audience shares? What is her purpose?

Writing Topics

1. "Handgun ownership need not turn us into gunslingers. But it can be part of believing in, and relying on, *ourselves* for protection." Write an essay attacking or defending this point of view.
2. Write a cause-and-effect analysis of a current news event. You might, for example, analyze what the results of a current political crisis might be or what reasons lie behind the current success or failure of a sports team.
3. Write a cause-and-effect analysis of a current sociopolitical issue. You might, for example, analyze the handgun control issue. What causes people to oppose or favor handgun control? What effect would tightening or not tightening control have?

Cause and Effect ———
Writing Topics

1. What would you say is the primary difference between a process analysis and a cause-and-effect analysis? Explain your answer in an essay that illustrates its points by describing both how a certain process works and why it works the way it does.

2. Write an essay on the effects of rock music on personal identity. Limit your topic to an aspect of the subject that you can discuss specifically.

3. Write an essay analyzing how and why one of your dreams has had an important effect on your life.

4. Select a contemporary social problem that interests you such as teenage suicide, violence in schools, AIDS, or pollution, and speculate about its effects. List as many effects as you can think of. Make sure that your purpose is clear and your tone is consistent.

5. Choose an influential rock or movie star popular with your generation. Review your tapes of him or her, and write an essay analyzing the causes and effects of his or her influence on your age group. Support your analysis with creative, specific examples.

13

Persuasion

PERSUASION USES ALL THE RESOURCES of the other three types of prose—narration, description, and exposition—but for its own purpose: to convince the reader to take a specific course of action or to believe a point of view. Even when it explains, it aims to persuade. It sets out clearly what is to be done or thought and proceeds to tell why, how, when, and so on, in the most compelling fashion. It engages the heart as well as the head. It aims to sell. It uses lively vocabulary and examples and illustrations that are most vivid for its particular audience. More than narration, description, or exposition per se, **argumentation** is prose whose effectiveness can be tested because it calls for a more or less definite and immediate reaction from the audience. It asks for commitment, and it requires commitment from the author. If it succeeds, the writer's rewards can be immediate and substantial.

Because the primary purpose of persuasive essays is to create in an audience the desire to do or believe something, they usually appeal to the reader's emotions, moral values, or logic. All of these appeals are ways of answering the question "Why should one think or act as I propose?" and are most closely associated with one of the methods of ex-

338

position, cause and effect. In this chapter, Martin Luther King's "I Have a Dream" speech, presented to a huge outdoor audience at the Lincoln Memorial in Washington, D.C., appeals largely to the emotions of his audience. The speech's logic is too evident to need elaboration: One hundred years after emancipation is too long to wait for full citizenship. The speech is a challenge to Americans to live up to their ideals. It spends little time winning acceptance for the truth or validity of these ideals; its purpose is to inspire courage and hope. For its emotional appeal it relies on rhythm, repetition, biblical quotations and vocabulary, historical parallels, and its author's personal identification with his audience and their problems.

If you were participating in a live debate, you would have to convince the judges that your evidence is sound and your conclusions correct. Your opponents in the debate would be trying to do the same thing, and you can't pretend that they don't exist; you must acknowledge and refute their arguments if you are to win the judges' votes. The writer of an argumentative or persuasive essay is also facing an unseen opponent, and one of the most effective ways you can establish your right to debate, your credentials, is to show that you know the arguments for both sides. Sydney Pollack in "The Way We Are" begins his speech at a conference on the influence of media in American culture by disagreeing with his opponents who claim that contemporary films are contributing to a decline in moral values. He strengthens his case and establishes his credentials by presenting evidence to support his thesis that "society's values have changed" and that the "kind of scrupulous, ethical concern for the sanctity of human life doesn't exist in the same way, and that fact is reflected in the movies." He concludes by stating that the economics of the contemporary film industry mandate that directors make movies that entertain their audiences. Your audience, like Pollack's, will accept your conclusions to the extent that they believe your claims to knowledge, honesty, and trustworthiness. They will be on the alert for your sense of ethics, your fairness, and consistency between what you say and how you say it—in a word, your **tone.**

Argumentation is a type of persuasion that appeals to your reader's sense of logic. Without going into the fine points of logic, we can say that logical thought moves in one of two directions, either from the general to the particular (*deduction*), or from the particular to the general (*induction*). In deduction, *logic* means reaching valid conclusions from valid premises, The model in deductive thinking is the **syllogism,** consisting of two premises and a conclusion:

All men are mortal.
Socrates is a man.
Therefore Socrates is mortal.

A syllogism assumes the truth of both premises and focuses on arriving at a *valid* conclusion within the system; the conclusion is valid if it correctly draws out the implications of the two interacting premises on the same principle as that used in geometry, that things equal to the same thing are equal to each other. The conclusion will be valid and *true* if both premises are true, but the closed system of a syllogism has no way of ascertaining the truth of its premises: that proof is left for *induction*.

How do we know that "All men are mortal" is true? By observation. Induction does not assume but arrives at its concluding generalization by the observation of particular facts or events, which it accepts as *evidence*. It is the method of science, and its generalizations are called *hypotheses* because they are always subject to review, to later observation. But don't scientists apply hypotheses to particular cases? They do indeed, and at that point they are using deduction. When scientists reach a conclusion that explains the observed facts, they apply that conclusion, however hypothetical. For example, the discovery of DNA, the mechanism of genetics, led scientists to seek ways to produce in large quantities substances such as interferon and insulin through genetic recombination.

So the two, deduction and induction, are continually coexisting, alternating, in the thought of scientists and nonscientists too. Consider the following mixture of induction and deduction:

Over a period of time you observe ten girls working on their cars.
All are poor mechanics.
You generalize that girls make poor mechanics.
You meet an eleventh girl.
You conclude—without observation—that No. 11 will be a poor mechanic.

The syllogism is as follows:

Girls make poor mechanics.
No. 11 is a girl.
Therefore No. 11 will make a poor mechanic.

The deductive conclusion here is valid—logically correct—but is it true? Obviously the truth of statement 3 above depends on the quantity and quality of your inductive observation. Ten girls is not a large enough sample to establish the truth of 3; if you accept it, you commit the common fallacy of *hasty generalization*. If you use 3 as your first premise, your deductive conclusion (statement 5) cannot be true. You have committed the fallacy of *causal oversimplification* by attributing an effect (poor mechanical ability) to the wrong cause (sex), a fallacy discussed in the previous chapter.

Dorothy L. Sayers opens "Are Women Human?" with an examination of the fallacy of *stereotyping,* which may also derive from causal oversimplification. The rest of her essay, a discussion of **clichés** about women, is a logical deduction from the premise that "*all* one's tastes and preferences [do not] have to be conditioned by the class to which one belongs." Logic is the substructure of her essay; but you will also find Sayers appealing to her readers' emotions and their trust in her credibility.

WRITING PERSUASIVE ESSAYS

1. Choose the appeal or appeals that suit your purpose, audience, and subject—emotional, ethical, or logical.
2. Acknowledge and refute the opposition.
3. In a logical appeal, choose the method for reasoning that suits your purpose and subject—induction or deduction. Check the validity of deductive conclusions.
4. Support your side with evidence, reasons, statistics, precedents, and the opinion of authorities.
5. Draw valid and significant conclusions from valid premises.
6. Cover the bare bones of your logic with graceful narration, description, and all the modes of exposition that suit your subject.

Are Women Human?

Dorothy L. Sayers (1893–1957), one of the most popular authors of the Golden Era, was born in England and educated at Oxford, where she received a degree in medieval literature. After graduation, she published two volumes of poetry. She began to write mystery stories to make money. Her first novel, Whose Body? *(1923), introduced Lord Peter Wimsey, the character for which she is best known. Sayers also edited several mystery anthologies collected under the heading* The Omnibus of Crime *(1929). Her early novels include* Clouds of Witness *(1926),* Unnatural Death *(1927),* The Unpleasantness at the Bellona Club *(1928),* Lord Peter Views the Body *(1928),* Strong Poison *(1929), and* The Documents in the Case *(1930).* Five Red Herrings *(1931),* Have His Carcase *(1932),* Murder Must Advertise *and* Hangman's Holiday *(1933),* The Nine Tailors *(1934), and* In the Teeth of the Evidence *(1939) are some of her later mysteries. "Are Women Human?" is one of the essays she wrote on philosophical and social issues collected in* Unpopular Opinions *(1947). She spent the last years of her life working on an English translation of* Dante's Divine Comedy.

IT IS THE MARK of all movements, however well-intentioned, that their pioneers tend, by much lashing of themselves into excitement, to lose sight of the obvious. In reaction against the age-old slogan, "woman is the weaker vessel," or the still more offensive, "woman is a divine creature," we have, I think, allowed ourselves to drift into asserting that "a woman is as good as a man," without always pausing to think what exactly we mean by that. What, I feel, we ought to mean is something so obvious that it is apt to escape attention altogether, viz.: not that every woman is, in virtue of her sex, as strong, clever, artistic, levelheaded, industrious and so forth as any man that can be mentioned; but, that a woman is just as much an ordinary human being as a man, with the same individual preferences, and with just as much right to the tastes and preferences of an individual. What is repugnant to every human being is to be reckoned always as a member of a class and not as an individual person. A certain amount of classification is, of course, necessary for practical purposes: there is no harm in saying that women, as a class, have smaller bones than men, wear lighter clothing, have more hair on their heads and less on their faces, go more pertinaciously to church or the cinema, or have more patience with small and noisy babies. In the same way, we may say that stout people of both sexes are commonly better-tempered than thin ones, or that university dons of both sexes are more pedantic in their speech than agricultural labourers, or that Communists of both sexes are more ferocious than Fascists—or the other way round. What is unreasonable and irritating is to assume that *all* one's tastes and preferences have to be conditioned by the class to which one belongs. That has been the very common error into which men have frequently fallen about women—and it is the error into which feminist women are, perhaps, a little inclined to fall into about themselves.

Take, for example, the very usual reproach that women nowadays always want to "copy what men do." In that reproach there is a great deal of truth and a great deal of sheer, unmitigated and indeed quite wicked nonsense. There are a number of jobs and pleasures which men have in times past cornered for themselves. At one time, for instance, men had a monopoly of classical education. When the pioneers of university training for women demanded that women should be admitted to the universities, the cry went up at once: "Why should women want to know about Aristotle?" The answer is NOT that *all* women would be the better for knowing about Aristotle—still less, as Lord Tennyson seemed to think, that they would be more companionable wives for their husbands if they did know about Aristotle—but simply: "What women want as a class is irrelevant. *I* want to know about Aristotle. It is true that most women care nothing about him, and a great many male undergraduates turn pale and faint at the thought of him—but I, eccentric individual that I am, do want to know about Aristotle, and I submit that there is nothing in my shape or bodily functions which need prevent my knowing about him."...

So that when we hear that women have once more laid hands upon something which was previously a man's sole privilege, I think we have to ask ourselves: is this trousers or is it braces? Is it something useful, convenient and suitable to a human being as such? Or is it merely something unnecessary to us, ugly, and adopted merely for the sake of collaring the other fellow's property? These jobs and professions, now. It is ridiculous to take on a man's job just in order to be able to say that "a woman has done it—yah!" The only decent reason for tackling any job is that it is *your* job and *you* want to do it.

At this point, somebody is likely to say: "Yes, that is all very well. But it is the woman who is always trying to ape the man. She *is* the inferior being. You don't as a rule find the men trying to take the women's jobs away from them. They don't force their way into the household and turn women out of their rightful occupations." 4

Of course they do not. They have done it already, 5

Let us accept the idea that women should stick to their own jobs—the jobs they did so well in the good old days before they started talking about votes and women's rights. Let us return to the Middle Ages and ask what we should get then in return for certain political and educational privileges which we should have to abandon. 6

It is a formidable list of jobs: the whole of the spinning industry, the whole of the dyeing industry, the whole of the weaving industry. The whole catering industry and—which would not please Lady Astor, perhaps—the whole of the nation's brewing and distilling. All the preserving, pickling and bottling industry, all the bacon-curing. And (since in those days a man was often absent from home for months together on war or business) a very large share in the management of landed estates. Here are the women's jobs—and what has become of them? They are all being handled by men. It is all very well to say that woman's place is the home—but modern civilization has taken all these pleasant and profitable activities out of the home, where the women looked after them, and handed them over to big industry, to be directed and organized by men at the head of large factories. Even the dairy-maid in her simple bonnet has gone, to be replaced by a male mechanic in charge of a mechanical milking plant. 7

Now, it is very likely that men in big industries do these jobs better than the women did them at home. The fact remains that the home contains much less of interesting activity than it used to contain. What is more, the home has so shrunk to the size of a small flat that—even if we restrict woman's job to the bearing and rearing of families—there is no room for her to do even that. It is useless to urge the modern woman to have twelve children, like her grandmother. Where is she to put them when she has got them? And what modern man wants to be bothered with them? It is perfectly idiotic to take away woman's traditional occupations and then complain because she looks for new ones. Every woman is a human being—one cannot repeat that too often—and a human being *must* have occupation, if he or she is not to become a nuisance to the world. 8

I am not complaining that the brewing and baking were taken   9
over by the men. If they can brew and bake as well as women or better,
then by all means let them do it. But they cannot have it both ways. If
they are going to adopt the very sound principle that the job should be
done by the person who does it best, then that rule must be applied
universally. If the women make better office-workers than men, they
must have the office work. If any individual woman is able to make a
first-class lawyer, doctor, architect or engineer, then she must be allowed to try her hand at it. Once lay down the rule that the job comes
first and you throw that job open to every individual, man or woman,
fat or thin, tall or short, ugly or beautiful, who is able to do that job
better than the rest of the world.

Now, it is frequently asserted that, with women, the job does not   10
come first. What (people cry) are women doing with this liberty of
theirs? What woman really prefers a job to a home and family? Very
few, I admit. It is unfortunate that they should so often have to make
the choice. A man does not, as a rule, have to choose. He gets both. In
fact, if he wants the home and family, he usually has to take the job as
well, if he can get it. Nevertheless, there have been women, such as
Queen Elizabeth and Florence Nightingale, who had the choice, and
chose the job and made a success of it. And there have been and are
many men who have sacrificed their careers for women—sometimes,
like Antony or Parnell, very disastrously. When it comes to a *choice,*
then every man or woman has to choose as an individual human being,
and like a human being, take the consequences.

As human beings! I am always entertained—and also irritated—   11
by the newsmongers who inform us, with a bright air of discovery,
that they have questioned a number of female workers and been told
by one and all that they are "sick of the office and would love to get
out of it." In the name of God, what human being is *not,* from time to
time, heartily sick of the office and would *not* love to get out of it? The
time of female office-workers is daily wasted in sympathizing with dis-
gruntled male colleagues who yearn to get out of the office. No human being likes work—not day in and day out. Work is notoriously a
curse—and if women *liked* everlasting work they would not be human
beings at all. *Being* human beings, they like work just as much and just
as little as anybody else. They dislike perpetual washing and cooking
just as much as perpetual typing and standing behind shop counters.
Some of them prefer typing to scrubbing—but that does not mean that
they are not, as human beings, entitled to damn and blast the typewriter when they feel that way. The number of men who daily damn

and blast typewriters is incalculable; but that does not mean that they would be happier doing a little plain sewing. Nor would the women.

I have admitted that there are very few women who would put their job before every earthly consideration. I will go further and assert that there are very few men who would do it either. In fact, there is perhaps only one human being in a thousand who is passionately interested in his job for the job's sake. The difference is that if that one person in a thousand is a man, we say, simply, that he is passionately keen on his job; if she is a woman, we say she is a freak. It is extraordinarily entertaining to watch the historians of the past, for instance, entangling themselves in what they were pleased to call the "problem" of Queen Elizabeth. They invented the most complicated and astonishing reasons both for her success as a sovereign and for her tortuous matrimonial policy. She was the tool of Burleigh, she was the tool of Leicester, she was the fool of Essex; she was diseased, she was deformed, she was a man in disguise. She was a mystery, and must have some extraordinary solution. Only recently has it occurred to a few enlightened people that the solution might be quite simple after all. She might be one of the rare people who were born into the right job and put that job first. Whereupon a whole series of riddles cleared themselves up by magic. She was in love with Leicester—why didn't she marry him? Well, for the very same reason that numberless kings have not married their lovers—because it would have thrown a spanner into the wheels of the State machine. Why was she so bloodthirsty and unfeminine as to sign the death-warrant of Mary Queen of Scots? For much the same reasons that induced King George V to say that if the House of Lords did not pass the Parliament Bill he would create enough new peers to force it through—because she was, in the measure of her time, a constitutional sovereign, and knew that there was a point beyond which a sovereign could not defy Parliament. Being a rare human being with her eye to the job, she did what was necessary; being an ordinary human being, she hesitated a good deal before embarking on unsavory measures—but as to feminine mystery, there is no such thing about it, and nobody, had she been a man, would have thought either her statesmanship or her humanity in any way mysterious. Remarkable they were—but she was a very remarkable person. Among her most remarkable achievements was that of showing that sovereignty was one of the jobs for which the right kind of woman was particularly well fitted.

Which brings us back to this question of what jobs, if any, are women's jobs. Few people would go so far as to say that all women are well fitted for all men's jobs. When people do say this, it is particularly exasperating. It is stupid to insist that there are as many female musicians and mathematicians as male—the facts are otherwise, and the most we can ask is that if a Dame Ethel Smyth or a Mary Somerville turns up, she shall be allowed to do her work without having aspersions cast either on her sex or her ability. What we ask is to be human individuals, however peculiar and unexpected. It is no good saying: "You are a little girl and therefore you ought to like dolls"; if the answer is, "But I don't," there is no more to be said. Few women happen to be natural born mechanics; but if there is one, it is useless to try and argue her into being something different. What we must *not* do is to argue that the occasional appearance of a female mechanical genius proves that all women would be mechanical geniuses if they were educated. They would not.

Where, I think, a great deal of confusion has risen is in a failure   14 to distinguish between special *knowledge* and special *ability*. There are certain questions on which what is called "the woman's point of view" is valuable, because they involve special *knowledge*. Women should be consulted about such things as housing and domestic architecture because, under present circumstances, they have still to wrestle a good deal with houses and kitchen sinks and can bring special knowledge to the problem. Similarly, some of them (though not all) know more about children than the majority of men, and their opinion, *as women,* is of value. In the same way, the opinion of colliers is of value about coal-mining, and the opinion of doctors is valuable about disease. But there are other questions—as for example, about literature or finance— on which the "woman's point of view" has no value at all. In fact, it does not exist. No special knowledge is involved, and a woman's opinion on literature or finance is valuable only as the judgment of an individual. I am occasionally desired by congenital imbeciles and the editors of magazines to say something about the writing of detective fiction "from the woman's point of view." To such demands, one can only say, "Go away and don't be silly. You might as well ask what is the female angle on an equilateral triangle."...

A man once asked me—it is true that it was at the end of a very   15 good dinner, and the compliment conveyed may have been due to that circumstance—how I managed in my books to write such natural conversation between men when they were by themselves. Was I, by any chance, a member of a large, mixed family with a lot of male friends? I replied that, on the contrary, I was an only child and had practically never seen or spoken to any men of my own age till I was about twenty-five.

"Well," said the man, "I shouldn't have expected a woman [meaning me] to have been able to make it so convincing." I replied that I had coped with this difficult problem by making my men talk, as far as possible, like ordinary human beings. This aspect of the matter seemed to surprise the other speaker; he said no more, but took it away to chew it over. One of these days it may quite likely occur to him that women, as well as men, when left to themselves, talk very much like human beings also.

Indeed, it is my experience that both men and women are funda-   1(
mentally human, and that there is very little mystery about either sex, except the exasperating mysteriousness of human beings in general. And though for certain purposes it may still be necessary, as it undoubtedly was in the immediate past, for women to band themselves together, as women, to secure recognition of their requirements as a sex, I am sure that the time has now come to insist more strongly on each woman's— and indeed each man's—requirements as an individual person. It used to be said that women had no *esprit de corps;* we have proved that we have— do not let us run into the opposite error of insisting that there is an aggressively feminist "point of view" about everything. To oppose one class perpetually to another—young against old, manual labor against brainworker, rich against poor, woman against man—is to split the foundations of the State; and if the cleavage runs too deep, there remains no remedy but force and dictatorship. If you wish to preserve a free democracy, you must base it—not on classes and categories, for this will land you in the totalitarian State, where no one may act or think except as the member of a category. You must base it upon the individual Tom, Dick and Harry, on the individual Jack and Jill—in fact, upon you and me.

Questions on Meaning

1. Sayers does not object to "a certain amount of classification." What *does* she object to? Do you see any inconsistency in this position? Why or why not?
2. How does Sayers defend women's takeover of jobs formerly held only by men? How does Sayers answer those who say women don't like jobs outside the home?
3. What fields, according to Sayers, do women seldom excel in? Do you think she is right?
4. On what subjects should one look for "the woman's point of view"? Why? Do you agree that there can't be a woman's point of view on literature or finance? Why or why not?

5. Sayers began by accusing "feminist women" of the same error into which men had fallen. What is that error? Why do you suppose she began this way?
6. Is this a good title for this essay? Explain your answer.

Questions on Method

1. Does Sayers support her thesis that men and women are individuals rather than members of a class, or does she assume it? Is the essay based on induction, deduction, or both?
2. What modes of exposition does Sayers use in presenting her ideas? Cite at least two and discuss their effectiveness.
3. Choose two paragraphs from the essay and analyze how Sayers supports her topic sentences. Does she, for example, give evidence for her points? Is it sufficient?
4. The topic sentence of Sayers's concluding paragraph is striking. How does she support it in the rest of the paragraph? Does her conclusion convince you? Why or why not?

Writing Topics

1. Sayers writes: "Indeed, it is my experience that both men and women are fundamentally human, and that there is very little mystery about either sex, except the exasperating mysteriousness of human beings in general." Write a persuasive essay agreeing or disagreeing with Sayers's point of view. Review your paper for sufficient convincing evidence to win your reader's support for your answers.
2. According to Sayers, "There is perhaps only one human being in a thousand who is passionately interested in his job for the job's sake." To what extent do you agree? How would you characterize your own goals with regard to work? Do you think being ambitious is more important than enjoying work? Can you imagine doing both? Write an essay defining your attitudes toward work, indicating the factors that influenced them.
3. Write an essay in which you argue either that you would rather be male than female or that you would rather be female than male.

The Way We Are

Sydney Pollack (b. 1934) was born in Lafayette, Indiana, during the Depression. His father, David, was a pharmacist and professional boxer. The young Pollack sought a career as an actor in New York City and studied under Sanford Meisner at the Neighborhood Playhouse. He served in the United States Army and worked as an acting instructor from 1954 to 1960. He appeared on the New York stage in A Stone for Danny Fisher *in 1954 and in* The Dark is Light Enough *in 1955. He later toured with the road company of* Stalag 17. *He also performed in television drama.* Shot Gun Slade *(1959) was his first assignment as a television director. From 1960 to 1965, he directed television shows. His first major box-office success was* They Shoot Horses, Don't They? *(1969). In 1972 he directed* Jeremiah Johnson, *which was entered in the Cannes Film Festival and chosen by Stanley Kauffman and other film authorities as the year's best film. He directed* The Way We Were *in 1973 and the spy thriller* Three Days of the Condor *in 1975, for which he won the Edgar Allan Poe mystery writers award. In 1977* Bobby Deerfield *was the surprise hit of the Deauville Festival in France. His other films include* The Electric Horseman *(1979);* Absence of Malice *(1981), for which he was voted best director by the New York Film Critics Circle, which also cited the film for its screenplay and supporting actress; and* Tootsie *(1982). He received the Golden Globe award from the Hollywood Foreign Press Association and was honored by the Los Angeles Film Critics. In 1980 he coproduced* Honeysuckle Rose *with Willie Nelson and produced both* Songwriter *(1984) and* Out of Africa *(1985). His latest films include* Husbands and Wives *(1992),* Death Becomes Her *(1992),* The Firm *(1993),* Sabrina *(1995), and* Random Hearts *(1999).*

SIX WEEKS AGO, I thought I was going to be happy to be a part of this conference, which shows you how naive I am. The agenda—for me at least—is a mine field. Normally, I spend my time worrying about specific problems and not reflecting, as many of you on these panels do. So I've really thought about this, and I've talked to anyone who would listen. My colleagues are sick and tired of it, my wife has left for the country, and even my agents—and these are people I pay—don't return my phone calls. By turns, I have felt myself stupid, unethical, a philistine, unpatriotic, a panderer, a cultural polluter, and stupid. And I've completely failed to solve your problems, except in one small way. You have delayed by at least six weeks the possibility of my contributing further to the problems you see.

I know your concerns have to do with American values and whether those values are being upheld or assaulted by American entertainment—by what I and others like me do. But which values exactly?

In the thirties, forties, and fifties, six men in the Valley, immigrants really, ran the movie industry. Our society was vastly different. The language of the movies was a language of shared values. If you put forward a virtuousness on the part of your hero, everybody responded to it.

When Sergeant York, played by Gary Cooper, refused to endorse a breakfast cereal, knowing he'd been asked because he'd won the Medal of Honor, he said: "I ain't proud of what I've done. You don't make money off of killing people. That there is wrong." We expected him to behave that way.

But society's values have changed. That kind of scrupulous, ethical concern for the sanctity of human life doesn't exist in the same way, and that fact is reflected in the movies. There's a nostalgia now for some of the old values, but so many people embrace other expressions of values that it's hard to say these other expressions aren't reality.

Their idea of love, for example, is a different idea of love. It's a much less chaste, much less idealized love than was depicted in the earlier films. We are seeing some sort of return to the ideal of marriage. There was a decade or two when marriage really lost its popularity, and while young people are swinging toward it again, I don't believe one could say that values have not changed significantly since the thirties, forties, and fifties.

Morality, the definitions of virtue, justice, and injustice, the sanctity of the individual, have been fairly fluid for American audiences in terms of what they choose to embrace or not embrace.

Take a picture like *Dances With Wolves*. You could not have made it in the thirties or forties. It calls into question every value that existed in traditional Westerns. It may not reflect what everybody thinks now, but it expresses a lot of guilty re-evaluation of what happened in the West, the very things shown in the old Westerns that celebrated the frontier.

If we got the movies to assert or talk about better values, would that fix our society? Well, let me quote Sam Goldwyn. When he was told by his staff how poorly his studio's new—and very expensive—film was doing, Sam thought a minute, shrugged, and said, "Listen, if they don't want to come, you can't stop them."

Now that's as close to a first principle of Hollywood as I can come. It informs everything that we're here to discuss and it controls every solution that we may propose.   10

OUT OF HOLLYWOOD

Before they can be anything else, American movies are a product. This is not good or bad, this is what we've got. A very few may become art, but all of them, whatever their ambitions, are first financed as commodities. They're the work of craftsmen and artists, but they're soon offered for sale.   11

Whether we say that we're "creating a film" or merely "making a movie," the enterprise itself is sufficiently expensive and risky that it cannot be, and it will not be, undertaken without the hope of reward. We have no Medicis here. It takes two distinct entities, the financiers and the makers, to produce movies, and there is a tension between them. Their goals are sometimes similar, but they do different things. Financiers are not in the business of philanthropy. They've got to answer to stockholders.   12

Of course, the controlling influence in filmmaking hasn't changed in 50 years: it still belongs to the consumer. That's the dilemma and, in my view, what we're finally talking about. What do you do about culture in a society that celebrates the common man but doesn't always like his taste?   13

If you operate in a democracy and you're market-supported and -driven, the spectrum of what you will get is going to be very wide indeed. It will range from trash to gems. There are 53,000 books published in this country every year. How many of them are really good? Tired as I may be of fast-food-recipe, conscienceless, simple-minded books, films, TV, and music, the question remains, Who is to be society's moral policeman?   14

Over the course of their first 30 or 40 years, the movies were a cottage industry, and the morality that was reflected in them was the morality of the early film pioneers. Now, film studios are tiny divisions of multinational corporations, and they feel the pressure for profits that happens in any other repeatable-product business. They look for a formula. Say you get the recipe for a soft drink and perfect it; once cus-   1.

tomers like it, you just repeat it and it will sell. More fortunes have been lost than made in the movie business pursuing such a formula, but unfortunately today, more junk than anything else is being made pursuing it. And film companies are folding like crazy.

Since we are in the democracy business, we can't tell people what they should or shouldn't hear, or support, or see, so they make their choices. The market tries to cater to those choices, and we have what we have. 16

MAKING FILMS

Are American films bad? A lot of them surely are, and so are a lot of everybody else's, the way a lot of anything produced is bad—breakfast cereals, music, most chairs, architecture, mail-order shirts. There probably hasn't been a really beautiful rake since the Shakers stopped making farm implements. But that is no excuse. 17

I realize that I am a prime suspect here, but I'm not sure that you really understand how odd and unpredictable a business the making of films actually is. It just doesn't conform to the logic or rules of any other business. It's always been an uneasy merger of two antithetical things: some form of art and sheer commerce. 18

If the people who make films get the money that is invested in them back to the people who finance them, then they'll get to make more. We know that the business of films is to reach as many people as possible. That works two ways; it's not just a market discipline. You have to remember that most of us who are doing this got into it for the romance, the glory, the applause, the chance to tell stories, even to learn, but rarely for the money. The more people you reach, the greater your sense of success. Given the choice, I'd rather make the whole world cry than 17 intellectuals in a classroom. 19

But, paradoxically, if you are the actual maker of the film—not the financier—you can't make films and worry about whether they'll reach a large audience or make money, first, because nobody really knows a formula for what will make money. If they did, I promise you we would have heard about it, and studios would not be going broke. Second, and much more practically, if you spent your time while you were making the film consciously thinking about what was commercial, then the real mechanism of choice—the mechanism that is your own unconscious, your own taste and imagination, your fantasy—would be replaced by constant reference to this formula that we know doesn't work. 20

So the only practical approach a filmmaker can take is to make a   21
film that he or she would want to see. This sounds arrogant, but you
try to make a movie for yourself, and you hope that as many people as
possible will like it too. If that happens, it's because you've done something in the telling of the story that makes people care. One of the
things that makes a film distinct from other American business products is this emotional involvement of the maker. A producer of auto
parts can become pretty emotional about a sales slump, but it isn't the
same thing. His product hasn't come from his history; it isn't somehow
in the image of his life; and it lacks mystery. It is entirely measurable
and concrete, which is certainly appropriate in the manufacture of
auto parts. I wouldn't want to buy a carburetor from a neurotic,
mixed-up auto manufacturer.

Fortunately for those of us in film, no such standards apply. Quite   22
the contrary, in fact. No matter what his conscious intentions are, the
best part of what the filmmaker does—the part, when it works, that
makes you want to see the film—doesn't come from a rational, consciously controllable process. It comes from somewhere inside the
filmmaker's unconscious. It comes from making unlikely connections
seem inevitable, from a kind of free association that jumps to odd or
surprising places, conclusions that cause delights, something that creates goose pimples or awe.

This conference has suggested a question: While you're actually   23
making the movie, do you think about whether or not it will be doing
the world any good? I can't answer it for filmmakers in general. For
myself, candidly, no, I don't.

I try to discover and tell the truth and not be dull about it. In that   24
sense, the question has no significance for me. I assume that trying to
discover the truth is in itself a good and virtuous aim. By truth I don't
mean some grand, pretentious axiom to live by; I just mean the truth
of a character from moment to moment. I try to discover and describe
things like the motives that are hidden in day-to-day life. And the truth
is rarely dull. If I can find it, I will have fulfilled my primary obligation
as a filmmaker, which is not to bore the pants off you.

Most of us in this business have enormous sympathy for Scheher-   25
azade—we're terrified we're going to be murdered if we're boring. So
our first obligation is to not bore people; it isn't to teach.

Most of the time, high-mindedness just leads to pretentious or   26
well-meaning, often very bad, films. Most of the Russian films made
under communism were of high quality in terms of craft, but they

were soporific because their intent to do good as it was perceived by the state or an all-knowing party committee was too transparent.

I'm sure that you think the person in whose hands the process ac- 27
tually rests, the filmmaker, could exert an enormous amount of control over the film's final worthiness. The question usually goes like this: Should filmmakers pander to the public, or should they try to elevate public taste to something that many at this conference would find more acceptable? Is the job of an American filmmaker to give the public what it wants or what the filmmaker thinks the public should have? This doesn't leave much doubt as to what you think is the right answer.

But framing your question this way not only betrays a misunder- 28
standing of how the filmmaking process works but also is just plain wishful thinking about how to improve society. I share your nostalgia for some of those lost traditional values, but attempting to reinstall them by arbitrarily putting them into movies when they don't exist in everyday life will not get people to go to the movies or put those values back into life. I wish it were that simple.

ENGAGING AN AUDIENCE

This conference is concerned with something called popular cul- 29
ture and its effect on society, but I am concerned with one film at a time and its effect. You are debating whether movies corrupt our souls or elevate them, and I'm debating whether a film will touch a soul. As a filmmaker, I never set out to create popular culture, and I don't know a single other filmmaker who does.

Maybe it's tempting to think of Hollywood as some collective 30
behemoth grinding out the same stories and pushing the same values, but it's not that simple. Hollywood, whatever that means, is Oliver Stone castigating war in *Born on the Fourth of July* and John Milius celebrating it in *The Wind and the Lion*. It's Walt Disney and Martin Scorsese. It's Steven Spielberg and Milos Foreman. It's *Amadeus* and *Terminator* and hundreds of choices in between.

I don't want to defend Hollywood, because I don't represent 31
Hollywood—I can't, any more than one particular writer can represent literature or one painter art. For the most part, the impulse toward all art, entertainment, culture, pop culture, comes from the same place within the makers of it. The level of talent and the soul, if you'll forgive the word again, is what finally limits it.

At the risk of telling you more than you need to know about my ³² own work, I make the movies I make because there is in each film some argument that fascinates me, an issue I want to work through. I call this a spine or an armature because it functions for me like an armature in sculpture—something I can cover up and it will support the whole structure. I can test the scenes against it. For me, the film, when properly dramatized, adds up to this idea, this argument.

But there are lots of other ways to go about making a film, and ³³ lots of other filmmakers who do it differently. Some filmmakers begin knowing exactly what they want to say and then craft a vehicle that contains that statement. Some are interested in pure escape. Here's the catch. The effectiveness and the success of all our films is determined by exactly the same standards—unfortunately, not by the particular validity of their message but by their ability to engage the concentration and emotions of the audience.

Citizen Kane is an attack on acquisition, but that's not why people ³⁴ go to see it. I don't have any idea if the audience that saw *Tootsie* thought at any conscious level that it could be about a guy who became a better man for having been a woman; or that *The Way We Were*, a film I made 20 years ago, may have been about the tension between passion, often of the moment, and wisdom, often part of a longer view; or that *Out of Africa* might be about the inability to possess another individual and even the inability of one country to possess another. That's intellectual and stuffy. I just hope the audiences were entertained.

I may choose the movies I make because there's an issue I want to ³⁵ explore, but the how—the framing of that issue, the process of finding the best way to explore it—is a much more mysterious, elusive, and messy process. I can't tell you that I understand it; if I did, I would have a pep talk with myself and go out and make a terrific movie every time.

I would not make a film that ethically, or morally, or politically ³⁶ trashed what I believe is fair. But by the same token, I feel an obligation—and this is more complicated and personal—to do films about arguments. I try hard to give each side a strong argument—not because I'm a fair guy but because I believe it's more interesting. Both things are going on.

I do the same thing on every movie I make. I find an argument, ³⁷ a couple of characters I would like to have dinner with, and try to find the most fascinating way to explore it. I work as hard as I can to tell the story in the way I'd like to have it told to me.

What is really good is also entertaining and interesting because it's 38 closer to a newer way to look at the truth. You can't do that consciously. You can't start out by saying, "I am now going to make a great film."

The virtue in making a film, if there is any, is in making it well. If 39 there's any morality that's going to come out, it will develop as you begin to construct, at every moment you have a choice to make. You can do it the honest way or you can bend it, and the collection of those moments of choice is what makes the work good or not good and is what reveals morality or the lack of it.

I've made 16 films. I've had some enormous successes and I've 40 had some colossal failures, but I can't tell you what the difference is in terms of what I did.

AN AMERICAN AESTHETIC?

In some circles, American films suffer by comparison with Euro- 41 pean films precisely because a lot of our movies seem to be the product of little deliberation and much instinct. It's been said of European movies that essence precedes existence, which is just a fancy way of saying that European movies exist in order to say something. Certainly one never doubts with a European film that it's saying something, and often it just comes right out and says it.

American films work by indirection; they work by action and 42 movement, either internal or external, but almost always movement. Our films are more narratively driven than others, which has a lot to do with the American character and the way we look at our lives. We see ourselves and our lives as being part of a story.

Most of our movies have been pro the underdog, concerned with 43 injustice, relatively anti–authority. There's usually a system—or a bureaucracy—to triumph over.

More often than not, American movies have been affirmative and 44 hopeful about destiny. They're usually about individuals who control their own lives and their fate. In Europe, the system was so class-bound and steeped in tradition that there was no democratization of that process.

There's no prior education required to assimilate American mov- 45 ies or American culture. American culture is general, as opposed to the specificity of Japanese or Indian culture. America has the most easily digestible culture.

Our movies seem artless. The best of them keep us interested 46 without seeming to engage our minds. The very thing that makes movies so popular here and abroad is one of the primary things that drives their critics to apoplexy, but seeming artlessness isn't necessarily mindlessness. There's a deliberate kind of artlessness in American movies that has come from a discipline or aesthetic long ago imposed by the marketplace. Our movies began as immigrants' dreams that would appeal to the dreams of other immigrants, and this aesthetic has led American films to transcend languages and cultures and communicate to every country in the world.

THE FILMMAKER'S RESPONSIBILITY

It has been suggested to some extent in this conference that I 47 ought to study my own and American filmmakers' responsibilities to the public and to the world. I realize I have responsibilities as a filmmaker, but I don't believe that they are as a moralist, a preacher, or a purveyor of values. I know it's tempting to use filmmaking as such, but utility is a poor standard to use in art. It's a standard that has been and is still used by every totalitarian state in the world.

My responsibility is to try to make good films, but "good" is a 48 subjective word. To me at any rate, "good" doesn't necessarily mean "good for us" in the narrow sense that they must elevate our spirits and send us out of the theater singing, or even that they must promote only those values that some think are worth promoting.

Good movies challenge us, they provoke us, they make us angry 49 sometimes. They present points of view we don't agree with. They force us to clarify our positions in opposition to them, and they do this best when they provide us with an experience and not a polemic.

Somebody gave the okay to pay for *One Flew Over the Cuckoo's* 50 *Nest, Driving Miss Daisy, Stand By Me, Moonstruck, Terms of Endearment,* and *Amadeus,* and despite conventional wisdom that said those films could not be successful, those decisions paid off handsomely because there are no rules. Studio executives and other financiers do exceed themselves. They take chances. They have to, and we have to hope that they'll do it more often.

What we see in movie theaters today is not a simple reflection of 51 today's economics or politics in this country but is a sense of the people who make the movies, and they vary as individuals vary. So what we really want is for this very privileged process to be in the best hands possible, but I know of no force that can regulate this except the moral climate and appetites of our society.

What we're exporting now is largely a youth culture. It's full of adolescent values; it's full of adolescent rage, love, rebelliousness, and a desire to shock. If you're unhappy with their taste—and this is a free market—then an appetite has to be created for something better. How do we do that? Well, we're back to square one: the supplier or the consumer, the chicken or the egg? Let's not even ask the question; the answer is both. 52

Of course filmmakers ought to be encouraged toward excellence, and audiences ought to be encouraged to demand it. How? That's for thinkers and social scientists to figure out. I have no idea. But if I had to play this scene out as an imaginary dialogue, I might say that you must educate the consumer first, and the best places to start are at school and at home. And then you would say that that is my job, that popular entertainment must participate in this education. And I would say, ideally, perhaps, but I do not think that will happen within a system that operates so fundamentally from an economic point of view. On an individual basis, yes, one filmmaker at a time; as an industry, no. An appetite or market will have to exist first. 53

That's not as bad as it sounds, because in the best of all possible worlds, we do try to satisfy both needs: entertain people and be reasonably intelligent about it. It can be done, and it is done more often than you might think. It's just very difficult. 54

It's like the two Oxford dons who were sitting at the Boarshead. They were playwrights, grousing because neither one of them could get produced, neither one could get performed. One turned to the other and said, "Oh, the hell with it. Let's just do what Shakespeare did—give them entertainment." 55

Questions on Meaning

1. To what extent do you agree with Pollack that the primary goal of a filmmaker should be to entertain his or her audience?
2. Review paragraph 8 of Pollack's essay. What points is he making about *Dances With Wolves*? If you have seen this film, do you agree or disagree with Pollack?
3. In paragraph 36, Pollack states that presenting both sides of an issue in a film is more challenging to the audience. What films can you think of to support his point of view?

4. Pollack discusses movies about youth culture in paragraph 52. How do you respond to his description of adolescent values? To exporting these films to the rest of the world?

Questions on Method

1. Pollack uses an analogy in paragraph 17. To what extent do you find it persuasive?
2. In paragraph 42, the author states that in American movies "we see ourselves and our lives as being part of a story." What evidence does he offer in paragraphs 43–46 to support his thesis?

Writing Topics

1. Rent one of Pollack's movies and write an analysis of its theme. To what extent does the film conform to Pollack's theories about American movies?
2. Pollack claims that movies reflect the values of society. Write an analysis of a film you saw recently. What aspects of contemporary American life does it reflect? To what extent do you agree or disagree with the film-maker's point of view?
3. Compare and contrast two recent films focusing on twentysomethings. What do they suggest about images of this age group in contemporary popular culture?

The Declaration of Independence

Thomas Jefferson (1743–1826), who became a governor, secretary of state, and president, is best known for his draft of the Declaration of Independence. Although Benjamin Franklin and John Adams made some small revisions, the document is essentially Jefferson's. As you read it, speculate as to how the author's understanding of his audience contributed to his effective communication of his message.

In Congress, July 4, 1776: The Unanimous Declaration of the Thirteen United States of America

WHEN IN THE COURSE of human events it becomes necessary for one people to dissolve the political bands which have connected them with another, and to assume among the powers of the earth, the separate and equal station to which the Laws of Nature and of Nature's God entitle them, a decent respect to the opinions of mankind requires that they should declare the causes which impel them to the separation.

We hold these truths to be self-evident, that all men are created equal, that they are endowed by their Creator with certain unalienable Rights, that among these are Life, Liberty and the pursuit of Happiness. That to secure these rights, Governments are instituted among Men, deriving their just powers from the consent of the governed. That whenever any Form of Government becomes destructive of these ends, it is the Right of the People to alter or to abolish it, and to institute new Government, laying its foundation on such principles and organizing its powers in such form, as to them shall seem most likely to effect their Safety and Happiness. Prudence, indeed, will dictate that Governments long established should not be changed for light and transient causes; and accordingly all experience hath shewn that mankind are more disposed to suffer, while evils are sufferable, than to right themselves by abolishing the forms to which they are accustomed. But when a long train of abuses and usurpations, pursuing invariably the same Object evinces a design to reduce them under absolute Despotism, it is their right, it is their duty, to throw off such Government, and to provide new Guards for their future security. Such has been the patient sufferance of these Colonies; and such is now the necessity which constrains them to alter their former Systems of Government. The history of the present King of Great Britain is a history of repeated injuries and usurpations, all having in direct object the establishment of an absolute Tyranny over these States. To prove this, let Facts be submitted to a candid world.

He has refused his Assent to Laws, the most wholesome and necessary for the public good.

He has forbidden his Government to pass laws of immediate and pressing importance, unless suspended in their operation till his Assent should be obtained; and when so suspended, he has utterly neglected to attend to them.

He has refused to pass other Laws for the accommodation of large districts of people, unless those people would relinquish the right of Representation in the Legislature, a right inestimable to them and formidable to tyrants only.

He has called together legislative bodies at places unusual, uncomfortable, and distant from the depository of their Public Records, for the sole purpose of fatiguing them into compliance with his measures.

He has dissolved Representative Houses repeatedly, for opposing with manly firmness his invasions on the rights of the people.

He has refused for a long time, after such dissolutions, to cause others to be elected; whereby the Legislative Powers, incapable of Annihilation, have returned to the People at large for their exercise; the State remaining in the mean time exposed to all the dangers of invasion from without, and convulsions within.

He has endeavored to prevent the population of these States; for that purpose obstructing the Laws for Naturalization of Foreigners; refusing to pass others to encourage their migration hither, and raising the conditions of new Appropriations of Lands.

He has obstructed the Administration of Justice, by refusing his Assent to Laws for establishing Judiciary Powers.

He has made Judges dependent on his Will alone, for the tenure of their offices, and the amount and payment of their salaries.

He has erected a multitude of New Offices, and sent hither swarms of Officers to harass our people, and eat out their substance.

He has kept among us, in times of peace, Standing Armies without the Consent of our legislatures.

He has affected to render the Military independent of and supe- 14
rior to the Civil Power.

He has combined with others to subject us to a jurisdiction foreign 15
of our constitution, and unacknowledged by our laws; giving his Assent
to their Acts of pretended Legislation: For quartering large bodies of
armed troops among us: For protecting them, by a mock Trial, from
punishment for any Murders which they should commit on the Inhabitants of these States: For cutting off our Trade with all parts of the world:
For imposing Taxes on us without our Consent: For depriving us in
many cases of the benefits of Trial by Jury: for transporting us beyond
Seas to be tried for pretended offences: for abolishing the free System of
English Laws in a neighboring Province, establishing therein an Arbitrary government, and enlarging its Boundaries so as to render it at once
an example and fit instrument for introducing the same absolute rule
into these Colonies: For taking away our Charters, abolishing our most
valuable Laws and altering fundamentally the Forms of our Governments: For suspending our own Legislatures, and declaring themselves
invested with power to legislate for us in all cases whatsoever.

He has abdicated Government here, by declaring us out of his 16
Protection and waging War against us.

He has plundered our seas, ravaged our Coasts, burnt our towns, 17
and destroyed the lives of our people.

He is at this time transporting large Armies of foreign Mercenaries 18
to complete the works of death, desolation and tyranny, already begun
with circumstances of Cruelty & Perfidy scarcely paralleled in the most
barbarous ages, and totally unworthy the Head of a civilized nation.

He has constrained our fellow Citizens taken Captive on the high 19
Seas to bear Arms against their Country, to become the executioners
of their friends and Brethren, or to fall themselves by their Hands.

He has excited domestic insurrections amongst us, and has en- 20
deavored to bring on the inhabitants of our frontiers, the merciless Indian Savages, whose known rule of warfare, is an undistinguished
destruction of all ages, sexes, and conditions.

In every stage of these Oppressions We have Petitioned for Re- 21
dress in the most humble terms: Our repeated Petitions have been answered only by repeated injury. A Prince, whose character is thus
marked by every act which may define a Tyrant, is unfit to be the ruler
of a free people.

Nor have We been wanting in attention to our British brethren. 22
We have warned them from time to time of attempts by their legislature

to extend an unwarrantable jurisdiction over us. We have reminded
them of the circumstances of our emigration and settlement here. We
have appealed to their native justice and magnanimity, and we have
conjured them by the ties of our common kindred to disavow these
usurpations, which would inevitably interrupt our connections and cor-
respondence. They too have been deaf to the voice of justice and of con-
sanguinity. We must, therefore, acquiesce in the necessity, which
denounces our Separation, and hold them, as we hold the rest of mankind, Enemies in War, in Peace Friends.

We, THEREFORE the Representatives of the UNITED STATES OF   23
AMERICA, in General Congress, Assembled, appealing to the Supreme
Judge of the world for the rectitude of our intentions, do, in the Name,
and by Authority of the good People of these Colonies, solemnly publish and declare, That these United Colonies are, and of Right ought to
be FREE AND INDEPENDENT STATES; that they are Absolved from all Allegiance to the British Crown, and that all political connection between
them and the State of Great Britain, is and ought to be totally dissolved;
and that as Free and Independent States, they have full Power to levy
War, conclude Peace, contract Alliances, establish Commerce, and to do
all other Acts and Things which Independent States may of right do.
And for the support of this Declaration, with a firm reliance on the protection of Divine Providence, we mutually pledge to each other our
Lives, our Fortunes, and our sacred Honor.

Questions on Meaning

1. What, according to the Declaration, is the purpose of government? How
   is this point important to the Declaration?
2. What, according to the Declaration, are people more likely to do, rebel
   or put up with injustice?
3. What does the last paragraph of the Declaration proclaim? How is this
   paragraph related to the rest of the document?
4. We have all heard the phrase "all men are created equal" so often that we
   don't really hear it anymore. What does it mean in this context? Is it true
   divorced from this context? In what sense is it true? Not true? In what
   sense was it true or not true at the time the Declaration was written?

Questions on Method

1. What is Jefferson's purpose in drafting the Declaration of Independence?

2. Who besides the King and "our British brethren" does Jefferson consider to be his audience?
3. Does Jefferson base his argument in the Declaration on induction or deduction?
4. Is Jefferson appealing primarily to his audience's emotions? Intellect? Both? Explain your answer.

Writing Topics

1. Jefferson declares that "all men are created equal," yet he continued to own slaves. How does this fact affect your response to Jefferson's document?
2. Compare and contrast the Declaration of Independence with Stanton's Declaration of Sentiments and Resolutions" (Chapter 7). Which document do you consider more relevant? Cite reasons for your point of view.

I Have a Dream

Born in Georgia, Martin Luther King Jr. (1929–1968) was the son and grandson of Baptist ministers. He was educated at Morehouse College, Crozier Theological Seminary, and Boston University. He was pastor of a Baptist church in Montgomery, Alabama, when Rosa Parks refused to relinquish her seat on a bus to a white person. King, influenced by the teachings of Mahatma Gandhi, led a nonviolent bus boycott in 1955 that attracted national attention. This incident led to the U.S. Supreme Court ruling that Alabama's bus segregation was unconstitutional. King wrote of the experience in Stride Toward Freedom *(1958).*

The message of passive resistance spread, and King and his followers organized many protests against segregation and injustice in the South. Although he was arrested, jailed, had his home bombed, and was stabbed, King continued to preach his philosophy and gained respect and admiration all over the world. In 1963 his Letter from Birmingham Jail *replied to those who criticized his methods and beliefs. King organized the March on Washington in 1963 and there delivered his memorable "I Have a Dream" speech. He was awarded the Noble Peace Prize in 1964—at age 35, he was the youngest recipient. King continued to lead protests and coupled his message about segregation with opposition to the Vietnam War. While preparing to march with striking workers in Memphis, Tennessee, in 1968, he was assassinated by James Earl Ray. His killer was sentenced to 99 years in prison. When Ray died in prison in 1998, he was fighting to prove his innocence and was supported by King's family, who wanted the case reopened, believing that there are questions about the crime that have remained unanswered.*

I AM HAPPY to join with you today in what will go down in history as the greatest demonstration for freedom in the history of our nation.

Five score years ago, a great American, in whose symbolic shadow we stand today, signed the Emancipation Proclamation. This momentous decree came as a great beacon light of hope to millions of Negro slaves who had been seared in the flames of withering injustice. It came as a joyous daybreak to end the long night of their captivity.

But one hundred years later, the Negro still is not free; one hundred years later, the life of the Negro is still sadly crippled by the manacles of segregation and the chains of discrimination; one hundred years later, the Negro lives on a lonely island of poverty in the midst of a vast ocean of material prosperity; one hundred years later, the Negro is still languished in the corners of American society and finds himself in exile in his own land.

So we've come here today to dramatize a shameful condition. In a sense we've come to our nation's capital to cash a check. When the architects of our republic wrote the magnificent words of the Constitution and the Declaration of Independence, they were signing a promissory note to which every American was to fall heir. This note was the promise that all men, yes, black men as well as white men, would be guaranteed the inalienable rights of life, liberty, and the pursuit of happiness.

It is obvious today that America has defaulted on this promissory note in so far as her citizens of color are concerned. Instead of honoring this sacred obligation, America has given the Negro people a bad check, a check which has come back marked "insufficient funds." But we refuse to believe that the bank of justice is bankrupt. We refuse to believe that there are insufficient funds in the great vaults of opportunity of this nation. And so we've come to cash this check, a check that will give us upon demand the riches of freedom and the security of justice.

We have also come to this hallowed spot to remind America of the fierce urgency of now. This is no time to engage in the luxury of cooling off or to take the tranquilizing drug of gradualism. Now is the time to make real the promises of democracy; now is the time to rise from the dark and desolate valley of segregation to the sunlit path of racial justice; now is the time to lift our nation from the quicksands of racial injustice to the solid rock of brotherhood; now is the time to make justice a reality for all of God's children. It would be fatal for the nation to overlook the urgency of the moment. This sweltering summer of the Negro's legitimate discontent will not pass until there is an invigorating autumn of freedom and equality.

Nineteen sixty-three is not an end, but a beginning. And those who hope that the Negro needed to blow off steam and will now be content, will have a rude awakening if the nation returns to business as usual. There will be neither rest nor tranquility in America until the Negro is granted his citizenship rights. The whirlwinds of revolt will continue to shake the foundations of our nation until the bright day of justice emerges.

But there is something that I must say to my people, who stand on the worn threshold which leads into the palace of justice. In the process of gaining our rightful place, we must not be guilty of wrongful deeds. Let us not seek to satisfy our thirst for freedom by drinking from the cup of bitterness and hatred. We must forever conduct our struggle on the high plain of dignity and discipline. We must not allow our creative protests to degenerate into physical violence. Again and again we must rise to the majestic heights of meeting physical force with soul force. The marvelous new militancy, which has engulfed the Negro community, must not lead us to a distrust of all white people. For many of our white brothers, as evidenced by their presence here today, have come to realize that their destiny is tied up with our destiny. And they have come to realize that their freedom is inextricably bound to our freedom. We cannot walk alone. And as we walk, we must make the pledge that we shall always march ahead. We cannot turn back.

There are those who are asking the devotees of Civil Rights, "When will you be satisfied?" We can never be satisfied as long as the Negro is the victim of the unspeakable horrors of police brutality; we can never be satisfied as long as our bodies, heavy with the fatigue of travel, cannot gain lodging in the motels of the highways and the hotels of the cities; we cannot be satisfied as long as the Negro's basic mobility is from a smaller ghetto to a larger one; we can never be satisfied as long as our children are stripped of their selfhood and robbed of their dignity by signs stating "For Whites Only"; we cannot be satisfied as long as the Negro in Mississippi cannot vote and a Negro in New York believes he has nothing for which to vote. No! No, we are not satisfied, and we will not be satisfied until "justice rolls down like waters and righteousness like a mighty stream."

I am not unmindful that some of you have come here out of great trials and tribulations. Some of you have come fresh from narrow jail cells. Some of you have come from areas where your quest for freedom left you battered by the storms of persecution and staggered by the winds of police brutality. You have been the veterans of creative suffering. Continue to work with the faith that unearned suffering is redemptive. Go back to Mississippi. Go back to Alabama. Go back to South Carolina. Go back to Georgia. Go back to Louisiana. Go back to the slums and ghettos of our Northern cities, knowing that somehow this situation can and will be changed. Let us not wallow in the valley of despair.

I say to you today, my friends, so even though we face the diffi- 11
culties of today and tomorrow, I still have a dream. It is a dream deeply
rooted in the American dream. I have a dream that one day this nation
will rise up and live out the true meaning of its creed, "We hold these
truths to be self-evident, that all men are created equal." I have a
dream that one day on the red hills of Georgia, sons of former slaves
and the sons of former slave owners will be able to sit down together at
the table of brotherhood. I have a dream that one day even the state of
Mississippi, a state sweltering with the heat of injustice, sweltering
with the heat of oppression, will be transformed into an oasis of freedom and justice. I have a dream that my four little children will one
day live in a nation where they will not be judged by the color of their
skin, but by the content of their character.

I HAVE A DREAM TODAY! 12

I have a dream that one day down in Alabama—with its vicious 13
racists, with its Governor having his lips dripping with the words of in-
terposition and nullification—one day right there in Alabama, little
black boys and black girls will be able to join hands with little white
boys and white girls as sisters and brothers.

I HAVE A DREAM TODAY! 14

I have a dream that one day every valley shall be exalted, and ev- 15
ery hill and mountain shall be made low. The rough places will be
plain and the crooked places will be made straight, "and the glory of
the Lord shall be revealed, and all flesh shall see it together."

This is our hope. This is the faith that I go back to the South 16
with. With this faith we will be able to hew out of the mountain of
despair a stone of hope. With this faith we will be able to transform the
jangling discords of our nation into a beautiful symphony of brotherhood. With this faith we will be able to work together, to pray together, to struggle together, to go to jail together, to stand up for
freedom together, knowing that we will be free one day. And this will
be the day. This will be the day when all God's children will be able to
sing with new meaning, "My country 'tis of thee, sweet land of liberty,
of thee I sing. Land where my fathers died, land of the pilgrims' pride,
from every mountainside, let freedom ring." And if America is to be a
great nation, this must become true.

So let freedom ring from the prodigious hilltops of New Hamp- 17
shire; let freedom ring from the mighty mountains of New York; let
freedom ring from the heightening Alleghenies of Pennsylvania; let
freedom ring from the snow-capped Rockies of Colorado; let freedom

ring from the curvaceous slopes of California. But not only that. Let freedom ring from Stone Mountain of Georgia; let freedom ring from Lookout Mountain of Tennessee; let freedom ring from every hill and mole hill of Mississippi. "From every mountainside, let freedom ring." And when this happens, and when we allow freedom to ring, when we let it ring from every village and every hamlet, from every state and every city, we will be able to speed up that day when all of God's children, black men and white men, Jews and Gentiles, Protestants and Catholics, will be able to join hands and sing in the words of the old Negro spiritual: "Free at last. Free at last. Thank God Almighty, we are free at last."

Questions on Meaning

1. King uses the word *freedom* several times in his speech. What do you think he means by it? Consider the different possible meanings of freedom to the various members of his audience. What does it mean to you?
2. When King speaks of "cash[ing] a check" or "insufficient funds," is he talking about money? Explain.
3. "You have been the veterans of creative suffering." Can suffering be creative? How?
4. What events in Mississippi in the early 1960s might have caused King to single out that state? Why would he specifically mention Georgia? Why Alabama?

Questions on Method

1. Why is the phrase "Five score years ago" more appropriate than a hundred years ago or in 1863? Why does he later repeat the phrase "one hundred years later" so often?
2. What evidence is there that King is addressing an audience that included whites?
3. One characteristic of persuasion is that it uses connotative diction and figurative language to appeal to the reader's emotions. What words or expressions do you find that make you react emotionally?
4. Characterize the tone of the speech. Is it objective, angry, neutral? Explain your answer.

Writing Topics

1. King says his dream is "rooted in the American Dream." What is that? King's quotation connects it with the Declaration of Independence. Is the American dream more than the hopes and rights expressed in that document? If so, in what way?

2. King was arrested several times for civil disobedience. Is there a cause for which you too would be willing to break the law? Under what circumstances can you imagine making such a choice? Write a persuasive essay explaining your reasons for so doing.

3. In his essay, King imagines that "one day on the red hills of Georgia, sons of former slaves and the sons of former slave owners will be able to sit down together at the table of brotherhood." To what extent has his dream been realized?

A Modest Proposal

Jonathan Swift (1667–1745) is considered one of the best English satirical prose writers. He served for several years as dean of St. Patrick's church in Dublin. His most famous satirical work on human foibles is Gulliver's Travels *(1726). One of his best known essays is "A Modest Proposal."*

IT IS A MELANCHOLY OBJECT to those who walk through this great town,[1] or travel in the country, when they see the streets, the roads, and cabin-doors crowded with beggars of the female sex, followed by three, four, or six children, *all in rags,* and importuning every passenger for an alms. These mothers, instead of being able to work for their honest livelihood, are forced to employ all their time in strolling, to beg sustenance for their helpless infants, who, as they grow up, either turn thieves for want of work, or leave their dear Native Country to fight for the Pretender in Spain, or sell themselves to the Barbadoes.

I think it is agreed by all parties that this prodigious number of children, in the arms, or on the backs, or at the heels of their mothers, and frequently of their fathers, is in the present deplorable state of the kingdom a very great additional grievance; and therefore whoever could find out a fair, cheap, and easy method of making these children sound useful members of the commonwealth would deserve so well of the public as to have his statue set up for a preserver of the nation.

But my intention is very far from being confined to provide only for the children of professed beggars; it is of a much greater extent, and shall take in the whole number of infants at a certain age who are born of parents in effect as little able to support them as those who demand our charity in the streets.

As to my own part, having turned my thoughts, for many years, upon this important subject, and maturely weighed the several schemes of other projectors, I have always found them grossly mistaken in their computation. It is true a child, just dropped from its dam, may be sup-

[1]Dublin.

ported by her milk for a solar year with little other nourishment, at most not above the value of two shillings, which the mother may certainly get, or the value in scraps, by her lawful occupation of begging, and it is exactly at one year old that I propose to provide for them, in such a manner as, instead of being a charge upon their parents, or the parish, or wanting food and raiment for the rest of their lives, they shall, on the contrary, contribute to the feeding and partly to the clothing of many thousands.

There is likewise another great advantage in my scheme, that it will prevent those voluntary abortions, and that horrid practice of women murdering their bastard children, alas, too frequent among us, sacrificing the poor innocent babes, I doubt, more to avoid the expense than the shame, which would move tears and pity in the most savage and inhuman breast.   5

The number of souls in this kingdom being usually reckoned one million and a half, of these I calculate there may be about two hundred thousand couples whose wives are breeders, from which number I subtract thirty thousand couples who are able to maintain their own children, although I apprehend there cannot be so many under the present distresses of the kingdom, but this being granted, there will remain an hundred and seventy thousand breeders. I again subtract fifty thousand for those women who miscarry, or whose children die by accident or disease within the year. There only remain an hundred and twenty thousand children of poor parents annually born. The question therefore is, how this number shall be reared, and provided for, which, as I have already said, under the present situation of affairs, is utterly impossible by all the methods hitherto proposed, for we can neither employ them in handicraft, or agriculture; we neither build houses (I mean in the country), nor cultivate land: they can very seldom pick up a livelihood by stealing till they arrive at six years old, except where they are of towardly parts,[2] although I confess they learn the rudiments much earlier, during which time they can however be properly looked upon only as *probationers,* as I have been informed by a principal gentleman in the County of Cavan, who protested to me that he never knew above one or two instances under the age of six, even in a part of the kingdom so renowned for the quickest proficiency in that art.   6

I am assured by our merchants that a boy or a girl, before twelve years old, is no saleable commodity, and even when they come to this   7

[2]Innate abilities.

age, they will not yield above three pounds, or three pounds and half-a-crown at most on the Exchange, which cannot turn to account either to the parents or the kingdom, the charge of nutriment and rags having been at least four times that value.

I shall now therefore humbly propose my own thoughts, which I hope will not be liable to the least objection.   8

I have been assured by a very knowing American of my acquaintance in London, that a young healthy child well nursed is at a year old a most delicious, nourishing, and wholesome food, whether stewed, roasted, baked, or boiled, and I make no doubt that it will equally serve in a fricassee, or a ragout.[3]   9

I do therefore humbly offer it to public consideration, that of the hundred and twenty thousand children already computed, twenty thousand may be reserved for breed, whereof only one fourth part to be males, which is more than we allow to sheep, black-cattle, or swine, and my reason is that these children are seldom the fruits of marriage, a circumstance not much regarded by our savages, therefore one male will be sufficient to serve four females. That the remaining hundred thousand may at a year old be offered in sale to the persons of quality, and fortune, through the kingdom, always advising the mother to let them suck plentifully in the last month, so as to render them plump, and fat for a good table. A child will make two dishes at an entertainment for friends, and when the family dines alone, the fore or hind quarters will make a reasonable dish, and seasoned with a little pepper or salt will be very good boiled on the fourth day, especially in winter.   10

I have reckoned upon a medium, that a child just born will weigh 12 pounds, and in a solar year if tolerably nursed increaseth to 28 pounds.   11

I grant this food will be somewhat dear, and therefore very proper for landlords, who, as they have already devoured most of the parents, seem to have the best title to the children.   12

Infant's flesh will be in season throughout the year, but more plentiful in March, and a little before and after, for we are told by a grave author, an eminent French physician,[4] that fish being a prolific diet, there are more children born in Roman Catholic countries about nine months after Lent than at any other season; therefore reckoning a year after Lent, the markets will be more glutted than usual, because

---

[3]Stew.

[4]French humorist François Rabelais.

the number of Popish infants is at least three to one in this kingdom, and therefore it will have one other collateral advantage by lessening the number of Papists among us.

I have already computed the charge of nursing a beggar's child (in 14 which list I reckon all cottagers, laborers, and four-fifths of the farmers) to be about two shillings *per annum,* rags included, and I believe no gentleman would repine to give ten shillings for the carcass of a good fat child, which, as I have said, will make four dishes of excellent nutritive meat, when he hath only some particular friend or his own family to dine with him. Thus the Squire will learn to be a good landlord, and grow popular among the tenants, the mother will have eight shillings net profit, and be fit for work till she produces another child.

Those who are more thrifty (as I must confess the times require) 15 may flay the carcass; the skin of which, artificially dressed, will make admirable gloves for ladies, and summer boots for fine gentlemen.

As to our City of Dublin, shambles[5] may be appointed for this pur- 16 pose, in the most convenient parts of it, and butchers we may be assured will not be wanting, although I rather recommend buying the children alive, and dressing them hot from the knife, as we do roasting pigs.

A very worthy person, a true lover of this country, and whose 17 virtues I highly esteem, was lately pleased, in discoursing on this matter, to offer a refinement upon my scheme. He said that many gentlemen of his kingdom, having of late destroyed their deer, he conceived that the want of venison might be well supplied by the bodies of young lads and maidens, not exceeding fourteen years of age, nor under twelve, so great a number of both sexes in every country being now ready to starve, for want of work and service: and these to be disposed of by their parents if alive, or otherwise by their nearest relations. But with due deference to so excellent a friend, and so deserving a patriot, I cannot be altogether in his sentiments; for as to the males, my American acquaintance assured me from frequent experience that their flesh was generally tough and lean, like that of our schoolboys, by continual exercise, and their taste disagreeable, and to fatten them would not answer the charge. Then as to the females, it would, I think with humble submission, be a loss to the public, because they soon would become breeders themselves: And besides, it is not improbable that some scrupulous people might be apt to censure such a practice (although indeed very unjustly) as a little bordering upon cruelty, which, I confess,

---

[5]Slaughterhouses.

hath always been with me the strongest objection against any project, however so well intended.

But in order to justify my friend, he confessed that this expedient was put into his head by the famous Psalmanazar, a native of the island Formosa, who came from thence to London, above twenty years ago, and in conversation told my friend that in his country when any young person happened to be put to death, the executioner sold the carcass to persons of quality, as a prime dainty, and that, in his time, the body of a plump girl of fifteen, who was crucified for an attempt to poison the emperor, was sold to his Imperial Majesty's Prime Minister of State, and other great Mandarins of the Court, in joints from the gibbet, at four hundred crowns. Neither indeed can I deny that if the same use were made of several plump girls in this town, who, without one single groat to their fortunes, cannot stir abroad without a chair, and appear at the playhouse, and assemblies in foreign fineries, which they never will pay for, the kingdom would not be the worse.

Some persons of a desponding spirit are in great concern about that vast number of poor people, who are aged, diseased, or maimed, and I have been desired to employ my thoughts what course may be taken to ease the nation of so grievous an encumbrance. But I am not in the least pain upon that matter, because it is very well known that they are every day dying, and rotting, by cold, and famine, and filth, and vermin, as fast as can be reasonably expected. And as to the younger labourers they are now in almost as hopeful a condition. They cannot get work, and consequently pine away for want of nourishment, to a degree, that if at any time they are accidentally hired to common labour, they have not strength to perform it; and thus the country and themselves are happily delivered from the evils to come.

I have too long digressed, and therefore shall return to my subject. I think the advantages by the proposal which I have made are obvious and many, as well as of the highest importance.

For first, as I have already observed, it would greatly lessen the number of Papists, with whom we are yearly over-run, being the principal breeders of the nation, as well as our most dangerous enemies, and who stay at home on purpose with a design to deliver the kingdom to the Pretender, hoping to take their advantage by the absence of so many good Protestants, who have chosen rather to leave their country than stay at home, and pay tithes against their conscience to an Episcopal curate.

Secondly, The poorer tenants will have something valuable of their own, which by law may be made liable to distress, and help to pay their landlord's rent, their corn and cattle being already seized and *money a thing unknown.*

Thirdly, Whereas the maintenance of an hundred thousand children, from two years old, and upwards, cannot be computed at less than ten shillings a piece *per annum,* the nation's stock will be thereby increased fifty thousand pounds *per annum,* besides the profit of a new dish, introduced to the tables of all gentlemen of fortune in the kingdom, who have any refinement in taste, and the money will circulate among ourselves, the goods being entirely of our own growth and manufacture. 23

Fourthly, The constant breeders, besides the gain of eight shillings sterling *per annum,* by the sale of their children, will be rid of the charge for maintaining them after the first year. 24

Fifthly, This food would likewise bring great custom to taverns, where the vintners will certainly be prudent as to procure the best receipts for dressing it up to perfection, and consequently have their houses frequented by all the fine gentlemen, who justly value themselves upon their knowledge in good eating; and a skillful cook, who understands how to oblige his guests, will contrive to make it as expensive as they please. 25

Sixthly, This would be a great inducement to marriage, which all wise nations have either encouraged by rewards, or enforced by laws and penalties. It would increase the care and tenderness of mothers toward their children, when they were sure of a settlement for life, to the poor babes, provided in some sort by the public to their annual profit instead of expense. We should see an honest emulation among the married women, which of them could bring the fattest child to the market, men would become as fond of their wives, during the time of their pregnancy, as they are now of their mares in foal, their cows in calf, or sows when they are ready to farrow, nor offer to beat or kick them (as it is too frequent a practice) for fear of miscarriage. 26

Many other advantages might be enumerated: For instance, the addition of some thousand carcasses in our exportation of barrelled beef; the propagation of swine's flesh, and improvement in the art of making good bacon, so much wanted among us by the great destruction of pigs, too frequent at our tables, which are no way comparable in taste or magnificence to a well-grown, fat yearling child, which roasted whole will make a considerable figure at a Lord Mayor's feast, or any other public entertainment. But this and many others I omit, being studious of brevity. 27

Supposing that one thousand families in this city would be constant customers for infants' flesh, besides others who might have it at 28 merry-meetings, particularly weddings and christenings, I compute that Dublin would take off annually about twenty thousand carcasses, and the rest of the kingdom (where probably they will be sold somewhat cheaper) the remaining eighty thousand.

I can think of no one objection that will possibly be raised against this proposal, unless it should be urged that the number of people will be thereby much lessened in the kingdom. This I freely own, and it was indeed one principal design in offering it to the world. I desire the reader will observe, that I calculate my remedy for this one individual *Kingdom of Ireland, and for no other that ever was, is, or, I think, ever can be upon earth.* Therefore let no man talk to me of other expedients: *Of taxing our absentees at five shillings a pound: Of using neither clothes, nor household furniture, except what is of our own growth and manufacture: Of utterly rejecting the materials and instruments that promote foreign luxury: Of curing the expensiveness of pride, vanity, idleness, and gaming in our women: Of introducing a vein of parsimony, prudence, and temperance: Of learning to love our Country, wherein we differ even from* Laplanders,[6] *and the inhabitants of* Topinamboo:[7] *Of quitting our animosities and factions, nor act any longer like the Jews, who were murdering one another at the very moment their city was taken:*[8] *Of being a little cautious not to sell our country and consciences for nothing: Of teaching landlords to have at least one degree of mercy toward their tenants. Lastly, of putting a spirit of honesty, industry, and skill into our shopkeepers, who, if a resolution could now be taken to buy only our native goods, would immediately unite to cheat and exact upon us in the price, the measure, and the goodness, nor could ever yet be brought to make one fair proposal of just dealing, though often and earnestly invited to it.*

Therefore I repeat, let no man talk to me of these and the like expedients, till he hath at least some glimpse of hope that there will ever be some hearty and sincere attempt to put them in practice.

But as to myself, having been wearied out for many years with offering vain, idle, visionary thoughts, and at length utterly despairing of success, I fortunately fell upon this proposal, which as it is wholly new, so it hath something solid and real, of no expense and little trouble, full in our own power, and whereby we can incur no danger in *disobliging* ENGLAND. For this kind of commodity will not bear expor-

---

[6]A region of northern Europe on the Barents Sea, largely within the Arctic Circle.
[7]Part of Brazil inhabited by primitive tribes.
[8]Prominent Jews executed during Roman siege of Jerusalem.

tation, the flesh being too tender a consistence to admit a long contin-
uance in salt, *although perhaps I could name a country which would be glad
to eat up our whole nation without it.*

After all I am not so violently bent upon my own opinion as to
reject any offer, proposed by wise men, which shall be found equally
innocent, cheap, easy, and effectual. But before something of that kind
shall be advanced in contradiction to my scheme, and offering a better,
I desire the author, or authors, will be pleased maturely to consider two
points. First, as things now stand, how they will be able to find food
and raiment for an hundred thousand useless mouths and backs. And
secondly, there being a round million of creatures in human figure,
throughout this kingdom, whose whole subsistence put into a common stock would leave them in debt two millions of pounds sterling;
adding those, who are beggars by profession, to the bulk of farmers,
cottagers, and labourers with their wives and children, who are beggars
in effect; I desire those politicians, who dislike my overture, and may
perhaps be so bold as to attempt an answer, that they will first ask the
parents of these mortals whether they would not at this day think it a
great happiness to have been sold for food at a year old, in this manner
I prescribe, and thereby have avoided such a perpetual scene of misfor-
tunes as they have since gone through, by the oppression of landlords,
the impossibility of paying rent without money or trade, the want of
common sustenance, with neither house nor clothes to cover them
from the inclemencies of the weather, and the most inevitable prospect
of entailing the like, or greater miseries upon their breed for ever.

I profess in the sincerity of my heart that I have not the least personal interest in endeavoring to promote this necessary work, having
no other motive than the *public good of my country, by advancing our trade,
providing for infants, relieving the poor, and giving some pleasure to the rich.* I
have no children by which I can propose to get a single penny; the
youngest being nine years old, and my wife past childbearing.

Questions on Meaning

1. Characterize the speaker of Swift's essay.
2. What is his proposal?
3. At what point do you become aware of the discrepancy between the
   moderate tone of the essay and the violence of the speaker's proposal?
4. Why does Swift bring Americans into his essay? What significance do
   you attribute to the fact that cannibalism was an American proposal?

Questions on Method

1. State Swift's purpose in writing "A Modest Proposal." How does his use of satire and irony contribute to his purpose?
2. Is Swift's appeal to his audience emotional, ethical, or logical? Cite examples to support your point of view.
3. Who is the target of Swift's irony in paragraph 12? What examples of **pun** can you cite in this paragraph?

Writing Topics

1. Millions of children in the United States live below the poverty line. Interview your classmates to determine what responsibility, if any, members of the larger society have to these children. Analyze their responses and write an editorial for your college paper based on your findings.
2. Compare and contrast the rhetorical strategies used by King and Swift to create support for their causes. Consider such techniques as vocabulary, tone, and audience as well as examples selected to appeal to the reader's emotions and intellect.

A View of Affirmative Action in the Workplace

Michael Gnolfo (b. 1951) was born in Brooklyn, New York. He grew up in Queens and lives in Nassau County on Long Island with his wife and son. He works for a major utility company as a customer-service supervisor. He returned to college after a sixteen-year absence and graduated from Empire State College (SUNY) in 1999 with a Bachelor's degree in history.

AFFIRMATIVE ACTION is by definition any plan or program that promotes the employment of women and of members of minority groups. This has come about to right all the wrongs suffered by these groups in the past. It is intended to be a positive force for civil rights. 1

Directly or indirectly, because of Affirmative Action women and minorities have increasingly found more opportunity where none existed for them. Traditional role separation is disappearing. Society is realizing an untapped wealth of talent and business is reaping a whirlwind of benefits from this new diversity. 2

Jobs that were traditionally male dominated have had major inroads by women. Bus drivers, construction workers, telephone technicians and pilots now count women among their numbers as do the management staffs of many corporations. The reverse is also true. Men have increasingly entered such fields as nursing, secretarial sciences and flight attendants which have been traditionally female occupations. It seems that no barriers exist to an individual with the skills to perform a job. 3

While all of this is good and the proper course to pursue, there are problems. We can all agree that the protection and promotion of one group in society is wrong. So, when does a program designed to promote fairness become discriminatory? When capable people are neglected at the expense of less capable or similarly capable politically correct/connected candidates. A glaring example of this is the New York City Police exam and requirements. A comparison of physical requirements from today versus thirty years ago reveals a less demanding 4 test of strength and physique. The requirements were relaxed to allow lesser physical candidates to pass. Minority candidates with lower written test marks are also taken over other candidates if a certain percentage of those minorities are not represented on the force. We are legislating mediocrity at best. What is more desirable, a competent organization or a gender/racially correct structure?

Private business is doing just the same. It is especially true in any large company that is contractually obligated to the government or is regulated by it. Those not included in Affirmative Action become less likely to be successful despite qualification. They are fast becoming a new oppressed minority. Companies are zealous in their adherence to Affirmative Action not out of altruism but of fear of loss of contract or stiffer regulation. Remember that while there has been much progress by minorities in business there is a dearth of minority CEOs in the major corporations and that says so much about the reality of Affirmative Action.

The time is right for another step in the evolution of American society. We all realize the positive contributions of the groups protected by Affirmative Action. They have been valuable additions to our society. But abuses have now surfaced. Let's not make the same mistakes we made before. We need a Positive Fairness principle to replace Affirmative Action. Qualification and achievement should be the deciding factors in society and business. Quotas are abhorrent. Discrimination is bad, be it directed toward a race, gender, religion or anyone for any reason. Affirmative Action is becoming a racist, sexist instrument that is quickly turning into a tool of those who would replace one form of dominance with another. Contrary to the belief of feminists, the best man for the job is not a WOMAN but the most qualified individual.

Questions on Meaning

1. Gnolfo says that the purpose of Affirmative Action has been "to right all the wrongs suffered by these groups in the past." If this was once a worthwhile goal, has the goal been met? Are there perhaps other reasons for Affirmative Action (such as diversification) that make it still worthwhile?
2. What is the relationship between economic hard times and Affirmative Action in the workplace?
3. What is the legal status of Affirmative Action? Gnolfo says that companies don't practice Affirmative Action out of "altruism." What difference

would it make if it were voluntary? Would it still accomplish its goal without the "abuses" Gnolfo attributes to it?

Questions on Method

1. Gnolfo assumes that his readers will understand "politically correct/ connected candidates." Has he correctly judged his audience? Political correctness—or PC—has become a frequently encountered shorthand or code designation for what set of ideas or beliefs? How does political correctness relate to Affirmative Action? To freedom of speech and other Bill-of-Rights issues?
2. Comment on the relationship between Gnolfo's first three paragraphs and the rest of the essay. How effective is this two-part organization?
3. "Affirmative Action is becoming a racist, sexist instrument that is quickly turning into a tool of those who would replace one form of dominance with another." To what extent do you agree or disagree? What evidence does Gnolfo offer to support his point of view?

Writing Topics

1. Affirmative Action is a controversial issue. If you are a member of a minority group who could benefit from Affirmative Action, write an essay citing reasons why your choice to do so is ethical. If you are in a position to be hurt by Affirmative Action, write an essay citing reasons why Affirmative Action programs offer unfair opportunities to minorities. Be as specific as you can.
2. Respond to Gnolfo's thesis that, "Contrary to the belief of feminists, the best man for the job is not a WOMAN but the most qualified individual."
3. Write an essay analyzing the causes and effects of women's entry into the workplace in the nineties. You might focus on *one* of the following issues: the responsibility of the employer or the state to provide adequate child care, or the impact of working mothers playing multiple roles.

Persuasion
Writing Topics

1. How different are the techniques used to write an argument that appeals to reason from the techniques used to write an argument that appeals to emotion or ethics? Write an argumentative essay that appeals strictly to logic and reason. Using a different color ink, make additions to the essay that broaden its argumentative appeal emotionally or ethically.

2. Does an argument have to be true to be convincing? Does a lawyer, for example, necessarily have to be defending an innocent client to argue successfully that his or her client is innocent? Write an essay in which you argue when, if ever, the method may be more important in making an argument convincing—whether or not the argument is true.

3. *Apocalypse Now, Born on the Fourth of July, Coming Home,* and *The Deer Hunter* all take strong positions against the Vietnam War, but their focuses are not identical. Compare and contrast any three of these movies, and write a persuasive essay aimed at convincing your reader why one movie is better than the other two.

4. Write an essay about one of the following topics. In your paper, argue for or against the issue—do not take both sides!

   disseminating birth control information in high schools
   censoring books in school libraries
   allowing children with AIDS to attend public schools
   giving the death penalty to drug dealers
   legalizing assisted suicide
   requiring mandatory testing for AIDS
   educating children in their native language

   Try to base your case on an ethical appeal. To persuade your audience, you might write from the perspective of a lawyer, doctor, teacher, or cleric; in other words, create a **persona** (see Glossary) who uses ethical appeal.

5. Write an essay attacking or defending the statement that "advertisments are designed to exploit the discontentments fostered by the American dream, the constant desire for social success and the material rewards that accompany it." You may use commercials on television or advertisements from magazines as supporting evidence for your point of view.

14

Further Reading

MARY WOLLSTONECRAFT

from *A Vindication of the Rights of Woman*

Mary Wollstonecraft (1759–1797) was born in Hoxton, England. In 1788 she wrote her first novel, Mary, *a fictional account of the life of her childhood friend Fanny Blood. In 1792 she went to Paris to investigate the French Revolution and witnessed firsthand the Reign of Terror. In France she met an American military captain, Gilbert Imlay, by whom she had a daughter. Later she married William Godwin, a liberal social reformer who published his* Political Justice *in 1793. She died soon after giving birth to their daughter Mary, who married the poet Percy Bysshe Shelley and wrote the novel* Frankenstein. *Wollstonecraft is best known for the first great feminist manifesto,* A Vindication of the Rights of Woman *(1792).*

...THE PREPOSTEROUS DISTINCTIONS of rank, which render civiliza- 1
tion a curse, by dividing the world between voluptuous tyrants and
cunning envious dependents, corrupt, almost equally, every class of
people, because respectability is not attached to the discharge of the

relative duties of life, but to the station, and when the duties are not fulfilled the affections cannot gain sufficient strength to fortify the virtue
of which they are the natural reward. Still there are some loop-holes out
of which a man may creep, and dare to think and act for himself; but for
a woman it is an herculean task, because she has difficulties peculiar to
her sex to overcome, which require almost superhuman powers.

A truly benevolent legislator always endeavours to make it the interest of each individual to be virtuous; and thus private virtue becoming the cement of public happiness, an orderly whole is consolidated by
the tendency of all the parts towards a common centre. But the private
or public virtue of woman is very problematical, for Rousseau, and a
numerous list of male writers, insist that she should all her life be subjected to a severe restraint, that of propriety. Why subject her to propriety—blind propriety—if she be capable of acting from a nobler spring,
if she be an heir of immortality? Is sugar always to be produced by vital
blood? Is one half of the human species, like the poor African slaves, to
be subjected to prejudices that brutalize them, when principles would
be a surer guard, only to sweeten the cup of man? Is not this indirectly
to deny woman reason? for a gift is a mockery, if it be unfit for use.

Women are, in common with men, rendered weak and luxurious
by the relaxing pleasures which wealth procures; but added to this they
are made slaves to their persons, and must render them alluring that
man may lend them his reason to guide their tottering steps aright. Or
should they be ambitious, they must govern their tyrants by sinister
tricks, for without rights there cannot be any incumbent duties. The
laws respecting woman…make an absurd unit of a man and his wife;
and then, by the easy transition of only considering him as responsible,
she is reduced to a mere cipher.

The being who discharges the duties of its station is independent;
and, speaking of women at large, their first duty is to themselves as rational creatures, and the next, in point of importance, as citizens, is
that, which includes so many, of a mother. The rank in life which dis-
penses with their fulfilling this duty, necessarily degrades them by
making them mere dolls. Or should they turn to something more important than merely fitting drapery upon a smooth block, their minds
are only occupied by some soft platonic attachment; or the actual management of an intrigue may keep their thoughts in motion; for when
they neglect domestic duties, they have it not in their power to take
the field and march and counter-march like soldiers, or wrangle in the
senate to keep their faculties from rusting.

I know that, as a proof of the inferiority of the sex, Rousseau has   5
exultingly exclaimed, How can they leave the nursery for the camp!
And the camp has by some moralists been proved the school of the
most heroic virtues; though I think it would puzzle a keen casuist to
prove the reasonableness of the greater number of wars that have
dubbed heroes. I do not mean to consider this question critically; because, having frequently viewed these freaks of ambition as the first
natural mode of civilization, when the ground must be torn up, and
the woods cleared by fire and sword, I do not choose to call them
pests; but surely the present system of war has little connection with
virtue of any denomination, being rather the school of *finesse* and ef-
feminacy than of fortitude.

Yet, if defensive war, the only justifiable war, in the present ad-   6
vanced state of society, where virtue can show its face and ripen amidst
the rigours which purify the air on the mountain's top, were alone to
be adopted as just and glorious, the true heroism of antiquity might
again animate female bosoms. But fair and softly, gentle reader, male or
female, do not alarm thyself, for though I have compared the character
of a modern soldier with that of a civilized woman, I am not going to
advise them to turn their distaff into a musket, though I sincerely wish
to see the bayonet converted into a pruning-hook. I only re-created an
imagination, fatigued by comtemplating the vices and follies which all
proceed from a feculent stream of wealth that has muddied the pure
rills of natural affection, by supposing that society will some time or
other be so constituted, that man must necessary fulfil the duties of a
citizen, or be despised, and that while he was employed in any of the
departments of civil life, his wife, also an active citizen, should be
equally intent to manage her family, educate her children, and assist
her neighbours.

But to render her really virtuous and useful, she must not, if she   7
discharge her civil duties, want individually the protection of civil laws;
she must not be dependent on her husband's bounty for her subsistence during his life, or support after his death; for how can a being be
generous who has nothing of its own? or virtuous who is not free? The
wife, in the present state of things, who is faithful to her husband, and
neither suckles nor educates her children, scarcely deserves the name
of a wife, and has no right to that of a citizen. But take away natural
rights, and duties become null.

Women then must be considered as only the wanton solace of   8
men, when they become so weak in mind and body that they cannot

exert themselves unless to pursue some frothy pleasure, or to invent some frivolous fashion. What can be a more melancholy sight to a thinking mind, than to look into the numerous carriages that drive helter-skelter about this metropolis in a morning full of pale-faced creatures who are flying from themselves! I have often wished, with Dr Johnson, to place some of them in a little shop with half a dozen children looking up to their languid countenances for support. I am much mistaken, if some latent vigour would not soon give health and spirit to their eyes, and some lines drawn by the exercise of reason on the blank cheeks, which before were only undulated by dimples, might restore lost dignity to the character, or rather enable it to attain the true dignity of its nature. Virtue is not to be acquired even by speculation, much less by the negative supineness that wealth naturally generates.

Besides, when poverty is more disgraceful than even vice, is not morality cut to the quick? Still to avoid miscontruction, though I consider that women in the common walks of life are called to fulfill the duties of wives and mothers, by religious and reason, I cannot help lamenting that women of a superior cast have not a road open by which they can pursue more extensive plans of usefulness and independence. I may excite laughter, by dropping a hint, which I mean to pursue, some future time, for I really think that women ought to have representatives, instead of being arbitrarily governed without having any direct share allowed them in the deliberations of government.

But, as the whole system of representation is now, in this county, only a convenient handle for despotism, they need not complain, for they are as well represented as a numerous class of hard-working mechanics, who pay for the support of royalty when they can scarcely stop their children's mouths with bread. How are they represented whose very sweat supports the splendid stud of an heir-apparent, or varnishes the chariot of some female favourite who looks down on shame? Taxes on the very necessaries of life, enable an endless tribe of idle princes and princesses to pass with stupid pomp before a gaping crowd, who almost worship the very parade which costs them so dear. This is mere gothic grandeur, something like the barbarous useless parade of having sentinels on horseback at Whitehall, which I could never view without a mixture of contempt and indignation.

How strangely must the mind be sophisticated when this sort of state impresses it! But, till these monuments of folly are levelled by virtue, similar follies will leaven the whole mass. For the same character, in some degree, will prevail in the aggregate of society; and the refinements of luxury, or the vicious repinings of envious poverty, will equally banish virtue from society, considered as the characteristic of that society, or only allow it to appear as one of the stripes of the harlequin coat, worn by the civilized man.

In the superior ranks of life, every duty is done by deputies, as if duties could ever be waived, and the vain pleasures which consequent idleness forces the rich to pursue, appear so enticing to the next rank, that the numerous scramblers for wealth sacrifice everything to tread on their heels. The most sacred trusts are then considered as sinecures, because they were procured by interest, and only sought to enable a man to keep *good company*. Women, in particular, all want to be ladies. Which is simply to have nothing to do, but listlessly to go they scarcely care where, for they cannot tell what.

But what have women to do in society? I may be asked, but to loiter with easy grace; surely you would not condemn them all to suckle fools and chronicle small beer! No. Women might certainly study the art of healing and be physicians as well as nurses. And midwifery, decency seems to allot to them though I am afraid the word midwife, in our dictionaries, will soon give place to *accoucheur,* and one proof of the former delicacy of the sex be effaced from the language.

They might also study politics, and settle their benevolence on the broadest basis; for the reading of history will scarcely be more useful than the perusal of romances, if read as mere biography; if the character of the times, the political improvements, arts, etc., be not observed. In short, if it be not considered as the history of man; and not of particular men, who filled a niche in the temple of fame, and dropped into the black rolling stream of time, that silently sweeps all before it into the shapeless void called—eternity.—For shape, can it be called, "that shape hath none"?

Business of various kinds, they might likewise pursue, if they were educated in a more orderly manner, which might save many from common and legal prostitution. Women would not then marry for a support, as men accept of places under Government, and neglect the implied duties; nor would an attempt to earn their own subsistence, a most laudable one! sink them almost to the level of those poor abandoned creatures who live by prostitution. For are not milliners and mantuamakers reckoned the next class? The few employments open to women, so far from being liberal, are menial; and when a superior education enables them to take charge of the education of children as governesses, they are not treated like the tutors of sons, though even clerical tutors are not always treated in a manner calculated to render them respectable in the eyes of their pupils, to say nothing of the private comfort of the individual. But as women educated like gentlewomen, are never designed for the humiliating situation which necessity sometimes forces them to fill; these situations are considered in the light of a degradation; and they know little of the human heart, who need to be told, that nothing so painfully sharpens sensibility as such a fall in life.

Some of these women might be restrained from marrying by a proper spirit of delicacy, and others may not have had it in their power to escape in this pitiful way from servitude; is not that Government then very defective, and very unmindful of the happiness of one-half of its members, that does not provide for honest, independent women, by encouraging them to fill respectable stations? But in order to render their private virtue a public benefit, they must have a civil existence in the State, married or single; else we shall continually see some worthy woman, whose sensibility has been rendered painfully acute by undeserved contempt, droop like "the lily broken down by a plowshare."

It is a melancholy truth; yet such is the blessed effect of civilization! the most respectable women are the most oppressed; and, unless they have understandings far superior to the common run of understandings, taking in both sexes, they must, from being treated like contemptible beings, become contemptible. How many women thus waste life away the prey of discontent, who might have practised as physicians, regulated a farm, managed a shop, and stood erect, supported by their own industry, instead of hanging their heads surcharged with the dew of sensibility, that consumes the beauty to which it at first gave lustre; nay, I doubt whether pity and love are so near akin as poets feign, for I have seldom seen much compassion excited by the helplessness of females, unless they were fair; then, perhaps, pity was the soft handmaid of love, or the harbinger of lust.

How much more respectable is the woman who earns her own bread by fulfilling any duty, than the most accomplished beauty!—beauty did I say!—so sensible am I of the beauty of moral loveliness, or the harmonious propriety that attunes the passions of a well-regulated mind, that I blush at making the comparison; yet I sigh to think how few women aim at attaining this respectability by withdrawing from the giddy whirl of pleasure, or the indolent calm that stupefies the good sort of women it sucks in.

Proud of their weakness, however, they must always be protected, guarded from care, and all the rough toils that dignify the mind. If this be the fiat of fate, if they will make themselves insignificant and contemptible, sweetly to waste "life away," let them not expect to be valued when their beauty fades, for it is the fate of the fairest flowers to be admired and pulled to pieces by the careless hand that plucked them. In how many ways do I wish, from the purest benevolence, to impress this truth on my sex; yet I fear that they will not listen to a truth that dear bought experience has brought home to many an agitated bosom, nor willingly resign the privileges of rank and sex for the privileges of humanity, to which those have no claim who do not discharge its duties.

Those writers are particularly useful, in my opinion, who make   20
man feel for man, independent of the station he fills, or the drapery of factitious sentiments. I then would fain convince reasonable men of the importance of some of my remarks; and prevail on them to weigh dispassionately the whole tenor of my observations. I appeal to their understandings; and, as a fellow-creature, claim, in the name of my sex, some interest in their hearts. I entreat them to assist to emancipate their companion, to make her a *helpmeet* for them.

Would men but generously snap our chains, and be content with   21
rational fellowship instead of slavish obedience, they would find us more observant daughters, more affectionate sisters, more faithful wives, more reasonable mothers—in a word, better citizens. We should then love them with true affection, because we should learn to respect ourselves; and the peace of mind of a worthy man would not be interrupted by the idle vanity of his wife, nor the babes sent to nestle in a strange bosom, having never found a home in their mother's.

Understanding Natural Selection

Charles Darwin (1809–1882) was an English naturalist who expounded the theory of evolution. He studied medicine at Edinburgh University in Scotland. As a naturalist, he sailed on the Beagle *from 1831 to 1836 on an expedition to South America and Australia. In 1859 he published* On the Origin of Species, *which is still considered one of the most important books in natural philosophy.*

IT MAY BE SAID that natural selection is daily and hourly scrutinizing, throughout the world, every variation, even the slightest; rejecting that which is bad, preserving and adding up all that is good; silently and insensibly working, whenever and wherever opportunity offers, at the improvement of each organic being in relation to its organic and inorganic conditions of life. We see nothing of these slow changes in progress, until the hand of time has marked the long lapses of ages, and then so imperfect is our view into long past geological ages, that we only see that the forms of life are now different from what they formerly were.

Although natural selection can act only through and for the good of each being, yet characters and structures, which we are apt to consider as of very trifling importance, may thus be acted on. When we see leaf-eating insects green, and bark-feeders mottled-grey; the alpine ptarmigan white in winter, the red-grouse the color of heather, and the black-grouse that of peaty earth, we must believe that these tints are of service to these birds and insects in preserving them from danger. Grouse, if not destroyed at some period of their lives, would increase in countless numbers; they are known to suffer largely from birds of prey; and hawks are guided by eyesight to their prey—so much so, that on parts of the Continent persons are warned not to keep white pigeons, as being the most liable to destruction. Hence I can see no reason to doubt that natural selection might be most effective in giving the proper color to each kind of grouse, and in keeping that color, when once acquired, true and constant. Nor ought we to think that the occasional destruction of an animal of any particular color would produce little effect: we should remember how essential it is in a flock of white sheep to destroy every lamb with the faintest trace of black. In plants the down on the fruit and the color of the flesh are considered by botanists as characters of the most trifling importance: yet we hear from an excellent horticulturist, Downing, that in the United States smooth-skinned fruits suffer far more from a beetle, a curculio, than those with down; that purple plums suffer far more from a certain disease than yellow plums; whereas another disease attacks yellow-fleshed peaches far more than those with other colored flesh. If, with all the aids of art, these slight differences make a great difference in cultivating the several varieties, assuredly, in a state of nature, where the trees would have to struggle with other trees and with a host of enemies, such differences would effectually settle which variety, whether a smooth or downy, a yellow or purple fleshed fruit, should succeed.

In looking at many small points of difference between species, 3 which, as far as our ignorance permits us to judge, seem to be quite unimportant, we must not forget that climate, food, and so on probably produce some slight and direct effect. It is, however, far more necessary to bear in mind that there are many unknown laws of correlation to growth, which, when one part of the organization is modified through variation, and the modifications are accumulated by natural selection for the good of the being, will cause other modifications, often of the most unexpected nature.

As we see that those variations which under domestication ap- 4 pear at any particular period of life, tend to reappear in the offspring of the same period; for instance, in the seeds of the many varieties of our culinary and agricultural plants; in the caterpillar and cocoon stages of the varieties of the silkworm; in the eggs of poultry, and in the color of the down of their chickens; in the horns of our sheep and cattle when nearly adult; so in a state of nature, natural selection will be enabled to act on and modify organic beings at any age, by the accumulation of profitable variations at that age, and by their inheritance at a corresponding age. If it profit a plant to have its seeds more and more widely disseminated by the wind, I can see no greater difficulty in this being effected through natural selection, than in the cotton-planter increasing and improving by selection the down in the pods on his cotton-trees. Natural selection may modify and adapt the larva of an insect to a score of contingencies, wholly different from those which concern the mature insect. These modifications will no doubt affect, through the laws of correlation, the structure of the adult; and probably in the case of those insects which live only for a few hours, and which never feed, a large part of their structure is merely the correlated result of successive changes in the structure of their larvae. So, conversely, modifications in the adult will probably often affect the structure of the larva; but in all cases natural selection will ensure that modifications consequent on other modifications at a different period of life, shall not be in the least degree injurious: for if they became so, they would cause the extinction of the species.

Natural selection will modify the structure of the young in relation to the parent, and of the parent in relation to the young. In social animals it will adapt the structure of each individual for the benefit of the community; if each in consequence profits by the selected change. What natural selection cannot do, is to modify the structure of one species, without giving it any advantage, for the good of another species; and though statements to this effect may be found in works of natural history, I cannot find one case which will bear investigation. A structure used only once in an animal's whole life, if of high importance to it, might be modified to any extent by natural selection: for instance, the great jaws possessed by certain insects, and used exclusively for opening the cocoon—or the hard tip of the beak of nesting birds, used for breaking the egg. It has been asserted, that of the best short-beaked tumbler pigeons more perish in the egg than are able to get out of it; so that fanciers assist in the act of hatching. Now, if nature had to make the beak of a full-grown pigeon very short for the bird's own advantage, the process of modification would be very slow, and there would be simultaneously the most rigorous selection of the young birds within the egg, which had the most powerful and hardest beaks, for all with weak beaks would inevitably perish: or, more delicate and more easily broken shells might be selected, the thickness of the shell being known to vary like every other structure.

SEXUAL SELECTION

Inasmuch as peculiarities often appear under domestication in one sex and become hereditarily attached to that sex, the same fact probably occurs under nature, and if so, natural selection will be able to modify one sex in its functional relations to the other sex, or in relation to wholly different habits of life in the two sexes, as is sometimes the case with insects. And this leads me to say a few words on what I call sexual selection. This depends, not on a struggle for existence, but on a struggle between the males for possession of the females; the result is not death to the unsuccessful competitor, but few or no offspring. Sexual selection is, therefore, less rigorous than natural selection. Generally, the most vigorous males, those which are best fitted for their places in nature, will leave most progeny. But in many cases, victory will depend not on general vigor, but on having special weapons, confined to the male sex. A hornless stag or spurless cock would have a poor chance of leaving offspring. Sexual selection by always allowing the victor to breed might surely give indomitable courage, length to the spur, and strength to the wing to strike in the spurred leg, as well as the brutal cock-fighter, who knows well that he can improve his breed by careful selection of the best cocks. How low in the scale of nature this law of battle descends, I know not; male alligators have been described as fighting, bellowing, and whirling round, like Indians in a war dance, for the possession of the females; male salmons have been seen fighting all day long; male stag-beetles often bear wounds from the huge mandibles of other males. The war is, perhaps, severest between the males of polygamous animals, and these seem oftenest provided with special weapons. The males of carnivorous animals are already well armed; though to them and to others, special means of defence may be given through means of sexual selection, as the mane to the lion, the shoulder-pad to the boar, and the hooked jaw to the male salmon, for the shield may be as important for victory, as the sword or spear.

Amongst birds, the contest is often of a more peaceful character.   7
All those who have attended to the subject, believe that there is the severest rivalry between the males of many species to attract by singing the females. The rock-thrush of Guiana, birds of Paradise, and some others, congregate; and successive males display their gorgeous plumage and perform strange antics before the females, which standing by as spectators, at last choose the most attractive partner. Those who have closely attended to birds in confinement well know that they often take individual preferences and dislikes: thus Sir R. Heron has described how one pied peacock was eminently attractive to all his hen birds. It may appear childish to attribute any effect to such apparently weak means: I cannot here enter on the details necessary to support this view; but if man can in a short time give elegant carriage and beauty to his bantams, according to his standard of beauty, I can see no good reason to doubt that female birds, by selecting, during thousands

of generations, the most melodious or beautiful males, according to their standard of beauty, might produce a marked effect. I strongly suspect that some well-known laws with respect to the plumage of male and female birds, in comparison with the plumage of the young, can be explained on the view of plumage having been chiefly modified by sexual selection, acting when the birds have come to the breeding age or during the breeding season; the modifications thus produced being inherited at corresponding ages or seasons, either by the males alone, or by the males and females; but I have not space here to enter on this subject.

Thus it is, as I believe, that when the males and females of any animal have the same general habits of life, but differ in structure, color, or ornament, such differences have been mainly caused by sexual selection; that is, individual males have had, in successive generations, some slight advantage over other males, in their weapons, means of defence, or charms; and have transmitted these advantages to their male offspring. Yet, I would not wish to attribute all such sexual differences to this agency: for we see peculiarities arising and becoming attached to the male sex in our domestic animals (as the wattle in male carriers, horn-like protuberances in the cocks of certain fowls, and so on), which we cannot believe to be either useful to the males in battle, or attractive to the females. We see analogous cases under nature, for instance, the tuft of hair on the breast of the turkey-cock, which can hardly be either useful or ornamental to this bird; indeed, had the tuft appeared under domestication, it would have been called a monstrosity.

ILLUSTRATION OF THE ACTION OF NATURAL SELECTION

...Let us take the case of a wolf, which preys on various animals, securing some by craft, some by strength, and some by fleetness; and let us suppose that the fleetest prey, a deer for instance, had from any change in the country increased in numbers, or that other prey had decreased in numbers, during that season of the year when the wolf is hardest pressed for food. I can under such circumstances see no reason to doubt that the swiftest and slimmest wolves would have the best chance of surviving, and so be preserved or selected—provided always that they retain strength to master their prey at this or at some other period of the year, when they might be compelled to prey on other animals. I can see no more reason to doubt this, than that man can improve the fleetness of his greyhounds by careful and methodical selection, or by that unconscious selection which results from each man trying to keep the best dogs without any thought of modifying the breed.

Even without any change in the proportional numbers of the animals on which our wolf preyed, a cub might be born with an innate tendency to pursue certain kinds of prey. Nor can this be thought very improbable; for we often observe great differences in the natural tendencies of our domestic animals; one cat, for instance, taking to catch rats, another mice; one cat...bringing home winged game, another hares or rabbits, and another hunting on marshy ground and almost nightly catching woodcocks or snipes. The tendency to catch rats rather than mice is known to be inherited. Now, if any slight innate change of habit or of structure benefited an individual wolf, it would have the best chance of surviving and of leaving offspring. Some of its young would probably inherit the same habits or structure, and by the repetition of this process, a new variety might be formed which would either supplant or coexist with the parent-form of wolf. Or, again, the wolves inhabiting a mountainous district, and those frequenting the lowlands, would naturally be forced to hunt different prey; and from the continued preservation of the individuals best fitted for the two sites, two varieties might slowly be formed. These varieties would cross and blend where they met; but to this subject of intercrossing we shall soon have to return. I may add, that...there are two varieties of the wolf inhabiting the Catskill Mountains in the United States, one with a light greyhoundlike form, which pursues deer, and the other more bulky, with shorter legs, which more frequently attacks the shepherd's flocks.

Genius and Originality

John Stuart Mill (1806–1873) was an English philosopher and economist. He was educated at home by his father and learned Greek and Latin before age fourteen. He published essays in Westminister, Monthly Repository, *and* London Review. *In his book* Logic, *he developed his theories of Utilitarianism, advocating individual dignity and requiring a reexamination of production, socialist solutions, and the role of the working class, especially the condition of women. In particular Mill believed in the exercise of human reason, and he endorsed the empirical school of philosophy, which advocated the search for evidence as a necessary step toward reaching conclusions. His most radical and influential book,* The Subjection of Women, *was published in 1869.*

IT WILL NOT BE DENIED by anybody, that originality is a valuable element in human affairs. There is always need of persons not only to discover new truths, and point out when what were once truths are true no longer, but also to commence new practices, and set the example of more enlightened conduct, and better taste and sense in human life. This cannot well be gainsaid by anybody who does not believe that the world has already attained perfection in all its ways and practices. It is true that this benefit is not capable of being rendered by everybody alike; there are but few persons, in comparison with the whole of mankind, whose experiments, if adopted by others, would be likely to be any improvement on established practice. But these few are the salt of the earth; without them, human life would become a stagnant pool. Not only is it they who introduce good things which did not before exist; it is they who keep the life in those which already existed. If there were nothing new to be done, would human intellect cease to be necessary? Would it be a reason why those who do the old things should forget why they are done, and do them like cattle, not like human beings? There is only too great a tendency in the best beliefs and practices to degenerate into the mechanical; and unless there were a succession of persons whose everrecurring originality prevents the grounds of those beliefs and practices from becoming merely traditional, such dead matter would not resist the smallest shock from anything really alive, and there would be no reason why civilization should not die out, as in the Byzantine Empire. Persons of genius, it is true, are, and are always likely to be, a small minority; but in order to have them, it is necessary to preserve the soil in which they grow. Genius can only breathe freely in an *atmosphere* of freedom. Persons of genius are, *ex vi termini* [by definition], *more* individual than any other people—less capable, consequently, of fitting themselves, without hurtful compression, into any of the small number of moulds which society provides in order to save its members the trouble of forming their own character. If from timidity they consent to be forced into one of these moulds, and to let all that part of themselves which cannot expand under the pressure remain unexpanded, society will be little the better for their genius. If they are of a stronger character, and break their fetters, they become a mark for the society which has not succeeded in reducing them to commonplace, to point at with solemn warning as "wild," "erratic," and the like; much as if one should complain of the Niagra river for not flowing smoothly between its banks like a Dutch canal.

I insist thus emphatically on the importance of genius, and the 2 necessity of allowing it to unfold itself freely both in thought and in practice, being well aware that no one will deny the position in theory, but knowing also that almost every one, in reality, is totally indifferent to it. People think genius a fine thing if it enables a man to write an exciting poem, or paint a picture. But in its true sense, that of originality in thought and action, though no one says that it is not a thing to be admired, nearly all, at heart, think that they can do very well without it. Unhappily this is too natural to be wondered at. Originality is the one thing which unoriginal minds cannot feel the use of. They cannot see what it is to do for them: how should they? If they could see what it would do for them, it would not be originality. The first service which originality has to render them, is that of opening their eyes: which being once fully done, they would have a chance of being themselves original. Meanwhile, recollecting that nothing was ever yet done which some one was not the first to do, and that all good things which exist are the fruits of originality, let them be modest enough to believe that there is something still left for it to accomplish, and assure themselves that they are more in need of originality, the less they are conscious of the want.

In sober truth, whatever homage may be professed, or even paid, 3 to real or supposed mental superiority, the general tendency of things throughout the world is to render mediocrity the ascendant power among mankind. In ancient history, in the Middle Ages, and in a diminishing degree through the long transition from feudality to the present time, the individual was a power in himself; and if he had either great talents or a high social position, he was a considerable power. At present individuals are lost in the crowd. In politics it is almost a triviality to say that public opinion now rules the world. The only power deserving the name is that of masses, and of governments while they make themselves the organ of the tendencies and instincts of masses. This is as true in the moral and social relations of private life as in public transactions. Those whose opinions go by the name of public opinion, are not always the same sort of public: in America, they are the whole white population; in England, chiefly the middle class. But they are always a mass, that is to say, collective mediocrity. And what is a still greater novelty, the mass do not now take their opinions from dignitaries in Church or State, from ostensible leaders, or from books. Their thinking is done for them by men much like themselves, addressing them or speaking in their name, on the spur of the moment, through the newspapers. I am not complaining of all this. I do not assert that anything better is compatible, as a general rule, with the present low state of the human mind. But that does not hinder the government of mediocrity from being mediocre government. No government by a democracy or a numerous aristocracy, either in its political acts or in the opinions, qualities, and tone of mind which it fosters, ever did or could rise above mediocrity, except in so far as the sovereign. Many have let themselves be guided (which in their best times they always have done) by the counsels and influence of a more highly gifted and instructed One or Few. The initiation of all wise or noble things, comes and must come from individuals; generally at first from some one individual. The honor and glory of the average man is that he is capable of following that initiative; that he can respond internally to wise and noble things, and be led to them with his eyes open. I am not countenancing the sort of "hero-worship" which applauds the strong man of genius for forcibly seizing on the government of the world and making it do his bidding in spite of itself. All he can claim is freedom to point out the way. The power of compelling others into it, is not only inconsistent with the freedom and development of all the rest, but corrupting to the strong man himself. It does seem, however, that when the opinions of masses of merely average men are everywhere become or becoming the dominant power, the counterpoise and corrective to that tendency would be, the more and more pronounced individuality of those who stand on the higher eminences of thought. It is in these circumstances most especially, that exceptional individuals, instead of being deterred, should be encouraged in acting differently from the mass. In other times there was no advantage in their doing so, unless they acted not only differently, but better. In this age, the mere example of nonconformity, the mere refusal to bend the knee to custom, is itself a service. Precisely because the tyranny of opinion is such as to make eccentricity a reproach, it is desirable, in order to break through that tyranny, that people should be eccentric. Eccentricity has always abounded when and where strength of character has abounded; and the amount of eccentricity in a society has generally been proportional to the amount of genius, mental vigor, and moral courage which it contained. That so few now dare to be eccentric, marks the chief danger of the time.

from *Incidents in the Life of a Slave Girl*

Harriet Jacobs (c. 1813–1897) was born a slave in Edenton, North Carolina. She was sexually abused by her master, James Norcom. In order to escape sexual slavery, she became the mistress of another white man with whom she had two children. Norcom, however, continued to pursue Jacobs, so she was forced to hide for years in her grandmother's house. In 1842 she escaped to the North. She found work, and eventually both her children joined her. In 1861 she published her story in Incidents in the Life of a Slave Girl, *a narrative of her life.*

A SMALL SHED had been added to my grandmother's house years ago. Some boards were laid across the joists at the top, and between these boards and the roof was a very small garret, never occupied by anything but rats and mice. It was a pent roof, covered with nothing but shingles, according to the southern custom for such buildings. The garret was only nine feet long and seven wide. The highest part was three feet high, and sloped down abruptly to the loose board floor. There was no admission for either light or air. My uncle Phillip, who was a carpenter, had very skillfully made a concealed trap-door, which communicated with the storeroom. He had been doing this while I was waiting in the swamp. The storeroom opened upon a piazza. To this hole I was conveyed as soon as I entered the house. The air was stifling; the darkness total. A bed had been spread on the floor. I could sleep quite comfortably on one side; but the slope was so sudden that I could not turn on the other without hitting the roof. The rats and mice ran over my bed; but I was weary, and I slept such sleep as the wretched may, when a tempest has passed over them. Morning came. I knew it only by the noises I heard; for in my small den day and night were all the same. I suffered for air even more than for light. But I was not comfortless. I heard the voices of my children. There was joy and there was sadness in the sound. It made my tears flow. How I longed to speak to them! I was eager to look on their faces; but there was no hole, no crack, through which I could peep. This continued darkness was oppressive. It seemed horrible to sit or lie in a cramped position day after day, without one gleam of light. Yet I would have chosen this, rather than my lot as a slave, though white people considered it an easy one; and it was so compared with the fate of others. I was never cruelly over-worked; I was never lacerated with the whip from head to foot; I was never so beaten and bruised that I could not turn from one side to the other; I never had my heel-strings cut to prevent my running away; I was never chained to a log and forced to drag it about, while I toiled in the fields from morning till night; I was never branded with hot iron, or torn by blood-hounds. On the contrary, I had always been kindly treated, and tenderly cared for, until I came into the hands of Dr. Flint. I had never wished for freedom till then. But though my life in slavery was comparatively devoid of hardships God pity the woman who is compelled to lead such a life!

My food was passed up to me through the trap-door my uncle   2
had contrived; and my grandmother, my uncle Phillip, and aunt Nancy would seize such opportunities as they could, to mount up there and chat with me at the opening. But of course this was not safe in the daytime. It must all be done in darkness. It was impossible for me to move in an erect position, but I crawled about my den for exercise. One day I hit my head against something, and found it was a gimlet. My uncle had left it sticking there when he made the trap-door. I was as rejoiced as Robinson Crusoe could have been at finding such a treasure. It put a lucky thought into my head. I said to myself, "Now I will have some light. Now I will see my children." I did not dare to begin my work during the daytime, for fear of attracting attention. But I groped round; and having found the side next to the street, where I could frequently see my children, I stuck the gimlet in and waited for evening. I bored three rows of holes, one above another; then I bored out the interstices between. I thus succeeded in making one hole about an inch long and an inch broad. I sat by it till late into the night, to enjoy the little whiff of air that floated in. In the morning I watched for my children. The first person I saw in the street was Dr. Flint. I had a shuddering, superstitious feeling that it was a bad omen. Several familiar faces passed by. At last I heard the merry laugh of children, and presently two sweet little faces were looking up at me, as though they knew I was there, and were conscious of the joy they imparted. How I longed to *tell* them I was there!

My condition was now a little improved. But for weeks I was tormented by hundreds of little red insects, fine as a needle's point, that pierced through my skin, and produced an intolerable burning. The good grandmother gave me herb teas and cooling medicines, and finally I got rid of them. The heat of my den was intense, for nothing but thin shingles protected me from the scorching summer's sun. But I had my consolations. Through my peeping-hole I could watch the children, and when they were near enough, I could hear their talk. Aunt Nancy brought me all the news she could hear at Dr. Flint's.

From her I learned that the doctor had written to New York to a colored woman, who had been born and raised in our neighborhood, and had breathed his contaminating atmosphere. He offered her a reward if she could find out any thing about me. I know not what was the nature of her reply; but he soon after started for New York in haste, saying to his family that he had business of importance to transact. I peeped at him as he passed on his way to the steamboat. It was a satisfaction to have miles of land and water between us, even for a little while; and it was a still greater satisfaction to know that he believed me to be in the Free States. My little den seemed less dreary than it had done. He returned, as he did from his former journey to New York, without obtaining any satisfactory information. When he passed our house next morning, Benny was standing at the gate. He had heard them say that he had gone to find me, and he called out, "Dr. Flint, did you bring my mother home? I want to see her." The doctor stamped his foot at him in a rage, and exclaimed, "Get out of the way, you little damned rascal! If you don't, I'll cut off your head."

Benny ran terrified into the house, saying, "You can't put me in jail again. I don't belong to you now." It was well that the wind carried the words away from the doctor's ear. I told my grandmother of it, when we had our next conference at the trap-door; and begged of her not to allow the children to be impertinent to the irascible old man.

Autumn came, with a pleasant abatement of heat. My eyes had become accustomed to the dim light, and by holding my book or work in a certain position near the aperture I contrived to read and sew. That was a great relief to the tedious monotony of my life. But when winter came, the cold penetrated through the thin shingle roof, and I was dreadfully chilled. The winters there are not so long, or so severe, as in northern latitudes; but the houses are not built to shelter from cold, and my little den was peculiarly comfortless. The kind grandmother brought me bed-clothes and warm drinks. Often I was obliged to lie in bed all day to keep comfortable; but with all my precautions, my shoulders and feet were frostbitten. O, those long, gloomy days, with no object for my eye to rest upon, and no thoughts to occupy my mind, except the dreary past and the uncertain future! I was thankful when there came a day sufficiently mild for me to wrap myself up and sit at the loophole to watch the passers by. Southerners have the habit of stopping and talking in the streets, and I heard many conversations not intended to meet my ears. I heard slave-hunters planning how to catch some poor fugitive. Several times I heard allusions to Dr. Flint, myself, and the history of my children, who, perhaps, were playing near the gate. One would say, "I wouldn't move my little finger to catch her, as old Flint's property." Another would say, "I'll catch *any* nigger for the reward. A man ought to have what belongs to him, if he *is* a damned brute." The opinion was often expressed that I was in the Free States. Very rarely did any one suggest that I might be in the vicinity. Had the least suspicion rested on my grandmother's house, it would have been burned to the ground. But it was the last place they thought of. Yet there was no place, where slavery existed, that could have afforded me so good a place of concealment.

Nature

American poet, essayist, and philosopher Ralph Waldo Emerson (1803–1882) earned a degree from Harvard in 1821. He then entered divinity school and was ordained but soon abandoned the ministry. After a year in Europe, he returned to America to bring his philosophy directly to the American people, urging self-reliance and the integrity of the individual. His first book, Nature, *advanced his theories on transcendentalism, and for two years (1842–1844) Emerson edited the transcendentalist journal* The Dial. *His other famous works include* Representative Men *(1850),* The Conduct of Life *(1860), and* English Traits *(1865). His most influential addresses are "The American Scholar" (1837) and "The Divinity School Address" (1838).*

TO GO INTO SOLITUDE, a man needs to retire as much from his chamber as from society. I am not solitary whilst I read and write, though nobody is with me. But if a man would be alone, let him look at the stars. The rays that come from those heavenly worlds will separate between him and vulgar things. One might think the atmosphere was made transparent with this design, to give man, in the heavenly bodies, the perpetual presence of the sublime. Seen in the streets of cities, how great they are! If the stars should appear one night in a thousand years, how would men believe and adore; and preserve for many generations the remembrance of the city of God which had been shown! But every night come out these preachers of beauty, and light the universe with their admonishing smile.

The stars awaken a certain reverence, because though always present, they are always inaccessible; but all natural objects make a kindred impression, when the mind is open to their influence. Nature never wears a mean appearance. Neither does the wisest man extort all her secret, and lose his curiosity by finding out all her perfection. Nature never became a toy to a wise spirit. The flowers, the animals, the mountains, reflected all the wisdom of his best hour, as much as they had delighted the simplicity of his childhood.

When we speak of nature in this manner, we have a distinct but 3
most poetical sense in the mind. We mean the integrity of impression
made by manifold natural objects. It is this which distinguishes the stick
of timber of the wood-cutter from the tree of the poet. The charming
landscape which I saw this morning is indubitably made up of some
twenty or thirty farms. Miller owns this field, Locke that, and Manning
the woodland beyond. But none of them owns the landscape. There is
a property in the horizon which no man has but he whose eye can in-
tegrate all the parts, that is, the poet. This is the best part of these men's
farms, yet to this their land-deeds give them no title.

To speak truly, few adult persons can see nature. Most persons do 4
not see the sun. At least they have a very superficial seeing. The sun il-
luminates only the eye of the man, but shines into the eye and the
heart of the child. The lover of nature is he whose inward and outward
senses are still truly adjusted to each other; who has retained the spirit
of infancy even into the era of manhood. His intercourse with heaven
and earth becomes part of his daily food. In the presence of nature, a
wild delight runs through the man, in spite of real sorrows. Nature
says,—he is my creature, and maugre all his impertinent griefs, he shall
be glad with me. Not the sun or the summer alone, but every hour and
season yields its tribute of delight; for every hour and change corre-
sponds to and authorizes a different state of the mind, from breathless
noon to grimmest midnight. Nature is a setting that fits equally well a
comic or a mourning piece. In good health, the air is a cordial of in-
credible virtue. Crossing a bare common, in snow puddles, at twilight,
under a clouded sky, without having in my thoughts any occurrence of
special good fortune, I have enjoyed a perfect exhilaration. Almost I
fear to think how glad I am. In the woods too, a man casts off his years,
as the snake his slough, and at what period soever of life is always a
child. In the woods is perpetual youth. Within these plantations of
God, a decorum and sanctity reign, a perennial festival is dressed, and
the guest sees not how he should tire of them in a thousand years. In
the woods, we return to reason and faith. There I feel that nothing can
befall me in life,—no disgrace, no calamity (leaving me my eyes,)
which nature cannot repair. Standing on the bare ground,—my head
bathed by the blithe air and uplifted into infinite space,—all mean ego-
tism vanishes. I become a transparent eyeball. I am nothing. I see all;
the currents of the Universal Being circulate through me; I am part or
particle of God. The name of the nearest friend sounds then foreign

and accidental: to be brothers, to be aquaintances,—master or servant, is then a trifle and a disturbance. I am the lover of uncontained and immortal beauty. In the wilderness, I find something more dear and connate than in streets or villages. In the tranquil landscape, and especially in the distant line of the horizon, man beholds somewhat as beautiful as his own nature.

The greatest delight which the fields and woods minister is the suggestion of an occult relation between man and the vegetable. I am not alone and unacknowledged. They nod to me and I to them. The waving of the boughs in the storm, is new to me and old. It takes me by surprise, and yet is not unknown. Its effect is like that of a higher thought or a better emotion coming over me, when I deemed I was thinking justly or doing right. 5

Yet it is certain that the power to produce this delight does not reside in nature, but in man, or in a harmony of both. It is necessary to use these pleasures with great temperance. For nature is not always tricked in holiday attire, but the same scene which yesterday breathed perfume and glittered as for the frolic of the nymphs is overspread with melancholy today. Nature always wears the colors of the spirit. To a man laboring under calamity, the heat of his own fire hath sadness in it. Then there is a kind of contempt of the landscape felt by him who has just lost by death a dear friend. The sky is less grand as it shuts down over less worth in the population. 6

Glossary

Abstract An abstract word describes a concept or quality that has no physical, tangible existence in itself; a concept such as truth or a quality such as beauty. A "child," for example, is a concrete object that our senses can perceive; but "childishness" is an abstract quality. *See* "Concrete."

Allegory A narrative that has a second meaning in addition to the obvious one. The meaning may be religious, moral, or political.

Analogy An analogy is a comparison that points out a resemblance between two essentially different things. Sleep and death are analogous, although certainly not identical. Often an analogy is drawn to explain something that is complex or abstract by pointing out one way it resembles something that is simpler or more concrete. For example, to explain how the mind processes and stores information in its memory, an analogy might be drawn to the way a bank processes and stores deposits.

Antonym An antonym is a word of opposite meaning from another word. "Good" is an antonym of "bad." *See* "Synonym."

Argumentation In persuasive essays, a unit of discourse meant to prove a point or to convince; the process of proving or persuading.

Audience   Audience refers to an author's concept of who his or her readers will be, which affects the style and tone. An author may write more technically, for example, if the intended audience is composed of specialists in a certain field and may write less technically if the writing is for the general public.

Cause and Effect   *See* Chapter 12.

Chronology   The time sequence of a narrative or description. The two most popular ones are straight chronology (from beginning to middle to end) and flashback (end to beginning to middle to end). By withholding information and manipulating chronology, writers are able to create suspense.

Classification   *See* Chapter 9.

Cliché   A cliché is an expression that has been so overused it has lost its ability to affect us as a bright and picturesque way of conveying an idea. Clichés, such as "busy as a bee," make writing less clear and precise. Because we are so used to hearing them, they become little more than vague generalizations to us.

Coherence   Coherence refers to a sense of connection and interrelationship among the parts of an essay. In a coherent piece of writing, each sentence leads reasonably to the next sentence, and each paragraph follows reasonably from the previous paragraph. A lack of coherence is evident when there are gaps between parts of an essay, when a reader begins to ask, "Why does the writer say this here?" or "How did the writer get to this idea from the previous idea?" *See* "Transition" and "Unity."

Comparison and Contrast   *See* Chapter 11.

Conclusion   A conclusion sums up or restates the writer's thesis; it should give a well-rounded sense of completion and finality to a piece of writing. It may be no more than a sentence in a short essay, or it may be many paragraphs in a long report. A short conclusion may restate the writer's thesis in a memorable way, place the specific topic being discussed within or against a broader framework, or suggest answers to questions raised in the essay. A summary of the writer's main points may be effective as the conclusion to a long paper, but in a short essay it will seem unnecessarily repetitious.

Concrete   A concrete word describes something specific and tangible as opposed to something general and abstract. "Wealth" is an abstract concept, of which "gold" is a concrete form. The use of concrete details, examples, and illustrations is a key to clear and effective writing. *See* "Abstract."

Connotation   The connotations of a word are its implications and overtones and the qualities, feelings, and ideas it suggests beyond its literal meaning or dictionary definition. The word *sunshine* literally signifies the lightrays of the sun, but it connotes warmth, cheer, happiness, and even prosperity. *See* "Denotation."

Deduction   Deduction is a mental process in which one first assumes that a broad generalization is valid, then reasons that its validity is applicable to more specific instances. For example, if we assume that cigarette smoking causes cancer, we may deduce that a person who smokes is liable to contract the disease. *See* "Induction" and "Syllogism."

Definition   *See* Chapter 10.

Description   *See* Chapter 6.

Diction   Diction is the writer's choice of words. A writer is said to employ proper diction when the words he or she chooses to express ideas are accurate and appropriate, that is, when what he or she writes says exactly what he or she means. Poor diction stems from choosing words whose denotation does not accurately convey the author's intended meaning or from choosing words regarded as inappropriate because they are nonstandard ("ain't"), colloquial, or obsolete.

Epigram   A witty or clever saying, concisely expressed.

Exposition   Exposition is a mode or form of discourse that is designed specifically to convey information, give directions, or explain what is difficult to understand.

Figure of Speech   A figure of speech is an imaginative phrase and comparison that is not meant to be taken literally. "He ran as fast as the wind," for example, is a figure of speech known as a simile. *See* "Analogy," "Hyperbole," "Metaphor," "Personification," "Simile," and "Understatement."

Generalization   A generalization is a broad statement, idea, or rule that holds a common truth or applicability. For example, it is generally true that a soldier's job is to fight in wars, although there may be many specific exceptions to such a generalization. Writing that relies too much on generalization is likely to be vague and abstract. *See* "Specificity."

Hyperbole   Hyperbole is obvious exaggeration, an extravagant statement, intentionally designed to give the reader a memorable image. A fisher who tells you that the one that got away was "big as a whale" probably is speaking hyperbolically. *See* "Understatement."

Illustration and Example   *See* Chapter 7.

Induction   Induction is a mental process in which one draws a generalized conclusion from specific, factual evidence. For example, if it is a fact that a high percentage of people who die from cancer each year also smoke cigarettes, one might induce that cigarette smoking is a contributing cause of the disease. *See* "Deduction."

Introduction   An introduction sets forth the writer's thesis or central themes, establishes the tone (the attitude toward the subject), and, particularly in a long paper, suggests the organizational plan. The introduction or opening of an essay should be designed to capture a reader's attention and interest. Like the conclusion, it may be no more than a sentence in a short essay or many paragraphs in a long paper.

Irony   Irony is the undercutting or contradicting of someone's expectations. It may be either verbal or dramatic; verbal irony involves a discrepancy, sometimes intentional, sometimes not, between what is said and what is meant; for example, if a dog tries to bite you, you may say, "What a friendly dog!" Dramatic irony involves a discrepancy between what someone expects to happen and what does happen; it would be ironic, for example, if the dog who seemed so unfriendly to you saved your life. *See* "Sarcasm" and "Satire."

Metaphor   A metaphor is a figure of speech in which through an implied comparison one object is identified with another, and some qualities of the first object are ascribed to the second. *See* "Simile."

Mode   A mode is a conventional form or usage. In writing there are four customary modes of discourse: descriptive, narrative, expository, and persuasive or argumentative.

Narration   *See* Chapter 5.

Objectivity   Objectivity is freedom from personal bias. A report about a scientific experiment is objective insofar as the facts are explained without reference to the writer's feelings about the experiment. But not even the most factual piece of writing is completely objective, completely uncolored by the writer's attitudes and impressions. Objectivity tends to be a matter of degree, increasing as the writer acts as an observer who distances himself or herself from whatever he or she is writing about. *See* "Subjectivity."

Pacing   The rate at which a writer reveals the details of his or her narrative. Unimportant details should be glossed over; essential events need to be carefully explained.

Paradox   A paradox is a statement that sounds self-contradictory, even absurd, and yet expresses a certain truth. For example, it is paradoxical, though nonetheless true, to say that one person can feel both love and hatred for another person at the same moment.

Parallel Structure   Parallel structure is the association of ideas phrased in parallel or similar ways, thus giving a piece of writing balance and proportion. "He loves wine, women, and singing" lacks parallel structure; "He loves wine, women, and song" is more balanced.

Parody   A humorous imitation of a usually serious work. It can take any fixed or open form, because parodists imitate the tone, language, and shape of the original in order to deflate the subject matter, making the original work seem absurd.

Persona   The mask or voice that the author creates to tell a story.

Personification   Personification is a figure of speech in which abstract concepts or inanimate objects are represented as if they had human qualities. To write that "death rides a pale horse," for example, is to personify death.

Persuasion   *See* Chapter 13.

Point of View   The point of view is the vantage point from which an author writes. In expository prose an author may adopt a first-person or a third-person point of view. *See* "Style" and "Tone."

Process Analysis   *See* Chapter 8.

Pun   A play on words based on the similarity of sound between two words differing in meaning. For example, "Ask for me tomorrow and you will find me a *grave* man."

Satire   Satire is a form of writing that makes use of irony, sarcasm, ridicule, and humor in order to expose, denounce, and possibly correct the follies and evils of human beings and institutions. The satirist's tone may range from gentle mockery and amused wit to harsh contempt and moral indignation.

Simile   A simile is a figure of speech in which a direct, explicit comparison is made between two different things. One thing is expressly *like* or *as* another thing: he ate *like* a pig; her heart felt light *as* a feather. *See* "Metaphor."

Slang   Slang refers to colloquialisms and jargon that are deemed inappropriate not only in formal writing but also in the standard speech of educated conversation. Whether a word or phrase is considered colloquial or slang is often a matter of personal taste. A word such as *uptight,* which was once considered slang by many cultivated people, is now an acceptable colloquialism.

Specificity   Specificity is precision, particularity, concreteness. The more detailed a person's writing is, the more specific and hence the less general, vague, and abstract it will be. Specificity, like generalization, is a matter of degree; the word *horse,* for example, is more specific than the word *animal* but more general than the word *stallion.* See "Generalization."

Subjectivity   Subjectivity in writing is the personal element. The more subjective a piece of writing, the more it will focus on the opinions and feelings of the writer. *See* "Objectivity."

Syllogism   A syllogism is a highly formalized version of deductive logic. Syllogistic reason argues that if a generalization (major premise) is true and a specific case of the generalization (minor premise) is also true, then whatever conclusion deduction reaches is necessarily true. For example, if the major premise is "smoking causes cancer" and the minor premise is "John Doe smokes," then the conclusion is "John Doe will contract cancer." A syllogism may sound logical yet not be true because one or both of its premises are faulty. *See* "Deduction."

Symbol   A symbol is something that stands for something else. An eagle is a conventional symbol of America. The word *eagle* may bring to mind different images or ideas in different contexts or to different people; it may connote freedom or power or solitude. Any word, image, or description, any name, character, or action, that has a range of meanings and associations beyond its literal denotation may be symbolic, depending on who is interpreting it and the context in which it appears.

Synonym   A synonym is one of two or more words having approximately the same meaning. *Happiness* and *joy,* for example, are synonyms. *See* "Antonym."

Thesis   The thesis of an essay is its main idea or central theme. In expository prose the writer usually will want to state the thesis clearly in the introduction. The thesis statement should establish the point of view, the primary point(s) intended for discussion, and the writer's attitude or tone toward it.

Tone   The tone of voice indicates an author's attitude toward the subject and, at times, the audience. The tone is caught in the "sound" of the writing. The voice of an essay may be angry, resigned, humorous, serious, sentimental, mocking, ironic, sarcastic, satirical, reasonable, emotional, philosophic—anything, in short, that the voice of the author can be. One tone may predominate or many tones may be heard in any single work. *See* "Style."

Topic Sentence   The topic sentence is the sentence in a paragraph that states clearly the central theme or point of the paragraph.

Transition   A transition is a bridge between one point or topic or idea and another. The transitional movement from sentence to sentence and paragraph to paragraph should be easy to follow if a piece of writing is to achieve coherence. The logic of moving from one point to the next often is emphasized by means of transitional expressions such as "therefore," "hence," "similarly," "however," "but," "furthermore," "also," and "for example." *See* "Coherence."

Understatement   An understatement is an obvious downplaying or underrating of something. It is the opposite of a hyperbole, although similarly designed to create a memorable image or an ironic effect. To say that "after they ate the apple, Adam and Eve found life a bit tougher" is to understate the case. *See* "Hyperbole."

Unity   Unity refers to the way a basic focus or theme permeates a single piece of writing, lending the piece a sense of wholeness and completeness. The words and sentences and paragraphs, the images and ideas, the explanations and examples, the characters and actions, the descriptions and arguments—all in some way should be relevant to the overriding purpose or point of the work. *See* "Coherence."

Index